Ferranti. Your foundation for advanced technology in Scotland.

The name Ferranti is synonymous with technology in Scotland.

We are, after all, the largest science based company north of the Border.

And our activities are widespread.

You'll find our name on aircraft navigation, radar and display systems, precision industrial measuring machines, computer graphics systems, petrol pumps, workshop cutting lasers, microwave components for satellites, telecommunication systems and other advanced equipment.

For technology in Scotland you can safely build on Ferranti.

Ferry Road
Edinburgh EH5 2XS Scotland
Telephone: 031-332 2411
Telex: 72141

SC01/44/036/BJ

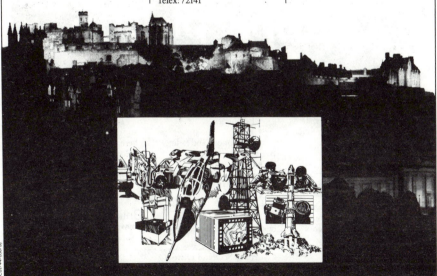

FERRANTI

3

4

TABLE OF CONTENTS

The Yearbook is edited on behalf of the Unit for the Study of Government in Scotland at The University of Edinburgh. Additional copies of the Yearbook, backcopies of the nine previous volumes and further information about The Unit's activities can be obtained from Mrs. Helen Ramm at 31 Buccleuch Place, Edinburgh EH8 9JT, Scotland.

A COMMENTARY

The Editor

Nineteen eighty six was not a year of miracles. Scotland slid further into the pit of economic recession, unemployment climbed inexorably, the end of deep-mining in Scotland grew more likely, and the new industries of oil and 'hi tech' suffered in the global slump. Readers of *Scottish Government Yearbook* should not be surprised that the new dawn has been slow to happen, for our contributors have been pointing out throughout the 1980s that Scotland has little control over its economic affairs which are ruled from the boardrooms of multinational companies or from the inner recesses of Whitehall. The failure of the much-vaunted 'Scottish lobby' to influence the Guinness shareholders is proof of that. The role of the Scottish Office and its agencies is too often to provide some trimmings and garnishing at the edges. And now even the limited powers of the SDA are threatened by Treasury cuts.

What impact does this economic gloom have on the governance of Scotland? Since our last edition, Scotland has a new Secretary of State in Malcolm Rifkind. He too has found it an uncommon bed of nails much like his predecessor genial George Younger who has at last been allowed to move to the gentler world of the Defence Ministry. Rifkind is an Edinburgh advocate and well versed in that breed's professional capacity to argue a threadbare brief. He has little to work on, for most of the problems of his successor he has inherited, and they show a stubborn refusal to go away. Of the three issues we identified last year, none has been resolved. The teachers' dispute smoulders on and is given piquancy by the threat that the England and Wales teachers might strike a better bargain than their Northern colleagues. The schools are entering their third year of discontent, and it will take a major reversal of political philosophy to grant the teachers what they would settle for. Public sector workers do not figure much in the Thatcherite pantheon. Ravenscraig too remains a threatening shadow over Scotland's industrial base and over Rifkind's credibility, but it is probably safe until after the next general election. Only the rates issue has been tackled head-on, and there is a suspicion that the cure might be worse than the disease. The solution, the euphemistically sounding 'community charge' or 'poll tax', is a creature of its time. It is hard to imagine that such a regressive piece of taxation would have been introduced ten or twenty years ago, for it is an unashamed appeal to the pockets of the middle class owner occupiers who have been deserting the Tories in droves in Scotland. It may be too late to stop them, and there is the possibility that the government will encounter great difficulties getting it through on the current parliamentary timetable.

Being a Tory Secretary of State is a thankless task. The lack of a political mandate, and, more importantly, of a political base in Local Government, makes it probably an impossible job even for so skilled and consummate a politician as Malcolm Rifkind. In the recent round of ministerial musical chairs, there has been a redrawing of responsibilities, and the freshening of Rifkind's team with new and unfamiliar faces. It seems the belief that there is nothing wrong with government policies that 'presentation' will not cure has ushered in a team of smooth, pinstripe-suited youngish men. And yet the Tory decline in Scotland is more deep-seated and longer term.

Why should this be so? Malcolm Rifkind used to be fond of pointing out that only the Tory Party has ever received 50% of the popular vote in a general election in Scotland (in 1955). This remarkable event has become an embarrassing boast to a party which got all of 17% in the Regional Elections in May, and who struggle to reach even that in the opinion polls. The general election in 1983 when the party got 28% of the vote begins to look a very good result, for since then the Tories have managed to get 20% of the opinion polls only once in the last 15 months. While the talk of the party being exterminated in Scotland makes good journalistic copy, it is unlikely to happen. What cannot be denied is that since 1955, the fortunes of the Tories in Scotland have slumped dramatically while in England they culminated in 1983 in the re-election of a Thatcher government with a landslide majority. It was this election which saw the greatest divergence between Scotland and England with regard to the fortunes of the Tory Party. As Hutchison has pointed out in an important political history of Scotland* published recently, the Tories' support in Scotland was quite stable between 1924 and 1955. Even the historic victory of Labour in 1945 saw the Tories receive a greater share of the vote in Scotland (41%) than in the UK as a whole (36%). Nineteen fifty nine saw a reversal of this trend and the beginning of Labour hegemony. Gradually the gap between Conservative performance in Scotland and in the rest of the UK has grown so that in 1983 it stood at its widest margin of a 14 percentage point difference.

It might seem straightforward enough to see this as the corollary of the rise of the SNP which took off after the famous victory of Winnie Ewing in Hamilton in a 1967 by-election. We would be mistaken, for the SNP did none too well in 1979 and 1983, while the gap between Tory support in Scotland and the rest of the UK has grown. Nevertheless, it would be a mistake to claim that there was no relationship. It simply is more complicated than a siphoning away of Tory support to the SNP (or the Alliance for that matter). The success of the SNP seems to have fed off the rising expectations of the relatively young and socially mobile at the end of the 'long boom' in the early 1970s encouraged by North Sea oil and

8

amplified by the media in Scotland. Its success in achieving 30% of the popular vote in October 1974 has not been repeated, and is unlikely to be in this form, for much of that depended upon a belief in the post-war period that the state could deliver the economic goods. Thatcherism is both a creature and a cause of the death of this belief. As Thatcher has confronted public spending, so a new pessimism that the state (be it a British state or a Scottish state) could create economic development has grown. It is an irony that her government has used powerful state machinery to drive down expectations and in so doing has resorted to an increasingly nationalistic ideology fed off the Falklands debacle. At each turn of this Thatcherite ratchet, so Scotland is more alienated for two reasons. Firstly, it has a higher level of state-driven investment in economic and social infrastructure, and secondly, as John Mackintosh pointed out so perceptively, Scots have two national identities, British and Scottish, which allows them to opt out of the former as pride (and pay-off) wanes. This thesis of dual nationalism was confirmed by a poll carried out in July 1986 for the *Glasgow Herald* which showed that 39% of respondents regarded themselves as Scottish not British, 30% more Scottish than British, and 19% equally Scottish and British. Only 4% felt themselves to be more British than Scottish, and 6% British not Scottish. This commitment to 'Scottishness' is fairly evenly distributed among supporters of all parties, even Conservatives. Only 20% replied that they were more British than Scottish, or simply British, compared to 6% of Labour supporters, 10% Alliance, and 5% SNP (exactly why *they* should vote SNP is a puzzle).

We should be careful, of course, in jumping to conclusions about these data, because how they are tied into political and social identities is very unclear. They provide the raw materials around which identities are constructed, rather than the finished political articles. Similar observations can be made about opinion poll data, particularly on constitutional options which are outlined by Allan Macartney in this issue. The February 1986 MORI poll findings have been seized upon to show that around one third of Scots want 'independence' and a further 47% want an assembly. Such data are being bandied about to show that home rule is round the corner. Careful scrutiny of the questions should council caution. 33% replied that they wanted a 'completely independendent Scottish assembly separate from England', a cunning fusion by the pollsters of 'separatism' and 'devolution'. We cannot simply read off the conclusion that one third of Scots want independence, although to say that around three quarters are dissatisfied with the 'status quo' is nearer the mark. Such a conclusion receives support from the fact that SNP support bobs along at around 15-20%, considerably short of the magical 'third'.

What does seem more of a conundrum, is that the SNP should do so badly given these straws in the political wind, given the English flavour of Thatcher's government, and the inability of Labour to do anything about it. It is the failure of the SNP to exploit economic and political conditions which run in their favour which is much more interesting than the jump in the polls of 1 or 2 percentage points. After all, in fully 37 opinion polls taken in Scotland since the 1983 election, the SNP have taken 4th place on 31 occasions, making it undoubtedly the fourth party. Labour came first in every poll with between 40 and 52% of support, the Tories second in 23 polls and third in 11 (all in the last 15 months), and the Alliance, the dark and ignored horse of Scottish politics, second in 16 polls and third in 20. The SNP, of course, protest that their support in the polls underestimates their true electoral standing. Did they not come second in the popular vote in the Regional elections in May 1986, their leader has pointed out? Well, not really. To be sure, the SNP took 18% of all votes cast in the regional elections of May 1986 but this reflected the number of seats it contested as Bochel and Denver show. Taking only *contested* seats, the SNP (with 19.8%) was pushed into a narrow *fourth* place behind the Tories and Alliance (at 22.5% and 20% respectively), a result closer to its opinion poll position. The fact remains that Scotland has a political system in which Labour dominates both elections and polls with around 45%, and the others three parties contest the remainder of political support.

The Tory Party in Scotland resembles a once-stately airplane (one is tempted to label it 'British Imperial Airways') which once dominated the skies. Now it bumps and scrapes its way along the runway in search of former glory, but succeeds only in digging itself further into the sand. There is more than a suspicion that its lack of flight derives from inappropriate instructions from the control tower. The SNP is a much lighter and more modern contraption which launches itself down the runway at fairly frequent intervals with much skirling and commotion, and then fails to get very far in strong, prevailing winds. Why Labour in Scotland flies at all is a bit of a mystery to theorists of political flight. Its crew don't seem to do much at the controls preferring to try to gain influence with the control tower. Nevertheless, it outflies all the others, and seems at times to be held together merely by its own weight. The Alliance in Scotland is an almost ghostly machine which has gained flight before anyone has really noticed, although its destination is a bit of a mystery. It has a fairly old and well tested Liberal wing, and a new fangled and smaller SDP one which threaten now and again to flap out of unison. Above all, for all parties there is the suspicion that flying at all is a remarkable feat in skies over which they have little control, and while they receive instructions from the ground which threaten mid-air collision or encourage self-destruction.

The next twelve months may see a general election, although the polls will have to run more strongly the Tory way for Mrs Thatcher to take a chance. A minority government led by her and seeking support from smaller parties does not accord with her political instincts and is not an attractive proposition for the leaders of these parties. Whatever happens, Scotland will stand on the sidelines as the key skirmishes are fought out elsewhere, particularly in the English Midlands. It will take another party to break the log-jam of Scottish political expectations which have built up over Home Rule, and then we may be entering a more exciting and exacting form of politics.

The 1987 edition of the *Yearbook* analyses unemployment in Scotland and local responses to it; and the media which has played such a key role in Scotland's political distinctiveness. The politics of education remains a central importance. How Scotland copes with government legislation is an important theme, and we focus on rating revaluation, social security, and transport policy in remote areas. Neglected areas of Scottish governance, notably police complaints procedures and political education in Scottish schools, are examined, as well as Scotland's electronics industry upon which so many expectations rest. Party politics in Scotland are described and analysed both with regard to happenings at Westminster and in the Regional elections of May which confirmed the weakness of the government in Scotland to an unprecendented degree.

All our contributors have given freely and generously of their talents and time, and we are indebted to them. Our regular writers continue to provide a unique and invaluable service. The editor is particularly grateful to Helen Ramm who manages to cope with our ridiculous timetable with efficiency and good humour. Our readers make the whole exercise worthwhile, and we hope that the **Scottish Government Yearbook** continues to expand its readership as it has done in the last few years.

*I G C Hutchison, *A Political History of Scotland, 1932-1942: parties, elections and issues*, John Donald, Edinburgh, 1986.

September 1986

THE YEAR AT WESTMINSTER

Martin Dowle

The Westland whirlwind

On January 9, 1986, Malcolm Rifkind was at his Duddingston home suffering from a bout of 'flu when the Prime Minister telephoned out of the blue to tell him he had been elevated to the post of Scottish Secretary and catapulted into the Cabinet at the relatively young age of 39 within one hour of the dramatic walk-out by Michael Heseltine.

A stunned Rifkind told reporters of his "absolute amazement" at Mrs Thatcher's call when he said: "It was not one of the things I woke up to this morning expecting to happen."

Despite his surprise, the transition from the long reign of George Younger to that of Malcolm Rifkind was about the only orderly and predictable moment of the strange Westland affair.

After Heseltine had collected his papers in the midst of an arcane discussion on the meaning of collective responsibility and had marched out of the Cabinet room, a rather stunned Prime Minister adjourned the meeting and called Younger into her study.

He at last was given the job he had sought for at least two years, and replaced Heseltine at Defence. There was then no doubt in the mind of either Younger or Thatcher over the credentials of Rifkind to succeed him, and he was appointed within the hour.

Rifkind had more than won his spurs as Minister of State at the Foreign Office, a gruelling job carrying much of the day-by-day work of foreign affairs, but also requiring immense diplomatic skills and a sharp knowledge of a range of issues from East-West tensions to arms control negotiations and the thorny question of South Africa.

His track record in Scotland before his move to the Foreign Office in that earlier crisis of the Falklands in May 1982 was also considered excellent by both Thatcher and Younger. For the first three years of the Thatcher Government, Rifkind had handled the tricky area of local government during a severe period of economic contraction when the squeeze was on public spending, with consummate skill and much wit.

If any doubts had lingered in her mind over the appointment, they centred around his age (the Prime Minister had contemplated elevation in earlier reshuffles and been concerned about this point) rather than his earlier support for devolution or his mild tendency towards the Wet wing of the Conservative Party.

Rifkind took over at an unhappy moment for the Scottish Tories, with the Government facing a number of seemingly intractable problems, in particular the teachers' dispute, reform of the rating system and the row over the closure of the Gartcosh steel rolling mill.

The morale of his party was low, and there was a general feeling that the Younger technique of placating endless delegations of councillors, trade unionists and businessmen by expressing genial sympathy while being unable to do more than sweeten the bitter pill of central government action, had begun to wear a bit thin.

Thus it was more than just a passing reference to Rifkind's heavy cold when Younger, in preparing to hand over the Great Seal of Scotland, joked: "I hope he will be well enough to carry it because it's very heavy."

The New broom at Dover House

When Winston Churchill took over from Neville Chamberlain in 1940, it was said that civil servants began to run down the corridors of power as the new Prime Minister galvanised the Government machine into action. Though Scottish Office officials may not have broken into a trot, there was very swiftly a new mood of urgency about the approach to the Government's problems in the offices of St Andrew's House in Edinburgh and at Dover House in Whitehall.

The expression 'Action this Day' could well have been applied to Rifkind's first few months in office. Rifkind decided that the best hope of recovery for the Conservatives in Scotland lay in attack, and in a move designed to lift his party from the depths of despair which accompanied its drop to the low 20s and high teens in the opinion polls, set the Conservatives the target of reaching 30 per cent by the next election – 2 per cent higher than in 1983.

Rifkind's task amounted to trying to deal with a number of running sores before he could embark on his own initiatives, and indeed the first of these was dealt with by the Cabinet within his first hour as Secretary of State, and, inevitably, in his absence.

Grasping the nettle of rates reform

When the rather shaken Cabinet of January 9 resumed, the question of rating reform was at the top of the agenda. The proposed Green Paper had undergone a rather difficult and stressful gestation period given the rather different levels of enthusiasm for the concept of a poll tax, or as it was to be labelled, a community charge.

The pressure for reform on domestic rates had, of course, been strengthened inside the ranks of the Scottish Conservative Party by the rates revaluation crisis of 1985, and only partly alleviated by the promise of up to £50 million directly from the Treasury for additional assistance to hard-hit ratepayers.

But that pressure was not replicated in England and Wales, largely because of the continued postponement of revaluation. In addition, there seemed to be a built-in suspicion inside the Department of the Environment at the prospect of another upheaval in local government finance.

Younger therefore pushed the public pace of reform at the Blackpool conference in October 1985. It had become clear that any reform south of the border would be, to say the least, leisurely. Despite earlier refusals by Downing Street to contemplate a two-speed programme in which the Scottish legislation was introduced ahead of the English by at least one year, Younger floated the proposition behind the scenes at Blackpool.

He immediately contradicted suggestions by Kenneth Baker, then the Environment Secretary and the chairman of the Ministerial rating reform committee, that Scotland could not have separate legislation, arguing that Scottish Office Ministers were simply "working in tandem" with their English counterparts on the issue, and expected legislation to be on the Statute Book by the time of the general election.

Younger's difficulty proved to be a formidable resistance to change in a combination of UK departments. The Department of the Environment's doubts centred not only around the practicality of a poll tax, but more specifically around disparities of income district-by-district and around the question of business payments, an issue far more accentuated in England's large cities than in Scotland.

The Home Office, initially under Leon Brittan and then under Douglas Hurd, expressed concern over the correlation of the duty to pay a local government tax with the right to vote. The Department of Health and Social Security inevitably had an interest in the question over the extent of rebates for those paying the poll tax.

Above all, the Treasury viewed the plan for the great leap in the dark to voter accountability as the key method of controlling local government expenditure as a rather inadequate replacement for the armoury of controls which it had built up since 1979 to keep a grip on high-spending local councils.

In the end, these differences could only be resolved by the formulation under Baker's guidance of a putative timescale for introduction of the community charge under which Scotland would have its Bill in the 1986/7 session and the English a Bill in the following one – which would conveniently fall with the dissolution of Parliament, if Thatcher decided to go through the final winter of the term.

Within that, there would be a further differential timetable inside England which would enable the community charge system to be implemented more quickly in some local authority areas than in others. The problems with the Home Office were ironed out by agreeing to a separate roll for community charge, while Thatcher herself forced the pace on the question of accountability of voters by insisting on a clause in the Social Security Bill (implementing the Fowler reforms) which would oblige all ratepayers to pay 20 per cent of their rate bills regardless of their means.

Despite considerable misgivings inside the Department of the Environment over the practicality of the community charge proposals – and much concern over the impact which they may have on many lower-income Tory-voting families – the discussion on January 9 was relatively smooth. In a delicious irony, one of the lead speakers in the discussion was Younger, putting the Scottish Office view in his last act before moving across the road to the Ministry of Defence.

If Rifkind ever viewed the proposals as a poisoned chalice, then he never betrayed it. He threw himself into the role of key promoter of the measure with all the skills of an Edinburgh advocate.

But when the Green Paper, *Paying for Local Government*, was published in late January, the striking point was the immediate opposition of most of local government in Scotland and the luke-warm response with which the plan was greeted in England.

In their enthusiasm, the Scottish Conservatives brushed aside Opposition complaints that a community charge, averaging at £207 per adult in Scotland, amounted to a strongly regressive tax for most citizens.

Indeed, Rifkind, in his statement to the Commons on the day after publication, clearly thought that the best form of defence was attack and accused his Labour opponents of being "wedded to a corrupt and out-of-date system" in concluding that the proposals should be rejected.

Donald Dewar, the Shadow Scottish Secretary, described the proposals as an "anti-social fraud" which would hit those least able to bear the burden. Sir Russell Johnston, the Scottish Liberal leader, described the poll tax as "a stride back into the Middle Ages", while Gordon Wilson, the SNP chairman, argued that the system was unrelated to the ability to pay, was expensive to implement and very hard to enforce.

Although the Scottish Office established a special group of civil servants to tackle what was seen by leading officials as one of the thorniest problems it had had to handle since devolution, it was clear that by mid-summer many of the problems had still not been ironed out, that the proposals were still implacably opposed by the bulk of local authorities and that they had won no consensus in Scotland at large.

The teachers' dispute: breaking the log-jam

Rating reform was not however as big a headache for Rifkind as the long-running teachers' dispute, and it was clear that his ability to lift Scottish education out of its downward spiral would prove to be the greatest challenge of his first few months in office.

Younger had been unlucky in the closing months of 1985 over the dispute. His attempts, along with Chris Patten, the Minister of State for Education, to persuade Thatcher to change her mind over a review of teachers' pay ran into the sands as Ministerial committee after Ministerial committee. A highly-secret initiative by Patten to convince Thatcher of a new attitude towards separate but parallel disputes in Scotland and England foundered over her instinctive distaste for such inquiries, which had led to huge pay problems for the Government in its early months in office.

The Patten-Younger initiative was also dogged by the early discovery by the media of the mission, and despite attempts to revive it during the Christmas recess, Younger found Thatcher as implacable as ever during his last few days in office.

Rifkind quickly spotted that the key to any settlement inevitably involved the concession of an independent inquiry by the Government in exchange for the teachers accepting that conditions should be examined as well as pay. But laying the groundwork for Cabinet acceptance of the committee of inquiry, and the probability of acceptance by the unions, proved to be a much slower and more arduous process.

The latter was achieved through the arrangement of low key meetings with relevant figures in Scotland, the former by a well-judged campaign inside the Government pointing out the need for a strong political initiative in Scotland to pull both the education system and the Tory Party out of the morasses in which they found themselves. Perhaps the most important point in the package was the acceptance that the inquiry, which was chaired by the former Boots chairman, Sir Peter Main, should take into account what the Government could afford.

The initiative, announced just two days short of Rifkind completing his second month in office, marked a signal personal victory which was capped by the subsequent calling off of industrial action by the Educational Institute for Scotland (EIS) and only slightly marred by the subsequent penalties on education authorities for the 1985/6 settlement which fell outside the parameters set by the Scottish Office.

Gartcosh: the doomed campaign

The most curious aspect about the fight to save the Gartcosh steel rolling mill with its 750 jobs was that it was only mounted after the Government had decided that it could not intervene in what was essentially a management issue for British Steel.

The campaign could never have gained the same impetus as the successful fight to save the main complex of Ravenscraig itself mainly because the Government insisted it had no locus and additionally because even if it had, it could legitimately point out that the decision had been taken before the political storm broke.

In part, the timing was to blame. The Cabinet's consideration of the BSC corporate plan had taken place during the summer recess, so the *post facto* campaign in essence coincided with the build-up to the annual conference season and just after Leon Brittan had taken up the reigns from Norman Tebbit as Trade and Industry Secretary in September 1985.

In the Opposition parties, there were no doubts about the importance of Gartcosh as an integral part of the Ravenscraig plant, and their fears that the closure of the mill, which took place in March 1986, were the prelude to the destruction of the entire Scottish steel industry were supported by many Tory MPs and activists.

But hopes that an all-party campaign on the lines of the successful Ravenscraig fight of 1982 could be repeated were swiftly dashed. For a start, it could not be led by Younger who had been a party to the original Cabinet decision on the corporate plan. He was only able to tell the campaigners that he would pass on any fresh evidence over why the mill should be retained to British Steel in the hope that they would review the planned closure.

The revolt in Conservative ranks appeared more damaging to the party at the start than at the finish. It began with the resignation of Iain Lawson, a former parliamentary candidate, from the party, and threats of disaffiliation by two constituency parties in the west of Scotland. But when the vote was finally taken in the Commons on January 24th, only two Conservatives (Sir Hector Monro and Anna McCurley) voted against, and only one other abstained.

In an attempt to give impetus to the campaign, the Scottish Affairs Select Committee launched itself into an investigation of the role of Gartcosh which, much like an earlier examination of the future of Scott Lithgow shipyard, collapsed in much acrimony among its members.

Coup and counter-coup

Although the select committee could in theory boast a majority in favour of the retention of Gartcosh of nine to four, internal Conservative Party wrangles eventually made that impossible. Indeed, so bitter were the divisions, that Westminster saw the bizarre spectacle of a Right-wing campaign to oust Monro from his post as chairman of the Scottish Conservative Backbench Committee, only to be restored at a subsequent, and better attended, meeting of Tory MPs.

In a remarkable putsch in late November, a small group of English Tories belonging to the so-called St Andrews school of economics and masterminded by Michael Forsyth, the MP for Stirling, turned up to vote in the annual elections for the chairmanship of the Backbench Committee and elected Bill Walker, the populist Right-wing member of North Tayside.

Moderate and Wet Scottish Conservative MPs were outraged at the move, and wrote to Cranley Onslow the chairman of the 1922 Backbench Committee which oversees the elections, demanding a re-run. Their fear was that Walker's would be able to claim the much more important role of leader of the Conservative side in the Select Committee, a powerful negotiating post given the Government's majority of eight members to five.

Onslow ordered the re-run, and also clarified the rules to prevent any future participating of English MPs in the contest. Although Monro was restored to his position (ironically, he gave up the post in June 1986 claiming pressure of work), the real reverberations of the split were felt when Forsyth was able to take advantage of an ill-conceived attempt by Monro to heal the wounds on his own side.

Labour had been convinced that it had secured a consensus with the pro-Gartcosh Tory members of the committee with the proposal that there should be a three-year moratorium on the closure of Gartcosh to coincide with the Cabinet review of all steel-making in Britain in September 1988.

But the committee was thrown into chaos when Monro surprised colleagues by producing an amendment suggesting yet another inquiry into the future of Gartcosh, in place of the three-year commitment. It was an ill-judged attempt to buy unity which left the fundamentalist Right unimpressed and alienated West of Scotland MPs who could accept nothing less than the moratorium plan.

The manoeuvres caused wilderment and anger in Scotland, and David Lambie, the Labour chairman, swiftly agreed with Monro that the package should be put back together again if possible. The committee produced a second report after threats by Forsyth and Walker to mount a lengthy filibuster which would have kept it sitting until Christmas was dropped at the last minute.

By the time Rifkind had taken over, the Gartcosh issue, was despite the famous march to London, effectively a dead political issue. In opening the debate in the Commons at the end of January, Rifkind marked out his own stand on the future of steel in Scotland, warning the BSC that the Government took very seriously its pledge that the future of Ravenscraig was not tied up with the closure of Gartcosh. Thus the rather inglorious parliamentary end of the campaign to save the mill came to its inevitable end.

The state of the parties

While 1986 could be viewed as yet another year of electoral grief for the Scottish Conservatives as their leaders tried to make some impact on the party's poor poll ratings, it could only really be categorised as a year of waiting for the Opposition.

In the end, the prediction of Rifkind on taking office that "a change of personnel will change opinion not as much as some would hope but more than others would fear" had not borne fruit for the Conservatives by the time of the regional election in May, which were much worse than the Tories had feared.

Labour started the year anxious to protect its flank from the unknown quantity of the SNP, which had shown a mini-revival in a number of council by-elections in the central belt without the results feeding through into the opinion poll ratings. In fact, the local elections proved that Labour's domination of the political scene was by-and-large unchallenged, but that left the party with the old headache of how best to use that dominant position.

Perhaps with one eye on the SNP, the party sharpened up its devolution proposals with Neil Kinnock, the party leader, flying north to the Perth conference in March to knock away residual doubts about his new-found support for Home Rule which he told journalists (but strangely, not the conference itself) would be included in the first Queen's Speech of an incoming Labour Government.

It was a performance designed to convince the most sceptical of the Doubting Thomases who feared that he remained as opposed to devolution as leader as he did as an opponent of the ill-fated Wales Act in 1979. To back it all up, John Smith, the Shadow Trade and Industry Secretary, chaired a special committee to draw up draft plans for the Scottish devolution legislation which, it was argued, could be dealt with constitutionally for the most part in a committee and not block up the party's legislative programme on the floor of the Commons as in the 1974 to 1979 Labour Governments.

The SNP also had its sights on the electoral future, choosing to place much of its energy in the year in concluding a pact with Plaid Cymru in the hope of returning at least 13 MPs between them at the next election.

Under it, the two parties pledged full support in a future Parliament for each other's constitutional demands. Its weakness as a strategy lay not only in the hope of a hung Parliament after the election, but in a certain configuration of seats which would make the Nationalists more important or attractive to deal with than any other third grouping.

Similarly for the Alliance, which suffered some adverse publicity for its differing views on nuclear power and the Dounreay European prototype reprocessing plant, 1986 was more a year of preparation for the next election than anything else.

Conclusion

The publication of the inquiry by Sir Peter Main on teachers' pay and conditions left Ministers with a major headache when they returned to Westminster after the summer recess. Its recommendation of a 16.4 per cent increase over 18 months in exchange for concessions on working conditions let to an immediate split in the Cabinet sub-committee dealing with parallel disputes in Scotland and England.

The recommendations were broadly accepted by Malcolm Rifkind, and by Kenneth Baker, the Education Secretary, who saw implementation of the proposed award, with similar payments in England, as the Government's way out of a long and damaging dispute. Their argument was strengthened by the view that the Government could ill-afford another winter of disruption in the schools, particularly in the run-up to a General Election.

But implementation was strongly opposed by the Chancellor, Nigel Lawson, and by the Environment Secretary, Nicholas Ridley, also member of the ad hoc committee. They argued against on two grounds: the danger of a knock-on effect elsewhere in the public sector; and the question of cost. Although the cost of a settlement on the lines of Main for Scotland alone would cost just £234 million, an equivalent deal in England and Wales would cost the Exchequer around £2.5 billion.

The relatively large contingency reserve of £6 billion had already been heavily denuded by other local government costs, and Lawson was anxious to ensure that a teachers' pay deal affected the fund as little as possible.

The Prime Minister, who chaired the committee, was said to have blown "hot and cold", swithering between a desire to see the long-running and damaging disputes settled to assist Baker and Rifkind to start turning education into a positive election issue for the Tories, and her pathological dislike of Clegg-style commissions which caused her much anguish on the inflation front after coming to office in 1979.

In the event, the two sides reached an old-fashioned compromise at the end of October and proposed to fund a slower staging-in of the proposals that recommended by Main. Rifkind argued that the deal was exceptionally favourable at a time of very low inflation, and that there was ample precedent for phased introductions of such recommendations when the police, nurses, doctors and dentists had been awarded large "catch up" increases.

But the Government's proposals found a hostile response in Scotland. Donald Dewar argued that a starting date for the first payment of January 1, 1987 (in place of October 1, 1986) and other adjustments suggested by Rifkind would rob the teachers of £50 million of pay.

The episode demonstrated both the strength and weakness of Rifkind's position. The former had been shown by his capacity to reverse Thatcher's long-held opposition to an independent inquiry on pay and conditions, securing approval for the setting up of Main where Younger had argued in vain. But the latter was illustrated by his inability to deliver the full recommended settlement, even though the Government continued to argue that Main should be treated "as a package" by the teachers in every other respect.

Martin Dowle, Chief Political Correspondent of *The Scotsman*,

LABOUR PREDOMINANCE REASSERTED: THE REGIONAL ELECTIONS OF 1986

John Bochel & David Denver

There can be little doubt that the most significant development in Scottish Regional elections since the formation of the Regional Councils in 1984 has been the steady incursion of political parties into local electoral competition. By 1982 all four major parties (Conservative, Labour, Alliance and SNP) were heavily involved in Regional elections. In the six 'partisan' Regions (Grampian, Tayside, Fife, Lothian, Central and Strathclyde) containing about 90.0 percent of the electorate, party competition was overwhelmingly the norm. In Scotland as a whole too, the proportion of Independent candidates had more than halved. These developments, along with the formation of the Liberal/SDP Alliance and its strong intervention in local elections, led us to give our report on the 1982 elections the title: Towards a Four Party System?

The results of the general election of 1983 suggested that this question was a fair one since Scotland returned MPs from all four parties to Westminster, and in some respects the 1986 Regional elections suggest that the question is still pertinent. Table 1 shows the number of candidates each party put forward in 1986 compared with 1982. In the partisan Regions increases in the number of Labour (3), Alliance (14) and SNP candidates (62) more than offset the small decline (-16) in the number of Conservative candidates. In these Regions the SNP contested 92.0 percent of the divisions, Labour 89.0 percent, the Conservatives 73.0 percent and the Alliance 69.0 percent.

While the Alliance and the Conservatives have room for advances, Labour and the SNP are close to saturation point in terms of candidacies of partisan Regions. The record number of candidates in 1983 was partly a product of the presence of a large number of Green Party representatives (69) but it is difficult to know whether this represents the first appearance of a new political force or merely a temporary flurry of ecological interest which will not be repeated. The higher level of party participation has important consequences for the nature of the choices facing electors. Table 2 shows the incidence of various forms of electoral competition in 1982 and

23

1986, again distinguishing partisan and non-partisan Regions.

TABLE 1

Party of Candidates 1982-86

	Partisan Regions		Non-Partisan Regions		Total	
	1982	1986	1982	1986	1982	1986
Con	259	243	24	16	283	259
Lab	294	297	28	20	322	317
Alliance	217	231	13	14	230	245
SNP	245	307	21	23	266	330
Ind	29	23	111	118	140	141
Others	53	97	–	1	53	98
Total	1097	1198	197	192	1294	1390
Divisions	331	335	110	110	441	445

TABLE 2

Forms of Electoral Competition 1982-86

	Partisan Regions		Non-Partisan Regions		Total	
	1982 %	1986 %	1982 %	1986 %	1982 %	1986 %
Major Party Contest	92	96	18	13	74	75
Major Party Unopposed	6	2	12	11	7	4
Major party v Ind/Other	2	2	27	28	9	9
Ind/Other Contest	–	*	15	18	4	5
Ind Unopposed	–	–	28	30	7	7

Note: * = less that one percent. The numbers of divisions are as in Table 1.

In partisan Regions, the proportion of divisions that witnessed a contest between at least two major party candidates rose from 92.0 to 96.0 percent between 1982 and 1986. Put another way, only 14 of 335 divisions in these Regions did not have such a contest in 1986. In contrast, in non-partisan Regions the percentage of major party contests declined and a pattern of unopposed returns of Independents remained common.

TABLE 3

Percentages of Divisions Uncontested 1974-86

	1974 %	1978 %	1982 %	1986 %
Partisan Regions	7.3	10.7	5.7	1.5
Non-partisan Regions	17.1	52.4	40.0	41.0
Total	9.7	20.9	14.3	11.2

The trend in unopposed returns since 1974 is shown in Table 3. It is clear that as party competition has increased in the partisan Regions, the incidence of unopposed returns has steadily diminished. In contrast, following the first flurry of activity in 1974, unopposed returns in non-partisan Regions seem to have stabilised at around two-fifths of divisions. Those who deplore 'politics' in local government should recognise that at least 'politics' promotes electoral competition. A somewhat similar point can be made with reference to turnout in contested divisions. Table 4 shows the trend in this case.

TABLE 4

Percentage Turnout in Contested Divisions 1974-86

	1974 %	1978 %	1982 %	1986 %
Partisan Regions	50.7	44.8	43.0	45.9
Non-partisan Regions	49.6	43.3	40.2	40.1
Total	50.4	44.7	42.9	45.6

In every round of Regional elections the turnout of voters has been greater in the partisan Regions and the gap between these and the non-partisan Regions has been widening. In 1986 areas with party competition had a turnout almost five points higher than the others despite the fact that Grampian, a partisan Region, had the lowest turnout of any individual Region (as it has had in all four sets of elections).

A small proportion of uncontested seats and higher turnouts are by-products of party competition. Our final piece of evidence about the changing nature of party competition in Scotland is given in Table 5. Thus far we have referred only to 'party contests' defining these as any contest involving two or more candidates of the major parties. Such contests can take many forms however and the table shows how these have changed since 1974.

TABLE 5

Forms of Party Contest (Partisan Regions)

	1974 %	1978 %	1982 %	1986 %
Four-way Contests				
Con v Lab v Lib/All v SNP	5	6	45	51
Three-way Contests				
Con v Lab v SNP	21	52	16	12
Con v Lab v Lib/All	12	3	9	3
Other Three-way	1	0	10	15
All Three-way	34	55	35	30
Two-way Contests				
Con v Lab	42	18	5	0
Lab v SNP	14	11	8	15
Other Two-way	5	9	7	5
All Two-way	61	38	20	20
Total Party Contests	254	279	304	321

In 1974 straight fights between Labour and the Conservatives were the commonest form of party contest, accounting for two-fifths of such contests, while other straight fights accounted for another fifth. Only five percent of party contests involved all four parties. Four years later the situation changed markedly. The number of SNP candidates rose sharply and as a result there were many more triangular contests. More than half of these were of the Conservative v Labour v SNP variety. Four-way contests remained rare, however. In 1982, following the formation of the SDP and its alliance with the Liberals there was another sea change. Four-way contests were now the commonest (45.0 percent of contests) and there were corresponding declines in three-way and two-way battles. This trend continued in 1986. More than half of the contests involved all four parties. The only form of straight fight to have occurred in significant numbers was Labour v SNP and these contests were concentrated in just two Regions (Central and Fife). Not a single division in the partisan Regions had a straight fight between Labour and Conservative – a clear indication of the change in the form of party competition at Regional elections since 1974. If, then, party systems could be adequately characterised on the basis of candidatures there would be good grounds for arguing that the 1986 Regional elections saw a continuation of the trend towards competitive four-party politics in Scotland. But of course candidatures tell only one side of the story and when we consider the outcome of the elections a rather different picture emerges.

Patterns of Party Support

The most significant influence on the results of the 1982 Regional elections was the intervention of the Alliance for the first time on a large scale. In addition the Labour Party nationally was in disarray and was tumbling in the polls as the Conservatives benefitted from the government's handling of the Falklands war. Despite these portents, Labour held its own in the 1982 elections and it was the Conservatives and the SNP who suffered losses, though the Conservative losses may have been dampened by the Falklands and the 'Lothian' affair.

In the run up to the 1986 elections things looked different. Labour under its new 'realistic' leadership seemed to be back on the rails and the party was benefitting in the polls from the more centrist image being projected. The Conservatives, in contrast, were in the doldrums. The government had committed a series of gaffes – beginning with the Westland affair – and in Scotland in particular there was much discontent – within as well as outside the Conservative Party – over the government's handling of the teachers' dispute, rating revaluation, the closure of the Gartcosh steel plant and the question of heating allowances during severe weather. In all of these cases the Conservatives appeared indifferent to Scottish interests.

Both the SNP and Alliance, on the other hand, had some cause for optimism. The SNP had been slowly creeping up in Scottish opinion polls and had gained a number of council seats in local by-elections. The Alliance had also performed well in local by-elections in England and were in a strong position in national opinion polls. Its strength in Scotland, however, remained more problematical.

The distribution of votes at the 1982 and 1986 elections is shown in Table 6.

TABLE 6

Party Share of Votes in Regional Elections 1982-86

	Partisan Regions		Non-Partisan Regions		Total	
	1982 %	1986 %	1982 %	1986 %	1982 %	1986 %
Con	25.8	17.3	13.1	9.6	25.1	16.9
Lab	39.2	45.6	9.6	12.1	37.6	43.9
All	18.4	15.5	13.4	7.1	18.1	15.1
SNP	13.7	18.6	9.5	11.5	13.4	18.2
Ind	2.3	2.0	54.4	59.2	5.1	4.8
Other	0.6	1.1	–	0.5	0.6	1.1

Clearly the Conservatives suffered a major setback. In partisan Regions their vote fell to 17.3 percent, by far their worst performance at local level in Scotland since reorganisation. They were outpolled by the SNP whose slight recovery in popular support was confirmed as they increased their vote share to 18.6 percent. The SNP also overtook the Alliance whose vote declined to 15.5 percent, although the Alliance's disappointment could be tempered by the fact that this was a slight improvement upon their performance in the 1984 District elections. It is Labour's showing which catches the eye, however. From an already predominant position Labour's vote increased sharply. They obtained their largest level of support to date at Regional elections, far outstripping their competitors.

Due to the small numbers of votes involved, changes in patterns of support in non-partisan Regions are not very significant although it is worth noting how Independents maintained their dominance while falling further back over the country as a whole.

As we have cautioned in previous analyses of local election results, the figures in Table 6 are 'raw', taking no account of variations in candidatures and unopposed returns. The SNP as we have seen, for example, sharply increased its number of candidates between 1982 and 1986 and that might partly explain its apparent recovery. But its average vote per candidate did increase.

A check on the trends identified in Table 6 is made in Table 7 which shows the four parties' shares of the votes in divisions which all four contested in both 1982 and 1986, of which there were 108.

TABLE 7

Change in Party Support in 108 Four-Party Divisions 1982-86

	1982 %	1986 %	Change %
Con	28.7	19.9	−8.8
Lab	37.5	47.0	+9.5
All	23.2	18.6	−4.6
SNP	10.7	14.4	+3.7

While the precise percentages are, of course, slightly different from those given in Table 6, trends are similar although these data suggest an even stronger Labour advance than the 'raw' figures and (not unexpectedly given their increased number of candidates) a rather more modest SNP gain.

Noting trends from one local election to the next is, of course, largely of interest to local government specialists or local politicians. Most political commentators and national politicians are more concerned about trends in relation to general elections. Table 8 gives an indication of these trends by comparing the 1983 General Election results in Scotland with the distribution of votes in all wards (166) having a four-party contest in the 1984 District elections and all divisions (165) having a four-party contest in the 1986 Regional elections.

Clearly the Conservatives are in steep decline in Scotland while Labour has recovered from its relatively poor performance in the 1983 general election The SNP seems to be staging something of a comeback while the Alliance, though suffering a drop in support are hanging on to a respectable share of the Scottish vote. It would be unwise, however, to extrapolate from these figures to make predictions about the outcome of the next general election, although the MORI poll published in *The Scotsman* on May 5th 1986 closely reflects the figures in the third column of Table 8. The electorate is highly volatile and the next election may be still two years away. In addition, voters will be confronted with a different set of tactical situations in a general election and this is likely to affect their behaviour. It does seem clear, however that if the Conservatives do not do something to improve their electoral fortunes in Scotland they face the prospect of losing a significant number of the 21 parliamentary seats they now hold. The Conservatives do not now control a single Regional council, they have a majority on only 4 of the 53 District councils (with only 5.0 percent of the Scottish electorate) and in only one of the non-partisan Regions (Dumfries and Galloway) can they boast a Member of Parliament.

TABLE 8

Trends in Party Support in Scotland 1983-86

	General Election 1983 %	District Election (4 way Contest) 1984 %	Regional Election (4 way Contest) 1986 %	MORI Poll 5 May 1986 %
Con	28.5	25.8	20.8	21.0
Lab	35.2	45.9	45.8	45.0
All	24.6	17.5	18.5	19.0
SNP	11.8	10.8	14.9	14.0

The impression conveyed by the voting figures of overwhelming Labour predominance in the 1986 Regional elections is emphasised when the distribution of seats won is considered. These data are shown in Table 9.

TABLE 9

Regional Council Seats Won

	Partisan Regions		Non-partisan Regions		Total	
	1982	1986	1982	1986	1982	1986
Con	106	57	13	8	119	65
Lab	177	209	9	14	186	223
All	18	31	7	9	25	40
SNP	18	27	5	9	23	36
Ind	11	10	76	69	87	79
Others	1	1	–	1	1	2
Total	331	335	110	110	441	445

In partisan Regions, the number of seats won by the Conservatives was almost halved. Labour, on the other hand, advanced to over 60.0 percent of the seats at stake. Advances were also made by the Alliance and the SNP, but both still have a relatively minor presence in regional councils. Once again the number of Independent councillors declined. Labour now has an absolute majority of seats in four Regions (Fife, Lothian, Central and Strathclyde) which together contain some 74.0 percent of the Scottish electorate and they are the largest party in two others (Grampian and Tayside). The remaining three Regions (Highland, Borders and Dumfries and Galloway) are 'controlled' by Independents. The trend towards four-party politics as indicated by contests and candidatures is, then, rather superficial. As at District level, Regional politics is best characterised as a system of one-party predominance with three 'also-rans'.

It remains to be seen whether the other parties become disheartened by Labour's apparent impregnability or whether they will continue to plug away in the hope that something will turn up which may undermine Labour's position.

John Bochel, Department of Political Science and Social Policy, The University of Dundee.

David Denver, Department of Politics, University of Lancaster.

RATING REVALUATION REVISITED

Arthur Midwinter, Colin Mair and Charles Ford

Introduction

The political significance of the Scottish rating revaluation of 1985 was that of a catalyst for change. The Government had come under increasing internal pressure (i.e. from its own supporters) in 1984, some simply protesting about the growth of rate bills and the political consequences of that for the Conservatives, others concerned about the inability of the Government's control system to discriminate between 'prudent' and 'profligate' authorities.[1] The impact of revaluation was to increase demands from conservative groups for reform. Although much was made in the media of widespread public dissatisfaction, in our view the pressure was confined to a small but vociferous and active number of pressure groups, both of the ratepayer and business variety. For example, in Lothian, only around 5% of domestic ratepayers challenged their new assessments. This is certainly an increase from the 3% of 1978, but when one takes into account the change in incidence of taxation from non-domestic to domestic, it is hardly evidence of widespread discontent. Moreover, although the non-domestic sector benefited as a whole from the changeover, there were some dramatic individual increases. Non-domestic ratepayers appeals by contrast rose from 19% to 25% in 1985.[2]

Yet the impression given in the media was of a nation in revolt. In part, this is because of the general misconception that revaluation will be to the detriment of all ratepayers. A more accurate picture would be of a minority in revolt. Those who were gaining had no reason to.

The search for an alternative system of local government finance began in the Conservative Government's first term. This focussed on domestic property and in January 1982, the Secretary of State announced that the revaluation due to be held in 1983 would apply to non-domestic property only, the intention being not to have a domestic revaluation whilst the future of the domestic rating system was being considered.

Following strong representations by the Convention of Scottish Local Authorities and others that this would create anomalies, the Government decided to defer the revaluation completely for two years. Some commentators interpreted this decision as reflecting the expectation that revaluation would have adverse electoral consequences for the

Government. The revaluation postponement aroused no great political opposition. One senior official voiced to us the view that this is only because "– revaluation is used as a political whipping-boy, the convenient raw material for the making of political capital, and all political parties are guilty in this respect. It is my view that the real reason was that a partial revaluation was administratively impossible".

By the late summer of 1984, early indications of the likely effects of revaluation were available. By October, a report of the Distribution Committee of the Working Party on Local Government Finance recommended an increase in the domestic element of the Rate Support Grant, which would mitigate the effects of revaluation on domestic ratepayers. Government ministers took a series of interim measures to ameliorate the effect of revaluation.

In December, 1984, the Minister announced that Industrial Derating was reduced from 50% to 40%, and increased the domestic element of the rate support grant from 1p to 5p in the pound (on the new valuation). Thereafter protests grew, both within the Conservative party and amongst its natural supporters, owner-occupiers and sections of the business community. Early in 1985, the Government made it clear that revaluation would not be postponed, and in February announced a further increase in domestic rate relief to 8p in the pound, the equivalent of about £1 per week per household.

This second subsidy was achieved by generating savings in other elements of the Scottish Office expenditure block, namely regional aid, roads and transport, prisons, health and housing. The total now consumed by Domestic Rate Relief was £102 millions, compared to £14.3 millions in 1984-5. The final stage in the process was responding to the pressure from the small business sector. Whilst the overall effect of revaluation was broadly neutral on the commercial sector, within that category considerable variation in the revaluation factor occurred. So the Scottish Office had a strong political card to play and managed to obtain concessions from the Treasury out of the Contingency Fund. The sum of £50 million was allocated for further rebates for those whose valuation had increased at least threefold (in contrast to the national 2.3 times increase) with an individual limit of £10,000 placed on this particular subsidy. The special legislation to allow this was assisted by opposition parties in Parliament.

It should not be assumed, however, that these adjustments were painless. There is some evidence that the reduction in industrial derating caused hardship to some small industrialists. Moreover, the increase in the domestic element of the rate support grant reduced the amounts available for the needs and resources element. That is, it redistributed grant income away from poorer, needier areas, to wealthier ones. Finally, these changes denied industry the full benefits of revaluation. These changes we suspect will be temporary, and a gradual reduction of the domestic relief will take place. (It was reduced to 7p in the current year).

Revaluation in Scotland gave an additional impetus to the Government's efforts to find an alternative to the rating system. Indeed, revaluation was presented in the latest Green Paper as providing further evidence of the unfairness and unacceptability in the rating system (Scottish Office 1986). Whilst we are sceptical of this view, we have little doubt that, combined with the reduction in the rate support grant, and the budget conflict in Edinburgh, it strengthened Ministers' resolve to find a politically acceptable alternative. We shall address some of these issues later, but at this point, an account of the mechanics of the system is necessary, for it became clear that even active lobbyists are confused over how the system works.

The basis of domestic rates is a valuation placed by the Assessor on rateable value, and that valuation is an estimate of the rent at which a property might reasonably be expected to be let for a one year period with a reasonable expectation of continuance (based on the contractor principle). It is based on a survey of the property market, rental evidence, and some other general factors. Thomson[3] lists these as the age, degree of attachment, construction, amenity and quality of a house.

The Assessor enters properties in the Valuation Roll showing annual value. In the case of domestic properties these are valued to a Gross Annual Value, and a statutory allowance is deducted to cover the upkeep of the property to arrive at Net Annual Value. All other subjects are valued direct to Net Annual Value.

The amount of rates payable by each ratepayer is determined by the rateable value of the property multiplied by the Regional and District Rates. The combined rate is reduced by a statutorily determined sum (7p per £ of Rateable Value in 1986-7) for domestic ratepayers. People on low incomes have their rates taken into account in a system of housing benefits, and therefore treated as part of their housing costs. Domestic water rates are levied separately, but paid with the rate payments.

Given the basis of the rating system, it is clear that frequent revaluations are necessary. In this respect, we are in full agreement with the former Scottish Secretary, George Younger, who told the House of Commons,

"It is the precise purpose of having a revaluation to reflect changes in values both upwards and downwards. It was never the purpose to ensure that nobody had an increase and nobody had a reduction. That would merely perpetuate the unfairness which revaluation is designed to reduce."

The changes in liability are the consequence of valuation from rental. In Scotland, house rentals have moved upwards in steady progression for the past twenty years. Levels depend very much upon public authority housing and on rents set by Rent Assessment Committees and Rent Officers. However, the industrial and commercial sector are more sensitive to changes in the economic climate. Industrial depression causes industrial rents to fall, in real terms, and the level of value in the commercial sector ebbs and flows from place to place. This explains the changes which occurred in 1985. In 1978, the changes benefited domestic ratepayers, and as a result, domestic rate relief was reduced from 31p to 3p (The relief of 3p in 1977-8 was equivalent in terms of the new valuations applicable to 1978-9 to 11p in the pound.)

According to law in Scotland, a revaluation must take place every five years. In 1983, with the agreement of other political parties and COSLA, the revaluation was postponed for two years, on the grounds that plans to reform the rating system were underway. In fact, the recommendations of the 1981 Green Paper (Department of the Environment 1981) suggested only minimal change, and the Government proposed the retention of rating as the major form of local taxation.[4]

Whatever the reason, the end result was that revaluation was taking place after seven years of fairly traumatic changes in the British economy, and it would inevitably reflect those trends. The major change has been the rapid decline in manufacturing industry, and by contrast, the growth in the service sector and new technology. The rental value of properties will change with the capacity of those different sectors to pay, in short, it will reflect the operation of supply and demand mechanisms in a mixed economy.

The second related change was the growth of unemployment. Areas experiencing high unemployment will likewise have reduced capacity to pay rents, and house prices will also be affected. For those in work, however, the picture has been somewhat different, and in particular in families where the growth of working spouses has led to increased family income and aspirations. The demand for home ownership has increased and, therefore, the putative 'rental value' of privately owned houses relative to the public sector.

The end result was inevitably going to be changed tax liabilities for many ratepayers. There is also a difference in the basis of the valuation for the commercial sector. Housing is valued on the principle of a 'balanced market' (the assumption that supply equals demand for housing), whereas the value of shops for rating purposes is accordingly governed by a straightforward comparison of rents actually paid.

There has been rapid fluctuation in the level of value of shops, particularly with the developments of new shopping centres, which redirect the flow of potential value from one part of the town to another, often lowering the value of other shops. Revaluation is necessary to reflect this, otherwise shops with reduced income will be left with higher values. Shop rents themselves vary in the regularity with which rents are fixed, some on an annual basis, others on long-term basis. Rents fixed more recently will provide a much more accurate basis for reflecting current economic conditions as shop rental values reflect location, trading and the flow of potential customers.[5]

From the official papers, it is clear that the provisional estimates showed that rateable value would increase on average by 2.3 times. There was, however, a significant range of variation between the four sectors (domestic, industrial, commercial, others), with domestic subjects increasing by 2.6 times on average and industry by 1.7 times on average. These estimates suggested an increase of 16.5% in the share of total rateable value borne by domestic subjects with decreases of 24% for industry and freight subjects and 6% for 'other' subjects.

This prompted the early responses on industrial derating and the increase of domestic rate relief. The effect that had on potential increases is indicated below, and slight modifications were made to these figures later when errors in assessment were corrected.

TABLE 1

(October)

	Before Adjustment	After Adjustment
Domestic	+17%	+ 8 %
Industrial	−25%	−10.7%
Commercial	− 1%	− 1.3%
Others	−11%	−10.5%

Source:Geddes[6]

However, the actual rates increases have also to take into account overall changes in grant income and the spending decisions of local councils. A COSLA paper produced in March 1985, and based on the further increase in the Domestic Rate Relief, local budgets, and the reductions in grant, presented the following picture

TABLE 2

Potential changes in Rating Liabilities of Different Sectors Based on budget Decisions of Local Authorities

	%of RV (1984)	£m	% of RV (1985)	£m	% Change
Domestic	36.9	£533	42.2	£652	+18
Industrial	11.8	£181	10.4	£186	+ 3
Commercial	28.2	£434	27.2	£486	+12
Other	23.1	£356	20.2	£361	+ 1

Source: Convention of Scottish Local Authorities.

The Political Response to Revaluation

As authorities were finalising their budgets in 1985, and as the new assessments were being delivered to ratepayers, pressure grew on the Government, in the main from Conservative Party supporters, ratepayers groups, and small businessmen. During this period, the notion that the Government faced widespread electoral disaster in Scotland unless they took action to mitigate the effects of revaluation became commonplace, and was widely alluded to in the media. For example, the Chairman of the Scottish Conservative Party, Sir James Goold led the pressure to suspend revaluation as "a huge vote loser",(*Glasgow Herald* 23.2.86), and Brian Meek, then Conservative Convener of Lothian Region, expanded this argument into the issue of wider reforms of local government finance.

> "We should stop tinkering with this unfair system and replace it with a more equitable form of local taxation. I cannot recall anything that a Tory Government has done that has been so massively unpopular as this." (quoted in *Glasgow Herald* 7.3.85).

This view was put even more forcibly by Jim O'Neill, former

Conservative leader of Renfrew District Council, who predicted that revaluation would put a lot of small businesses out of business, and have adverse effects for the Conservative Party.

"I have met many people in the business community who supported the party because it backed owner-occupation and small business. But with one move they have destroyed the dreams of many. I don't think Mr Younger, the Scottish Conservative Party, or the Government itself, have any idea of the depth of anger over this issue. At future elections there will be a terrible backlash."(quoted in *The Scotsman* 15.3.85)

What is ironic about all this of course is that the trends in rental value merely reflect economic trends in the market. The growth of owner-occupation and the service sector would inevitably be reflected in tax liabilities. And indeed the Government did share many of these preconceptions of the political consequences as the subsidies to domestic and non-domestic ratepayers show. Public misunderstanding was prevalent in the view that the Government was to blame. One senior local government officer questioned this view.

"However misguided such conceptions may have been, Central Government decided to retreat in the face of the onslaught and it was subsequently announced that an extra £50 million had been found which would be made available to stave off the disaster which apparently was threatening the credibility of the party in power who had evidently assumed responsibility for the outcome of the revaluation. This was surprising as such results were quite predictable and would have been the same no matter what shade of Government had been in St Andrews House or in the House of Commons for that matter. Nevertheless, the dice had been cast."[7]

There is no doubt that potentially the highest increases were faced by the Government's 'natural' supporters, owner-occupiers and small businessmen. The highest increases in the domestic sector, where rental values had risen three times on average for owner-occupied houses compared to 2.6 for all houses, and 2.3 times for Scotland as a whole. This was noted in the recent Green Paper.

"Average movements at the regional level mask even more dramatic increases falling on individual ratepayers. The average domestic valuation in Scotland increased on revaluation by a multiplier of almost 2.7, but 130,000 Scottish householders faced multipliers of more than three times their previous rateable values."

Increasing domestic rate relief provided the biggest subsidies to those occupying houses with the highest rateable value. (In short, the subsidy was a regressive one.)

It is also true that some of the highest increases were faced in the commercial sector, but it is unclear that job losses would result. One Officer questioned this view.

> "Revaluation has *not* put many small businesses out of business, and though it has caused many small businesses to tell the press and me that they could be put out of business, but I have yet to see evidence of this."

In his opinion, job losses result from technological changes in retail practice rather than simply from revaluation. New shopping centres are designed for more efficient profit-making by reducing overheads, and such developments have offsetting effects in traditional shopping centres, whose retail values will also drop. The matters are interconnected.

> "But on the simpler basis of looking at a retail shop, no case has been brought to my attention where a shopkeeper has had to pay off staff because his rent or valuation has increased. I can recall one such 'demonstrative' case, but the very needs of the business involved re-engagement of staff who had been temporarily laid off."

Public protest centred around three key themes.

First, it was argued that revaluation demonstrated that rating was unfair and ought to be replaced.

Second, it was argued that revaluation discriminated against Scottish ratepayers vis-a-vis English ratepayers.

Third, it was widely believed that revaluation caused rates increases. The third theme does have some credence and will form the third part of this paper. The other two themes represent misunderstanding of the system by lobbyists, and we will only make a brief comment about each of these.

The notion that rates are unfair was invoked regularly, both in attempts to delay revaluation, *and* in the pressure mounted for the abolition of the rating system. The National Federation of Self Employed and Small Businesses have been powerful and persistent critics of rating's unfairness. One of the worst hit areas by revaluation was the Borders Region, and their NFSESB spokesman, John Curtis, adopted that line.

"It must be remembered that rate increases and demands bear no relation to the ratepayers' ability to find the money.......the rating system is unfair and completely out of date but, despite election promises, the Government has done nothing to introduce alternative methods of raising local finance."(quoted in *The Scotsman* 8.2.85)

The Scottish Conservative Party Chairman, Sir James Goold, argued that the revaluation experience showed that "the rating system, with a reducing industrial base and with not all that many people paying rates, is not the proper system for financing local government."(quoted in *The Scotsman* 8.2.85)

Let us now address some of these assumptions. Firstly, we should be clear as to the *actual* impact of revaluation. It does not increase the *rating income* of local authorities, but updates the rateable values to take account of changes in inflation and circumstance since the previous revaluation. What it does do is alter the balance between *ratepayers*, and indeed *local authorities*, because it affects their entitlement to rate support grant. Those with above average increases in rateable values will have their grant income reduced, as the resources element seeks to equalise grant income per penny rate poundage, and those with below average incomes will have their grant increased. For the small number of authorities who receive no resources element, their position is that if they had above average increases in rateable value, their tax raising *potential* is increased (i.e. they can raise more for a penny rate) and vice-versa.

The notion that revaluation demonstrated that rates are an unfair tax is mere tautology, for all that revaluation showed was that if you change the basis of calculation then you change the outcome in terms of tax liability. The mere fact that these changes took place is no more evidence that rates are an unfair tax than the previous pattern of tax liabilities were *per se*.

The notion that revaluation does not take account of ability to pay is only true in a narrow sense. Certainly values ignore income considerations, but indirectly, as these are based on comparisons with actual rental and property market evidence, the system does so. The Green Paper[8] distinguishes between the 'redistributive' and 'beneficial' principles in rating. The redistributive principle "sees the value of property as the measure of the taxpayer's ability to pay. The ratepayer, in living in a more valuable house than he truly needs, has exercised choice, knowing that one of the consequences is an increased tax liability."[9]

As noted earlier, the basis of valuing shops for rating purposes is governed broadly by a straightforward comparison of rents actually paid. In a market economy, one has to assume that the buyer (the renter of the property) is willing to assume the consequent rent and rates costs of doing so, and if the highest increased values were in sectors and locations experiencing relative economic prosperity, it is difficult to see this as unfairness. It is possible to argue that there are similarities in principle between the income tax system and the rating system, particularly for non-domestic ratepayers, if income tax is viewed as a share of the profits of employment, and rent as an appropriate share of the profits of occupation of property. (This view was put to us by a Chartered Surveyor in private correspondence).

In terms of logic, it would be wrong to argue that revaluation showed that rating is an unfair system. Those who argued in this way were simply transferring their own general criticisms of the rating system *per se*, to revaluation itself.

The second recurring theme was the notion that revaluation was unfair to Scotland vis-a-vis the rest of Britain. Mrs Mary Whitehouse, Chairman of the Scottish Ratepayers Federation, made this point frequently in the press. Sir James Goold, Scottish Conservative Party Chairman, used this argument when calling for the suspension of revaluation, as "it demonstrates the way in which Scotland suffers, whilst England does not." More expectedly, Donald Stewart MP, President of the SNP, also calling for revaluation to be shelved, stated that revaluation continued the Government's policy of direct discrimination against Scotland, using Scots "as guinea pigs for measures which would be unacceptable in the Tory shires or the Home Counties."(quoted in *The Scotsman* 6.4.85). By contrast, John Davidson, of the Scottish CBI, believed that revaluation had gone some way to rectifying imbalance between industrial/commercial rates and domestic rates, whilst arguing that industry and commerce still pay more than similar interests in England.

Again, there are serious problems with these assumptions. It is certainly the case that there has been no revaluation in England since 1973. In part this is for technical reasons. With the growth of owner-occupation, and the decline of the private rented sector, it was stated in the Layfield Report of 1976 that the point had been reached in England and Wales where enough rental evidence to support another revaluation of domestic properties on a rental basis would not be available.[10] A recent study argued that only 1.7% of private dwellings in the Borders Region had rents which were useable for valuation purposes.[11] However, this study wrongly ignored the public rented sector.

There are problems of comparing the outcomes of the two systems, as they are based on different principles. And the data does not exist to allow a comprehensive comparative analysis of the tax liabilities of non-domestic ratepayers North and South of the border.

Certainly, the selectivity exercised by pressure groups for purposes of political lobbying (e.g. Celtic and Manchester United, or Frasers and Harrods) provides no sound basis for conclusions. In terms of domestic ratepayers, there is consistent evidence of higher average rates in England vis-a-vis Scotland, both per house and as a proportion of average incomes.[12] There are reasons for expecting this to be the case. Scotland has a higher level of central government support for local government finance than in England. England has a higher level of owner- occupation, with consequent higher rateable values, and thus higher rates.

As the two systems have different principles, it is wrong to assume that an English revaluation would settle what real anomalies do occur anyway. Only when a uniform system of valuation is introduced will this be so. What has to be clear, however, is that a revaluation in England would have *no direct* impact on rates in Scotland, nor vice versa. A revaluation in England would lead to some ratepayers paying more and others less, and in all probability, to use an American analogy, a shift in grant resources from the English "sun belt", the prosperous South and South East, to the English "frost belt", the industrial North.

The 1981 White Paper *Alternatives to Domestic Rates* predicted that an English revaluation would have the following shifts:

(a) Larger, older labour intensive industries in the Midlands and the North would have their relative rate burdens substantially reduced.

(b) Newer steelworks, local shops and older offices would receive a slight reduction.

(c) New offices and small factories on modern industrial estates would be slightly increased.

(d) Shops in primary locations and modern oil refineries would be substantially increased.

These are similar to the changes which occurred in Scotland. As a result, the political consequences for the Government could be more dramatic than in Scotland if a revaluation now took place in England. This does not conceal the fact that rates are lower in the South and higher in the North than they would be if revaluation took place. Whatever the position in England, apart from industries in *direct* competition, (i.e. *not* Frasers and Harrods) it is difficult to find any serious argument that revaluation was discrimination against Scotland as a whole. This would only be so if *all* Scottish ratepayers paid more as a result of the revaluation (which they do not) and as a result paid more for the same level of service as in England. What is surprising is the lack of knowledge of the system by political or pressure group activists seeking to affect change. One would have thought a sound knowledge of how the current system works is a necessary prerequisite to informed advocacy of change and reform.

Analysing the Impact of Revaluation on Rates

We have already stressed that revaluation does *not* increase the rating burden as a whole. It does, however, have relative effects between ratepayers and areas. We cannot examine detailed and individual cases, and whilst we know that, in general, industrial ratepayers gained and domestic ratepayers lost, and others were broadly neutral, there will always be exceptions to those general trends because of peculiar local circumstances. Ratepayers do not pay 'national' rates, so knowing the broad shifts for Scotland as a whole are only indicative.

The proportions of rateable value paid by the different classes of ratepayer varies between authorities, so one would expect any relative effect of revaluation on rates to vary also. There are two ways of analysing this effect. One is by suing direct measures of the change in rateable values. Table 3 below shows the wide range of changes incurred across Scotland within the total overall changes which ranged from 1.4 to 2.7.

TABLE 3

Range of Revaluation Multipliers by Sector

Domestic	2.4 to 2.9
Industrial	0.6 to 2.8
Commercial	1.3 to 3.4
Other	1.5 to 3.6

We can see the range is considerable. It may well be, however, that such indicators have a varied effect on rates. For example, an authority which had a high increase of rateable values for its industrial ratepayers, but which sector provided only a small proportion of its rateable income, would have a different effect from an authority with the same degree of increase but where that same sector accounted for a higher proportion of its rateable values. We know also that these proportions vary considerably between authorities. For example, Table 4 sets out the variations in domestic as a proportion of total income.

TABLE 4

Domestic as a Proportion of Total Rateable Income

Number of Authorities	Percentage Range
2	0–9%
Nil	10–19%
2	20–29%
18	30–39%
22	40–49%
10	50–59%
2	60% +

We have therefore constructed three measures which reflect the pattern of change nationally. If we are looking for explanations of variations in the effect of revaluation *between* authorities, then we know to concentrate on measures relative to the two classes of ratepayer where the most significant overall changes took place, namely domestic and industrial ratepayers.

We have suggested two indicators to take account of the effect of industrial decline. The first is simply the *percentage of industrial rateable value in the total of rateable value.* With the decline in industrial values, authorities with high proportions of industrial ratepayers will have greatly reduced rateable income which could affect the amount which needs to be raised in rates from other sectors *within* the authority, and may well bring them into the resources element and affect other authorities. Secondly, we propose using a simple measure of *population density* as industrial decline is thought to be greatest in urban areas.

The final problem is the choice of a dependent variable. We have already argued that revaluation does not in itself increase local authority expenditure, but what it does change is the rateable and grant income of authorities. As the greatest overall increase was faced by domestic ratepayers, we have chosen the *% growth in average domestic rate bill* as the domestic variable as this will vary directly with the effect of revaluation. The average domestic rate bill in Scotland grew by 19.5% in 1985-6, (after account is taken of selective action to reduce the rate in the City of Edinburgh).

We tested the relationship of these variables using the statistical technique of regression analysis. When used in data analysis, this is a versatile statistical procedure employed for exploring and testing the relationship between a dependent variable and a set of independent variables. The technique can be used to quantify the strength and nature of relationships among certain variables while controlling the effect of other variables in the regression formula. The statistical relationship between variables is sought in a linear model of prediction. It can, therefore, identify general relationships. It cannot be used for the explanation of features specific to a few observations.

TABLE 5

	Average Domestic Rate	% Domestic	% Industrial	% Commercial
Ave. Domestic Rate	1.000			
%Domestic	0.316**	1.000		
%Industrial	−0.257*	−0.262*	1.000	
%Commercial	0.057	0.267*	−0.198	1.000
%Other	0.061	0.167	−0.048	−0.286*
Population Density	0.487***	0.246	0.050	0.356**

* = Significant at .05 level
** = Significant at .01 level
*** = Significant at .001 level

The first stage of the analysis was simply the production of simple correlations, as set out in Table 5. It provides some statistical support for the hypotheses framed earlier, with one spectacular exception. The strongest correlation found was between population density and the average domestic rate increase. So whilst the simple correlations suggest that no general relationship exists between the percentage of commercial and the percentage of domestic rate increase, its close association with population density suggests that it was in urban residential and commercial centres that the greatest impact of revaluation was felt and that population density is not a surrogate for industrialisation as expected. We know that high increases occurred in residential Bearsden and Eastwood for instance, and the big commercial cities such as Aberdeen, Glasgow and Edinburgh. Importantly, there was a negative relationship (as expected) with the surrogate for industrial decline (percentage of rateable value for industrial ratepayers). In fact, the areas most likely to benefit from revaluation were areas of traditional Labour Party control.

There are obvious problems of multi-collinearity with the data. That is, simple correlations do not isolate completely the explanatory power of specific variables. For example, areas with a high dependence on domestic rateable income are also closely associated with high levels of income from commercial ratepayers.

We pursued this further by entering the variables into a stepwise, multiple regression, a technique for isolating the effects of individual variables and identifying those variables with the strongest explanatory power. That is, the analysis selects those variables most strongly associated with the dependent variable, the percentage increase in the average domestic rate payment.

The empirical findings confirm our theory. *Population density* was selected first, and explained 23% of the variance. The second variable selected was the *percentage of rateable values raised by industrial ratepayers*, and the relationship, as expected, was a negative one. This second variable added only a further 6% to the variance explained.

TABLE 6

**Stepwise Regression on Effect of Revaluation
on the Average Domestic Rates Payment**

Variable	Correlation Coefficient	Variance Explained
Population Density	0.487	23.73%
% Industrial in Rateable Values	−0.235	29.17%

None of the other variables adds any further explanations to those two variables, and are therefore rejected by the computer. This provides partial confirmation of our hypotheses. Areas with high proportions of industrial ratepayers are areas of relative economic decline, and this has been reflected in the movement of rental levels, and thus of rateable values. They would therefore receive additional resources element grant and, assuming no change in spending or grant levels, this would result in lower domestic rate payments than in residential areas. However, in the real world of local politics, changes in grant and spending occur as local authorities react to changes in their financial, social, economic and political context. Moreover, as we saw, less than 30% of the variance in increases in domestic rate payments were directly attributable to revaluation.

We can explore the issue further by widening the analysis to include other factors unaffected by revaluation, by seeking to explain changes in rateborne expenditure. Revaluation does not affect rateborne expenditure for local government as a whole. What it changes is the balance of contributions between classes of ratepayer and local authority area. We have already examined the effect of changes between classes of ratepayers on authorities. What matters here is the changes in revaluation overall. Authorities with high increases in rateable values will have consequent decreases in the resources element of the Rate Support Grant. In some cases, where authorities do not receive resources element, high revaluations would represent real growth in the financial raising capacity of a penny rate, and potential real growth in income to authorities (e.g. Grampian Region where the growth was above the Scottish average). Table 7 below sets out the changes in valuations for regional and island authorities. In the case of Orkney and Shetland, neither of whom receive resources element, revaluation resulted in a real loss of income per penny rate product, and this reflects the high proportion of non-domestic rateable income.

A similar picture emerged for districts where the range of changes varied from 2.1 to 2.7. Significantly, the highest increases overall were in areas where the Conservative Party is electorally strong. These were, Berwickshire (2.7), and Ettrick and Lauderdale, Roxburgh, Annandale and Eskdale, Kincardine and Deeside, Moray, Eastwood, Angus, and Perth and Kinross (all 2.6). In Eastwood, and Perth and Kinross District, the local Conservative MPs received considerable flak for the effect of both revaluation and government grant decisions on rates. The decision about absolute levels of grant would also affect the capacity of the resources element to compensate for relative changes in rateable income resulting from revaluation.

TABLE 7

Revaluation Multipliers 1985

Authority	Multiplier
Borders	2.6
Central	2.2
Dumfries and Galloway	2.5
Fife	2.4
Grampian	2.5
Highland	2.3
Lothian	2.3
Strathclyde	2.2
Tayside	2.5
Orkney	1.4
Shetland	1.7
Western Isles	2.3
Scotland	2.3

In this instance we will use the % *change in rateborne expenditure* as a measure of changes in local taxation, as the use of *rate poundages* would be complicated by the effect on poundages by revaluation. That is, the amount raised for a penny rate rose by 2.3 times in Scotland as a whole as a result of revaluation, thereby reducing the rate poundages fixed by authorities.

One variable likely to impact on rateborne expenditure is: *percentage change in the needs element* of the Rate Support Grant, the sum of money provided by central government as being indicative of need to spend. In 1985, the government decided to alter radically the balance of this grant between regions and districts, and whereas the total amount available to regional services fell by 1.86% (in part because of the increase in domestic rate relief), the sums available to districts fell by 27.83%. The effect of this is a cosmetic one, the intention being to increase the grant contribution to major services and assist more equitable use of grant between regional, therefore having very minimal impact on actual rates payments. But the effect of these changes needs to be isolated and controlled to examine the effects of revaluation on rateborne expenditure.

The next variable is the *percentage change* in *the resources element*, which is the direct result of revaluation. Some regions and islands get no such grant, and some such as Grampian did in the past, but revaluation

TABLE 8

	Rateborne Exp. (% Change)	Growth in Spending (% Change)	Balances	Change in Resources Grant (% Change)	Revaluation Multiplier	Change in Needs Grant (% Change)
Rateborne Expenditure	1.000					
Growth in Spending	0.553***	1.000				
Balances	0.467	−0.016	1.000			
Change in Resources Grant	−0.102	−0.167	−0.016	1.000		
Revaluation Multiplier	0.492***	0.260	0.139	−0.321**	1.000	
Change in Needs Grant	−0.346**	0.047	−0.140	−0.271*	0.073	1.000
Guideline Excess	0.252	0.649***	−0.234*	0.125	−0.123	−0.041
Growth in Guidelines	0.032	0.122	0.333**	0.036	−0.233*	0.133
Labour Control	−0.480***	−0.432***	−0.293*	−0.316**	−0.565***	−0.225*

*   = significant at .05 level
**   = significant at .01 level
***   = significant at .001 level

changed that.

For both the foregoing factors, we would assume a relationship that the greater the grant loss, the greater the increase in rateborne expenditure.

The third factor resulting from the decisions of the Secretary of State is current expenditure guidelines. Each year central government issues current expenditure guidelines to authorities to assist in their financial planning. Although described as indicative, these guidelines are crucial features of the penalty and rate-capping mechanisms. Guidelines are based on two sets of calculations. The first is the client group assessments of expenditure need, which form the basis of both guidelines and the distribution of the needs grant. The second is the operation of a safety net mechanism whereby assessments of need are adjusted to reflect past expenditure patterns. That is, authorities who would require to make dramatic savings to reach these assessments have them adjusted closer to their last year's budget in order to provide a more attainable guideline. The converse is also true.

Since the guidelines became linked to the penalty (or general abatement) system, the pressure to conform to them has increased. Indeed, some authorities whose needs assessment was growing lobbied hard to have the scale of the secondary adjustment modified to give greater prominence to the client group assessments in 1985-6. We have used % *growth in guidelines* as a potential explanatory variable.

We now turn to local factors. The first of these is simply the *revaluation multiplier* for each authority. It too, like the decisions of the Secretary of State, is a given. It does not in itself lead to changes in rateborne expenditure, but it can seriously constrain the choice. For example, an authority with a growing rateable income could choose either to use it to promote growth in spending, or reduce local taxation levels, whereas an authority with falling levels of income is less fortunate, dependent upon where it stands vis-a-vis its guidelines. So it could choose to increase its overall level to compensate for loss of income, or reduce spending, or some combination of these. At any rate, the key point is that the effect of revaluation would not be mechanical, but rather one of constrained choice.

The second variable relates to existing spending. Rateborne expenditure will be increased or reduced dependent upon the availability of unspent balances or accrued deficit in the previous year. The application of balances will reduce the level of rateborne expenditure, and rating for deficits will increase it. The variable used is the *percentage change in balances/deficits.*

Government ministers continually insisted that a major cause of increased rates was local 'overspending'. The Scottish Secretary stressed this, even after he announced the subsidies to both domestic and non-domestic ratepayers.

> "We are in no doubt that there are many in Scotland who even after the new rebates will continue to face hefty rates increases this year, especially in areas where the local authorities have been less than responsible in budgeting." (speech to the House of Commons, 3.6.85)

We have included three variables which reflect local spending decisions. One is the *percentage change in net expenditure* (that financed by grant and rates) with the expectation that higher increases than suggested by the RSG settlement will lead to higher rateborne expenditure. A second indicator is the *degree of excess above current expenditure guidelines.*

Thirdly, there is a widespread assumption that Labour-controlled councils are "high spenders". Our own view is that this is an over-simplification, and whilst we would accept that in terms of political philosophy one would expect Labour to be more favourably disposed to local spending than the Conservatives, the Labour Party has a wide diversity of philosophy and practice with regard to local government (as with other areas of public policy). From our own research, we are aware of several Labour authorities which exhibit great concern for rate levels and the avoidance of rate-capping.

The variable we have used is simply *Labour control.* This is consistent with previous academic research[13], which argues that it is the fact of party control of the council which matters rather than the size of the majority. We have assumed therefore that Labour councils would be more prone to increase spending than either Conservative, Independent, or hung councils, and that the one authority controlled by the SNP would not be of statistical significance anyway. Our detailed knowledge of that authority (Angus) is such that we are aware of that Group's concern for fiscal prudence and in fact it met the government guidelines in 1985-6.

We have again examined these factors in two stages. Table 9 sets out the simple correlations found and reveals some strong associations. There is a negative correlation (-0.565) between Labour Party control and the revaluation multiplier. This confirms our previous findings that the areas of economic prosperity did have the expected higher valuations with adverse political consequences for the government.

In terms of explaining variations in rateborne expenditure, the strongest association was with growth in spending (0.552) and secondly, with the revaluation multiplier (0.492). Both of these are consistent with the government view that revaluation and spending growth were important factors. What is perhaps unexpected is the strong *negative* relationship between Labour control and both growth in rateborne expenditure and net expenditure. If authorities were being "less than responsible in their budgeting", then these do not seem to have been Labour controlled authorities.

Further examination shows the availability of balances to be quite strongly associated with growth in spending. Loss of needs grant is also related to growth in rateborne expenditure (the financing decision), though not to growth in net expenditure (the spending decision).

Some of these findings are really quite important. Already it appears that changes in *income* had a much greater effect on the financing decision of local authorities than the expenditure decisions. There are only two significant relationships identified with growth in spending. Budgeting to spend above guidelines is strongly related (0.649), which is not surprising, as guidelines now reflect past spending, but the real surprise again is the negative relationship between Labour control and spending growth. Labour councils lost needs grant, and gained resources grant in 1985-6, but these appear to have had little impact on the spending decision. Importantly, however, although guidelines growth had no impact on either the spending or the financing decision *overall*, it was weakly negatively associated with Labour control, and suggests Labour councils were constrained by this because of its implication for grant penalties.

As expected there was a negative relationship between the revaluation multiplier and the change in resources grant. There was no relationship at all between the needs grant and the revaluation multiplier. This can be interpreted as demonstrating that those authorities with the most buoyant local economies had less need to spend on local public services.

Again, many of these factors are interrelated, so we sought to isolate the effects through stepwise multiple regression. 31% of the variance in rateborne expenditure was attributable to growth in spending, 23% due to changes in the availability of balances from the previous year (i.e. rating for spending previously funded from balances) 9% was negatively related to growth in expenditure need (as reflected in the needs grant) and 10% because of revaluation. In total these four variables explain 73% of the growth in rateborne expenditure, and all the other variables tested are rejected.

TABLE 9

Explanations of Change in Rateborne Expenditure

Variable	Correlation Coeficient	Variance Explained
Growth in Spending	.553	30.6%
Availability of Balances	.475	53.2%
Change in Need	−.313	62.8%
Revaluation	.337	73.2%

Conclusions

Revaluation did have considerable impact on the tax liabilities of individual ratepayers. Domestic ratepayers as a whole paid more, commercial ratepayers approximately the same (with greater variations) and industrial ratepayers paid less.

Its relative effects between authorities were minimal in comparison to other factors. In general, industrial areas with high levels of public housing gained central government resources from the changes. Areas of traditional Conservative support lost grant, and had higher rates increases as a result.

Whilst the spending decisions of local authorities were important, so also was the effect of changes in available balances perhaps because these were heavily used in 1984 to keep down district rates in the election year. Labour party control, contrary to expectations, proved unimportant. Labour councils were less likely in 1985-6 to finance higher spending, perhaps because of potential grant penalties. Other councils appear to have been less concerned about penalties and guidelines.

So whilst revaluation could be crucial in determining individual rates bills, its significance was much less in explaining rates increases between local authorities. As the biggest effect was on domestic ratepayers in general, and private house owners in particular, the political problems for the government were considerable. The more exaggerated claims about revaluation have little substance. Revaluation did not prove that Scotland was suffering vis-a-vis England, nor that rating is an unfair system. Indeed, the provision of additional grant for areas of social and economic decline has been a direct consequence of revaluation, and one which would not have occurred without it. In England, this problem can only be overcome by a revaluation, but this will not happen in the lifetime of the present Parliament.

Arthur Midwinter is senior lecturer in administration at Strathclyde Business School, and Director of the School's Public Sector Management Unit.

Colin Mair is lecturer in administration at Strathclyde Business School.

Charles Ford is research fellow in administration at Strathclyde Business School.

References

1. Martin Dowle "The Year at Westminster", in D McCrone (ed.) *The Scottish Government Yearbook* (Unit for the Study of Government in Scotland, University of Edinburgh) (1986), pp.5-20.

2. John Gardener "Rating Reform" paper presented to a Seminar organised by the Royal Institute of Chartered Surveyors, Edinburgh, (14 February 1986).

3. James Thompson Guide to Home Valuation (Department of Regional Assessor, Fife House, Glenrothes) (1985).

4. Department of the Environment *Alternatives to Domestic Rates*, Cmnd 8449, (London HMSO) (1981).

5. John Gilchrist *Report on the 1985 Rating Revluation in the Borders Region*, Report prepared for Borders Regional Council (1985).

6. Eric Geddes "Note on Revaluation in Scotland", in *Municipal Journal* (November 1985).

7. Eric Geddes, *op cit*.

8. Department of Environment *Paying for Local Government*, Cmnd 9714 (London HMSO) (1986).

9. John Gardener, *op cit*.

10. Layfield *Local Government Finance* (Report) Cmnd 6453 (London HMSO) (1976)

11. John Gilchrist, *op cit*.

12. Department of Environment 1986, *op cit*.

13. L J Sharpe "Does Politics Matter", in K Newton (ed.) *Urban Political Economy* (Francis Pinter (Publishers) Ltd London) (1981) pp.1- 26.

IBM in Scotland-more than three decades of growth.

IBM has been an integral part of the Scottish economy since 1951 – the year IBM United Kingdom was formed. That year, IBM UK established its first manufacturing plant at Greenock on the banks of the Clyde, where 100 people built typewriters and accounting machines.

Today, 2,700 people work there producing advanced information technology products including Display Systems and the IBM Personal Computer. Over 85 per cent of IBM Greenock's production is exported to countries in Europe, the Middle East and Africa.

Through branch offices in Edinburgh, Glasgow and Aberdeen, IBM UK serves more than 4,000 Scottish customers; from banking and insurance to North Sea oil and gas; from manufacturing to retailing and distribution; from education to local and central government administration.

IBM's operations in Scotland, those of our customers and of the 2,000 British suppliers to the Greenock plant, contribute significantly to the prosperity and welfare of Scotland and to the economy as a whole.

IBM

IBM UNITED KINGDOM LIMITED, BUCHAN HOUSE, 21 ST. ANDREW SQUARE, EDINBURGH EH2 1AY.

THE SCOTTISH "ELECTRONICS" INDUSTRY[1]

Jim Walker

1. Introduction - The Three Waves

In the mid-1980s the electronics industry has been hailed as the Scottish manufacturing success story. According to one source (Firn & Roberts[2]) it represented 1.1% of total Scottish manufacturing employment in 1959 whereas by 1983 it accounted for 9.9%. However, this nine-fold increase in share of total manufacturing employment only reflects an absolute increase in employment terms of 5.7 times ("electronics" employment growing from 7,400 in 1959 to 42,500 in 1983). Furthermore, one firm, Ferranti, accounts for over 7,500·of this total, or 17.6%. In the following chapter we shall discuss in turn a number of important aspects of the Scottish electronics industry e.g. employment, output and trade, as well as some of the disturbing issues which have been ignored in the euphoria surrounding the industry's 'rapid growth'. These will be examined presently but first a brief history of the development of electronics in Scotland is in order.

The first wave

The forerunners of the modern Scottish electronics business appeared in two distinct waves of inward investment. The first wave started during the second world war when Ferranti set up its first Scottish factory in Edinburgh to manufacture gunsights. After the war there was an influx of US multi-national enterprises (MNEs) which located right across the industrial central belt of Scotland – from National Cash Register in Dundee to International Business Machines in Greenock. NCR arrived in 1947 and was followed by Honeywell (1948), Burroughs (1949) and IBM (1951) amongst others. These MNEs were primarily involved in manufacturing electro-mechanical products, from time-clocks and cash registers to the first generation of computers. As such they employed mostly skilled and semi-skilled male labour with a predominantly engineering background. Unlike more recent start-ups in the electronics industry, this male domination has stayed with these companies to the present day. Also in contrast to more recent 'incomers' the majority of these firms were, and still are, unionised (the most notable exception being IBM[3]). In the past, Burroughs, Honeywell and NCR have had their fair share of labour difficulties which have contributed to the long-held fears on the other side of the Atlantic that Scotland was a country of militant trade unionists and, therefore, not a good investment option. While there seems to be no doubt that the experiences of these firms did have an effect on the investment decisions of a number of their more timid compatriots the record of IBM in Greenock has done much to dispel the myth. IBM maintains that it is not anti-union (indeed, some of its workforce remain members of trade unions) but equally, it refuses to recognise single or joint trade union negotiating rights. There have been no major disputes in the company's thirty-odd years on Scottish soil a record which largely reflects the firm's package of benefits, rates of pay and guarantee of a job-for-life. In the second wave of inward investment, the non-union IBM model was adopted by most of the incoming firms.

The second wave

The first wave of inward investment had established some of the strongest original equipment manufacturers (OEMs) in Scotland. However, most of the components and sub-contract work required to service these giant electro-mechanical firms was, by necessity, imported. In contrast, the second wave of inward investment in the late 1960s brought with it the basis for the important components industry which is still strong in Scotland today. Again the inflow was dominated by US firms – Motorola, General Instruments, Hughes Microelectronics, National Semiconductor and Hewlett Packard. While the last named added to the industrial products and information systems sector of the Scottish industry the other four all brought with them the new 'solid-state technology' which was replacing the old diodes, valves and wiring of the early giant (in physical terms) computers. These companies utilised semi-conductor materials to manufacture transistors – the immediate predecessor of today's integrated circuit or microchip.

This period of active inward investment took place during the phase of strong regional policy as enacted by the Wilson government. Retrenchment in the industry followed in the early to mid-1970s and employment fell from a peak of around 49,000 in 1970 to just under 31,000 in 1978 (Crawford[4]). Latest estimates (Industry Department for Scotland[5]) place employment in the industry at 45,800 still some way short of the 1970 peak.

The third wave

Perhaps one of the major factors drawing attention to the electronics industry over the last few years has been the sector's continuing growth while other manufacturing industries have declined or stagnated (thus accounting for the industry's ninefold increase in the share of Scottish manufacturing employment since 1959 while in absolute numbers the workforce has increased by less than sixfold). The IDS claims that output in the industry more than doubled in the period 1978 to 1984 (although difficulties with definitions and re-classifications open this figure to some question). At the same time the Scottish Development Agency has been successful in attracting well-known, established names in the electronics industry world-wide to Scotland. As in the other investment waves these firms have been mostly American but two notable Japanese enterprises – Nippon Electric Company and Shin-Etsu Handotai – have been among them. All major aspects of the electronics industry have emerged in Scotland; from electronic data processing equipment to optical precision instruments. Expansion in existing electronics firms has been a characteristic of this development.

The predominant position of electro-mechanical engineering became a casualty of the disinvestment of the 1970s and the picture in Scotland today is of a highly electronic-orientated workforce concentrated mainly in the defence, industrial and semiconductor/components sectors.

2. The structure of the industry today

One of the most important aspects of the phenomenon known as 'Silicon Glen' is the concentration of electronics and electronics-servicing firms in an area 80 miles long by 30 miles wide. There are now around 300 firms in this central belt of the country which is similar in size to one county in the large American states. This concentration can be contrasted with the fact that in the US these counties often have one, or at most, two firms located in them. In this section the main features of the industry, employment, output and trade, will be reviewed.

Employment

It should be noted first that, in discussing changes in employment in the Scottish electronics industry over time, there have been a number of revisions and re-classifications of the government's Minimum List Headings (i.e. the most detailed breakdown of employment and output available from official sources). Under the 1980 Standard Industrial

Classification the electronics industry is split into 10 Activity Headings as shown in Table 1.

TABLE 1

Current electronics industry Activity Headings

3302	Electronic data processing equipment
3433	Alarms and signalling equipment
3441	Measuring, checking and precision instruments and apparatus
3442	Electrical instruments and control systems
3443	Radio and electronic capital goods
3444	Components other than active components
3453	Active components and electronic sub-assemblies
3454	Electronic consumer goods
3710	Optical precision instruments
3732	Telegraph and telephone apparatus and equipment

With respect to these headings the IDS (IDS[6]) have estimated electronics employment for selected years between 1978 and 1984 using the Census of Employment and Regional Data Systems. These data are shown in Table 2.

TABLE 2

Estimated electronics employment 1978-84 : by industry grouping

	Employees in employment from:			
	Census of Employment		Regional Data Systems	
Industry groupings	1978	1981	1983	1984
Electronic data processing equipment*	8,100	7,100	8,700	9,400
Electronic components**	9,600	8,400	9,700	10,500
Electronic instruments engineering‡	6,600	5,700	5,400	5,400
Other electronics‡‡	13,000	17,100	20,100	20,500
All electronics sector	37,300	38,300	43,900	45,800

Note: *   Activity Heading 3302
     ** Activity Headings 3444, 3453
     ‡   Activity Headings 3710, 3732
     ‡‡ Activity Headings 3433, 3441, 3442, 3443, 3454

Source: IDS Statistical Bulletin

The resulting estimates suggest increases in employment in all industry groupings except electronic instruments engineering over the period 1978-84, with the increase for electronics as a whole being of the order of 23%. However, the extent of employment expansion in the sector is a subject of some debate. Data from an alternative source, the Engineering Industry Training Board, paint quite a different picture (see Table 3).

TABLE 3

Electronic and related industries employment, 1978/83 (SIC, 1980)

Industry grouping	Employment in Scotland	
	April 1978	April 1983
Office & data processing equipment	10,940	8,671
Basic electrical equipment	7,881	5,151
Electronics*	23,997	24,480
Other electrical engineering	18,407	6,185
Instrument engineering	11,806	7,656
Total‡	**73,031**	**52,143**

Note: *   EITB definition
         ‡   Office machinery and data processing equipment,
              Electronic amd electrical engineering and Instrument
              engineering

Source: EITB Statutory Returns

Using a wider SIC definition, the EITB estimates employment in electronics and related industries as having fallen from 73,031 in April 1978 to 52,143 in April 1983 (a decrease of 28.6%). Only the electronics sector displayed an increase in employment over the period, and that of only 2%. How can these two sets of figures be reconciled? The stock answer is that they cannot. There are, however, sufficient grounds for caution with respect to the considerably more optimistic IDS figures which, as IDS concedes, are compiled from a number of sources and are subject to reclassification according to current production patterns[7]. It is worrying from the point of view of forecasters and serious commentators on the Scottish economy that two reputable sources of information should provide such widely differing estimates. However, given that most previous employment estimates have been based on IDS figures we must accept these for the purposes of comparison. In so doing, a picture of the regional distribution of electronics employment in Scotland in the two years 1976 and 1984 can be drawn (see Table 4).

TABLE 4

Estimated employment in electronics in Scotland by Local Authority Region, 1976/84

| | Estimated total electronics employment | | | |
| Region | 1976 | | 1984 | |
	Number	%	Number	%
Strathclyde	18,000	50	19,100	42
Lothian	8,640	24	11,000	24
Fife	6,120	17	8,500	. 19
Tayside	1,080	3	4,300	9
Borders	1,080	3	2,900	6
Rest of Scotland	1,080	3	—	—
	36,000	100	45,800	100

Sources: 1976, Scottish Economic Bulletin No.16
1984, IDS, Statistical Bulletin

This table displays that there was a fairly high degree of stability in the proportions of employment in each region between the two years. However, there was a slight shift in employment from the west to the east coast regions. Whereas Strathclyde's employment share has dropped by 8% (although in absolute terms the number employed has increased marginally), the Fife and Tayside shares have increased by 2% and 6%, respectively. Within all of these regions employment is concentrated in a number of towns and industrial estates e.g. the new towns of Glenrothes (Fife), Livingston (Lothian), Cumbernauld, East Kilbride and Irvine (all Strathclyde) have successfully attracted many inward investment companies. One of the main reasons for the shift in proportions from west to east coast regions is the fact that Glenrothes and Livingston have attracted mainly new, high growth electronics firms during the third wave of investment. On the other hand, many of the first and second wave electro-mechanical employers settled in the new towns on the west coast (nearest Prestwick airport and America) and therefore Strathclyde has experienced a much slower rate of employment growth because incoming electronics firms are often making up the job numbers which the electro-mechanical producers have shed.

Employment is also concentrated in the industry in a number of sectors. A sectoral breakdown of employment was provided for 1983 by the Scottish Development Agency (SDA[8]) and is shown in Table 5.

TABLE 5

Sectoral spread of electronics employment (1983)

Source	%
Industrial, commercial and telecommunications	25
Defence electronics	25
Information Systems	22.5
Semiconductors and components	17.5
Sub-contracting	7.5
Consumer sector	2.5
	100.0

Source: Scottish Development Agency

Highlighted in this table is Scotland's relative weakness in sub-contracting – an indication of the central buying policy of many of the OEMs sited in the country. However, it is also the case that many large electronics concerns (e.g. IBM), restrict the amount of sub-contracting services they buy from any one supplier to between 20-30% of the sub-contractor's output. This safeguards the sub-contractor in that it reduces the risk of closure born of dependency on one or two major customers but, at the same time, makes it difficult for small, indigenous firms of this type to emerge. The SDA and government are now focussing attention on ways of alleviating this imbalance but it is too early yet to detect real signs of success.

McCulloch points to another important feature of the Scottish industry:

"It should be noted that employment in the defence systems, information systems and semiconductor market sectors is primarily with large MNCs, whereas in the industrial and commercial support components sectors, the average company size is very much smaller."(McCulloch[9])

During 1984 there was rapid growth in the semiconductor and

components sectors which appeared to establish the potential for a higher employment share than 17.5%. However, the semiconductor industry experienced considerable difficulties during 1985 (see section 3) and over 1,000 jobs were lost in this sector alone. It must also be borne in mind that the majority of jobs in the defence sector is due to three firms – Ferranti, Barr & Stroud and Racal-MESL – whereas around 300 firms account for the employment in the remaining sectors.

The heterogeneity of the industry is perhaps best illustrated by breaking down employment by country ownership as in Table 6.

TABLE 6

Employment by country ownership and number of firms, 1983

Location of ownership	Number of firms	Average number of employees
Japan	2	179.0
Europe	6	66.5
U.S.A.	34	511.4
Rest of UK	49	354.5
Scotland	178	39.4
Total	**269**	

Source: Scottish Development Agency

From the table it can be estimated that although there were only 34 US firms (not plants) in Scotland, they accounted for 40% of electronics employment i.e. they are large employers. On the other hand, the 178 Scottish-owned firms accounted for only 17% of employment and had by far the lowest average number of employees.

Two final features concerning the composition of employment in the Scottish electronics industry are worth considering: the degree of technical and support staff and the ratio of female to male labour.

The SDA (SDA[10]) claimed that, in 1978, scientists, technologists and technicians accounted for 22% of the electronics workforce. By 1981 this figure had reached 26% and was expected to touch 30% in 1985. Evidence from the Engineering Industry Training Board goes some way towards reinforcing these claims for electronics, and office machinery and data processing equipment in particular. The occupational structure of electrical, electronic and instrument engineering in Scotland as at April 1983 is shown in Table 7. From this table we can see that the two sectors –

electronics, and office machinery and data processing equipment – have 22.1% and 27.8% of their workforces classified as scientists, technologists and technicians (the sum of rows 2 and 3). This is noticeably more than, for instance, basic electrical equipment (10.6%), a more traditional sector serving the electricity supply industry which reflects the craft and occupational structure of industries such as mechanical engineering.

TABLE 7

Occupational structure of electrical, electronics and instrument engineering in Scotland (April, 1983)

	Off.mach/ry & data processing	Basic electrical equipment	Percentage in each occupation Electronics*	Other electrical engineering	Instrument engineering
1 Managerial	8.7	5.3	4.7	5.1	3.9
2 Scientists & technologists	16.7	1.0	7.1	1.5	6.2
3 Technicians	11.1	9.6	15.0	4.8	10.7
4 Admin. & Prof.	11.0	4.8	5.9	7.2	6.4
5 Clerks, typists etc.	12.7	8.0	9.6	9.5	9.6
6 Supervisors & foremen	3.6	4.2	4.7	5.4	3.9
7 Craftsmen	4.4	30.8	9.0	9.5	14.1
8 Operators	27.4	32.6	39.3	53.7	40.2
9 Others	4.4	3.5	4.7	3.3	5.0
Total	**100.0**	**100.0**	**100.0**	**100.0**	**100.0**

Note*: Definition of electronics used by EITB. It excludes data processing equipment, alarm and signalling equipment, measuring and optical instruments but includes records and pre-recorded tapes.

Source: Engineering Industry Training Board

If, as the SDA claim, the occupational structure of the electronics industry (corresponding roughly to columns 1 and 3 in Table 7) is becoming more highly skilled, then a number of issues are raised. Most importantly, it must be considered whether Scotland is well-equipped to meet the demand for higher skills. Secondly, there is the question of whether if high wage, skilled labour is taking an increasing share of total electronics employment, other occupations are being squeezed to make way for them. The first question will be re-addressed in section 3 but here we shall concentrate briefly on the second.

It is not necessarily the case that, as the proportion of scientists, technologists and technicians grows, the absolute numbers in other occupational grades will fall. However, one of the main reasons for a growing high skill element in the workforce is the degree of automation being introduced into the industry. In the present day electronics industry automation is particularly affecting the labour intensive assembly operations e.g. automatic machine insertion is taking over from hand population of printed circuit boards and the surface mounting technique of fixing microchips to these boards growing at the expense of flow-soldering and manual operations. One section of the workforce which these developments are likely to hit first is that dominated by female workers – the semi-skilled assembly tasks area.

In some firms in the industry (especially in integrated circuit and assembly unit production) the female component of the labour force is as high as 75%. Often the tasks women are asked to perform require a high degree of manual dexterity and repetition. Many managers believe that women cope better with the high boredom factor in these operations although this appears to be based on amateur psychology rather than scientific fact.

In assisted areas, of which Scotland is one, official figures, contained in Cooke et al[11], have estimated female employment at 74% of all manual production workers (falling to 48% in non-assisted areas). However, developments in the industry are leading larger electronics firms to shed unskilled labour and increase the demand for semi-skilled and skilled technicians and engineers. The future demand, therefore, for unskilled female (and male) labour looks set to fall and, indeed, current employment levels may be difficult to maintain.

Ownership

It follows from the development of the Scottish electronics industry that much of the ownership of the industry lies outwith Scottish and, indeed, UK hands.

TABLE 8

Employment by country of ownership (%)

Country	Employment
Japan	1
Europe	1
Scotland	17
US	40
UK	41

Source: Scottish Development Agency

Only 17% of electronics employment is in indigenous Scottish companies and the US rivals the UK for top spot in employment share (as Table 8 shows). This share mix is in part a reflection of the success of the SDA's campaign to bring inward investment in high technology companies to Scotland but, as we have seen, multinational investment (particularly from the United States) predates by a long way the Scottish Development Agency.

Many worries have been expressed at the degree of multinational control in the Scottish electronics industry. Politicians and trade unions, in particular, seem concerned at the influence these companies have and their 'notorious' nomadic qualities. While it is the case that a number of MNEs have closed or reduced their operations in recent years (e.g. Standard Telephone and Cable, ITT, Singer, Hoover, Burroughs, Honeywell, General Instruments and Timex) this is true also of a vast number of indigenous, UK and public firms. Indeed, Rada[12] makes it quite clear that the electronics and information technology markets are singularly distinguished from past innovations in that only if they operate on a world level can they become economically efficient. The price for a reduced role of MNEs in the Scottish industry would be a loss of status in the world market and the possible collapse of the servicing and components elements of the industry altogether.

Furthermore, there is little or no evidence to date to suggest that US multinationals regard Scotland as merely a 'staging post'. They have, more often than not, located in Scotland to serve not only the UK but the European market (as the fact that in 1983 Scotland was producing 21% of Western Europe's semiconductor output while having only 1.5% of its population clearly shows). The US multinational presence in Scotland is a mature and welcome feature of our economic and industrial life. In the electronics business it has acted as a catalyst to research and development (which has led to world leadership in areas such as optoelectronics and artificial intelligence) while in the economy in general it has not only brought much needed jobs and investment but new work practices and managerial philosophies which, if not always successful or desirable, are at least stimulating and thought-provoking.

Major products and markets

The electronics industry is, like most industry groupings, heterogeneous. As Levidow and Young[13] point out, heterogeneity stretches to the spatial dimension also.

> "...software production is focused on the high-wage areas such as London and the Home Counties in the UK, whereas micro-electronic hardware production has been drawn to the low-wage areas such as South Wales and Scotland." (Levidow and Young (eds))

This quotation indicates exactly where Scotland's product strength lies – in hardware and systems manufacture. Disaggregation reveals that the 'big four' product areas, in terms of employment, are industrial products, information systems, defence and avionics, and electronic components (see Table 9). Together these accounted for 77.6% of total electronics employment in 1983. The defence and avionics component is comprised mostly of mature investment and has expanded little in recent years. The electronic component product area (including semiconductors) is also technically very well advanced. Every semiconductor firm in Scotland undertakes wafer fabrication i.e. they are located at least at stage 3 in the stylised 'sophistication' ladder shown in Table 10.

In many less developed countries semiconductor producers operate mainly at stages 1 and 2. A mark of the sophistication or maturity of a country's semiconductor industry is indicated by movement through the various stages of product development. In Scotland's case some firms have even reached stage 5 e.g. Motorola and National Semiconductor, but to the best of our knowledge stage 6 is still confined to parent firms in the US and Japan.

The SDA considers that there are four areas where future electronics developments in Scotland will be particularly strong: semiconductors, very large scale integration (VLSI), artificial intelligence (AI) and opto-electronics. NEC and Digital are carrying out research into VLSI and

Edinburgh University's Wolfson Institute (now Wolfson Microelectronics Limited) has built up world leading expertise in AI and optoelectronics over the last 15 years. Furthermore, the SDA have also forecast growth rates in the European market over a range of products (see Table 11). These forecasts were based on market size in 1983 and project the then expected total increase in demand to 1986.

TABLE 9

Scottish electronics industry by produce area, 1983

Main product area	Number of companies	Number of employees	% share of total electronics employ
Industrial products	82	8,984	21.1
Information systems	24	8,880	20.9
Defence and avionics	9	7,739	18.2
Electronic components	52	7,406	17.4
Telecommunications	14	3,961	9.3
Electric sub-contracting	46	2,507	5.9
Consumer products	11	2,048	4.8
Design services	17	596	1.4
Medical electronics	14	402	1.0
	269	42,523	100.0

Source: SDA Survey [14]

Table first published in Firn and Roberts

TABLE 10

The semiconductor industry: stages of development in inward investment receiving countries

1. Warehousing and marketing functions

2. Assembly plant

3. Low-volume wafer fabrication

4. High-volume wafer fabrication

5. Silicon foundry work and design capability

6. World product responsibility

TABLE 11

European market increase in demand 1983-86 by product

Product	Demand increase %
Data processing equipment	63
Office equipment	27
Control and instrumentation	25
Medical and industrial	23
Communication and military	30
Telecommunications	26
Component	34
Consumer	19

Source: SDA slide presentation

Undoubtedly the current recession in the semiconductor market has adversely affected the estimate for components. If, however, the other forecasts are at all accurate Scotland is in a good position to further increase the size of its electronics industry as a result of its relative strength in the reputedly fast-growing product areas of data processing and communication and military equipment.

Firn and Roberts[15] claim that, in total, 38% of Scottish electronics production is exported whereas a further 55% goes to the UK market other than Scotland. These estimates are somewhat different from the corresponding proportions derived from the two Scottish Input-Output studies for 1973 and 1979 as indicated in Table 12.

In 1973 imports from the rest of the UK formed 71.4% of total Scottish electronic and communications equipment inputs. By 1979 this had fallen to 23.8% reflecting the upsurge in Scottish component, sub-contracting and service firms. The rest of the world import content had stayed fairly stable at 19-20%. However, exports to the rest of the world in the two years were substantially higher than the Firn and Roberts estimates i.e. rising from 45% of output in 1973 to 52.2% in 1979, with RUK exports falling back from 43.4% to 34.5% over the same period. Since the electronics industry has become, if anything, more export-oriented in the last few years the Firn and Roberts figure for ROW exports begins to look like an under-estimate. The discrepancy is most probably explained by the fact that some of the rest of the UK (RUK) trade reported in the Firn and Roberts study may be exported at a later date.

It is clear that the Scottish electronics industry enjoys a healthy trading surplus. Exports to the rest of the world outweighed imports from the rest of the world in both 1973 and 1979 and the trade balance with the rest of the UK moved from deficit to surplus between the two years.

TABLE 12

Scottish electronics industry trade flows 1973 and 1979
(% of total output)

	1973*	1979**
Imports (RUK)	71.40	23.80
Imports (ROW)	19.00	20.00
Exports (RUK)	43.40	34.50
Exports (ROW)	45.00	52.20
Total Output/Input‡	£326.47m	£813.40m

Note   *Comprises communications equipment and computers and electronics
    **Includes activity headings 3302, 3433, 3442, 3443, 3444, 3453, 3710, 3732
    ‡These figures are in current year prices as at the date of the study.

Sources: Input-output tables for Scotland[16]

It appears, therefore, that the electronics industry is a major contributor to the health and robustness of the Scottish economy in terms of employment, investment, trade, research and development as well as with respect to the less tangible aspects of new work philosophies. However, the industry has suffered a variety of 'growing pains' and setbacks. It is to these that we now turn.

3. Growing pains and other maladies

As mentioned in the introduction to this chapter, there have been a number of disturbing issues recently which have tempered claims that the Scottish electronics industry is in an unstoppable virtuous growth circle. In the following section three constraining aspects of the industry are considered.

The semiconductor slump

The semiconductor industry worldwide had its best ever year for sales and growth in 1984. Sales worth around $25bn were recorded and a further

22% growth was forecast by the Semiconductor Industry Association for 1985. Orders (bookings as they are referred to in the industry) exceeded $1,200m in the United States at the beginning of 1984. However, by January 1985 orders had slumped to around $600m in the worst market fall in the industry's history. Particularly badly hit were the giant US multinationals, many of whom form the backbone of the Scottish industry.

The slump was caused by a mismatch of demand and supply which resulted as a consequence of one of the congenital weaknesses of the electronics industry – over-optimism. The central problem arose in the home and personal computers market. Around 20 or so manufacturers were each aiming to take 25-50% of the market in the US and planned production accordingly[17]. As personal computer makers increased production, lead-times on the supply of microchips increased. This in turn caused other manufacturers, such as mainframe computer makers and telecommunications suppliers, to re-order early thus exacerbating the position. When the expected boom failed to materialise in the PC market excess demand quickly shifted to excess supply and, even with cuts of 40-50% in the price of a single chip, the market collapsed. The position for semiconductor firms was made even worse by the appearance of a large resale market made inevitable by the bankruptcies of the unsuccessful PC makers. The American market felt the recession most keenly. Up to August 1985 over 5,000 US jobs had been lost in semiconductor firms: 3,000 at Texas Instruments, 1,000 at National Semiconductor, 900 at Intel and 600 at Micron Technology. Scotland too suffered. However, contrary to the conventional wisdom on the 'branch plant syndrome' Scottish-based MNEs have faired better than their US bases.

The first casualties of the recession were the proposed expansionary investments at Motorola (£60m) and National Semiconductor (£100m). The firms maintain that these are just postponements and that the commitments to invest still stand but only time will tell. As 1985 progressed a variety of schemes were introduced in semiconductor firms to cut down output and reduce stocks. For example, short-time working, longer holidays, a reduction in shiftwork and voluntary severance schemes were all implemented. Nevertheless National Semiconductor announced 450 job losses at their Greenock plant during the summer thus bringing the workforce down to 1,100 (200 additional jobs had been lost through natural wastage). At the same time Timex in Dundee announced 400 redundancies due to the fall-off in orders for the Sinclair home computers produced in the factory. By the end of the year, the worst seemingly over, the bombshell of the first major closure in the Scottish semiconductor industry burst. General Instruments, based in Glenrothes, was one of the first semiconductor firms to arrive in Scotland during the 1960s and their position in the market relative to the large, standardised chip manufacturers such as Motorola and National Semiconductor, seemed fairly secure. Like Hughes Microelectronics and Burr-Brown, General

Instruments produced custom and semi-custom made chips for the 'higher end' of the market. One reason forwarded for their closure was that standard chip prices had fallen by so much that it was cheaper for customers to array a number of these chips in a certain way than to pay the price for the more specific, customised components. Whatever the reason, the General Instruments closure shook confidence in the industry.

The largely unforeseen recession demonstrated the dangers of forecasting in such a 'leading edge' industry. In 1983 it was estimated that the Scottish semiconductor workforce of 3,564 would almost double by 1986 (SDA Locate in Scotland[18]). Levels of employment in 1983 and the SDA projections are shown in Table 13 along with employment in the sector as at January 1986.

TABLE 13

The Scottish Semiconductor industry

Company	1983 Employment level	1986‡ Projection	1986 Actual
Motorola	1,259	2,100	1,200*
National Semiconductors	1,300	1,800	1,100*
NEC	170	650	250*
General Instruments	250	650	–
Hughes Microelectronics	547	600	600*
Burr-Brown	38	700	150*
	3,564	6,500	3,300

Note: ‡ Projections taken from SDA/LIS
Asterisks represent estimates from recent announcements where possible.

As the table shows, rather than the projected doubling of employment in the industry some workforces were more or less static and others had grown by much less than forecast. In the case of General Instruments the firm had closed completely.

There have been some signs that the worst of the recession may be over. In September 1985 the book-to-bill ratio (the industry's leading indicator) moved up for the first time in a year. The Semiconductor Industry Association forecast rapid sales growth worldwide of 18% in 1986 (although of only 7.8% for the European market which the Scottish industry serves). Furthermore, in the first quarter of 1986 National Semiconductor began to re-employ some of its workers laid-off during the previous year. In the medium to long term, however, employment prospects in the Scottish-based industry may be diminished by developments on two fronts. First, there is the threat to US firms and their branch plants posed by the recent heavy investment undertaken by competing Japanese firms such as NEC and Hitachi. NEC have developed the 'V' series of microchips which are compatible with IBM products and as such will be in direct competition with Motorola's 'H' series. Although NEC has a facility in Scotland it is possible that if the Japanese were to take a large share of the semiconductor market, the job gains at NEC would be outweighed by job losses in US plantsserving the European market. Secondly, there have been fairly widespread developments in the automation of wafer fabrication and other processes. These are likely to reduce the degree of labour intensity in the industry and thus eventually lead to job losses.

Manpower limitations

Semiconductor firms are not the only examples where automation is proceeding apace in the electronics industry. In many respects this automation entails the application of microprocessor technology to the very industry which produces it. Apart from the fact that this development might cost jobs in assembly and testing it requires a higher level of skilled manpower to operate and develop the new processes. One of the questions asked of companies in the Scottish Business Survey produced by the Fraser of Allander Institute is, which of a number of factors is likely to limit your output over the next three months. In April 1986 14% of companies responded skilled labour and, in July 9%. Although this is anecdotal evidence in that the survey has only been running for two year, it is worth bearing in mind. Indeed, it has been a response which has occured systematically throughout the life of the survey. The Scottish Office (Scottish Economic Bulletin[19]) has given much emphasis to the question of manpower shortages, as has the UK Government. The report on electronics manpower in the mid-1980s suggested that over the decade up to 1983 the composition of electronics manpower had shifted towards graduate and technician manpower and this, coupled with similar demands from other industrial groups, had placed pressure on the supply of these skill groups.

For example, the Scottish Office estimated that in 1979, 1,900 engineers and 2,500 technicians were employed in electronics (representing 5.1% and 6.7% of the workforce, respectively). By 1985 these numbers were expected to have risen to over 3,000 in each of the categories (representing 8.3% of the total workforce in both cases) i.e. an increase in actual numbers of 37%. Furthermore, over the same period the demand for electronics staff in other manufacturing industries was expected to rise by 25%.

To accommodate these demands there are basically three sources of supply of skilled electronics manpower. First, there are graduates from degree courses in the universities and technical colleges. In 1981/82 the intake for electronics degree courses was 780 (double that of 1975/6). More recently the government has made large scale finance available for just this type of course. Edinburgh, Glasgow, Heriot-Watt and Strathclyde Universities all shared in £28m worth of assistance advanced in 1984-85. Secondly, there are Higher National Diploma qualifications available at nine centres in Scotland and, although not considered on a par with a degree course, are more practical in nature. The student intake in 1982/83 for the electronics course was 345 (130 more than in 1979/80) and 166 awards were made in the same year. Lastly, SCOTEC courses (in electrical and electronic engineering) provide the main technical qualifications and are taught on a day-release or sandwich course basis. Over 1,000 certificate awards and around 500 higher certificate awards were expected between 1983 and 1987.

Despite these efforts the fact remains that strains are appearing on the Scottish skilled-labour market. These strains may lead to two things; first, higher salary offers to prospective and existing skilled staff in order to keep them, but secondly, to Scotland becoming a less attractive location for further investment as the manpower pool dries up and the labour cost increases.

The leading edge

One phrase often applied to the Scottish electronics industry is that it sits at the 'leading edge' of technology. This is meant to convey the ideas of frontier research, novel developments and sunrise industry. Indeed, the SDA and Scottish Office have used the electronics industry as a shining example of the new booming, thrusting Scottish economy. The former even employed the term 'critical mass', thus making the analogy that the Scottish industry has reached the stage of self perpetuation. Analogies between controlled natural science phenomena and the uncertain world of human relations, business and industry are always fraught with danger and deletion of this term from the SDA's publicity over the recent difficult period is of little surprise. Industries relying on leading edge technology face a double-edged sword. New ideas, high growth business and explosive profits have their counterpoint in the contribution of rapid technological change to uncertainty and the development of a highly volatile market. The 'leading edge' of technology, regardless of which industry is being examined, brings with it a high casualty rate as well as the opportunity for exceptional success.

Many firms in the electronics business find it difficult to keep abreast of new technology. They also require to be committed to continuing research, development and marketing efforts. It is therefore necessary, if the electronics industry is to remain as a countervailing force to the decline experienced in Scotland's traditional industries, that some public sector involvement be forthcoming. One suggestion has been that the SDA should assist in providing venture capital for the fledgling domestic firms in the industry. In this way failures might be written-off without frightening off the investment trusts, banks and financiers indefinitely (or at least for the period of the crisis, recession or slump). In order that the SDA might play this role the government would have to remove the financial burden of achieving a high commercial rate of return on investments that it has placed on it. This type of commercial constraint breeds caution and inaction in the public agency and deprives leading-edge industries of the necessarily risky support they need. The SDA and government seem content to recognise only one leading edge – the successful one – but in order to maintain and nurture the industry the other edge must also be contemplated and accepted, if not welcomed.

4. Conclusion

The electronics industry is extremely important for the Scottish economy. Since 1975 the electrical and electronic engineering industry's output has doubled, although employment growth has been much less impressive. During the same period other manufacturing sectors have grown very slowly or indeed, declined e.g. mechanical engineering, shipbuilding, textiles and coal mining. But how has Scotland managed to attract such activity in this sunrise industry? Is it all down to public sector efforts?

Government policy has played a part. Until November 1984 almost all of Scotland was designated an assisted area under UK regional policy. In financial terms *regional development grants* of 22% on capital expenditure were available to companies announcing investment plans in Special Development Areas (this has now been cut to 15% on *new* investment only). This was complemented by the existence of *selective financial assistance* (available to both special development areas and intermediate areas) the level and composition of which was decided on various grounds, e.g. desirability of the new investment, number of jobs it would create, degree of complementarity it might bring to the region's existing industries, support for innovation etc. This measure still exists in designated areas. *Advanced factories* were also available in designated industrial estates (often near New Towns) and other incentives such as assistance with training and tax allowances were allowed on a discretionary basis. In Scotland the SDA, through the Locate in Scotland bureau, has a special role in detailing these financial and other incentives for potential inward investors in a fully-integrated package.

Since 1980 selective financial assistance from a number of central government schemes (eg. **Product and Process Development Scheme (PPDS)** and the **Micro-electronics Industry Support Programme (MISP)** the latter of which is now in limbo) has become available to non-UK electronics companies. Indeed, Cooke et al [20] have shown that, especially US, inward investors have become the largest recipients of these funds. Despite this fact these firms claimed that such financial assistance has little impact on their future development or investment plans.

The new towns of Cumbernauld, East Kilbride, Glenrothes, Irvine and Livingston have development corporations which supervise the provision of industrial estates and the complementary amenities (including advanced factories) which go with them. Scotland also has three designated enterprise zones in Clydebank, Dundee and Invergordon, which offer further inducements to potential investors eg. rate-free letting for a period of years. In addition there are a number of area action schemes (eg. Glasgow Eastern Area Re-development project, Garnock Valley Action Area, Motherwell and District LIFE project) which are supported by the SDA and European Community grants as well as special funds such as the British Steel Corporation enterprise trust in the Garnock Valley. All of these quasi-public groups and funding sources are involved in increasing the level of amenities in various areas which help to make them attractive to industrialists and commercial concerns.

However, although such public sector support is important to inward investing firms other factors enter into the location decision.

For example, Scotland's traditionally skilled engineering labour force was a major attraction for the first and second waves of inward investment in electronics and electro-mechanical production. It is also the case that Scotland is a relatively labour-abundant region of the UK and as such has tended to be a relatively low wage region. These factors, high skill levels, (pressures on which now appear to be emerging as discussed in section 3), labour abundance and low wages (especially for unskilled and female labour), have been strong incentives for MNEs to locate in the area.

Academic reputation has also been a pull factor. The eight Scottish universities have a good reputation in both engineering and electronic research. In particular Edinburgh, Glasgow, Heriot-Watt and Strathclyde Universities have strong departments of direct relevance to the electronics industry, ranging from electrical engineering, computer science and physics to high quality research in artificial intelligence and opto-electronics. There is an active university-industry interface which involves academics in consultancy work, research projects in firms and industrialists participating in teaching courses at the various institutions.

One of the most important factors in Scotland's favour has been membership of the EEC. As a member Scotland falls within the tariff wall of the Common Market. The advantage of EEC membership is clearly shown in Table 14 which lists the current tariff rates on selected electronics products imported from non EEC sources.

TABLE 14

EEC tariff on electronic components and equipment

Product	Tariff (%)
Radio and communications equipment	9.3
Industrial control equipment	12.3
Electronic calculation machines	13.3
Semiconductors	17.0

Source: SDA presentation

Semiconductor firms in particular gain an advantage from being located within the EEC.

Further factors such as a plentiful pure water supply, a reliable supply of electrical power and good transport and communications links all add to Scotland's attractiveness as a location option.

Finally, a major inducement factor (if not incentive in itself) is the SDA and, in particular, its two divisions which are active in attracting overseas investment into the electronics industry – the *Electronics Division* and *Locate in Scotland*. The Agency gives fast access to detailed information on supplier companies, industrial developments and manufacturing processes in Scotland. It also screens companies as to their suitability for specific areas.

Firn and Roberts draw some conclusions about the way high technology industries should be supported:

> "...co-ordination of policy measures and attitudes across a wide range of activities including research, teaching and administration in all levels of education, the provision of more venturesome and flexible capital and management assistance from financial institutions, enhancing of management education and employee training, continued improvement of the physical environment, encouragement of changing social attitudes."[21]

To a large extent Scotland and the SDA are already meeting these challenges but more can always be done. To promote the sunrise into a new day will require money, patience and concerted government action.

Jim Walker, The Fraser of Allander Institute for Research on the Scottish Economy.

References

1. The term "electronics" industry must be used with some caution. Up until the late 1970s and early 1980s this industry was dominated by electro-mechanical and electrical engineering – which, in more ways than one, bore a strong resemblance to the mechanical engineering industry. Only since the third wave of investment has the "electronics" sector taken over as the major employer in the industry although, as is shown in the text, there are some doubts about the true definition of this term. These comments notwithstanding, it has become commonplace in Scotland to refer to the electrical and instrument engineering industry (which includes electronics) as the "electronics" industry.

2. Firn, J R and D Roberts, 'High-Technology Industries' in N Hood and S Young (eds.) *Industry Policy and the Scottish Economy*, Edinburgh University Press, 1984, p.298.

3. In a survey of electronics firms in the UK in 1984 it was found that trade unions were strongest in Scotland – more than 10% of the workforce was unionised in 59% of firms (Electronics Location File 1984).

4. Crawford, R "The Electronics Industry in Scotland", *Fraser of Allander Institute Quarterly Economic Commentary*, May 1984.

5. Industry Department for Scotland *The Electronics Industry in Scotland*, Statistical Bulletin, No C1.1, January 1986.

6. *ibid*

7. The IDS figures for 1983 and 1984 are based on Department of Employment estimates, *given production levels*, for those years. It is likely that these represent over-estimates of employment due to the spectacular growth in indices of production demonstrated by the Scottish electronics industry i.e. it has doubled over the period 1978-84.

8. Scottish Development Agency *Electronics in Scotland: The Leading Edge* 1983.

9. McCulloch, N A "The Structure of the Scottish Electronics Industry", *University of Edinburgh School of Engineering (Electrical Engineering)*, BSc Hons Dissertation HD314, May 1985.

10. Scottish Development Agency *Electronics Industry in Scotland (Profile)*, Spring 1985.

11. Cooke, P, Morgan, K and Jackson, D "New Technology and Regional Development in Austerity Britain: the case of the semiconductor industry". *Regional Studies*, vol 18.4, August 1984.

12. Rada, J *The Impact of Micro-Electronics*, International Labour Office, Geneva 1980.

13. Levidow, L and Young, B (eds.) *Science Technology and the Labour Process*, CSE Books, London, 1981, pp.172-207.

14. SDA (*op.cit*).

15. Firn and Roberts (*op.cit*).

16. Fraser of Allander Institute, Scottish Council (Development and Industry) and IBM (UK) Ltd *Input-Output Tables for Scotland, 1973*, Scottish Academic Press (1978).

17. To a lesser extent a similar over-optimism emerged in the UK market with firms like Sinclair, Acorn, Dragon, Oric etc. expecting to make much larger sales than they eventually realised. This led to massive discounting in the price of home computers and the eventual disappearance of Dragon and Oric.

18. Scottish Development Agency, Locate in Scotland, *The Semiconductor Industry in Scotland* 1983.

19. Scottish Economic Bulletin "Electronics Manpower in Scotland in the mid-1980s", *The Scottish Office*, No 28, December 1983.

20. Cooke et al (*op.cit.*).

21. Firn and Roberts (*op.cit.*)

THE POLITICS OF POVERTY IN SCOTLAND

Stephen Maxwell

This chapter is in two parts. The first part offers an assessment of the Scottish debate on poverty over the last fifteen years, and attempts to relate some of the key features of the debate to political developments of the period. The second part offers an overview of the Scottish response to the Government's proposals for the reform of the social security system which culminated in the Social Security Act of July 1986.

Four broad conclusions are suggested by the material surveyed. First, and most obviously, the poverty debate in Scotland has been more tightly confined by practical considerations of policy and politics than the debate south of the Border. Second, and partly as a consequence, the mainstream tradition of poverty analysis in Scotland has been largely derivative with no significant contribution to the theoretical debates initiated by Professor Peter Townsend and others. Third, an important stimulus to the development of the debate in Scotland has been an arms-length dialogue between Nationalists and unionists in the shape of Labour Party members and supporters which neither set of protagonists has been keen to acknowledge. Fourth, over the fifteen year period there has been a distinct though limited strengthening of the Scottish dimension of the debate.

For two decades after the Second World War British opinion believed that the creation of a social security system based on Beveridge with a National Assistance Board as a final safety net had eliminated poverty in Britain. Scottish doubts were slower to appear on the agenda of public debate than south of the border where from 1965 the orthodoxy was under attack by the Child Poverty Action Group.

The first major public breach of the conventional wisdom in Scotland did not come until 1973 and then not from a Scottish source but from a report by the National Children's Bureau *Born to Fail*[1]. The report claimed that while one in sixteen children in Britain were severely disadvantaged by their social and economic circumstances in Scotland the proportion was one in ten.

The National Children's Bureau figures were released at a time when Scottish political and economic perspectives were adapting to the prospect of Scotland becoming a major oil producer. In the Govan by-election of 1973 the Scottish National Party's emphasis on the contrast between the wealth potentially available to Scotland from the North Sea oil and the poverty and dilapidation so evident in many parts of the constituency was widely held to have been an important factor in SNP's surprise victory.

The SNP developed the contrast between Scottish poverty and Scottish wealth in its two General Election campaigns of 1974 and in the *War on Poverty* policy document launched at the Party Conference of June 1974.[2] Adapting estimates by the Child Poverty Action Group that one in five in the United Kingdom lived on incomes below 140% of the supplementary benefit rate, *War on Poverty* claimed that when Scotland's higher unemployment, lower incomes, higher costs and harsh climate were taken into account "the proportion of the Scottish population enduring a real standard of living below or very close to the supplementary benefit rate must be substantially higher than in the United Kingdom".

In response to the rise of the SNP, the Left in Scotland[3] published *The Red Paper on Scotland*. In his introduction editor Gordon Brown presented the Paper as an effort to "transcend" the "barren, myopic, almost suffocating consensus" of the "great debate" provoked by Nationalism. On a slightly less exalted level the book was an attempt to restore to the Labour Left in Scotland that degree of initiative on social and economic issues which had been lost to radical Nationalists in the early 1970's, and in so doing to re-establish the primacy of social and economic inequalities over the Nationalist division between England and Scotland.

In the chapter which dealt most directly with poverty, the author Ian Levitt confirmed, without acknowledging, SNP's estimate of the scale of Scotland's poverty problem.[4] But he adopted the standard United Kingdom 'income measure' of poverty without even a footnote acknowledgement that differences in price levels and in volume need in Scotland for some basic commodities such as fuel might have a significant impact on the incidence of 'real' as opposed to 'income' poverty.

The extent and distribution of Scottish poverty was further illuminated in 1977 by the publication of the Child Poverty Action Group pamphlet *Poverty: the Facts in Scotland*.[5] The pamphlet represented the first significant intervention in the Scottish debate by the London-based poverty lobby.

Although forthright in its acknowledgement of the political dimension of Scotland's poverty debate, Norris's pamphlet remained firmly in the unionist mainstream in its analysis. It did indeed acknowledge that as a standard money measure the supplementary benefit rate was defective as a measure of poverty. But because of the absence of Regional Price Indices and the paucity of other information on price levels it retained the income standard as its measure.

In the autumn of 1975 SNP launched a series of posters affirming the right to Scotland's oil wealth of four representative groups of deprived Scots – the unemployed, children in disadvantaged families, the low-income housewife enduring run-down housing and the pensioner. The plight of the latter group was illustrated by the claim that five thousand elderly Scots were dying each year from hypothermia. The claim provoked an outraged response from the Labour Party. In the Commons Scottish Secretary Willie Ross asserted that only nine Scots had died of hypothermia in the preceding year. In a controversy which turned largely on the distinction between deaths from hypothermia and deaths from cold-related diseases, SNP supported its claims by quoting estimates by Age Concern Scotland that between three and five thousand deaths from cold-related diseases occurred in Scotland each year. In the unusually cold Spring of 1976 the SNP developed its case by calling for some financial acknowledgement by the Government of the particular problems and dangers faced by old people in Scotland. Its credibility on the issue was enhanced in 1978 by the publication by an independent academic analyst of an estimate that 70,000 Scots pensioners were at risk from hypothermia[6], and in 1979 by the estimate by a Scottish based expert that it took 20% more fuel to heat a house to a given temperature in Glasgow than in Bristol and 30% more in Aberdeen.[7]

The publicity generated by the SNP around its hypothermia claims fell in the middle of a period of rapid increases in domestic fuel prices. In 1975, the peak year of increase, electricity prices increased by 41%, gas prices by 35.2%, coal by 26.8%, oil by 28.3% and paraffin by 19.4%.[8] Concern about the impact which such price rises were having on the ability of low-income households to provide themselves with adequate heating contributed to the creation of the Scottish Fuel Poverty Action Group in 1978.

The Scottish Fuel Poverty Action Group is the nearest thing that Scotland has had to a nationally organised poverty lobby. Although it focusses on one dimension of poverty, the status of fuel as entirely a market commodity and the importance it has in the budgets of low-income households make its price an important determinant of income poverty in general.

The SFPAG identified specifically Scottish factors – the higher rate of increase of fuel prices, defects in the construction of much of Scotland's post-war public housing and, of course, climatic differences – as contributing to the exceptionally high level of disconnections of electricity supply in Scotland due to non-payment of bills. While its first two publications had general United Kingdom policy targets – the repeal of legislation giving fuel boards the right to disconnect, a comprehensive fuel allowance scheme, the raising of building standards and a programme of improved insulation – the third concluded with a call for a Scottish Fuel

Policy embracing SNP MP Gordon Wilson's Bill for a Cold Climate Allowance adjusted to differences in the cost of heating a home to a standard temperature in different areas of the United Kingdom.[9]

The mainstream of Scottish writing on poverty continued remarkably resistant to the significance of the hypothermia and fuel poverty controversies. Its most recent expression *The Real Divide: Poverty and Deprivation in Scotland*[10], edited by two Scottish Labour MP's Gordon Brown and Robin Cook, contains valuable up-dates of the statistics traditionally deployed in the mainstream discussions as well as important new information on low pay in Scotland and on changes in Scotland's occupational structure. But its analysis of poverty is conservative, if not regressive. It adopts the standard United Kingdom income-measure of poverty without comment. The issue of price differentials is simply ignored. Fuel poverty receives only a passing reference in the chapter on poverty among pensioners and there is no discussion of the special problem of rural poverty.

There are, of course, methodological reasons for cleaving to a standard United Kingdom income measure of poverty. The absence of official regional price indices means that there is no official standard on which to base regional comparisons of purchasing power of the sort that the supplementary benefit rate provides for comparisons of income levels. Furthermore regional differences in prices tell us little by themselves about the standard of living or 'welfare' which a standard income can purchase. As the example of fuel shows, the quantity of the commodity required to achieve the agreed standard of welfare may be more important than the price. In Scotland fuel prices are generally lower than in England but the greater quantity of fuel required to heat a house to the same level as a house in the south of England makes the cost of heating in Scotland higher than in the south by a factor of 20% or more. And differences in volume of other basic commodities – most obviously clothing and footwear but also food and housing – may interact with prices to extend the differences in the purchasing power of standard incomes.

Even if standardised information were available on these factors the quantification of their impact would be an impossible task. The extension of poverty can be measured but not its intensity. The suffering of a pensioner in Scotland who endures lower room temperatures than her counterpart in the south of England cannot be measured on any common scale. No more can the loss of vitality suffered by children in low-income Scots families where a standard United Kingdom welfare income fails to cover the greater volume needs for heating, or wet weather wear or food. Sickness rates and mortality rates can be no more than suggestive: they cannot measure the 'intensity' of poverty of those who survive in some approximation to health.

Yet these methodological difficulties or incompatibilities do not excuse the neglect which the underlying issues have suffered from writers on Scottish poverty. There is a reputable if unofficial series of regional price indices for different socio-economic groups (Reward Regional Surveys).[11] The concept of 'purchasing power parity' is available to guide the researcher on at least one stage of inquiry. It is disappointing that social scientists in the Scottish universities have not shown greater curiosity.

The Government's Green Paper *The Reform of Social Security* was published in June 1985.[12] It proposed the abolition of State Earning Related Pensions (SERPS) and the replacement of supplementary benefit by a system of income support supplemented by client group premiums advertised as absorbing the standard additional allowances. Family Income Support (FIS) was also to be replaced by a Family Credit payed through the employer. Children in families receiving Family Credit would no longer be eligible for free school meals or milk and local authorities were to lose their discretion to give free school meals to children not on benefit. Single payments for special needs were to be replaced by discretionary loans or grants from a Social Fund. Single people under twenty five living independently were to suffer a major cut in benefit. Housing benefit was to be rationalised but everyone however low their income would be expected to pay at least 20% of their rates. The proposals were widely interpreted as weakening the 'universalist' foundations of the welfare state and forcing people to a greater reliance on the market for social provision in the name of rationalisation and superior targetting of resources.

This account of the Scottish response to the Green Paper and the assessments it offers is largely impressionistic. The only quantitative evidence on which to assess the strength of the Scottish response is provided by a computer print-out of the titles of those organisations which made formal responses to the Green Paper, supplied by the DHSS in December 1985. Of the 1,742 entries, 149 – 8.5% – were from identifiably Scottish organisations suggesting a ratio of response from Scotland approximately proportionate to Scotland's share of the United Kingdom's population.

Some tentative generalisations are suggested by a reading of a sample of the English and Scottish responses. The Scottish response is weaker on expert analysis, no doubt a consequence of the concentration of research bodies and specialist lobbies in London. On the other hand the reader receives a strong impression that the Scottish response is more uniform and 'solidaristic'. The sources of that impression are clear enough. Conspicuously absent from the list of Scottish respondents are the Scottish branches or counterparts of the Institute of Directors, the Monday Club or the Association of British Chambers of Commerce which in an analysis of the response of 60 British organisations carried out by the Child Poverty Action Group were the chief sources of support for the Government's proposals.[13]

The second source of the impression of a more 'solidaristic' Scottish response is the presence among the Scottish respondents of organisations such as the Church of Scotland, the Scottish Trades' Union Congress (STUC) and the Convention of Scottish Local Authorities (COSLA) with a plausible claim to be representative if not of a Scottish consensus at least of large segments of Scottish opinion.

When the Government's Green Paper was published in June 1985 Scotland was no better equipped organisationally to make a strong and distinctive response than it was intellectually. Scotland had no national poverty lobby to perform the educational and lobbying role which the Child Poverty Action Group carried out in London. The research institutes with a specialised interest in social policy issues – the Policy Studies Institute, the Family Policy Studies' Centre, the Low Pay Unit, the Institute for Fiscal Studies – were all London based. While the departments of social administration in the Scottish universities offer courses in social policy, there are no social policy units at Scottish universities comparable to the Policy Units at York and Bristol universities and few specialists in social security issues. The Scottish media were conspicuously lacking in expertise on social issues. Indeed the entire Scottish media could boast only a single designated correspondent in the shape of a Social Services' Correspondent with *The Glasgow Herald*.

There were, however, some positive factors. One was the presence in positions of influence within Labour-controlled local authorities of a younger generation of Party members, some professionally trained in social work or community education or with a specialised interest in urban deprivation, many of whom were familiar with the poverty debate as it had developed in Britain since the late 1960's. Another was the not unconnected growth in parts of central Scotland at least, of a network of Welfare Rights Officers supported by local authorities. Another was the established presence of a group of specialised voluntary organisations with sizeable reservoirs of information on the circumstances and problems of their particular client groups.

The Scottish response to the Government's proposals can be most conveniently considered under six headings – the voluntary sector response, the media response, the political response embracing Parliamentary and party responses, the local authority response, and the trade union and Church response.

The voluntary sector

Among the national voluntary sector organisations which responded actively were Scottish Women's Aid, the Royal Scottish Society for the Prevention of Cruelty to Children, Shelter Scotland, the Scottish Council for Single Parents, the Scottish Council for the Single Homeless, Age Concern Scotland, the Scottish Council on Disability and Scottish Neighbourhood Energy Action.

Age Concern Scotland was among the most active of these specialist voluntary organisations and its activity spans the range of initiatives taken by the other organisations.

Prior to the publication of the Green Paper, Age Concern organised a delegation including senior Church representatives to Westminster for meetings with parliamentary groups of MP's. Its formal response to the Green Paper focussed on a number of issues of particular Scottish concern including cuts in housing benefit estimated to cost 150,000 Scots pensioners £1-£2 weekly, the requirement to pay a minimum 20% of rates costing 200,000 Scots pensioners an average of £1.25 weekly, and the abolition of heating additions claimed at the higher rate by 36,000 Scots. Under the campaign slogan *The Pen is Mightier than the Sword* Age Concern encouraged its supporters and local groups to press the case against the reforms with their MP's. Early in 1986 the organisation circulated a response to the Government's White Paper of December, *In Jeopardy: Dignity In Old Age*, to all Scottish MP's. At the legislative stage beginning in February 1986, it sent suggestions for amendments to Scottish MP's and embarked on a campaign to encourage the take-up of benefits. Throughout the period its officers maintained close contact with the Scottish media and secured a steady flow of coverage for its initiatives.

The other leading specialist voluntary organisations pursued the same range of initiatives – briefings to members and MP's, press contacts, the circulation of recommended amendments – each focussing on those proposals which most directly threatened their particular client group – Scottish Women's Aid the payment of Family Credit through the employer, the Scottish Council for Single Parents the loss of single payments, the Scottish Council for Single Homeless cuts in benefits for the under-25's, Shelter Scotland the impact of the 20% minimum rates' payment, the Royal Scottish Society for the Prevention of Cruelty to Children the loss of free school meals.

In addition to their individual activities the leading specialist organisations were members of a group of national voluntary organisations co-ordinated by the Scottish Council for Community and Voluntary Organisations.

The Scottish Council for Community and Voluntary Organisations (SCCVO) had taken an active interest in the social security reforms since 1984 when it had objected to the fact that none of the four Review groups established by Social Services' Secretary Norman Fowler planned to hold a hearing outside London. When in response to the complaints the

Supplementary Benefits Review group visited Edinburgh the Scottish Council gave evidence arguing, *inter alia*, for a general increase in the value of benefits and the extension of long-term supplementary rates to the long-term unemployed.

In early 1985 the SCCVO convened a meeting of interested voluntary organisations to discuss how the voluntary sector's interest in the social security debate could be advanced. Agreement was reached that the Council should have a dual role – first to ensure that its own two hundred very diverse members were adequately briefed on the reform proposals, on their likely impact on clients, and on the opportunities for making representations to the policy makers, and second to service a grouping of national voluntary organisations which would have the task of co-ordinating voluntary sector publicity at Scottish and United Kingdom levels and providing a network for the exchange of information.

The grouping of national voluntary organisations agreed that their activities should be guided by two principles. One was that the group should focus on the distinctively Scottish impact of the reforms, on the understanding that the London-based Social Security Consortium co-ordinated by the Child Poverty Action Group would base their lobbying on the overall United Kingdom impact of the reforms. The second was that the impact of the voluntary sector's representations on Conservative opinion would be reinforced if voluntary organisations which traditionally remained aloof from campaigns on politically controversial issues could be mobilised in support.

The group of national voluntary organisations opened its activities by lobbying the Scottish media, by deputation or letter, with the argument that the proposed reforms merited the extensive and critical coverage appropriate to an issue of major national import. In the political arena, it sent deputations to meet party representatives, in the House of Commons prior to the Social Security Bill's first reading in January 1986, and in the House of Lords prior to the committee stage of the Bill in June 1986. In addition the Group maintained contact with the two Scottish members of the Standing Committee on the Bill, encouraged its members to provide the MP's with suggestions for amendments and with briefing materials, and organised a meeting in Edinburgh with Social Security Minister Tony Newton to put to him the by then familiar litany of Scottish concerns.

Meantime the SCCVO was active in its own name. Prior to the publication of the Green Paper the Council began the publication of a short series of briefing papers[14] which described the extent and characteristics of poverty in Scotland, summarised the key proposals of the Green Paper and of the White Paper and identified their impact on vulnerable groups of Scots. SCCVO's formal response to the Green Paper described the factors which contributed to the particular severity of Scotland's problem of poverty and suggested that for "cultural, social and institutional reasons" Scotland was ill-equipped to benefit from measures designed to strengthen the role of the market in social provisions. Among the particular dangers for Scotland which the submission highlighted were the replacement of single payments by a discretionary Social Fund, the proposal for a minimum 20% rates contribution, the loss of heating additions, the continued discrimination against the long-term unemployed, and the lowering of benefit levels for the under twenty-five year olds. The submission concluded that the Government's proposals failed to offer any hope of halting let alone reversing the spread of poverty in Scotland.

The Council also made its assessment of the proposals known to the Social Security Advisory Committee through a meeting with the Chairman and a series of meetings with its then sole Scottish member.

The Council's estimate of the number of Scots in poverty – 970,000 or 18.7% of the population living at or below supplementary benefit rates and 1,641,000 (31.7%) living below 140% of the supplementary rate – was accepted as standard by the Scottish respondents. But the Council's most purposeful intervention was the organisation of an Open Letter to Scottish Secretary George Younger emphasising the dangers for Scotland of the Green Paper's proposal to replace single payments and additional allowances by loans from a discretionary Social Fund and urging him to bring to the Cabinet's attention the problems which such a change could cause in a part of the United Kingdom in which both the incidence and the value of single payments were twice the level in England. The letter which received full coverage in *The Scotsman* and *The Glasgow Herald* was subscribed by thirty-eight voluntary organisations, including the Royal British Legion Scotland, the Earl Haig Fund, the Scottish Women's Rural Institutes and fifteen local Councils of Social Service.

Another level of voluntary sector activity was represented by the grass-roots 'network' campaigns of the National Campaign Against Social Security Cuts (NCASSC) and the Scottish Campaign Against Social Security (SCASSC).

The Scottish Campaign was born from a meeting in mid-1984 between representatives of Claimants' Groups, Tenants' Advice Groups and Welfare Rights Officers to discuss the joint threat of the DHSS 'snoopers' operating in Scotland and the creation of the social security review groups. It was conceived as a facility for the exchange of information and contacts, and neither formulated its own views on the reforms nor directly initiated campaigning activity. Its role was undercut by the growth of locally based campaigning groups and by the consolidation of the National Campaign. After meeting eight times at the initiative of its volunteer secretary the Campaign was suspended in mid-1985.

The National Campaign was the successor to the National Campaign Against the Supplementary Benefit Review of 1978 which drew its active members from Claimants' Unions, Law Centres, and Citizens' Rights Offices. With the change of Government in 1979 it altered its name and widened its remit only to lose much of its momentum.

Like the Scottish Campaign the National Campaign was more concerned with organisation and campaigning than with policy assessment, but it differed from its Scottish counterpart in directly promoting the creation of local groups and organising campaign activities. Where the mainstream voluntary sector focussed on specific proposals – usually those with a Scottish impact – and directed its case mainly at opinion-leaders, the National Campaign reflected United Kingdom concerns and sought to encourage a mass opposition to the reforms.

The Scottish Media

The Scottish media face a double handicap in covering social security issues, one external and one self-imposed. The external handicap is its distance from the locus of policy-making and the consequent difficulty of obtaining 'insider' information. The self-imposed handicap is its failure – with one exception – to equip itself with specialist writers on social welfare issues. In discussion with voluntary organisation representatives, senior editorial staff identified two further obstacles to wide coverage specifically of the social security reforms – the technical complexity of the issues and the assumed resistance of their readers to a diet of stories about Scotland's social failures. The representations which the group of national voluntary organisations made to the Scottish media to recognise the national importance of the proposed reforms elicited more positive response from Scottish newspaper journalists than from Scottish broadcasters.

In addition to giving news coverage to the formal Scottish responses to the Green Paper and opening their columns to opinion pieces and round-robin letters from concerned organisations and individuals, both *The Scotsman* and *The Glasgow Herald* devoted several leader articles to the issue. *The Scotsman* carried six leaders in the year from June 1985, all hostile to the market philosophy and the ethical assumptions of the Government's reforms. The most critical of the articles acknowledged Scotland's especially vulnerability to the reforms and went on to complain that efforts by the SCCVO and others to co-ordinate a Scottish response were handicapped by the lack of any Scottish Office responsibility or capacity for assessing the effects of the reforms in Scotland.[15]

While *The Glasgow Herald* through its Social Services' Correspondent gave more extensive coverage to both the Scottish impact of the reforms and to the views of what it tentatively identified as the emerging Scottish 'poverty lobby', the tone of its leader articles was sceptical rather than condemnatory, focussing on the Government's failure to integrate the benefits system with the tax system, or challenging it to comment on a survey by Strathclyde Region of key groups of social work clients which showed a far higher proportion losing income than in the Government's own figures.

If the Scottish 'quality' papers did their duty by the issue the same cannot be said for Scottish broadcasters. Senior editorial staff were evidently unimpressed by representations by the voluntary organisations. There was no major feature or documentary style coverage of the issue on any Scottish radio or television channel. Coverage was limited on radio to news items and 'talk' shows such as the Jimmy Mack show and Colin Bell's 'Taking Issue', and on television to routine studio debate between party spokespersons on the weekly current affairs programmes late on Friday nights.

The trade unions

The distinctive element in the trade union response in Scotland was provided by the Scottish Trades' Union Congress. (STUC). The STUC had long had a recognised role as a national forum on industrial and employment issues, but has less often sought a major role on social issues. However in October 1985 the Congress added a new element to the Scottish debate by convening a day conference to discuss a draft *Charter of Welfare Rights*[16] setting out guidelines for an alternative reform of the social security system.

The STUC initiative was important for two reasons. If the Scottish response had been impressive in the variety of organisations contributing their opinions it had also been fragmented, with each group pursuing its own strategy. The STUC initiative succeeded in attracting support from all the major groups – voluntary sector, the Churches, tenants' associations and unemployed workers' centres, trades' unions and two political parties (Labour and the SNP). Furthermore by presenting an alternative strategy for reform it marked a departure from the defensiveness of the other responses. In its final version the STUC's Charter opened with a condemnation of the impact of the Green Paper's proposals on Scotland before proceeding to offer some basic principles for an alternative social security system based on a universal right to a minimum income sufficient to purchase a standard of living reflecting the standards and expectations of society as a whole.

However boldly conceived as an attempt to turn the tables on the Government, the STUC initiative was flawed. It strengthened the sense of national solidarity among committed Scottish opponents of the Government's proposals but failed either to transform the terms of debate or to extend the constituency of support. It came too late – four months after the publication of the Green Paper – to influence the responses of most Scottish organisations. The Charter itself was too selective and rhetorical to carry credibility as an alternative model. And unlike STUC initiatives on some key industrial issues it lacked the support of bodies such as the CBI Scotland and the Scottish Council (Development and Industry), not to speak of the Liberal Party the SDP and at least some elements of the Conservative party, which might have supported its claim to be the vehicle of an emerging Scottish consensus.

The local authorities

Of Scotland's sixty-five local authorities, twenty three are recorded as having submitted formal responses to the Green Paper in addition to the Convention of Scottish Local Authorities (COSLA) and the Association of Directors of Social Work (ADWS). Twenty-seven supported a STUC petition in support of the *Charter of Welfare Rights*.

Notable among the respondents was Strathclyde Region. Strathclyde had had the most consistent record of action on poverty issues, reflecting its size, its disproportionate share of Scotland's poor and Labour's monopoly of control. Among its notable initiatives have been the pioneering in Scotland of local authority provision of a Welfare Rights service and the raising of a Court action against the DHSS in an attempt to obtain increased benefits for recipients facing the inflated costs of living on remote islands. Strathclyde's response was both practical and educational. It gave support to the organisation of a Strathclyde Campaign Against Cuts in Benefit and financial support to a Strathclyde Poverty Alliance based on the voluntary sector and co-ordinated by Glasgow Council of Voluntary Service. Its most effective educational initiative was the publication of a survey by the Social Work Department of the effect of the reforms on local groups of clients which revealed that 87% of those surveyed would lose financially by the reforms compared to the Government's figures of 32% losers overall.[17] The Strathclyde figures were used to challenge Social Security Minister Tony Newton at meetings with the ASDW and with the group of national voluntary organisations. Another notable educational initiative by local authorities was the Lothian Review of Social Security supported by the Regional Council and four District Councils to survey the pattern of need in Lothian and pre-empt the anticipated Government cuts by presenting alternative reforms.[18] Among Conservative controlled Councils, Grampian Regional Council broadly echoed the criticisms of its fellow Councils with Tayside alone offering the Government positive support. The COSLA response was predictably condemnatory though, slightly less predictably, it complained that Scotland had not been treated by the Green Paper as the 'special case' which its exceptional problems warranted.

The Scottish churches

Four Scottish Churches made formal submissions to the DHSS on the Green Paper, all critical – the Church of Scotland, the United Free Church of Scotland, the Baptist Union of Scotland and the Roman Catholic Church. The Congregational Union of Scotland sent a representative to the first conference convened by the STUC. The notable absentees were the Episcopal Church and the Free Church, neither of which responded formally to the Green Paper or attended the STUC conference. Characteristically the Roman Catholic Church as represented by the Scottish National Commission for Catholic Social Care the official group appointed by the Roman Catholic Bishops of Scotland to deal with issues of social care was the least inhibited by the political identity of the STUC and was the only Church group to sponsor the completed Charter of Welfare Rights. The Church and Nation Committee of the Church of Scotland, an early enthusiast for the STUC initiative, felt constrained by political considerations to stop short of public sponsorship.

The political response

The responses of the Scottish political parties were unexpectedly low-key. The Scottish Council of the Labour Party made no formal response to the Green Paper. Instead it circulated to its associations and branches a briefing paper by Gordon Brown MP which included estimates of the Scottish impact of the reforms based on leaked DHSS documents. However eight Labour Party Associations or branches did submit responses largely on the lines of Brown's briefing.

The formal SNP response took the form of the submission to the DHSS of a highly polemical resolution adopted at its September 1985 conference explaining the background to Scotland's poverty and contrasting it with Scotland's wealth. The Scottish Liberal Party produced a response which in the course of calling on the Government to reconsider the reforms with the aim of integrating the tax and social security systems limited its Scottish references to a single paragraph acknowledging the greater extent and intensity of Scottish poverty. The SDP in Scotland made no formal response but circulated a briefing paper on the White Paper of December 1985 dismissing it as a 'hypocritically pious document' and noting that nearly one-fifth of Scots were living on or below the supplementary rate and one-third on incomes below 140% of the rate.

The downbeat response of the Labour Party was also evident in its Parliamentary conduct. The only Scottish Labour MP nominated for the Standing Committee of the Bill was Willie McKelvey MP for Kilmarnock who had no public record of interest or expertise in the isue. McKelvey was replaced on health grounds by Norman Godman MP for Greenock and Port Glasgow who prefaced his opening contribution to the Committee proceedings by disclaiming any expertise on the subject. It is surprising in view of the extent of Scotland's problem of poverty and the severe impact the reforms will have on large sections of Labour's traditional supporters that the Scottish Parliamentary Labour Group did not secure more senior representation on the Committee, in the shape perhaps of one of the Group's two poverty experts Gordon Brown and Robin Cook.

In the event Godman and the only other Scottish MP on the Committee, Liberal Welfare spokesman Archy Kirkwood, made powerful contributions to the work of the Committee, with Godman in particular proving a forceful champion of distinctive Scottish interests. Both MP's made frequent use of the briefing material and amendments supplied by Scottish voluntary organisations. Kirkwood introduced an amendment to the Social Fund requiring that payments from the Fund should reflect a "reasonable estimate" by the Secretary of State of the regional variations in the purchasing power of income support, though he withdrew it before testing whether Labour members were prepared to support it.[19] Norman Godman introduced an amendment restoring heating benefits at levels which reflected the different cost levels in different areas of the United Kingdom, supporting his case with figures made familiar by the debate on fuel poverty and carrying the support of the Labour members.[20] Little of the distinctively Scottish material aired in Committee penetrated to the floor of the House. The only three Scots MP's to make major contributions to the Common's debates were the two Committee members and SDP Welfare Spokesman Charles Kennedy, like his two colleagues a rather junior Parliamentarian. The only other Scottish contributors were Labour MP's Gordon Brown and Hugh Brown and SNP MP's Gordon Wilson and Donald Stewart. In addition to his limited contribution to the Commons debate Gordon Brown played an important role in eliciting up-to-date poverty statistics through Parliamentary questions and as a regular conduit for leaks of DHSS papers, though his press outlets for this information was *The Guardian* and not any Scottish paper. In the House of Lords the Scottish voice was fainter with only one resident Scottish peer making a contribution and that in support of a Government proposal removing local authority discretion on free school meals.

Throughout the period of public debate the Scottish Parliamentary committees ignored the Bill and the issues it raised. In spite of the sharper political profile which the poverty issue had had in Scotland since the mid-1970's, the Scottish Select Committee has never investigated any aspect of income poverty in Scotland. (It was invited to do so as essential background to the social security reviews by SCCVO in early 1985). More surprising perhaps the issue failed to win a place on the agenda of the Scottish Grand Committee even after the publication of the Green Paper. The closest the Committee came to the issue was a debate on reform of the rating system in April 1986 when the Scottish Secretary Malcolm Rifkind was challenged to comment on the effect on low income groups in Scotland of the combined imposition of the community charge and the 20% minimum rates' contribution, but declined to do so on the grounds that the 20% proposal had nothing to do with rating reform.[21]

The reluctance of Malcolm Rifkind as Scottish Secretary to be drawn into debate on the social security reform had been previewed by George Younger as Scottish Secretary. The letter of October 1985 criticising the Social Fund proposal sent to Mr Younger by thirty-eight Scottish voluntary organisations included a direct invitation to the Scottish Secretary to intervene in Cabinet on an issue which was outwith his Departmental responsibility but within his conventional remit as 'Minister for Scotland'. The first response, which came from the Social Work Services' Group in the Scottish Office, simply stated that responsibility for social security reviews lay with the Secretary of State for Social Services. A second response, from the Scottish Secretary's private office, repeated that social security was the responsibility of the Social Services' Secretary but promised that Mr Younger would bring the letter to Mr Fowler's attention. Indeed a leaked internal DHSS memorandum on the Social Fund reported a suggestion by the Scottish Secretary that the Fund's budget for Scotland be set to take account of the greater number of cases of special need likely to arise because of Scotland's particularly cold weather[22]. While denying the relevance of that particular consideration, the memorandum did concede that there might be other grounds, including the existing higher levels of single payments in Scotland, for a "proportionally higher share for Scotland" in the allocation of the Social Fund budget.[22]

Neither institutional nor constitutional factors alone explain the refusal of the Scottish Secretary to become involved in public debate on social security issues, nor his apparent refusal to make significant Cabinet interventions in defence of Scottish interests. By convention the Scottish Secretary has a licence to raise any issue of concern to Scotland. The Scottish Office's responsibility for services which powerfully influence Scotland's 'poverty profile' – housing, health, education, social work – provides a platform for intervention on social security issues as secure as the platform which the Scottish Office's economic and industrial planning functions affords for Ministerial intervention on industrial issues within the remit of Whitehall departments. If a Scottish Secretary can semi-publicly commit himself to oppose in Cabinet the closure of a major steel-making facility, why should he not commit himself to oppose social security cuts which in the course of depressing yet further the living standards of hundreds of thousands of the poorest Scots threaten to take some £50m of purchasing power out of the Scottish economy?

The reason, of course, lies in the politics of Scottish poverty. An industrial cause such as the retention of Upper Clyde Shipbuilders in the early 1970s or Ravenscraig today is capable of mobilising a formidable lobby of trade unions and business interests the STUC, the CBI, the Scottish Council (D and I), and Chambers of Commerce.

The marketing of a poverty issue presents problems of a quite different order. Even when a dramatic example of poverty – hypothermia deaths among the old, the plight of severely deprived children or of the young homeless – stirs the public conscience it cannot call on the standing army of lobbyists which a major industrial issue can command. Churches and voluntary organisations are usually no match for the heavy brigade of industrial interests. Poverty in consequence is far less attractive to politicians as a campaigning issue let alone as a matter for Cabinet ultimatums.

Conclusion

In terms of its effect on the outcome of the reforms, the Scottish response must obviously be accounted a failure. The significant concessions made by the Government – on SERPS, on Family Credit, the retention of two systems of taper for Housing Benefit, the institution of an internal appeals system for the Social Fund – were issues on which the input of the Scottish lobby was marginal to the efforts of the London based lobbies. On the substantive issues of concern to Scottish organisations the Government was adamant. The discretionary Social Fund, without any provision for independent appeal, will replace the single payments system on which so many of the poorest Scots are precariously dependent. Additional allowances will be absorbed into group premiums which are likely to be set at levels too low to compensate for the loss of the higher rate of heating allowances at least. The replacement of rates by the universal community charge will ensure that all Scots however low their income will be confronted by the need to pay 20% of the charge. Young single Scots will be forced by reductions in benefit to add to the competition in an already saturated youth labour market. Thousands of Scots children will be denied free school meals. The case for an indexation of benefits to the cost of living in different parts of the United Kingdom did not get closer to the agenda of reform than a brief hearing in Committee.

The only victories to put against the record of defeats are verbal assurances that the allocation of the Social Fund budget will take account of the exceptional level of demand in Scotland for single payments and that neighbourhood insulation schemes will receive compensation for the loss of single payment contributions.

As an exercise in public education the Scottish response can perhaps claim more success. The controversy around the Government's proposals served to expose the extent and intensity of Scotland's poverty to fuller discussion than it had received since the mid-1970s. The Committee debate on the Bill suggests that Scottish politicians can now urge recognition of the distinctive dimensions of Scottish poverty without immediately and automatically forfeiting the support of all their English colleagues.

Ruth Lister of the CPAG believes the social security reforms have boosted the poverty lobby to a new level of activity and commitment. In Scotland, the response has crystallised a new awareness of poverty and extended organisational links between interested bodies. Whether that is enough, in the absence of constitutional change giving the Scots more direct responsibility for their social condition, to generate a determined public will to combat poverty remains to be tested.

Stephen Maxwell, Scottish Council for Community and Voluntary Organisations, Edinburgh.

References

1. P Wedge and H. Prosser, *Born to Fail*, Arrow Books, London, 1973.

2. *War on Poverty*, Scottish National Party, Edinburgh, 1974.

3. *The Red Paper on Scotland*, ed. G Brown, EUPB, Edinburgh, 1975.

4. I Levitt, *Poverty in Scotland*, p.317, *op.cit.*

5. Geoff Norris, *Poverty: the Facts in Scotland*, Child Poverty Action Group, London, 1977.

6. Malcolm Wicks, *Hypothermia and Social Policy*, Heinemann, London, 1978.

7. T Markus, *The Architects' Journal*, May 23rd, 1979.

8. A Grimes, *Cold As Charity: Fuel Poverty in Scotland Today*, Scottish Fuel Poverty Action Group, Edinburgh, 1978.

9. SFPAG, Glasgow, 1981, *Not the Same Cold Story*, Sheila Mackay, Scottish Council for Community and Voluntary Organisations, Edinburgh, 1985.

10. *The Real Divide: Poverty and Deprivation in Scotland*, (ed.) G Brown and R Cook, Polygon, Edinburgh, 1983.

11. *Reward Regional Surveys*, (Twice yearly regional costs of living surveys), Stone, Staffordshire, 1972 –

12. *The Reform of Social Security: Programme for Change*, Cmnd. 9518, HMSO.

13. *Review*, Issue No.8, Nov.1985, London Advisory Services Alliance, Bethnal Green Library.

14. *Facing the Facts: Scotland and the Social Security Reviews*. Briefing Papers 1-3, 5. Scottish Council for Community and Voluntary Organisations, Edinburgh, 1985.

15. *The Scotsman*, September 10th, 1985.

16. Draft *Charter of Welfare Rights*, STUC, Glasgow, October 1985.

17. *Social Security Bill, Supplementary Report by Director of Social Work, Strathclyde Regional Council, Social Work Committee. March 1985.*

18. *Changing the Rules? First Findings of the Lothian Review of Social Security* (LOSS), February 1985: *Fowler Rules: Final Report of LOSS,* June 1985.

19. Standing Committee (B), Social Security Bill, April 10th 1985, HMSO.

20. Standing Committee (B), Social Security Bill, February 27th, 1985, HMSO.

21. Scottish Grand Committee, April 28th, *Paying for Local Government,* House of Commons Official Report, HMSO.

22. Internal DHSS memorandum (n.d.).

THE SCOTTISH POLICE COMPLAINTS PROCEDURE

Eileen Macpherson

In its Final Report (April 1985) The Police Complaints Board (England & Wales) which believed that 'Complaints are indivisible from the wider subject of accountability generally', commented

> 'It is perhaps ironic that while the complaints procedures in England & Wales have been in the public eye, the Scottish arrangements, which leave far more discretion to the Chief Constable than in England & Wales, have largely escaped criticism'.(1)

While it is true that during the '70s and early '80s attention has focussed mainly on the English procedures, resulting in the establishment of the Complaints Board (1976) and its successor, the Police Complaints Authority (1985) there has been some debate on the Scottish 'arrangements'. This debate however, has not resulted in substantive change in Scotland; no independent element has been introduced.

From the earliest days of professional police forces in Scotland it had been recognised that some machinery for dealing with complaints from the public was necessary. Alfred John List, the first Superintendent of Haddingtonshire Police Force (1832-40) wrote

> 'If complaints are made against any of his men, he (the Superintendent) will procede(sic) and investigate them, and report forthwith to the Police Committee, and if from the nature of the complaint, he finds it necessary, he may at once suspend the man until the decision of the Police Committee be known'.[2]

It is impossible to be certain whether such regulations were introduced in all of Scotland's independent forces, but List was influential and the instructions on complaints issued in Perthshire's Handbook of 1856 *The Constable's Vade Mecum* are almost identical to List's proposals. It could be argued that these early rulings provided some independent review of complaints against the police in that although the Superintendent investigated complaints all decisions were taken by the Police Committee (a much more powerful body in the 19th century than it is today).

Although there was no standardised approach to the handling of complaints, the authorities had developed ad hoc procedures which ensured some independent supervision of the investigation of complaints. However successive legislation increased the responsibility of the Chief Constable for discipline in his force, with the result that the police authority's role in complaints procedures became insignificant. It became the responsibility of the Chief Constable to investigate and make decisions about complaints. Scotland's legal system ensured that in complaints cases alleging a criminal offence, the police must report the offence to the Procurator Fiscal, who then took charge of the investigation, thus providing a degree of independent scrutiny of serious complaints.

There is no indication of general dissatisfaction with the system which had evolved. In Scotland until 1967 each police force dealt with complaints in accordance with Police Discipline Regulations issued by the Scottish Secretary. It was not until 1959 that the issue of complaints procedures emerged in Scotland after the 'Thurso boy' incident was raised in Parliament.[3] Allegations were made that no effective action had been taken to investigate complaints made by the boy's father that his son had been assaulted by two policemen. After heated debates, the government appointed a Tribunal of Enquiry which found that one policeman had unjustifiably assaulted the boy.[4]

This Scottish controversy occurred at a time when misgivings about policing in England & Wales were being voiced.[5] A Royal Commission was appointed to 'review the constitutional position of the police throughout Great Britain, the arrangements for their control and administration' and to consider among other topics 'the relationship of the police with the public and the means of ensuring that complaints by the public against the police are effectively dealt with'.

Despite conceding that,

'A system in which the investigation of complaints is the concern of the police alone may not give the appearance of justice being done'[6]

the Commission was satisfied that in general the relationship between public and police was good, and that the police dealt with complaints 'thoroughly and impartially'. No radical revision of the complaints system was recommended although proposals intended to standardise procedures were made.

Opinion, however, was not unanimous. Three of the Commissioners felt that because of 'the need that justice should be seen to be done' a Commissioner of Rights should be appointed as an 'independent external check on the actions of Chief Constables in handling complaints'.[7] Dr A L Goodhart was in disagreement with much of the report which he felt unable to sign. His major criticism of the complaints procedure was that 'it violates the basic principles of justice that no man shall be a judge in his own case'[8] and recommended the establishment of a legal department staffed by lawyers attached to each regional force which could deal with complaints.

Each of these proposals had the advantage that an independent element would have been introduced into the complaints procedure. The disadvantages were that substantial costs would be incurred, and the police were reluctant to see such proposals introduced. It was the majority view of the Commissioners that their limited proposals were sufficient to win the confidence of any 'reasonable member of the public' and that

'Above all we think that the interests of the public can best be served by resisting any innovation which may weaken the strength of the police in their fight against crime'.[9]

The majority view was accepted. The Police Act 1964 and the Police (Scotland) Act 1967 implemented most of their recommendations establishing broadly similar procedures in England & Wales and Scotland.

The 1967 Act formalised the Scottish complaints procedure and defined areas of responsibility. It became obligatory for

'Every police authority and inspectors of constabulary to keep themselves informed as to the manner in which complaints made by members of the public against constables are dealt with by the Chief Constable.'[10]

to ensure that the procedures were applied correctly.

A central role was allotted to the Secretary of State for Scotland. When there is concern about the policing of an area he may order a local enquiry to be held in public or private at his discretion. If the report is not published. the Secretary of State will divulge those findings he feels to be in the public interest. He is empowered to issue discipline regulations. Appeals by constables against decisions of the disciplinary procedure are considered by him.

The regulations issued in 1967 (*Statutory Instruments No.1021 (S 80)*)cover both complaints and disciplinary procedures. Complaints against police officers and the action taken must be recorded in a complaints book held at force or divisional headquarters. The deputy chief constable has overall responsibility for complaints and is required to appoint an investigating officer of the rank of inspector or above for each case. This officer (whenever practicable) must not be a member of the same division as the alleged offender, must not be a material witness nor have any personal interest in the case. Authority to bring disciplinary charges rests with the deputy chief constable. Although disciplinary proceedings are held in private, the Chief Constable may arrange for a complainer to attend, other than as a witness. The complainer will be informed of the Chief Constable's findings but not the punishment imposed.

When a complaint from which 'it may be reasonably inferred that a constable has committed a criminal offence' (*S.I. No 1021 (S 80) 2(2)*), is received the deputy chief constable must refer it to the regional Procurator Fiscal, a qualified solicitor or advocate, who is empowered to question the complainer and witnesses and to direct police investigations. The Fiscals' role in the procedure is seen 'as providing a full safeguard against any suspicion of police partiality in dealing with complaints'.[11]

Proposals for Change

Much of the demand for change to the complaints procedure originated in England. Organizations such as the National Council for Civil Liberties and Justice were critical of the 1964 Act and campaigned for the introduction of an independent element into the procedure.

By 1969 a Joint Working Party of the Police Advisory Boards for England & Wales and Scotland was appointed to examine the procedures and advise on any changes. Although their report was not published, it is evident that once again opinion was divided. Some members of the Working Party had suggested that the investigating officer's report should be referred to an independent solicitor for his opinion on whether disciplinary charges should be brought. Alternatively, it had been proposed that an outside body should conduct an ex post facto review of individual cases.

However the government took the view that there were 'considerable practical objections' to these suggestions and that they would not 'command a general confidence.' It was felt that

> 'where no possibility of a criminal charge is involved, the chief officer of police who is responsible for discipline, must be responsible for what is done about complaints subject of course to the continuing supervision of the police authority.'[12]

Because of the confidential nature of the report there was no real discussion of the matter. The government had decided that no change was required.

In 1971 there was little evidence of widespread dissatisfaction in Scotland, but the Scottish Council for Civil Liberties was (and continues to be) critical of the system, 'having pressed since 1970 for a review of the police complaints procedure'.[13]) However, as the Select Committee on Race Relations and Immigration discovered, there was widespread concern in England. From their witnesses they heard little in favour of the existing system and recommended that

'The Secretary of State take urgent steps to introduce a lay element into enquiries into complaints against the police, possibly by setting up independent tribunals to consider appeals by complainants or police officers dissatisfied with police enquiries into complaints'[14]

There was no government response to this appeal but a private member's Bill was introduced along the lines proposed by the Select Committee. Ronald King Murray drafted a second section of the Bill applicable to Scotland, providing for the appointment of police complaints commissioners for each Scottish region. During the debate on the Bill Russell Johnstone, spokesman for the Scottish Police Federation 'was dubious about part II.'[15] The Bill was withdrawn to facilitate fuller discussion about the introduction of a review procedure.

Two Working Groups were appointed, one for England & Wales and one for Scotland, to investigate the 'handling of complaints against the police.' In the meantime, Police Circular 16/1973 and Police (Chief Constables) Circular 27/1973 incorporating recommendations of the Police Advisory Boards' Joint Working Party, were issued with the aim of ensuring that the investigation of complaints was not only 'impartial but seen to be impartial'. Greater use was to be made of the power to appoint investigating officers from other forces; investigations were to be more closely supervised by the deputy chief constable; complainers were to be given a fuller explanation of how their complaints were disposed of; and police authorities were urged to develop their supervisory role. Evidence suggests that these recommendations were not universally adopted.

When the Scottish Working Group reported, proposals for an ex post facto review procedure were included, although the majority of the Group saw 'no need to introduce such a system at this stage.' Representatives of the three police associations on the Working Group believed that existing procedures were entirely satisfactory and were opposed to the introduction of an independent review body. While recognising that any change to the procedures was aimed at improving police/public relations, the Working Group maintained that the police were best qualified to investigate complaints and believed it essential that

'....the responsibility of Chief Constables for discipline within their forces should not in any way be affected.'[16]

Given this attitude it is not surprising that the Group's proposals were limited in scope.

Following the reports of the Working Groups in 1974, legislation was introduced and the Police Act setting up the Complaints Board (England & Wales) passed in 1976. The Scottish Bill, proposing a Police Complaints Panel, initially consisting of a chairman and two members to be appointed by the Scottish Secretary, was not put before the House until November 1976. The Panel was to have no role in cases alleging criminal behaviour, but would have had power to review cases referred by complainers when the deputy chief constable decided against pressing disciplinary charges. If the Panel disagreed with this decision, it could 'recommend' or after consultation, 'direct' that disciplinary charges be brought. In the case of disciplinary proceedings resulting from a complaint, if the accused officer denied the charge, the Panel would receive a copy of the complaint and a Panel member could attend the hearing as an observer. Although he could express his opinion on the case

'The function of deciding and imposing punishment shall be discharged only by the Chief Constable.'[17]

In view of the Police Complaints Board's failure to increase public confidence it is unlikely that the Scottish Panel would have proved any more successful. But it was never put to the test. The Bill was withdrawn on 27th May 1977, the official explanation being that

'......the parliamentary programme did not permit any prospect that it would make progress. Therefore it simply fell by the wayside because of the difficulties of legislation.'[18]

In 1977 the Labour government was indeed faced with problems but the S.C.C.L. offers an alternative explanation for the withdrawal of the Bill. They claim that

'The general understanding in Scotland was that the abandonment of the Bill was not unconnected with the fact that it was abandoned during strong pressure by the police for a pay increase which was not granted by the government.'[19]

Whatever the explanation, the whole history of proposals for change to the complaints procedure in Scotland seems to indicate a lack of commitment on the part of governments, a certain degree of complacency, and a reluctance on the part of the police to see changes implemented. Almost immediately after the withdrawal of the Bill, the then Scottish Secretary claimed, 'I am convinced of the need for legislation in this field and will introduce a Bill as soon as possible.'[20] But there the matter rested.

The 1981 inner-city riots in England provided an impetus for a review of policing. Evidence given to Lord Scarman during his investigation of the 'Brixton disorders' convinced him that

'.....there is a widespread and dangerous lack of public confidence in the existing system of handling complaints against the police. By and large, people do not trust the police to investigate the police.'[21]

Accordingly he recommended the early introduction of an independent element in the investigation of complaints.

The climate of opinion about the complaints procedure in England & Wales was changing. The Select Committee on Home Affairs conducted a rigorous examination of the system in England & Wales and although not convinced of the need for independent investigations, recommended the establishment of a complaints office in every region, headed by an independent assessor. Even the Police Federation of England & Wales had come round to the view that

'the time has come for the task of investigating complaints against the police from members of the public to be taken out of the hands of the police and passed in its entirety, to a body of independent investigators.'[22]

Although Scotland had not suffered the trauma of riots and Scottish policing methods were not called into serious question, some evidence from Scotland was considered by the Select Committee. The Memorandum submitted by the Scottish Home and Health Department stated that since the withdrawal of the 1976 Police (Scotland) Bill

'....the Secretary of State has not considered it necessary to make any change in the system of dealing with complaints against the police in Scotland.'[23]

a statement which appears to contradict the Labour Secretary of State's belief in 1977 in 'the need for legislation in this field.'

In 1982 factors influencing the Conservative Secretary of State's view were that the role of the Procurator Fiscal provided a safeguard against doubts of police partiality in serious complaints; there were fewer complaints pro rata in Scotland than in England & Wales; and there was little evidence of public concern about the Scottish procedures. However the Scottish Council for Civil Liberties challenged this assessment in their evidence to the Select Committee. The General Secretary of the S.C.C.L. expressed misgivings about the 'active investigatory role' of the Fiscals, claiming that

'The Procurator Fiscal is for one reason or another not able or willing to give sufficient attention to the case for it to be much more than a police investigation of the police by the police.'[24]

Paul Laverty also of the S.C.C.L., 'flabbergasted' as the small number of complaints recorded, commented

'This demonstrates clearly not so much that there are good relationships between the police and public in Scotland, but the fact that many people do not see the point in making complaints at all and certainly that has been my experience especially of people living in the outer housing schemes especially in Glasgow.'[25]

While agreeing that there appeared to be a lack of public concern about the topic in Scotland, the S.C.C.L. explained

'....it is because the people who should be concerned and that is the people it would most directly affect, are fed up complaining about it and those people are individuals and there tends not to be the same sort of organisations in Scotland to give voice to individual people's complaints as there are based here in London and other major urban centres.'[26]

Despite these criticisms the Select Committee was favourably impressed by the Scottish system. As some of their recommendations had implications for Scotland, the Scottish Secretary circulated a consultative note to the Convention of Scottish Local Authorities, individual police authorities, the police associations, and the Scottish Council for Civil Liberties inviting their views. This initiative resulted in no radical change because

'The general thrust of the comments received was that the existing arrangements should continue without being embodied in legislation; that the flexibility they allowed enabled minor complaints to be dealt with to the satisfaction of all parties without recourse to the full statutory disciplinary process; and that formalisation might simply serve to reduce their effectiveness and value.'[27]

Although the Scottish procedures have been discussed frequently since 1967, there has been no rigorous examination of the system. There has been no general review as in England, where opinions have been sought from a wide spectrum of society. Views which have been considered have been mainly those of people involved in the existing system. The Scottish Working Group (1974) consisted of five representatives from the Home and Health Department, five police representatives, HM Chief Inspector of Constabulary (Scotland) and one representative each from the Crown Office, the Association of County Councils, the Convention of Royal Burghs and Counties of Cities Association. The Scottish witnesses to the Select Committee (1982) were, an Undersecretary from the Home and Health Department, an Assistant Inspector of Constabulary, two representatives from the Crown Office the deputy chief constable of Strathclyde, two members of the Scottish Police Federation and three officers from the S.C.C.L.

Although the S.C.C.L. had suggested to the Select Committee that the Glasgow Bar Association, the Scottish Legal Action Group, and community and information groups would endorse their criticisms of the complaints system in Scotland, there is no indication that the views of these groups were sought. It is perhaps not surprising that the 'Scottish arrangements..... have largely escaped criticism.'

The Working of the Complaints Procedure

While attempts have been made to improve the efficiency and integrity of the complaints procedure in Scotland, there appear to be some weaknesses which invite criticism. Recommendations issued in Police Circulars cannot be enforced and reliance on this method of introducing improvements is not likely to inspire public confidence.

The recommendation that an explanatory leaflet should be made available at police stations (*Police Circular 6/84*) has been implemented in each force area and is a welcome innovation. If members of the public wish to make a complaint about the behaviour of a police officer, they have several options. Complaints may be made directly to a police station, by letter to the Chief Constable, or can be lodged with the local Procurator Fiscal. It is also possible to lodge a complaint with any reliable authority – for example, a Member of Parliament, a councillor or solicitor – who will refer the complaint to the Chief Constable. Whichever option is adopted, the complaint must be recorded and a detailed account of actions taken held at force headquarters.

While hearsay evidence cannot be regarded as proof, it suggests that when a direct approach is made to a police station, the potential complainer may feel intimidated or pressured not to proceed with a complaint. Obviously some complaints are frivolous or malicious and it is entirely justifiable that a warning is issued that the complainer may be reported to the Procurator Fiscal in such cases. Allegations about the difficulty of lodging complaints directly are largely undocumented but support the claim made by the S.C.C.L. that

> 'It is not uncommon for a complainer to go round to the local police office with a complaint and for that complaint not to be passed on but for an officer, perhaps at the level of sergeant, to visit the complainer at home instead of passing the complaint to the Chief Constable's office.'[28]

If the procedures are to be fair to complainers there should be no opportunity for junior officers to apply pressure. It is also unfair to officers, most of whom do act with integrity, that such doubts exist. Although some complaints against the police are made because of a misunderstanding of police powers and duties and the complainer may not wish to proceed when an explanation is given, it is essential that correct procedures are adhered to.

Even when this is done, and the complainer is visited by a senior officer suggestions have been made[29] that undue pressure may be exerted in order to have the complaint withdrawn. Since the interview is normally held in private it is difficult for the police to refute allegations of undue pressure.

The amended regulations (*Statutory Instruments 1982 (S 119 5(1)*) allow for complaints to be dealt with informally, if the deputy chief constable decides that the complaint is of a minor nature. In such cases the officer involved is allowed to comment on the complaint and may be given a warning about his behaviour. A senior officer explains the officer's behaviour and if the complainer is satisfied, the need for fuller investigation is obviated. Increasing use has been made of this procedure, and it has obvious advantages. However, once again it is possible for a complainer to claim he was pressured into accepting the explanation. This procedure could be improved quite simply and without legislation if the proposal

> '.....that the record of the interview should include a record of the investigating officer's presentation to the complainer: that this should form a distinct section of the report: and that it should be separately signed by the complainer.'[30]

were incorporated into the regulations.

When it appears that a more serious offence against the Police Discipline Regulations may have been committed, a senior officer is appointed by the deputy chief constable to investigate the complaint. While it is acknowledged

> '....that complaints can often be dealt with by an internal investigating officer without prejudicing the absolute need for impartiality'

the guidelines stress that the appointment of an outside investigating officer is

> '....justifiable and indeed preferable....for instance to satisfy an evident public expectation that there should be a demonstrably independent investigation.'[31]

The Scottish Office is obviously aware of some public disquiet about the investigation of complaints by members of the same force. It is difficult to ascertain how often outside investigating officers are appointed, but in 1973 the '...power to request an officer from another force (had) been seldom used.'[32]

During the investigation of complaints the officer involved is not required to make any statement which could be used against him, with the result that

> '...certain otherwise good and credible complaints founder on a police officer's right of silence.'[33]

An analysis of the 1985 statistics is revealing and suggests that there is difficulty in obtaining evidence to support a complaint. Of the 1,716 complaints dealt with, 186 (10.8%) were withdrawn, or abandoned, 279 (16.2%) were resolved by explanation and only 153 (8.9%) were found to be unsubstantiated. Yet on completion of investigation, action was taken on only 150 complaints, leaving 948 (55.2%), which had warranted investigation, resulting in no action. Since

> 'A citizen who suffers an abuse at the hands of the police is peculiarly helpless, from the powers exercised by officers, to collect and preserve evidence, or to have this done on his or her behalf'[34]

it is perhaps prudent to consider making it obligatory for the officer involved to give a full and satisfactory account of his conduct to the investigating officer.

A large number of complaints is referred every year to the Procurator Fiscal, (1985 57% of complaints dealt with) and it appears that the regulations requiring the deputy chief constables to refer are stringently applied. However, of these complaints, very few (1985 1.7%) result in criminal proceedings. Recent highly publicised cases in England have illustrated the police lack of success in investigating criminal allegations against the police which are obviously well founded. Theoretically, in Scotland, such investigations are undertaken by the Fiscals. Yet the Police Complaints Board thought that

> 'In Scotland though the Procurator Fiscal determines whether the evidence of an investigation justifies criminal proceedings, the investigation of complaints is in practice conducted by the police.' [35]

Doubts exist that the Fiscals cannot possibly carry out extensive investigations because of an excessive work-load. In 1982 the total strength of the Fiscal service was, '916 of whom 210 are legally qualified' (H C 98 VIII para 749). This does not seem an adequate number to fulfil both investigatory and prosecuting roles. As Desmond Browne of the S.C.C.L. pointed out,

> 'If the Procurator Fiscal is to be an investigator, then I would like to see the Procurator in the courts in which I work as investigator. In order to do that he and his five assistants would need some considerable time off from prosecuting the 10,000 cases they prosecute every single year in the summary courts'[36]

While in theory the role of the Procurator Fiscal may provide a safeguard against any suspicion of police partiality in dealing with complaints, the evidence on practice leaves grounds for concern. As long as this exists, the complaints procedure cannot be regarded as satisfactory.

When complaints have been investigated, by the police disciplinary process or by the Fiscals, the guidelines recommend that each complainer be given as full an explanation as possible of how his complaint has been looked into. Yet it appears that this is frequently not provided.

'It is normal for people to receive a letter which amounts to three lines each with a paragraph to itself stating simply that the Chief Constable or the Procurator has investigated...and found no grounds for action.'[37]

A complainer who is dissatisfied with the outcome of his complaint or with the explanation offered, has no right to a review of his case. Although the Scottish Office maintains that complainers are largely satisfied, the S.C.C.L.

'...can only conclude that... the Scottish Home and Health Department have mislaid substantial correspondence with the S.C.C.L. and other bodies and with individual complainers and their solicitors.'[38]

When such dissatisfaction exists the credibility of the complaints system is called into question.

The role of H M Inspectorate of Constabulary and Police Authorities

Since the Inspectors of Constabulary are bound to 'visit and inquire into the state and efficiency of the police force' under the 1967 Act they are in close contact with Chief Constables and police authorities and have access to all information on complaints held by each force. In his annual report the Chief Inspector includes a survey of the complaints received during the year.

Normally there is little comment apart from a general expression of approval of the way in which complaints are dealt with. In 1977 – the year in which the Police (Scotland) Bill was withdrawn – it was noted that

'During the past few years the standard of inquiry into and the disposal of complaints in Scotland has improved'[39]

an indication perhaps that the procedures previously had been neither as impartial nor as thorough as has been claimed. Full discussions were held with all Chief Constables and their deputies and, as a result, minor changes were agreed. It would therefore seem that the inspectorate can, by discussion and suggestion, exert some influence on how complaints are dealt with. The Chief Inspector (always an ex Chief Constable) provides a useful link between forces and the Scottish Office, which, when 'good practices' are identified may suggest their implementation throughout the country. It is evident however, that the inspectorate is limited to guidance only and has no power to compel Chief Constables to comply with recommendations. On the other hand, if regulations are flouted a report will be made to the Scottish Secretary. Although the inspectorate has a general supervisory role, supervision is not close since forces are inspected only once a year.

While it appears that the inspectorate has access to information on complaints procedures, the Chief Constable is not obliged to give the police authority access to all information.

> 'The amount of supporting detail furnished to the police authority is within the discretion of the Chief Constable, but....he should, consistently with observance of the principle that the police reports of enquiries are confidential, bear in mind the need to supply the police authority with the necessary information to enable them to carry out their statutory duty.'[40]

Therefore one would expect to find variations in the way in which authorities fulfil their obligations. Indeed the Scottish Office makes it clear that 'the interpretation of the statutory requirements is primarily a matter for individual authorities.' By implication it seems that the Scottish Office does not regard the 'duty' of police authorities to be a crucial one.

Information gleaned mainly from regional officials illustrates how the authorities 'keep themselves informed'. The authority areas have been numbered because definitive information is not available.

1. The committee receives quarterly statistical tables recording the number of complaints received, their outcome and the number of hours spent on investigation. The type of complaint is categorised. Questions are rarely asked. Since the issue of *Police Circular 6/84* two committee members visit Police Headquarters (the frequency of these visits was not revealed) to discuss complaints with the deputy chief constable.

2. A bi-monthly report is made by the Chief Constable to the committee and statistics supplied, similar to those in 1, but with no categorisation of complaints by type. The Complaints Book is open to inspection by the committee.

3. 'The responsibility is undertaken most fully by members of the...committee, examining the workings of the complaints system during regular visits to Police Headquarters.' (letter 5.3.86). Registers recording complaints and disciplinary matters are available and subject to the 'fullest scrutiny'. Discussions on specific complaints are held with the deputy chief constable. Regular statistical information is not considered necessary.

4. The committee is supplied with annual statistics which do not include a categorisation of complaints by type. The Complaints Book is submitted for inspection every six months. 'There has been no controversy about the complaints procedure in recent years.'

5. The committee receives detailed quarterly reports from the Chief Constable. Types of complaint are categorised for each division of the force. Reference was made in the latest report (6.1.86) to the appointment of an outside investigating officer for a complaint of alleged assault 'which had been brought to notice by a national newspaper.' The availability of detailed information is an innovation initiated by the Chief Constable in response to *Police Circular 6/84*.

6. The committee receives quarterly statistics which do not specify the number of hours spent on investigations nor a categorisation of complaints by type. The Complaints Book is presented for inspection at Committee meetings. A sub-committee discusses specific complaints with the deputy chief constable.

7. At the monthly meetings of the committee, attended by the deputy chief constable, the statistics, which do not include a categorisation of complaints by type, and the complaints book are examined. One member of the committee expressed dissatisfaction with the amount of information supplied and feels that the committee as a whole should play a more active role in the complaints procedure.

8. At monthly meetings of the committee, statistics detailing the type of complaint and the number of hours spent on investigation, are examined. Since 1985 four (all party) committee members visit police headquarters bi-monthly and discuss each complaint with the deputy chief constable. A representative of the Police Federation is present to ensure police confidentiality is maintained.

There is then a variety in the amount and nature of information supplied to police authorities in Scotland and it appears that the majority do not play an active role in the complaints procedure. Police authorities are dependent on their Chief Constables for information; they cannot compel him to divulge that information. No criticism of existing relationships between Chief Constables and their authorities is implied, but should an authority be dissatisfied about the way complaints are dealt with, it may only recommend improvements which a Chief Constable is not required to implement. If, as the Scottish Secretary has stated

> '....police authorities have an important role to fulfil in reassuring the public that complaints against the police are dealt with thoroughly and with complete impartiality'[41]

it is important that their role should be a meaningful one. Existing legislation does not define their powers clearly.

Complaints Procedures in England & Wales

Reforms of the complaints procedure in England & Wales were introduced as a result of a growing awareness, by the government and by the police themselves, of the lack of public confidence in the system and a realisation of the implications this lack of confidence has for policing in general. The first independent element, the Police Complaints Board was empowered to act in a supervisory capacity in complaints implying a breach of the discipline regulations. The Board had no investigatory role and critics claimed its brief was too limited in scope. An incoming chairman of the Board, Sir Cyril Philips was critical of its performance declaring that 'the existing Board had kept so low a profile that it has climbed into a ditch.'[42]

The flurry of investigations into policing in England & Wales – the Scarman Inquiry, the Select Committee on the Police Complaints Procedure, the Plowden Working Party, the Royal Commission on Criminal Procedure – had all concluded that changes in the complaints procedure were essential with the result that the Complaints Board was replaced by the Police Complaints Authority in 1985.

Under the terms of the *Police and Criminal Evidence Act 1984 (part IX)* the Authority appears to be a more powerful body than the Board. The Authority must be informed about complaints involving death or serious injury; can demand to be informed about any other type of complaint; has a supervisory role in the investigation of complaints; has the power of veto over the appointment of investigating officers; can order the appointment of outside investigating officers; and is empowered to order reports of investigations to the D.P.P. A report of the investigation into a complaint supervised by the Authority must be submitted to it for an opinion before any disciplinary charges are brought. If the Authority deems it desirable, disciplinary proceedings may be held before a Tribunal, composed of a chairman (the Chief Constable) and two members of the Authority. Evidence is considered by the Tribunal and the decision on the guilt or otherwise of the accused officer may be reached by a majority, although punishment is determined by the Chief Constable after consultation with the Tribunal members. Any accused officer, who may lose his job or rank as a result of disciplinary proceedings, has the right to legal representation at a disciplinary hearing – a right not allowed to the police in Scotland.

The complaints procedure in England & Wales now differs considerably from that in Scotland. It is more open, is subject to close supervision by an independent body empowered to direct investigations and order reports, and is fairer in disciplinary proceedings to accused officers. But the fatal flaw remains – investigations into complaints are still conducted by the police. It is too soon to pass judgement on the effectiveness of the new Complaints Authority, but Reiner suggests that 'It is unlikely that pressure in the area of complaints will cease'[43] until a procedure involving completely independent investigators is introduced.

Although there has been little public debate on the complaints procedure in Scotland, increasingly disturbing cases are being reported by the media, indicating perhaps that the topic may become more controversial. The number of complaints recorded in Scotland has been rising dramatically recently (see graph) increasing by 64% between 1979 and 1985. It would appear that there are no grounds for complacency, especially if a number of those who complain is not satisfied.

As the Scottish Office told the Select Committee in 1982, the number of complaints in Scotland, pro rata, is significantly lower than in England & Wales (see Table 1 line 2). But the ratio is changing. Over the period 1981-1985 the number of comlaints per 1,000 officers has risen from 83.1 to 129, while in England and Wales it has declined. On the basis of available statistics it seems that the upward trend in Scotland is likely to continue. Although there may be various possible explanations for this – for example, a heightened awareness of individual rights, or a more careful recording of complaints – such increases indicate that the public is becoming more critical of police behaviour.

The Scottish statistics do not include the number of complaints substantiated, (line 3), but if the number of complaints resulting in proceedings (Result by Outcome, sub-total) is treated as in England &

RECORDED NUMBER OF COMPLAINTS AGAINST THE POLICE (SCOTLAND) 1967-1985

COMPILED FROM H.M. CHIEF INSPECTOR OF CONSTABULARY (SCOTLAND) ANNUAL REPORTS 1967-1985.

TABLE 1: Comparative Table of complaints Against the Police in Scotland and in England & Wales 1981 to 1985

	SCOTLAND					ENGLAND & WALES (INCLUDING MET)				
	1981	1982	1983	1984	1985	1981	1982	1983	1984	1985
Total number of complaints										
1 Disposed of	1096	1085	1346	1598	1716	32443	32086	30681	31174	28253
2 Per 1000 officers	83.1	82.2	84.5	120.2	129.0	273.1	269.0	255.2	260.2	234.0
3 Substantiated	Figures	not	given in (Scotland)	HMI	Report	1542	1787	1448	1561	1155
as % of 1						4.8%	5.5%	4.7%	5.0%	4.1%
4 Unsubstantiated	648	618	159	154	153	15263	15395	14353	15992	11650
as % of 1	59.1%	56.9%	11.8%	9.6%	8.9%	47.0%	48.0%	46.8%	51.3%	41.2%
5 With no proceedings recommended by P.F.	*N/A	N/A	691	859	948					
as % of 1			51.3%	53.7%	55.2%					
6 Found to be trivial or unfounded	27	49	155	259	279					20+
as % of 1	2.4%	4.5%	11.5%	16.2%	16.2%					
7 Resolved by explanation(s)/informally (E. & W.)						–	–	–	–	2162⊕
as % of 1										7.6%
8 Withdrawn/abandoned	305	250	181	180	186	15638	14904	14880	13621	13266
as % of 1	27.8%	23.0%	13.4%	11.3%	10.8%	48.2%	46.5%	48.5%	43.7%	46.9%
Subtotal (Scotland) Total E & W	980	917	1186	1452	1566	32443	32086	30681	31174	28253
Result by outcome										
9 Resulting in disciplinary proceedings	5	12	16	12	10	213	238	182	158	212
10 Resulting in criminal proceedings	11	21	34	24	29	39	41	33	32	31
11 Resulting in criminal (traffic)			35	23	28	23	18	12	9	3
12 Resulting in formal warning			75	87	83	N/A	N/A	N/A	N/A	N/A
13 Resulting in corrective advice	32	47	N/A	N/A	N/A	–	–	–	–	–
14 Dealt with by other means	N/A	N/A	N/A	N/A	N/A	1282	1494	1231	1366	916
Sub Total	48	80	160	146	150	1557	1791	1458	1565	1162
as % of 1	4.4%	7.4%	11.9%	9.1%	8.7%	4.8%	5.5%	4.7%	5.0%	4.1%
Total Scotland	x1028	x997	1346	1598	1716					
15 Referred to Procurator Fiscal	612	694	707	883	977	Direct comparison cannot be made, as in England & Wales the number of **cases** (as opposed to the of complaints) sent to the D.P.D. is recorded.				
as % of 1	55.8%	64.0%	63.4%	55.5%	57.0%					
Number of officers found guilty (a) of criminal offences	2	3	.6	not given	not given	27	16	30	14	23
(b) of traffic offences	N/A	N/A	N/A	N/A	N/A	15	15	7	8	2

* in 1981 & 1982 included as unsubstantiated.
+ Recorded only by the Met in 1985
⊕ New procedure introduced by Police & Criminal Evidence act
x Figures, as given in HMI (Scotland) Reports, do not tally

Tables compiled from annual reports of
(1) Her Majesty's Chief Inspector of Constabulary (Scotland)
(2) Her Majesty's Chief Inspector of Constabulary
(3) The Commisioner of the Metropolitan Police 1981-1985.

Wales as the number substantiated (a necessary procedure in the absence of comparable statistics) it appears that the Scottish rate of substantiation has been consistently higher than in England & Wales. However, on closer inspection it can be seen that although in Scotland the number of complaints resulting in criminal proceedings (line 10) is substantially higher, pro rata, than in England & Wales, (force ratio E. & W. 9 to S. 1), a lower proportion of Scottish officers is found guilty. (line 16)

It is debatable whether criminal proceedings resulting in a not-guilty verdict can be regarded as substantiated complainnts. If not-guilty verdicts are discounted in both areas the rate of substantiation is; Scotland, 3.5% (1981) : 5.7% :1982 : 9.8% (1983), while in England & Wales the figures are as given in the table. (line 3) In 1983, the proportion of substantiated complaints (9.8%) was double that in England & Wales (4.7%). It may be that in 1983 police behaviour deteriorated, which does not seem on the face of it to be a reasonable conclusion, or that the complaints procedure 'clear-up' rate improved. Because the Scottish statistics no longer include the number of officers found guilty, it is impossible to ascertain if the substantiation rate in Scotland has remained higher than in England & Wales. There, the low rate of substantiation has been a contributary factor to the lack of public confidence in the complaints procedure.

Research carried out by Ken Russell[44] indicates that this lack of confidence is justified. In the force area studied 9% of complaints were substantiated but the senior officer involved in the project suggested that 38% should have been. Even if the Scottish rate has remained higher than England & Wales, it seems that there is still considerable scope for improvement.

There appears to have been a remarkable change in the proportion of complaints found to be unsubstantiated in Scotland (line 4). In 1981 and 1982, complaints which resulted in no proceedings being recommended by the Procurator fiscal were included as unsubstantiated. Since then these have been detailed separately (line 5). If these complaints are regarded as unsubstantiated, the proportion of unsubstantiated complaints in Scotland has been about 63% since 1983; much higher than in England and Wales. There the number has fluctuated, dropping considerably in 1985 to 41.2% (line 4). Interestingly this significant drop occurred when the informal resolution procedure was introduced in England and Wales, with 7.6% (line 7) of complaints being dealt with by this method in 1985.

It must be noted that the number of complaints withdrawn or abandoned in Scotland is markedly lower than in England & Wales. There the lowest figure recorded was 43.7% in 1984 (line 8), while in Scotland the proportion of withdrawn complaints has declined from 27.8% (1981) to 10.8% (1985). Perhaps the decrease in Scotland is the result of more careful supervision. But the decline in the withdrawal rate almost exactly coresponds to an increased use of informal resolution procedures (line 7). If complainers are genuinely satisfied by this method of resolution it is a welcome innovation.

Neither of these explanations can account for the fact that the withdrawal rate in Scotland is significantly lower than in England & Wales. Russell's research identified some reasons for withdrawn complaints which did not reflect badly on the system in England and presumably such reasons, (such as misunderstandings or distortion perceptions) also exist in Scotland. However other reasons included a fear of police reprisals and pressure by investigating officers. It may be the case that in Scotland complainers experience less pressure or intimidation (although evidence gathered by the SCCL indicates that such pressures exist) and for that reason the withdrawal rate is lower. On the other hand, it may be that the complainer is less likely to withdraw in Scotland are less likely to withdraw because a higher proportion of complaints are allegations of criminal behaviour.

During the two years when comparison is possible, the proportionof complaintes alleging assault in Lothian and Borders was considerably higher than in the Metropolitan force area. It is extremely unlikely that the Lothian and Borders police are more violent than those serving in the Metropolitan force. Consideration must be given to the view that 'tactical' complaints are made against the police by people who themselves have been charged with offences. Undoubtedly such complaints are made, but since the statistics do not detail the number of complaints found to be malicious or unfounded, it is impossible to ascertain whether there is a higher incidence of tactical complaints in Lothian and Borders. Again this seems unlikely.

In the Metropolitan force area the proportion of complaints alleging criminal behaviour was 28.7% (1984) and 32.7 (1985). The corresponding figures for Lothians and Borders were 47.7% (1984) and 43.1% (1985). These figures appear disturbingly high but it must also be noted that the Lothian and Borders figure is lower than the 57.% of complaints referred to the Procurator Fiscal in Scotland as a whole in 1985.

However as Table 2 illustrates, the number of complaints made in Lothian and Borders about other matters' is lower than in the Metropolitan area. From this limited evidence it is possible to argue that Scots complain less often about 'other matters'. This may account for the lower pro rata number of complaints recorded in Scotland. It may also partially explain the lower withdrawal rate. There may be cultural factors involved which result in a lower withdrawal rate in Scotland but a complainer is less likely to withdraw if he feels that a criminal offence has been committed.

TABLE 2:   Analysis of the nature of complaints against the Police

	Lothian and Borders		Metropolitan Police	
	1984	1985	1984	1985
Total Number of Complaints	254	353	6594	5462
Nature of Allegation as a percentage of Total Complaints	%	%	%	%
Criminal				
Assault	42.5	41.1	21.4	25.0
Other Criminal Conduct	5.1	2.0	–	–
Bribery	–	–	0.5	0.3
Perjury	–	–	2.0	1.8
Conspiracy	–	–	1.6	2.0
Theft	–	–	1.5	1.9
Traffic	–	–	1.7	1.4
Total Criminal	**47.6**	**43.1**	**28.7**	**32.4**
Other Matters				
Improper Attitude	9.4	11.6	17.5	16.3
Misconduct of Officer	25.6	30.9	–	–
Neglect of Duty	9.8	6.8	10.7	10.3
Unjustified Harassment	7.5	7.6	2.7	2.9
False Evidence	–	–	0.6	0.8
Irregularity	–	–	37.2	35.4
Mistaken arrest	–	–	0.1	0.1
Racial discrimination	–	–	0.8	1.1
Stops in Street	–	–	0.5	0.5
Miscellaneous	–	–	1.1	0.5
Total Other Matters*	**52.3**	**56.9**	**71.3**	**67.9**

*   Figure have been rounded up

Tables compiled from:
    Statistical Returns to the Lothian & Borders Police Board – 6th January 1986
    and Reports of the Commissioner of the Metropolitan Police – 1984 & 1985.

The examination of complaints statistics has revealed a number of differences between Scotland and England & Wales. In Scotland a higher proportion of complaints result in criminal proceedings. However in England & Wales, more officers who are prosecuted are found guilty. In England & Wales, pro rata, a much higher proportion of officers fact disciplinary proceedings (see Table 1 line 9) and more are dealt with by 'other means' (line 14) that the number of officers who receive formal warnings or corrective advice (lines 12 & 13) in Scotland. In both areas the number of substantiated complaints is low, as is the number of officers found guilty of criminal offences.

Because of the implications for police/public relations if complainers are not satisfied with the outcome of their complaints, the very high number of unsubstantiated complaints and the low number of withdrawals is Scotland are disturbing aspects of the Scottish statistics. Unfortunately, because the police conduct the investigations into complaints, the belief exists that they are less than meticulous in seeking evidence. It is believed that the 'police culture' inclines officers to close ranks to protect their fellow officers accused of offences.

On the other hand the police believe that they are best qualified to conduct investigations. They spend a great deal of time on this work and point out that it is in their interest that complaints should be dealt with to the satisfaction of the public. During 1985, in Lothian and Borders 5755 hours were spent investigating 353 complaints. Under the existing system many highly trained officers are diverted from operational duties to investigate complaints. For example, the Complaints and Discipline Branch of the Strathclyde force employs 16 officers above the rank of inspector. The cost of the complaints system in terms of police time, is high.

Although there has not, as yet, been any significant controversy about the complaints procedure in Scotland, there are several weaknesses in the system which have implications for policing in general. considerable changes in policing and in public attitudes have taken place since the Royal Commission reported in 1962. Rather than wait until controversy develops, it is preferable that a Royal Commission be appointed to review not only the complaints procedure in Scotland but also the wider issue of police accountability.

Eileen Macpherson, The University of Dundee, Department of Political Science and Social Policy.

References

1. Final Report of the Police Complaints Board, 1985. Cmnd. 9584. Appendix Para 7.

2. Alfred John List,*Treatise on the Rural Police*, 1841, p.42.

3. House of Commons Debates 1958/59, Vol.600, col.204.

4. Report of the Tribunal appointed to inquire into the Allegation of Assault on John Waters. Cmnd.718, April 1959.

5. House of Commons Debates. 1958/59, Vol.600, Cols.1239-1305.

6. Final Report of the Royal Commission on the Police. 1962. Cmnd.1728, Para.429.

7. *Ibid*

8. *Ibid* Memorandum of Dissent. Para. 63.

9. *Ibid*, Para.478.

10. Police (Scotland) Act, 1967, S.40.

11. Report from the Select Committee on Home Affairs. 1982. H.C. 98 VIII Para. 12.

12. House of Commons Debates. 1971/72. Vol.827. Col.654.

13. *Op.cit*. H.C. 98 IX. Para.1078.

14. *Report from the Select Committee on Race Relations & Immigration*, 1972, H.C.471.1. Para.333.

15. House of Commons Debates. 1972/73. Vol.851.Col.1012.

16. Report of the Working Group for Scotland. The Handling of Complaints against the Police. 1974. Cmnd. 5583. Para.11.

17. Police (Scotland) Bill, 1976. 6(3).

18. *Op.cit.*, H.C. 98.VIII. Para. 201.

19. *Ibid.* H.C. 98.IX. Para. 272.

20. House of Commons Debates. 1976/77. Vol.934, Col.316.

21. Lord Scarman. *The Scarman Report* p.139, Penguin Books 1981.

22. *Op.cit.*. H.C. 98 11.p.7.

23. *Ibid*. H.C. 98 VIII Para. 1988.

24. *Ibid*, Para. 1091.

25. *Ibid*. Para.1064.

26. *Ibid*. Para. 1080.

27. Police Circular 6/1984. Para.16.

28. *Op.cit*. H.C. 98. IX. Para 1055.

29. *Ibid*. Para. 1080

30. Enquiry into Police Complaints Procedures. p.4. SCCL Leaflet 1983.

31. *Op.cit*. P.C.6/84 Para 4.

32. Police Circular 16/1973. Para 3.

33. *Op.cit*. SCCL Enquiry. p.5.

34. *Ibid*

35. *Op.cit*. Cmnd.9584. Para 7.

36. *Op.cit*. H.C. 98 IX Para.1085.

37. *Ibid*, Para. 1065.

38. SCCL. Correspondence 12th August 1982.

39. Annual Report of H.M. Chief Inspector of Constabulary (Scotland) 1977. Cmnd.7306, Para. 37.

40. Scottish Home & Health Department. Consultative Note 1983. Para. 31.

41. *Op.cit*. P.C. 6/84, Para.23.

42. Robert Reiner. *The Politics of the Police*, Harvester Press, 1985, p.191.

43. *Ibid*. p.192.

44. Ken Russell, *Complaints Against the Police which are Withdrawn*, 1986.

THE POLITICS OF ISLAND TRANSPORT

Jean Didier-Hache

Although Scotland does not ranks among the larger European nations journeying to and from its outer islands is still nowadays a fairly lengthy affair. Trying to reach the Scottish central belt from any of the three Islands Regions keeps implying a fairly considerable journey for those who can only travel by land and by sea. Using the quickest routes and the best possible connections, an inhabitant of the Western Isles will thus take around 10 hours to reach Glasgow, an inhabitant of Orkney between 11 and 12 to get to Edinburgh, and a Shetlander up to 17 hours. This, of course, if he lives in one of the main harbours from his archipelago; for a resident in a remote rural area or small outlying island may easily take between one and two days.

Travelling by air – a necessity more than a luxury in the islands – saves a lot of time, but is financially crippling, as fares are converse to the distance. In 1984, the average fare per km on a major UK line (Glasgow/London) was around 09p. By comparison, fares on the main routes linking the islands to the Scottish mainland ranged between 15p and 20p per kilometre. On the inter-island routes the air fares reached between 20p and 36p per kilometre, albeit some of those are already subsidised quite substantially by the local authorities.[1] Obviously passengers travelling on very short routes (like some inter-island flights in Orkney, which last only a few minutes) have to face the static costs of the service (the plane, its maintenance, the pilot's wages, etc.). Nevertheless, the vast difference (4 to 1) in price per km shows a clear disadvantage for the communities which are the most dependent upon this kind of amenity.

Ferries are not cheap either. To give but one example, if in 1979 a passenger travelling to the islands by boat had been charged a fare equivalent to the then British Rail average of 5p/mile, he would have had to pay £10.40 instead of around £16 to go to Shetland, £1.24 instead of around £5 to go to Orkney, and £2.11 instead of around £4 to go to Stornoway, in the Outer-Hebrides.[2] Internal ferries, when they are managed by the local islands authority, are very low-priced, but they have to be heavily subsidised by the ratepayers. In Shetland and in the Western Isles, over

90% of the internal ferries' income comes from the Council.

Unsurprisingly, consumers do tend to suffer from a higher cost of living in the outer islands, but substantial differences exist between the main towns and the rural areas, or especially the smaller islands. In 1984, for a retail price index using Aberdeen figures as a yardstick (Aberdeen =100), the average prices in the Highlands & Islands was 110. In the outer islands, the scale varied between 104.9 and 118.5, according to the location. The island towns which offer a sizeable market with a reasonable amount of competition, provided the cheapest cost of living: 104.9 for Stornoway, 109.4 for Lerwick, 110.7 for Kirkwall; which compares favourably with the Highlands & Islands average, or indeed with the figures of some remote rural areas of the mainland (111.8 in a small Sutherland village). But the island's rural areas, or even more the smaller islands provided the worst figures of Scotland: 118.5 in Shetland, 115.8 in Orkney, or 116.4 in the Western Isles.[3]

Since around two-thirds of the islanders live in sparsely populated rural areas, retail prices still remain a major concern in the Islands. Moreover, this kind of discrepancy strengthens an already worrying trend of imbalance in infra-regional development.

For the island industries too, the consequences of transport costs can be dire, but there are important variations. As a rough rule, it can be said that the impact of transport is converse to the volume/value ratio of the goods carried. In other words, High volume/Low value goods (such as hay, bricks, fertiliser, etc.) will be crippled by them, while Low volume/High value goods (such as most shellfish, tweed, knitwear, etc.) will be comparatively unaffected.

The farming and building industries do consequently bear the brunt of insularity. Crofters in the Western Isles and in Shetland wishing to import hay from the mainland are faced with transport costs so high that its price may easily double. Even in Orkney, where the fertility of the soil, the size of farms, and the apparent proximity of the mainland should imply a more limited vulnerability to the cost of imports and exports, the consequences are spectacular. It has been estimated that an Orcadian farmer's income is around 35% lower than the income of an Aberdeenshire farmer, and in the northern isles of Orkney, the figure would be an extra 10% lower.[4] It must be noted that in all the archipelagoes, farming imports and exports already benefit from a variety of concessionary fares[5] without which some agricultural activities could perhaps not take place.

Similar observations can be made about the building industry. Take, for example, a ton of bricks sold for £34 a ton in Aberdeen. The transport costs to Stornoway, in the Western Isles, will add an extra £27 (80% of the original value). By comparison, transport costs to Wick will only fetch £11.4, not only because of the mainland location, but also because of the stronger competition amongst road hauliers.

The local authorities are also faced with a much higher level of expenditure per capita, since services, public buildings and other types of infrastructures will be more costly and the population more scattered. For example, in 1984/85, the housing expenditure reached £1.876 per head of population in Orkney, and £1.351 in the Western Isles, against £788 in Scotland as a whole. Education cost £390 in Shetland, £355 in the Western Isles, and £315 in Orkney, against £250 per head of population for the Scottish average.

Tourism is another industry strongly affected by transport costs. The archipelagic configuration of Western Isles, Orkney and Shetland restrict the movements of cars, and since the journey from the mainland has already proved very expensive (especially in comparison with the cost of an overseas holiday), tourists are often reluctant to come or when they do, tend to limit their visit to the bigger islands.

In other sectors, the impact of transport will nevertheless be felt differently. This is the case of the fishing industry, and in particular of the shellfish industry. The value of fish and shellfish may range from £220 per ton for winkles, to around £5,000 per ton for salmon, and even £6 or £7,000 for lobster[6] – this according to the size, the quality, the time of the year, etc. Consequently the impact of transport costs is in a number of cases, limited because the retail price of much island produce is very high anyway. Such exports have long been hindered by the communication difficulties, but the development of transport technologies, (special containers adapted to cooling or freezing the fish, etc.) has lifted a lot of the old difficulties. This is not to say that the fishing industry as a whole is indifferent to transport costs. Imports of salmon feed for the fishfarm, or of engines and spare parts for fishing vessels is still a heavy burden. Yet in many cases, the speed and punctuality of delivery of top quality produce is more important than a lowering of transport costs.

The case of fishing could well be extended to the various activities where the islands manufacture goods which bear a strong "island identity" and command high prices. The Harris Tweed industry in the Hebrides, the knitwear industry in Shetland, the distilleries in Orkney, export goods which have achieved a world-wide fame. Once again, the plight of these industries in terms of transport lies more with the quality and speed of deliveries than with the consequences of costs – albeit no one would certainly object to cheaper fares.

There are also a number of activities where lower fares may have a damaging effect upon the island communities, by making them become more and more dependant upon the import of mainland goods which they could readily produce themselves. Milk, for example, is for a large part imported to the Western Isles daily from Inverness or Oban on the mainland. One may wonder if the subsidising of milk imports should not be more efficiently replaced by the development of a local milk industry (with higher hay or cattlefeed subsidies). Such a development would not only benefit the consumers, but also help to lower the 20% rate of unemployment which plagues the Outer Hebrides. Hasty and simplified as it may be, this brief survey of the relationships between transport and the island economy shows us an extensive range of diverse implications. At one end of the scale, certain industries are severely affected by transport costs. At the other end, the same transport costs may prove a useful incentive to foster some forms of local development.

The management and subsidising of island transport

The complexity of the transport issue may once again be observed in the way island services are managed and subsidised. Central government has indirect responsibility for the management of most island/mainland air routes since these are serviced by the national airline, British Airways. Inter-islands routes, and a small number of mainland routes, are serviced by Loganair, which is a private company owned by British Midland Airways.

Since 1982, British Airways operates its Highlands & Islands routes through its "Highlands Division". Due to strict reorganisation, this Division has become profitable; but the fares, which are unsubsidised, are high. This is very damaging for the island communities which are relying on air communciations more than any other part of Britain.

Central government could subsidise air transport through the *Highland & Islands Air Services (Scotland) Act 1980*, but it only does so very sparingly, for a small number of routes operated by Loganair.

Loganair also gets various forms of subsidies from the Islands Authorities. In the Western Isles, the Council pays a third of the internal routes' running costs, and has a say over the number of weekly flights. Consequently, local authority spending cuts have had direct consequences over the quality of the internal air service, with flights being withdrawn for lack of subsidy. In Orkney, passengers from the northern isles travelling to Kirkwall are getting a direct rebate on their fares, paid by the local authority. In Shetland, the Council subsidises chartered planes to some of the outlying islands (Foula, Papa Stour ...) where there are no regular services. Last but not least, Loganair provides important services like the air ambulance, or in Shetland the watch over oil tankers to prevent pollution around the Sullom Voe area. Those services are financed either by central government funds or by the local authority.

Sea services between the islands and the mainland are operated privately, except in the case of Caledonian MacBrayne (a subsidiary of the Scottish Transport Group) which provides the services for all the West of Scotland.

With some exceptions (like the oil related traffic, the summer service between Shetland and the Nordic countries, or some bulk shipping companies), most of these services are subsidised. Subsidies are granted by the Scottish Development Department of the Scottish Office, through the powers of the *Highlands & Islands Shipping Services Act 1960*. The Scottish Office also subsidises a number of inter-island routes: in the Western Isles, because MacBrayne operate "triangular" routes linking the mainland with two islands at a time; in Orkney with the Orkney Islands Shipping Co.

The way these subsidies are granted differ very much from one case to another. In the Western Isles, Caledonian MacBrayne gets a lump sum which covers presently around one-third of its budget. With this assistance, it must plan its fare policy, but also all its infrastructural expenditure, as it does not get specific grants for ship replacements. In Orkney and Shetland, P&O fares are subsidised separately. The operator works out its standard fares, and then deducts from them a subsidy which is refunded by the Scottish Office. The rate of that subsidy differs according to the type of traffic : mainland/islands traffic gets a 15% rate, the islands/mainland one a rate which varies between 30 and 60% between the different categories (passengers, vehicles, freight, invalids, OAP's, etc.).

P&O also gets a Scottish Office subsidy for the replacement or overhaul of its vessels. This is negotiated case by case, as the company argues that the cost of purchasing new ferries out of its own resources would be unacceptable to the users or to the shareholders. A 40% subsidy was thus granted for the refurbishing of the "St Clair" which operates between Aberdeen and Shetland.

Bulk shipping to the islands is operated by private companies. The rate of subsidy differs again: in the Western Isles, it is 30% whatever the direction of traffic, in Orkney and Shetland it is 15% for mainland/island traffic, and 50% for the other way. The subsidy is not granted systematically, and some operators and some types of goods are excluded.

Internal ferry services are operated in most cases by the local authority in the Western Isles and in Shetland. The prices are kept very low by deliberate policy, and quality has improved dramatically during the last decade, but the heavy deficit (over 90%) is supported by the ratepayers. Small private operators also get local authority subsidy, or occasionally the assistance of the HIDB for purchasing vessel. The two main exceptions are the MacBrayne "triangular routes" in the Western Isles, and the OISC in Orkney as already stated. Nevertheless the responsibility for the OISC is presently being transferred to the Orkney Islands Council. Predictably, the Council is reluctant to take over the burden of a deficit running close to £1m, presently supported directly by the Scottish Office.

As for all the transport related infrastructures (piers, airports, airfields, jetties, etc...), we shall simply note that their management and subsidising is equally complex. Roughly, central government covers the heavy deficit of the Highlands and Islands airports, but the local authorities have responsibility over the smaller airfields. Piers and jetties are generally managed by the Islands or Regional Councils, but exceptions are numerous, such as the Stornoway Pier & Harbour Commission, the Lerwick Harbour Trust, or Caledonian MacBrayne, which owns a number of piers.

Trends and changes in island transport

If the present system of subsidy is complex in its functioning and limited in its efficiency, it remains to be seen how it could be changed. In that respect, the answers focus around three main points: who should be responsible for transport policies, how much money should be put into them, and to whom that money should be granted.

Who frames transport policies?

The passing of the 1973 Local Government (Scotland) Act has undoubtedly been a decisive step in the history of island transport, since in creating the three present Islands Regions it gave Western Isles, Orkney and Shetland the possibility to get more involved in the framing of transport policies.

The setting up of single tier islands authorities was a special boon to the Outer Hebrides. That archipelago had been administered by the two mainland counties of Ross & Cromarty (for Lewis), and Inverness-shire (for all the other islands). Transport-wise, the Western Isles were disunited, with the main axis of communication running from West to East, and not from North to South. Attending council meetings involved considerable journeys, and moreover the mainland authorities were in no way interested in developing a proper network of internal transport to service the smaller, outlying islands.

When the Wheatley Commission published its report in 1969, it advocated the setting-up of a single Highland region encompassing the whole of the Highlands and Islands. This meant that Orkney and Shetland which had their own County Councils, were on the verge of finding themselves in a situation similar to the Western Isles, with great communication difficulties to a relatively distant seat of local government.

Happily, through energetic campaigning on the islands' behalf, and a supportive "Minority Report" by Mrs Bettie Harvie Anderson and Mr Russell Johnston[7], the case for single-tier Islands Councils, blending the powers of the mainland Districts and Regions, prevailed. The Local Government Act, enforced in 1975, gave the three outer-islands regions a number of important powers. It allowed them to make all kinds of grants "to public passenger transport services (whether by land, water or air)", and "to maintain, improve and operate any ferry situated wholly or partly within their area...". In doing so, an islands council could incur capital expenditure, borrow money, lease or hire, enter into arrangements and fix fares and charges, etc.[8]

Financial constraints of course restrict considerably the field of application of the Act. If the islands councils have been able to improve dramatically the condition of their internal shipping and sometimes air services, central government remains firmly in control of all the other forms of communication by holding the strings of the purse.

As a result, the amount of control which the island communities may have over the functioning of the services, and the adaptation of fares policies is rather limited, although a number of bodies have been set up to ensure proper communications between the users and the operators. For example British Airways Highlands Division has a Consultative Committee, and Caledonian MacBrayne has created a number of Shipping Services Advisory Committees, but the role of these bodies is more to act as a forum than anything else; and they do not allow the islanders to influence the operator's fare policy.

It can thus be seen that there is little comparison between the powers of the Scottish Office, which not only pays for subsidies but also audits the operators' accounts (including P&O's), and those of the island communities. Except for the services which they run or subsidise directly themselves, the island authorities can only rely on the quality of relationships which they have established with the operators. As the operator's commercial interests are not always coincidental, with their own, this relationship often turns out to be of a "love-hate" nature.

Since 1975, the islands have pressed for a number of proposals seeking a stronger level of local control over transport. When recently, the Montgomery Committee of Inquiry investigated the condition of the islands authorities, it received a wide range of proposals.[9] The Western Isles Council asked for the possibility of taking over all the piers and harbours in the region, and for the right to set up its own air service if the need arose. Shetland asked for a right of say in the licensing of the air operators, and for an additional grant to run its internal ferry services. Orkney said they were ready to take over their internal ferries (managed by the Orkney Islands Shipping Co.), provided they got proper central government assistance. All the three authorities declared themselves ready to manage their own airports if granted proper financial support.

More radical proposals have even been advocated by the Shetland Movement and the Orkney Movement, whose aim is Home Rule status in the northern archipelagoes. Both Movements have declared themselves in favour of the setting-up of island based and island controlled shipping companies.[10]

So far, few of these demands have been successful, all being rejected by the Montgomery Committee, or when accepted, refused by the Scottish Office. Only the transfer of management of the state run Orkney Islands Shipping Company to the Orkney Islands Council is going through, but it remains to be seen whether the level of financial assistance that the OIC will get will prove satisfactory. If it is not, the transfer will only mean a shift of responsibility from the central government to the Orcadian ratepayers.

What kind of subsidy?

Central government commitment to financing the costs of island transport has been very slow and uneven. If Caledonian MacBrayne, or rather its predecessors, have managed to get a degree of financial assistance since the end of the 19th century, the northern archipelagoes did not get a proper level of subsidy till fairly recently.

Whatever their political creed, successive administrations have refused to pay heed to the islanders' case that their shipping routes, like the mainland trunk roads, had to be financed out of central government funds. In 1969, the then Labour Secretary of State for Scotland, Mr Willie Ross, declared for example

"...The government are not convinced of the validity of the argument that shipping charges should be fixed on the basis of a comparison with mainland costs..."[11]

Surprisingly, a more enlightened attitude was eventually expressed by the Conservatives who, in 1979 and again in 1982, committed themselves to the progressive introduction of "Road Equivalent Tariff" in the Scottish islands. Inspired by the Norwegian experience, the "RET" proposal had been originally suggested by the Highlands & Islands Development Board as early as 1974. Albeit the idea had attracted interest from various quarters (including MP John Corrie), it was not supported by the Scottish Office which limited its involvement to subsidising Caledonian MacBrayne and the OISC. Moreover, the level of these subsidies went down year after year in real terms, and sometimes even in actual terms: £2.99m in 1975/76, £2.74m in 1976/77, £3.05m in 1977/78 and £3.46m in 1978/79: this with a fast rising inflation.

The Conservative's commitment to RET – considered as a suitable anti-inflationary policy – brought marked changes. Shipping subsidies jumped from £3.46m in 1978/79 to £5.08M in 1979/80, and upwards. By 1984/85, they were totalling £11.92m. This increase benefitted primarily a number of operators, hitherto unsubsidised: P&O started to get government assistance in 1979/80, followed by the bulk shippers in 1980/81.[12]

Road Equivalent Tariff also got considerable support from the Committee on Scottish Affairs, who declared that the government should have it fully enforced by the end of 1984/85.[13] Yet the promise did not materialise for by February 1984 the Secretary of State for Scotland decided to withdraw from the government's pledge, and not to pursue RET anymore.[14]

This U-turn in government policy, which caused strong disappointment in the Scottish islands, put an end to the intricate debates which had taken place around the notion of Road Equivalent Tariff. In summary, the concept of RET is based upon the principle that travellers to the islands should be charged a fare similar to the cost of motoring a similar distance. Practically, complications quickly rise as the cost of motoring may be substantially different if considered as a "running cost" (e.g. fuel, tyres) or as an "operating cost" (that is, all the costs related to car ownership). Far from academic, the various understandings of RET mean that according to the method of calculation, cars or commercial vehicles – which have different running and operating costs per mile – may find themselves more or less advantaged. Moreover, RET could, under certain circumstances prove itself detrimental and not beneficial to the longer routes.[15]

Lengthy negotiations eventually brought the islands to support a "running cost" type of RET, with the proviso that the longer routes would be limited to a maximum of 80 kilometres to assist the remoter communities. The Scottish Office then withdrew its commitment, arguing officially that the system was too complex, ineffective in terms of assistance distribution, likely to generate increasing demands in terms of subsidies, that it would be unrelated to shipping costs etc. First and foremost, the government thought that, in times of public expenditure cuts, the whole affair was going to prove far too costly with an expected doubling of the existing subsidy.[16]

Another source of assistance has been the European Community. Sensitive to the fact that the islands were the most reluctant parts of Europe to European integration, and that they constituted a test case in terms of reducing the Community's economic discrepancies, the EEC has slowly become involved in the matter of island transport. Prodded by regional lobbies[17] and by the campaigning of Euro MPs like Winnie Ewing, (for the Highlands & Islands), the European Regional Development Fund has progressively extended its grants to various transport-related expenditures: piers, jetties, etc. and more recently ferries.[18]

Classically, part of the Community assistance has been diverted by central government. For example, when Caledonian MacBrayne bought its new ferry "Hebridean Isles" to the tune of £5.5m, it received a 40% grant by ERDEF. But CalMac does not get specific government grants for the purchase of its ships, and has to finance them through borrowing repaid through its annual budget, two thirds of which comes from the users' fares, and a third from a government subsidy. Consequently, two-thirds of this 40% grant went to relieve the users' burden, but one-third of it was no more than a saving for central government.

This discrete waylaying of community funds must be witnessed with some irony, when one recalls that one of the Scottish Office arguments for dropping RET was precisely the size of its financial effort to renew the islands ferry fleet.

Who is to be subsidised?

Rather than subsidising heavy deficits, should not the market be allowed to weed out the less efficient operators by a healthy system of competition?

This line of thought has led the government to question the ways in which many transport amenities are provided in the Highlands & Islands, and to consider the remedy of privatisation.

To a large extent, this policy has proved inapplicable. A well publicised attempt has been the offer for sale of all the Highlands and Islands airports, hitherto run by the Civil Aviation Authority with a yearly deficit approaching 40%. The extent of that deficit made the proposal so unattractive that barely an offer was put forward by the private sector, and the project had to be dropped. Proposals by the islands authorities to take over their individual airports with government assistance was turned down. The government eventually decided to take these unprofitable airports from the CAA's by running them through a newly created subsidiary, 'Highlands and Islands Airports Ltd'.

Serious efforts were also made in the direction of shipping services. Caledonian MacBrayne went through extensive scrutiny by the Monopoly and Mergers Commission. The Commission did not recommend privatisation, but it stated, that CalMac routes should be priced according to a set scale of fares reflecting the different costs involved, (pier duty, distance, loading and unloading...).

Privatisation nevertheless took place in the case of MacBrayne Haulage (a distinct company from CalMac, also a subsidiary of the Scottish Transport group).

Another attempt at limiting government intervention led in 1985 to proposals to "deregulate" the Highlands and Islands air routes. These met with strong opposition from the island authorities, which objected that the size of the market was too small to allow healthy competition. A fares war, they said, would be likely to mean a downgrading in the quality of services, or a short term improvement followed by an unchecked monopoly situation. The islands insisted that the CAA should continue to act as a safeguard through the licensing of the air operators.

In the near future the main concern lies with the sale of British Airways. Since British Airways Highland Division is unsubsidised, one could think that its takeover by a private undertaker should not mean any major change. Yet, this is not certain, as a private company may well think that its planes should achieve better profits on other routes servicing more frequented areas.

Central government has not been the only party interested in the introduction of more competition on the island routes. In the northern archipelagoes, attempts have been made to compete against P&O and the Orkney Islands Shipping Company, with limited assistance from the island authorities. New summer services have been started in the northern isles of Orkney and between Orkney and Shetland, but for a number of reasons, including lack of capital, absence of a regular subsidy and of course the fragility and limited size of the market, these ventures have floundered.

More decisive attempts have been considered with the proposed introduction of a new car ferry service between South Ronaldsay (in Orkney) and John O'Groats. This proposal has led to a delicately balanced situation. On one hand, the opening of a new shipping route to Orkney would allow a better circulation of tourism through the area, improve the communication facilities and compete with P&O's fares. On the other hand, P&O may claim that a new route "creaming off" its summer service would make its operations far less profitable, and thus would compel it to increase its fares to provide the non-profitable winter service. Since P&O provides so far the overwhelming part of the archipelago's links with the mainland and with Shetland, the threat would be far from negligible.

This would tend to demonstrate that in the field of island transport, the dividing line is not really between the private and public operators, but between those whose size allows them to control the market, and those who can't.

Towards a new system of transport subsidy?

A hypothetically ideal solution to the problems of island transport would presently have to face a large number of varying, and sometimes conflicting, conditions.

The way transport is now being operated as well as the way it is subsidised is characterised by total lack of homogeneity. What is public or private criss-crosses what is being subsidised or not.

The impact of transport costs also differs, not only geographically, but also in intensity according to the type of industry.

The conditions in which the services are operated result in most cases in confrontations between the wishes of the users (low fares and good quality), the desires of the operation (who follow their own management priorities) and the policy of the subsidy provider (who tends to wish for a limited involvement).

Except in a minority of cases (when local services are managed or controlled by the island authority) the antagonism is strong, and the user is far from always the winning party.

So far, the magic word uttered when references have been made to transport difficulties in the Scottish islands has been "RET".

But is Road Equivalent Tariff an appropriate solution?

Albeit for different purposes from the Scottish Office's, I would argue that it is not. First of all, RET is a blanket type of subsidy. That is, it is meant to assist all the users, irrespective of their needs. Such method does not take into account the fact that some industries would still be crippled by transport costs – even on a "road equivalent" basis, when others are relatively indifferent to the present fares because of the size/value ratio of the goods they ferry. Moreover, one must bear in mind that for an island industry, shipping costs are only a part of transport costs. One must also include the vehicles and the drivers, which are immobilised for long periods, and thus incur very heavy (and totally unsubsidised) extra costs. "RET" would consequently be not only indiscriminate, but also incomplete.

Another point is that lower fares are in a number of cases far less relevant than faster and more direct accessibility (for example with the provision of extra "unprofitable" sailings).

RET does not cover air fares, which are a most serious handicap for foot passengers to the islands.

RET also implies a direct handout to the operators, and as such does not contribute to strengthening the say of the island communities over the way services are run.

Summarily, it can be said that albeit there is undoubtedly a case for increased assistance to the Scottish islands, the concept of RET is stiff, centralised, and likely to be ill-adapted.

Strong words indeed, but what other option could outmatch RET to solve the islands' difficulties?

I shall argue that better solutions exist which, pound for pound, would outmatch RET. Yet, such solutions are unlikely to be found with the centralist approach to the problems. Of course, one could conceive a system where fares, retail prices, and trade would be set at a fixed level, ensuring that no discrimination besets the island communities. But such an approach is not feasible in Scotland for political, historical and institutional reasons. It would also remain to be proved that centralism is the appropriate way to deal with the problems of peripheral regions characterised by very specific conditions and identities.

The other option is a strong move towards the implementation of full direct control by the islands over their internal as well as external transport.

Such direct control could be achieved in two ways. One would consist in the islands' regions themselves operating all the sea and air services. This option is tempting, but not readily open to the Scottish archipelagoes, which are small in terms of population, and are already locked into an intricate frame of transport services. Skills and funds would also have to be readily available, and whether one likes them or not, the capacity, the means and the professional experience of Caledonian MacBrayne, P&O, or British Airways won't overnight be replaced.

This leaves the outer islands of Scotland with one possibility, namely the direct management of all transport subsidies. Such a scheme would have the merit of letting each island group operate in its own way, according to its own priorities; and to enforce the best adapted form of "territorial continuity" with the mainland. Such "territorial continuity" should not merely consist in lowering shipping fares, but seek to develop the island industries, and aim at achieving a degree of parity (social and economic) between these communities and the rest of Scotland.

Such a system implies a very large degree of freedom in the application of transport subsidies. Some archipelagoes will favour a single operator, others will prefer competition. Some will assist exports more than imports, others not. Some will favour a straightforward handout to the users, others will prefer to run an individual service themselves. These disparities already exist but they should be acknowledged and intensified. Moreover, the island authorities should be able to assist directly the island industries which they will have selected for their vulnerability to transport costs, and for their impact in the local economy. This system would mean that local firms would get a direct refund on their overall transport costs (sea, road or air) to bring them in line with their mainland competitors. In some other cases, the subsidy could be used not to lower fares, but to finance a traffic increase which, albeit "unprofitable" in shipping terms, may be of a vital necessity for some island industries.

As a whole, the scope must be left as wide as possible for experimentations and imaginative solutions. To give but one example (inspired from a subsidy scheme existing in Sicily), one could consider a system which would boost tourism and benefit entirely the island community. Tourist cars would be handed a nominative voucher with their ticket. Provided a set number of nights is spent in the island hotels and B&Bs, an extra free night is granted by the voucher. The transport subsidy thus encourages longer stays, and benefits the directly catering trade.

Achieving such radical changes in the system of transport subsidy in the Scottish islands would require a complete overhaul of the present set-up, which may prove a lengthy and politically intricate affair. Perhaps some initiative could be expected from the European community to encourage such development and experience its efficiency.

Since the Community transport policy has been notoriously lagging, one could suggest that inroads be made in the field of island transport, especially in coordination with other policies like the Integrated Development Programmes. For example, the Community could grant each Island Authority a lump sum (a kind of "subsidised rebate" over transport costs) with a broad degree of freedom in its distribution amongst the operators and the local industries – this, of course, in addition to the present level of government subsidy.

What are the main hurdles to such a scheme?

The first one is a contradiction with the Treaty of Rome, which prohibits discrimination within the Community. Since a locally controlled subsidy would precisely be used as an instrument of positive discrimination, such a scheme could be refused. Nevertheless, the Treaty of Rome specifies in its Article 80 (point 2) that in the field of road, rail and inland waterways transport "...The Commission shall (...) take into account the requirements of an appropriate regional economic policy, the needs of under-developed areas..." and allow the relevant exceptions. There is thus a perfectly legal possibility for the Commission to allow an extensive range of use of transport subsidies by an island authority, by extending the provisions of Article 80 to sea and air transport.

The second hurdle would come from central government, which would claim its right to control directly communications on all the "trunk" routes. But since this very notion of "trunk route" has been systematically rejected when the islands used it to see their ferries subsidised properly, this argument would be weak. Moreover, central government would be in a delicate situation to reject openly an EEC subsidy.

The third hurdle, which would perhaps be the most serious, would be difficulties related to the administration of the subsidy. Hard battles would take place between island interests on how the subsidy should be used. Tourism may compete with crofting, air services with shipping routes, and so forth. The management of transport subsidy would become the islands' hottest political potato, since it would be instrumental for economic and social choices of these communities, and not just an indifferent way of lowering fares.

But would such confrontations be really detrimental? I would argue that they would be beneficial. Transport problems exist in the islands not only for geography's sake, but as a consequence of the progressive loss of control by these communities over their economy, their culture and their politics over the last two centuries. This "loss of control" has left a spectacular trail of failures and wrong doings: massive depopulation, linguistic and cultural alienation, heavy dependence on the mainland, etc. Moreover, it has meant that for decades, the islands have had to wait for the mainland based centre of government to provide the (supposedly) best adapted solutions.

In gaining control over the management of transport subsidies – that is over the crux of transport services – the islanders may well be able to turn that trend dramatically. There is little doubt that meeting full force with the weight of hitherto inaccessible decisions will cause friction. Such is the price to pay, however, for the major advantage of a scheme of locally controlled subsidy: namely the reconquest of political responsibility by the most outlying periphery.

Since the late 1960's the outer islands of Scotland have begun a process of political awakening, and met with quite a few surprising successes. They have managed to achieve special recognition in the battle over the reshaping of Scottish local government. They have won, in the Northern archipelagoes more responsibilities and powers to confront oil development than any other local authority. They have, when in charge, acted effectively to provide cheap, modern and efficient transport services within their own territory. A further degree of control over transport, far from being an exorbitant privilege, would be simply a logical follow-up to the basic philosophy that only the islanders are well placed to solve the problems of insularity.

Jean Didier Hache, Honorary Fellow, Centre of European Governmental Studies, University of Edinburgh.

References

1. The air fares figures have been calculated by working out an average between the different routes, as well as an average between the cheapest rates and the standard ones.

2. A more recent comparison with British Rail fares is not feasible since BR's method of pricing has changed. One must also keep in mind that the pattern of subsidising has changed since 1979, and that fares per km vary considerably from one shipping line to another, from one route to another, and also according to the nature of traffic. The figures I have here provided nevertheless give a rapid glance at the discrepancies between the costs of island and mainland transport. For more detailed explanations, see for example the RPT Economic Studies Group report on *Sea Transport to the Scottish Islands*, Comhairle Nan Eilean (Western Isles Islands Council), July 1980.

3. See G A MacKay and Ann Gillies *Rural Scotland. Price Survey – 1984 Report*, HIDB, Inverness, August 1984, Part 2.

4. The various examples quoted have been communicated by the Islands Councils, or by representatives of the different industries.

5. In the Western Isles, for example, Caledonian MacBrayne has concessionary fares for the import of hay. Trailers pay half-fare provided that they return empty.

6. 1985 prices, these are of course rough estimates, open to seasonal variations.

7. See *Royal Commission on Local Government in Scotland 1966-1969*, HMSO, Cmnd 4150, September 1969, pp.176-180, and pp.287-295.

8. *Local Government (Scotland) Act 1973*, s.150-154.

9. Sir David Montgomery (Chairman), *Committee of Inquiry into the Functions and Powers of the Islands Councils of Scotland*, HMSO, Cmnd 9216, April 1984, Chapter 10.

10. See Shetland Movement, *Are you interested in Shetland's future? Summary of Policy Discussion*, Shetland, 1985; and *The Orkney Movement, 'Policy Paper 1986'*, Orkney, Chapter 4. On the history of both Movements, see Allan Macartney, "The Scottish Islands debate" in *Islands of Europe*, USGS, University of Edinburgh, 1984, pp.7-24.

11. *Shetland Times*, 15/8/69, p.8

12. In 1984/85, out of a total subsidy of £11.92m, Caledonian MacBrayne got £6.98m, P&O £2.11m, the OISC £0.90m and the Bulk Shippers £0.91m.

13. See Committee on Scottish Affairs, *Rural Road Passenger Transport and Ferries*, House of Commons, 1981-82, pp.21-32.

14. Hansard, *Parliamentary Debates*, 21.2.84, p.697.

15. See RTP Economic Studies Group, *op.cit*, or HIDB, *The future of Ferry Services in the Highlands & Islands*, Transport Research Paper No.6, May 1980.

16. The 1982 Select Committee on Scottish Affairs had estimated the cost of implementing RET at around £19m or £20m, twice the ongoing subsidy.

17. For further details on the island lobby in Europe, see my paper on 'Island representation in the EEC', in *Islands of Europe, op.cit*, pp.161-181.

18. Between 1975 and 1985, ERDEF has spent £328m for all kinds of infrastructure in Scotland, 14% in the Islands Regions.

THE SCOTTISH LABOUR FORCE IN RECESSION

Trends in Employment and Unemployment

Neil Fraser and Adrian Sinfield

Unemployment in Scotland doubled in the second half of the 1970s and again in the first half of the 1980s, and it is still rising. Indeed in July 1986 Scotland accounted for more than half of the month's total UK increase in unemployment revealed by the seasonally adjusted figures.

One month's results do not make a trend but no economic forecaster predicts any significant fall in the numbers out of work by the end of the decade, except perhaps as a result of special employment measures.

This chapter attempts to assess the significance of the recession for the Scottish labour force. In the first part we examine the distribution of unemployment and the experience of those most vulnerable to it and seek to assess the support they receive. In the second part we consider changes in the structure of employment, discussing the causes of change and decline and setting out the impact for the major industries. In the final section we suggest some directions for policy which might benefit the Scottish economy and reduce the extent and impact of unemployment in Scotland.

The Scale of Unemployment and its Growth

The extent of the increase in unemployment is not as evident as it was in the 1970s because of a flurry of changes to the official statistics which helped to provoke *The Scotsman* editorial 'There are now four kinds of lies. Lies, damned lies, statistics and government figures.'[1] The changes to the definitions of unemployment and the working population, to the collection of the statistics and to the benefit system now total sixteen or seventeen since 1979. All of these – with one exception – have had the effect of reducing the official number of unemployed and/or the rate of unemployment.[2] There has long been a need for a radical review of British unemployment statistics, their definition and collection, to improve their coverage and in particular reduce their dependence on administrative sources. However, most of these changes have made the count even more vulnerable to changes in the benefits system because of the decision in 1982 to transfer the count from those registering for work at job centres to those claiming benefit at unemployment benefit offices.

In Scotland the total effect has been to reduce the numbers

unemployed by almost one-fifth or over 68,000. In July 1986 the official total of unemployed was 358,988 on the new claimant count. The Unemployment Unit estimates that on the previous registrant count the total would have been 427,100.[3] The unemployment rate is 14.3% after the latest adjustment compared with an estimate of 18.6% for the old count. The difference between rates is even greater than between the numbers because of the change to a larger denominator including the self-employed and the armed forces – although few of the self-employed out of work appear in the claimant count because of their ineligibility for unemployment benefit.

The use of estimates based on the old count reveals that the doleful landmark of 400,000 was passed for the first time since the early 1930s in January 1985. The reaching of 200,000 in January 1980 and 300,000 in June 1982 attracted major debate but the extent of the rise since then has been concealed by the statistical changes.

Much has been made of the growth in the labour force in accounting for the high level of unemployment and its failure to decline with economic growth. The total labour force did increase by 7% between 1975 and 1985 with a 17% increase among women. However, a detailed comparative analysis of market economies in recession showed many countries with much lower unemployment and much higher growth in the labour force than Scotland and the UK as a whole. 'It is remarkable how little of the immediate increase in unemployment may be accounted for by economic growth (or its lack) and by labour-force growth.'[4]

In Scotland the labour force growth would undoubtedly have been greater had it not been for the recession, given the increase in the population of working age and the fact that married women had been entering the labour force in greater numbers throughout the 1970s. The participation rate for women rose from 43.6% to 49.8% up to 1979 but then dropped back to 46.8% by 1984.[5] In addition, the long term decline in the participation of older people has been accelerated by the recession, although the fall has not been as great as the increase in unemployment might have led one to expect.

The growth of the Scottish labour force has been no greater than that for the rest of the UK, in part because of substantial migration from Scotland, much of it in 1981-83 outside the UK. In the EC Labour Force Survey for 1983, Scotland had an 'economic activity' rate of 58.3 compared with 58.1 for the United Kingdom as a whole. Among men the higher rate in Scotland was entirely due to those under 25 which was nearly three percentage points higher. Each older age-group fell further below the UK figure. Among women only those under 25 and those aged 35-44 had higher rates than the rest of the UK.[6]

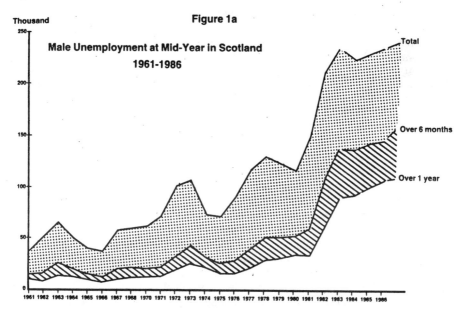

Source: 'Department of Employment data from Scottish Abstracts of Statistics'

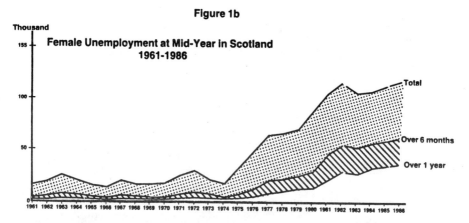

Source: 'Department of Employment data from Scottish Abstracts of Statistics'

The growth in Scottish unemployment over the last quarter of a century is shown in Figure 1. In 1961 unemployment in Scotland was still about twice the total UK level as it had been from the end of the Second World War. The gap was reduced by about a half during the second half of the 1960s. In recent years the difference between Scotland and the UK as a whole has been between 15% and 20%. The development of North Sea oil has provided some protection but there have been massive losses elsewhere which will be discussed later. The continuing migration from Scotland of course reduces the Scottish/UK difference.

The figure shows male and female unemployment separately to bring out the even sharper increase in unemployment among women. In recent years women have composed 30% of the claimant unemployed compared with about 20% a decade ago and earlier. The change is the result of two factors: the increase in labour force participation among married women and the changes in the National Insurance system with the phasing-out of the reduced contribution for married women from the mid-1970s. Nevertheless, married women out of work have always been undercounted in the regular monthly statistics and recent changes to the basis of the count have omitted many more, especially among the longer-term unemployed. Household surveys such as the EC Labour Force Survey show more women among those out of work : in the spring of 1985 women made up 39% of the unemployed in Great Britain as a whole.[7]

The Geography of Unemployment

The risk of unemployment varies considerably according to where one lives. In Table 1 the differences in the experiences of the regions is shown for selected years since 1967. The data for May 1983 and 1986 have been adjusted to make them comparable with earlier years but the rate and index are also included for May 1986 on the present claimant basis on the far right of the table.

The general Scottish pattern of unemployment doubling from 1967 to 1979, and again by 1983 with a smaller but continuing increase since then, masks considerable variation among the regions of Scotland and within them over that time. The rates of unemployment have actually fallen in Shetland and the Western Isles although the full scale of the reduction has been reduced since 1979. This still means a rate over 18% in the Western Isles, or 21% on the estimated old count, and they have only moved from worst to second worst in the ranking. Shetland by contrast has moved from second worst to best over the same period, reflecting the extra oil-related employment opportunities. Before 1979 there was more of a divergence

TABLE 1

Scottish Unemployment Rates by Regions, ranked by level in May 1986

	% rate	1967 = 100 as index of change						'New count'	
	May 1967	May 1971	May 1976	May 1979	May 1983	May 1986	%	May 1986 % rate	May 1986
Strathclyde	4.3	156	177	205	432	489	21.0	18.5	430
Western Isles	22.9	79	59	57	99	91	20.9	18.4	80
Fife	4.2	131	143	162	330	447	18.8	16.5	393
Central	3.1	155	184	200	536	594	18.4	16.2	522
Highland	5.2	119	106	161	277	335	17.4	15.3	294
Tayside	3.2	175	191	225	487	515	16.5	14.5	453
Dumfries & Galloway	5.4	100	131	142	263	282	15.2	13.4	248
Lothian	2.1	224	248	286	618	683	14.3	12.6	600
Orkney	4.6	89	56	126	279	295	13.5	11.9	259
Borders	1.3	231	277	269	804	840	13.2	11.6	738
Grampian	3.0	127	100	147	316	330	9.9	8.7	290
Shetland	8.3	58	35	32	96	83	6.9	6.1	73
Scotland	3.6	153	178	203	445	493	17.7	15.6	433

Sources: **Scottish Abstract of Statistics**, no. 9, 1980, p. 95 and Department of Employment press releases with estimates of the old registrant count by the authors based on data from the Unemployment Unit.

among areas with the rates actually falling in two regions and quite a wide dispersion among the others with Lothian and Borders rising significantly faster than the rest. Since 1979 it has increased in all areas with seven regions close to the national average. Borders, Central and Fife have experienced the worst increases.

In mid-1986 Strathclyde had the highest rate 18.4%, 21% old count, well ahead of the other mainland regions. Fife and Central were the only other regions above the national average. Strathclyde has borne the brunt of the economic decline in Scotland with the highest unemployment on the Scottish mainland throughout the 1970s and into the 1980s. With unemployment three points above the national average, Strathclyde had 45% of its unemployed out of work over a year compared with 36% in the rest of Scotland in April 1986.

The region lost 37% of its jobs in manufacturing industry within the decade 1971-1981, mostly within the last four years of that period. This made up 85% of the net fall in manufacturing employment in Scotland as a whole. When data on industry and region since 1981 becomes available, it is likely that the pattern will be shown to have continued. The losses reflect the importance of metal manufacturing and metal-using industries, especially engineering and ship building, in the Strathclyde economy, but there was also a 30% loss of jobs in the textile industry in the region.

The net effect of severe decline in manufacturing and limited growth elsewhere was a 12% loss in the total number of jobs in Strathclyde between 1971 and 1981. The increase in unemployment would have been even greater had it not been for a substantial movement of people out of the region – some 73,000 in the three years at the peak of the recession.[8]

By contrast unemployment in the Grampian region has been well below the Scottish average in recent decades. In 1970 the region began to move further below the average and with the Borders has kept closer to half the national rate since then. This did not however prevent Forres from having the very highest unemployment rate for a travel-to-work area in the whole of Scotland, 25% in July 1986. On the same date Aberdeen had 7.7% unemployment, the lowest rate on the mainland, very much in contrast to its experience of the interwar recession: it seems unlikely however that it will be able to maintain this position.

Grampian's generally stronger position during the recession is the result of oil development, now providing directly or indirectly over a quarter of all jobs in the region – more than three-quarters of all oil- related employment in Scotland according to official statistics. 'More than 500 firms depend wholly on the industry.' (*The Scotsman*, 10 April 1986). The dependence on oil is underlined by the fact that employment in the region grew by 30% between 1971 and 1981 despite an 11% fall in manufacturing. In consequence the slump in oil prices has led to much concern in 1986 'with the threat of job losses which in Scotland alone, could total 15,000 "according to" leading British oil supply and service companies.' (*The Press and Journal*, 31 May 1986). In Grampian itself '5,000 jobs could be lost by the end of the year' in the view of Alex Kemp, Professor of Political Economy at Aberdeen University.' (*The Press and Journal*, 20 May 1986). The Royal Bank of Scotland has predicted a strong recovery but only 'after a serious downturn over the next two or three years.' (*The Scotsman*, 31 May 1986) while others suggest an even greater collapse than the one currently feared, 'at the end of the 1990s when the second phase runs out with little prospect of a third.' (*Press and Journal*, 20 May 1986).

How the decline will actually affect Grampian and the rest of Scotland is not at all clear. Comparison of the first quarters of 1985 and 1986 show an increase of 162% in redundancies notified in Grampian and 33% in Tayside compared with a drop of 25% for the rest of Scotland.[9] The initial job losses are particularly expected to hit that quarter of Grampian's 51,000 oil-related workers whose homes are outside the region. As well as 3,000 workers from the United States, many have been attracted from areas such as Strathclyde, Tyneside, Merseyside, Teesside and the West Midlands already badly hit by the recession. Many of these workers are employed 'by a vast network of subcontractors' and will probably return home on the loss of their jobs. In addition employment elsewhere will be affected by the slump: at Clydebank for example redundancies have been announced for more than half of the core workforce of 530 and most of the 870 short term contract workers at the UIE offshore rig and platform yard.' (*The Scotsman*, 19 August 1986). In Grampian the indirect impact will be felt in the services that have grown up in response to high paid immigrant workers – hotels and lodgings, catering, leisure and the housing industry.

Comparison by regions alone conceals the extent to which unemployment varies within Scotland. There are significant differences among travel-to-work areas, though these are probably less than in the years of lower unemployment. In July 1986 only two areas – Aberdeen and Galashiels – had rates around half the national average in addition to the Shetland Islands. There were three areas – Forres in Grampian, Cumnock and Sanquhar in Dumfries and Galloway and Irvine in Strathclyde – with rates more than half as much again as the average: another six also had rates as high as 20%.

Marked variations within the travel-to-work areas is brought out by more detailed evidence for the cities of Edinburgh and Glasgow. Edinburgh as a whole had an unemployment rate of 13.1% in January 1986, over two points below the Scottish average. Ten of the sixty-two wards were below half the city's rate but another fourteen were more than one and half times the average rate. Twelve wards "accounted for 19% of the economically active population of the city but for 35% of all the unemployed and 41% of all those unemployed for a year or more".[10] The twelve wards were located within five blackspots in the inner city, peripheral council-housing estates and the port of Leith. 'An adult living in Craigmillar, is eight times as likely to be unemployed as an adult in Cramond' where unemployment was below 4%. In Craigmillar and Niddrie the longterm unemployment for males was over 20%. In Glasgow the scale of unemployment was much higher with an average rate of 21.4% in April 1986. Nine of the sixty-six wards had unemployment rates of 30% or more but only 3 were below 10%.[11]

The Unequal Impact of Unemployment

During the recession the burden has continued to be borne disproportionately by certain groups within areas. Young people unable to establish themselves in employment, older workers who are particularly prone to prolonged unemployment once they lose a job, those with less skills, the disabled and those in poorer health have all been more vulnerable.

Young people have been particularly affected by the increase in unemployment in the 1980s. In a special analysis in 1983 over a third of males aged 18 to 24 had been out of work at some time within the previous 12 months, more than twice as high a proportion as for older males.[12] In Scotland in October 1985 16% of Scottish males out of work were under twenty and 24% of females. The percentages were slightly larger than in England reflecting probably the greater proportion of young people entering the Scottish labour force.[13]

The full extent of the collapse of the youth labour market since 1979 is not revealed by the official statistics because of changes in the collection of statistics, in benefit entitlement for school-leavers, youth training and special programmes and the proportion staying in education. The reduction in employment opportunities is more clearly documented in the successive surveys of the Scottish School-leavers or Young People's Surveys (see Table 2). Approaching three-quarters of fourth-year students leaving school at the end of the summer term in 1978 had entered employment by the time of the survey in the following spring without any experience of YOP. Among the 1984 leavers the proportion going into jobs had fallen to below a third. While less than a twelfth were on YOP schemes in 1979, the proportion on YTS had risen to nearly two-fifths by 1985.

TABLE 2

Destinations of previous session's fourth-year summer-term leavers, at time of survey (percentages), Scotland

Leavers in: Survey year:	1978 1979	1980 1981	1982 1983	1983 1984	1984 1985
Males and Females					
Course	8.4	8.1	10.2	8.7	9.3
Full-time job	72.2	55.0	40.2	33.7	31.6
YOP/YTS	8.3	18.9	27.1	37.7	38.7
Unemployed	9.6	16.9	19.6	16.5	16.3
Others/NK	1.4	1.1	2.8	3.4	4.1
Males					
Course	3.0	2.5	4.4	3.7	4.6
Full-time job	76.8	60.6	46.8	35.7	32.3
YOP/YTS	9.6	19.4	27.2	41.8	43.2
Unemployed	9.4	16.8	19.5	15.7	16.5
Others/NK	1.2	0.7	2.0	3.1	3.4
Females					
Course	13.9	14.6	17.0	15.0	14.9
Full-time job	67.5	48.7	32.5	31.2	30.9
YOP/YTS	7.1	18.2	26.9	32.6	33.3
Unemployed	9.8	17.0	19.6	17.4	16.0
Others/NK	1.7	1.5	3.9	3.8	5.0

Note: 1978 leavers from grant-aided and independent schools without Highers or O grades at A-C are not included.

Source: David Raffe, Centre for Educational Sociology, University of Edinburgh, 1986.

For sixteen-year-olds therefore YTS has made a significant difference to the transition from school into the labour market. 'Seven in ten males and six in ten females in Scotland were offered places on the scheme in 1984-85; three-quarters of those offered places had accepted them. With the extension of the scheme from one year to two, the experience of unemployment under the age of seventeen is likely to be very much reduced but there is not enough evidence yet to indicate how the transition to employment will be affected, particularly if unemployment remains high. A disturbing finding from the Scottish Young People's Surveys is that those who left school without any educational qualifications were particularly likely to be unemployed rather than on YTS.'[14]

While the greater risk among young people is so widely recognised that it often monopolises concern about the social impact of unemployment, the unequal incidence by social class tends to be so taken for granted that it rarely provokes any comment. However, many people have assumed that the sharp rise in unemployment has led to a more even spread of the impact throughout the social classes and this view has been reinforced by 'discoveries' of the 'new' unemployed, out of work executives and managers.

In fact the inequality has increased – at least among men, for no comparable data are published for women (see Table 3). In 1983 men from unskilled or semiskilled jobs were four times as likely as men in non-manual work to have had any time unemployed in the previous twelve months: in 1975- 77 the incidence had been only three times greater. In 1983 the chance of any unemployment was one in three for the unskilled and semi-skilled, one in six for the skilled, one in ten for the routine non-manual and one in seventeen for the professional and managerial worker. The importance of the loss of traditional manufacturing jobs is borne out by the almost doubling of the experience of unemployment among men in skilled work as well as the marked increase in the already much higher rates among men in semi-skilled and unskilled work.

The increase in the unequal distribution of unemployment is particularly important for understanding its impact. Those who are shown to be more likely to be unemployed are also among those with the least resources. Their vulnerability to financial hardship and poverty will very much depend on the workings of the social security system which will be discussed below.

The Longterm Unemployed

Into the 1980s longterm unemployment climbed more speedily than total unemployment (see Figure 1). However, the government changes to

TABLE 3

Male Unemployment in the previous twelve months, 1975-1977 and 1983, Great Britain

Socio-economic group:	1975-77 %	1983 %
Professional Employers and managers	4	6
Intermediate and junior non-manual	8	10
All non-manual	6	8
Skilled manual	9	17
Semi-skilled and unskilled manual	18	32
All manual	12	23
All males aged 18-64	10	18

Source: General Household Survey in *Social Trends 1980,* Table 5.19 and *Social Trends 1985*, Table 4.26.

the statistics have particularly concealed the full growth of prolonged unemployment in comparison to the past. For some years now even the official figures have shown two in every five unemployed out of work for one year or more and well over one in five out of work for two years or more.

All groups have been affected by the marked increase in longterm unemployment although the impact on women is especially concealed by statistics based on claimants: most married women disappear from the count after their year's insurance benefit has ended. Older people have a higher risk of prolonged unemployment but the increase has been by far the greatest among those under 25. Since 1979 there has been a more than eightfold rise in the number out of work for a year or more.[15] Unemployment has been most likely to be prolonged in Strathclyde and Tayside and least likely in Grampian and Shetland, reflecting the patterns of employment decline and growth throughout Scotland.

As total unemployment remains high, longterm unemployment continues to increase. The MSC Scotland reported that 'nearly 70% of the overall increase in unemployment in 1985 was in longterm unemployment.'[16] Among the worst hit are the workers who lost their jobs in or before the sharp rise in unemployment in 1980 and 1981: this is borne out by the sharp increase of 55% among people out of work for five years or more who reached 25,000 in April 1986. Comparison over time is more reliable for men than women because of benefit and other changes, and among men the number out of work for five years or more in 1986 exceeded the number unemployed for as long as a year throughout the 1960s.

The chances of these people ever returning to work must be very remote given the evidence that the likelihood of re-employment diminishes with the length of time since previous work. Those out of work for less than 3 months were four times as likely as people unemployed for a year or more to cease being unemployed according to official statistics in January 1986. 'In Scotland an MSC survey of job search behaviour of the longterm unemployed, conducted in September 1984, indicated that at the average job application activity rate it takes a longterm unemployed person 2.5 years to find a job. On average 35 job applications and 9 interviews were required for such an outcome.'[17]

The longterm unemployed become caught by the combination of two pressures. The longer they are out of work and the more unsuccessful applications they make, the more discouraged they are made. Meanwhile employers generally prefer to take on people with recent work experience rather than those longer out of work. When unemployment is rising or remaining constant, both these tendencies are reinforced and the chances of re-employment are likely to be further reduced. In consequence those longterm unemployed who cease to become unemployed are more likely to have become ill or to have left the labour force altogether than to have obtained work.

Poverty Out of Work

The significance of the increase in longterm unemployment and its even longer duration is made all the greater by the increased risk of poverty and deprivation with the length of time out of work. And, when this is combined with the fact that the chances of both unemployment and prolonged unemployment are higher for those with lower pay, it is even more likely that any savings or credit become exhausted within the early months out of work.

One indication of deprivation is provided by the DHSS report on low-income families. This evidence used to be published yearly but it is now produced every other year as a result of government savings in public expenditure. The 1983 data were released after a long delay and many questions at the end of July 1986. These show that 72% of all families headed by an unemployed person had incomes no greater than the basic means-tested scheme of supplementary allowance and housing benefit supplement. In 1981 the proportion had been 56% and the increase reflects higher longterm unemployment and changes in the benefits system.[18]

Both Government and independent evidence has indicated the very limited standard of living available at this income level, especially for families with young children and the long-term unemployed.[19] Since much of that research was undertaken, benefits have been further reduced or restricted and so a standard set at the level of the basic means-tested benefit level may fairly be taken as a measure of poverty in contemporary British society.

Between 1979 and 1983 the number of unemployed families in poverty by this very limited measure increased three-and-a-half times. Unemployment therefore directly accounted for three-quarters of the total rise in poverty over that period. Many others have been affected indirectly: many women bringing up children on their own, older people and some in poor health have been unable to supplement meagre resources with part-time employment. Whenever the 1985 results are published, they should show a significant increase reflecting the continuing rise in the number out of work for increasingly long periods.

The Nature and Extent of Social Security

The evidence of increasing poverty and longterm unemployment underlines the importance of the state system of income support and maintenance for people out of work and their dependants. There is much confusion and ignorance about the availability of benefits. In fact, only three out of ten men and less than four out of ten women among the claimant unemployed were receiving National Insurance Benefit in Scotland in May 1985. For both men and women the proportions were slightly higher than the British average.[20]

The inadequacy of this first line of defence provided by the state's social security system is underlined by the fact that even more unemployed men than were currently receiving insurance benefit had exhausted it all because they had been out of work too long to qualify for any further payments. Insurance benefit has continued to be provided for only 12 months in a spell of unemployment despite the record levels of longterm unemployment. In consequence over two-thirds of men (68.4%) were receiving supplementary allowance, the means-tested benefit – more than twice as many as drew the insurance benefit.

Among women the proportion with supplementary allowance was lower (45.3%) but it still exceeded the proportion with insurance benefit. It is in fact surprisingly high since very many married women are not eligible for a means-tested allowance if their husband is in fulltime employment and others would generally be included as his dependant if he were unemployed and claiming and not as separate claimants themselves. Women were more likely to be ineligible for insurance benefit because they had not paid sufficient contributions than because they had exhausted the full year's entitlement.

It is often argued that the shortcomings of National Insurance are largely technical because most unemployed are entitled to more money if they apply for supplementary allowance and housing benefit. In consequence the transition from insurance to allowance upon exhaustion is seen as somewhat of a formality. However, income support only continues after exhaustion if the income and savings of the claimant and any spouse fall below a certain low level. In consequence, most men with working wives and virtually all women with working husbands are no longer eligible for any compensation for their continuing unemployment after a year.

The social security reforms of 1986 do little to help the unemployed. Many changes reflect the present government's concern to increase the incentive to find work despite the growing body of evidence on the hardships experienced by people out of work.[21]

Special Employment Measures

The Community Programme, which succeeded the Community Enterprise Programme in October 1982, is the largest special employment measure and is directed towards the longterm unemployed. It provides a maximum of one year's work experience on projects 'of benefit to the community'. Nearly 29,000 people were participants in Scotland in April 1986. This represented a 16% increase on the previous year and current plans forecast a total of 31,400 places by 1987. The scale of the programme in Scotland is shown by the fact that one in five job centre vacancies were for the CP in the first six months of 1986. In some areas its influence on the local labour market is considerable: in Clydebank, for example, CP is said to be the largest employer with 1,000 places, larger even than the District Council.[22] The scheme provides opportunities for people out of work over a year, or over six months for those aged 18-25. Eligibility has been narrowed to exclude those unemployed not receiving benefit, reducing the number of entrants from married women and older men.

Help from the CP has become concentrated on certain groups. Two-thirds of those on the schemes are under 25, and well over three-quarters male and the same proportion single. The extent and level of assistance have also become more limited. More than seventy per cent are returning to unemployment, underlining the lack of employment opportunities despite government emphasis on the need to improve incentives. In addition, the proportion reduced to working part-time on the schemes has always been high but it has risen to well over 80%. This is partly due to the government's failure to raise the average weekly payment in line with inflation or with the wage rates which have to be paid. The average has only been lifted twice in four years, from £60 to £63 in 1984 and again to £67 in 1986, although the MSC itself originally recommended £89 with annual reviews.[23]

New measures for the longterm unemployed have been introduced in 1986 based on the very early results of nine pilot schemes in different parts of Britain. Dundee was the location of one pilot for the Restart programme beginning in early January. By May over half the longterm unemployed had been interviewed and three-quarters of these were 'offered practical help' according to the MSC.[24] Details of the actual success in the pilots have been hard to locate. The first three months of *Jobstart* in Dundee, where there were nearly 6,000 people longterm unemployed, only resulted in fifteen applications being accepted according to the answer to a parliamentary question after the Budget announcement of the national scheme.[25]

Recession and Employment

To understand the full impact of the recession on the Scottish labour force it is necessary to examine the changes in employment as well as unemployment (see Table 4). Between 1979 and 1985 the number of employees fell by 7% (149,000). During the previous six years, when there had also been a major increase in unemployment, employment in Scotland had risen by 2.5% (52,000). In both periods manufacturing lost jobs and services gained. The great difference resulted from the very much sharper decline in manufacturing – by more than a quarter, and not just a twelfth – and an increase in services less than half the rate of the 1970s.

Male employment fell by one-eighth – a decline almost ten times as great as in the earlier period. Women were also work affected in the more recent period, an increasing number of labour force participants gaining only 2,000, not 69,000 jobs.

TABLE 4

Scotland's employment changes, 1973-85

	1973-9	1979-85	1973-9	1979-85
	absolute changes		% changes	
Total employees	+52000	−149000	+2.5	−7.1
Male employees	−16000	−151000	−1.3	−12.5
Female employees	+69000	+2000	+8.3	+0.2
Self-employed	+21000	+32000	+15.1	+20.0
Manufacturing	−54000	−166000	−8.2	−27.5
Services	+118000	+60000	+10.7	+4.9

Source: *Scottish Economic Bulletin*, June 1986.

The rise in part-time employment of 76,000 jobs between 1979 and 1985 was one of the highest in Britain. When this is taken into account, it is clear that there was also a sharp fall in full-time employment opportunities for women. The only other gain since 1979 has been in the number of self-employed which rose by 32,000.

The Explanation of Recession

Any attempt to explain Scotland's lack of success in generating enough jobs in the 1970s and 1980s must first take account of the longterm failure of industry to keep up with its competitors. In Britain as a whole, industry, particularly manufacturing, has steadily lost its share of markets at home and abroad. This has limited industrial output and therefore the jobs needed to make it. Scotland has shared in this failure: its economic performance resembles that of the rest of Britain much more than that of its other main competitors. The result, as David Bell has remarked, is 'Scotland slipping gradually into the economic backwaters of Europe.'[26] There are nevertheless some encouraging features for Scotland, at least in comparison with Britain, which we will go on to examine below.

It is difficult to explain the failure to maintain a share of the market. One major reason seems to be the failure to innovate. On the whole Scottish industry has been slow to change and research and development have been low even by UK standards.[27] There are exceptions to this conservatism, notably in electronics (mainly by foreign-owned firms) and to a lesser extent in knitwear and malt whisky.

A further impediment to British competitiveness in the 1970s and 1980s is the country's disorganised industrial relations system. Wage pressure, out of line with the slow growth in productivity, helped to make the 1970s international profit squeeze and inflation particularly severe in Britain, and is holding back job creation in the recovery.

These problems were exacerbated by the general slowdown in international trade and industrial output expansion with rising industrial costs at the end of the boom, with the oil crises of 1973 and 1979 and with the emergence of excess capacity in the world's manufacturing markets. Investment in periods of excess capacity tends to be of a cost-saving, particularly labour-saving, kind. Scotland's industry has invested more than the rest of the UK, but the effect has been a faster run-down of jobs. New products and new technologies, like electronics and information technology, have not so far been able to generate the jobs to take the place of other manufacturing jobs lost and may themselves displace jobs as much as they create them.

The final element contributing to the jobs failure has been British macroeconomic policy since the 1979 oil crisis. The Government refused to fight inflation with any form of incomes policy, in part because of a concern to bring a reduction in trade union power. In 1980, in spite of the loss of demand with the oil price rise, the Government fought inflation with a tight monetary squeeze which raised interest rates to unprecedented levels. Industry reacted by making major cuts in its investment in stock and there were many bankruptcies. In addition the response of the international money markets lifted the exchange rate which sharply raised the cost of British exports and weakened our competitive position even more.

North Sea oil, as well as providing some 4% of Scottish jobs, has shielded Britain from its manufacturing trade failure. For those in work, incomes have been kept higher and taxes lower than they would have been. The 1985-6 oil price collapse has already threatened to expose the failure in manufacturing, as does the decline in North Sea production due anyway by the 1990s. The jobs in oil and oil-related trades will then only be some of the Scottish victims. The danger is that many more jobs – public and private – will be lost in the squeeze which will be necessary to restore the post-oil balance of trade. This is the sense in which more jobs depend indirectly on our industrial competitiveness than do directly.

The number of jobs is not just a matter of aggregate production. It is also a matter of distribution. In principle, whether the future brings lower or higher aggregate production and income, jobs can be shared around more or left in their present grossly unequal state. Society could choose to have more of its national output in the labour intensive form of public services if it was willing to pay more taxes. More jobs might also be induced by tax incentives without loss of competitiveness, although only if there was a national willingness to share incomes.[28]

Output and Employment

The slow growth of output in the Scottish and the whole UK economy is illustrated in Table 5. Even including the output of oil, that growth is well below the output growth rates of France and Germany for both periods.[29] The output of oil is attributed in Government statistics to a separate region, the Continental Shelf, so that Scotland's figures have to be quoted without oil and compared with UK figures without oil.

TABLE 5

Growth in GDP (output measure), % per year

| | Without Oil | | With Oil |
	Scotland	UK	UK
1963-73	3.5	3.0	3.0
1973-84	0.6	0.5	1.0
73-9	0.8	0.7	0.8
79-81	−1.8	−2.7	−2.3
81-4	1.8	2.3	2.7

Source: Note 29.

A breakdown of Scottish economic output by sectors shows the importance of production and construction in the slowdown since 1973 (Table 6). The demand for many services also comes from production and construction, but the service sectors have not fared as badly, particularly business and public services.

The production and construction sector lost 61,000 jobs in the period 1973-9, its first sustained period of decline. In the next six years the loss has been more than three times greater: a fall of a further 204,000 jobs has meant a 25% drop between 1979 and 1985. A major reason is that this sector is the most vulnerable to international trade and to a monetary

TABLE 6

Growth in output by sector in Scotland, % per year

	Agriculture Forestry & Fishing	Production & Construction	Distribution Hotel, Catering & Repairs	Transport & Communication	Other Business & Public Services
Weighting (%)	3.3	40.4	13.2	7.6	35.6
63-73	3.2	4.1	3.1	3.7	2.9
73-84	1.4	−1.1	1.2	1.3	2.5
73-9	−1.4	−0.8	1.5	1.8	2.8
79-81	6.5	−5.3	−3.3	−1.2	2.2
81-84	4.0	1.2	3.5	1.8	2.0

Source: Note 29

squeeze such as was administered in 1980. Other sectors were not hit to the same degree, but their job performance could not make up for the disastrous record of production and construction (see Table 7).

TABLE 7

Employment change by sector, Scotland, 1979-86

	Share of jobs		Change of employment	
	1979	1985	Absolute	%
Agriculture	2.3	2.1	−7000	−15
Production & Construction	39.7	32.2	−204000	−25
Manufacturing	28.7	22.4	−166000	−28
Distribution & Catering	18.7	21.6	+29000	+7
Transport & Communications	6.3	5.8	−19000	−12
Business & Public Services	33.1	38.2	+50000	+4
Total	100	100	−151000	−7

Source: *Scottish Economic Bulletin* No. 33, Jun 1986 p. 52.

Scotland's comparative record in manufacturing deserves to be examined in more detail. The failure in competitiveness in Scotland, as in the UK as a whole has been so great that output has not recovered to its 1973 level. There have been two periods of severe falls in both output and employment, 1973-5 and 1979-81, with recoveries only in output, 1975-9 and 1981-5 (see Table 8). On each occasion Scotland's manufacturing output has suffered less in the recessions than the UK as a whole but has also performed more slowly in the recovery periods. However Scotland is out-performing the rest of the UK in manufacturing exports. Figures from a recent survey suggest that in terms of export sales per employee they were a third higher in Scotland in 1984. Scotland has continually lost proportionately more jobs than Britain as a whole since 1975, with a particularly notable loss since 1981 in spite of the recovery in output.

TABLE 8

Change in Manufacturing Output and Employment, % per year

| | % pa Output | | Employment | |
	Scotland	UK	Scotland	Great Britain
1973-5	−2.8	−4.6	−1.5	−2.2
1975-9	+0.2	+1.2	−1.6	−1.0
1979-81	−5.9	−7.8	−7.7	−7.0
1981-5	+2.2	+2.4	−3.9	−2.2

Note: Government statistics give output on a UK basis and employment on a Great Britain basis.

Source: Economic Trends, Scottish Economic Bulletins, various issues.

Productivity has risen much faster in Scottish manufacturing than in the rest of the UK. This is confirmed by evidence from the Fraser of Allander Institute. They calculate that Scottish manufacturing output per employee rose twice as quickly as the UK one between 1979 (quarter 2) and 1985 (quarter 1), 35.9% as against 17.3%.[30] The change appeared to be the result of two factors. Scotland has a larger share of the industries with faster growth in productivity, particularly electronics, and there have also been more total closures or reductions in employment in other Scottish industries. The engineering industry provides an example of both factors. Between 1979 and 1985 proportionately more jobs were lost in Scotland, 29% compared with 22% in Britain as a whole. At the same time overall output in Scotland grew by 9% (1984 compared with '79) against a fall of 8% in the UK. Within Scottish engineering, output growth was most marked in electrical and instrument engineering, up 71% in these five years, but employment still fell, except specifically in electronics. North Sea oil also provided output for Scottish engineering and some 14,000 jobs in mechanical engineering.[31] A third of the 180,000 jobs left in engineering in 1985 were in the two growth sectors, but the closures in other parts of engineering had a much greater impact on jobs (for example, car-making and shipbuilding).

Net investment, both per head of population and per employee, has been higher in manufacturing in Scotland than the UK at least since the 1960s. This difference has persisted through the recession. For example, in 1981 it was more than a third higher per employee than in the UK as a whole, including more than twice as much in the chemical industry and the data-processing equipment industry, and more than one and a half times as much in electrical and electronic engineering and in mechanical engineering.[32] In fact investment goods production did not fall in Scotland between 1979 and 1981 while it dropped 15% in UK as a whole. This helps to explain the productivity difference. In the recovery period investment goods production has also risen very much faster in Scotland than the UK[33], but the latest investment per employee figures show an alarming decline in Scotland in 1983, falling to equality with the rest of the UK with a particular failure in mechanical engineering.

The Employment Record of Particular Industries

1. *Production industries*: The distribution of employees between industries is generally quite similar in Scotland and the rest of the UK. Scotland has a heavier concentration of workers in mechanical engineering (particularly pumps, valves and industrial plant), office machinery (particularly computers), instrument engineering, shipbuilding, textiles and clothing, food and drink (particularly whisky), construction, and oil. The table below, from the Census of Production, gives examples of employment loss between 1979 and 1983, the latest data available.

The engineering industry is really a group of different industries making up some 46% of total Scottish manufacturing employment. The staple of Scottish engineering is heavy mechanical engineering and shipbuilding, but the emphasis has changed with the growth of electronics. Motor vehicles, the engineering sector which has lost jobs most in Britain of late, has never been as large in Scotland as in the rest of Britain, but it has still produced some of the biggest individual closures (at Linwood and Bathgate). Mechanical engineering in Scotland should have been revived by North Sea oil, but commentators all describe the response of the Scottish industry as disappointing.[34]

The two growth areas, electronics and oil-related supplies, have both depended heavily on incoming firms. About half of electronics

TABLE 9

Manufacturing industry job losses, Scotland 1979-83

	Jobs lost 79-83	% of 79 Employed	Jobs remaining '83
Textiles	19100	40	31000
Food, Drink	18500	21	73100
Mechanical Engineering	17900	23	59400
Motor Vehicles	14500	64	8200
Metal Manufacture	14200	51	13800
Clothing	9900	28	24900
Metal Goods	9100	34	17600
Electrical & Electronic Eng.	7800	17	37400
Paper, Publishing	7600	17	36400
Instrument Engineering	7600	50	7500
Shipbuilding & Other Transport	7300	17	36400
Chemicals	6300	23	21200
Mineral Products (Bricks etc)	6000	33	12300
Office Machinery	+1200	+17	8400
Manufacturing	156400	27	419200

Source: *Scottish Economic Bulletin* No. 33 June 1986, p. 39 and earlier issues.

employment is in overseas-owned plant, and more than half of the remainder have an English headquarters.[35] The UK share of total North Sea expenditure (not only engineering) has been estimated at only around 60%.[36] However it is worth noting that the number of jobs lost in overseas-owned firms in Scottish manufacturing between 1975 and 1985 appears to be slightly lower than for manufacturing as a whole, even though two of the largest closures, Talbot at Linwood and Singers at Clydebank, were foreign-owned.[37] The electronics industry, which is strongest in computers, semi-conductors, and defence systems, is discussed in greater detail by James Walker elsewhere in this volume. Scottish engineering – not only in electronics – is quite export-oriented e.g. 48.4% of the mechanical engineering output is exported.[38] Some firms have significant particular market niches, e.g. in pumps, valves, mining machinery, but it is doubtful if enough research is being done to retain them.

One feature of the Scottish engineering industry is that over 80% of the jobs are held by men – electronics is the only branch which employs many women – and strongly craft-based.[39] These features also apply to three other industries which have suffered many job losses – iron and steel, coal mining and construction. By 1983 iron and steel production in Scotland was down to only 36% of its 1973 level, a graphic indicator of both the slump in demand from the engineering industry and the world problem of over-capacity.[40] Closures have continued, with the cold strip rolling mill at Gartcosh closing in 1985 and the whole industry is vulnerable. The coal industry has also suffered a long-run decline in markets and is now very dependent on the electricity industry. The Scottish mines which remain are relatively high cost and under pressure to improve productivity, especially with the cheapening of oil.

Construction is a major industry in Scotland with a much larger share of production and construction output in Scotland (24%) than in the UK (16.6%). It employed 114,000 people in 1985, 27% less than in 1979. It has suffered from the slump in housebuilding, particularly in the public sector, and factory building, with output more depressed than the UK industry. It has had a share in the oil-related business but mainly in the development phase.

Textiles and clothing should not just be seen as a traditional declining industry in Scotland. It lost a lot of jobs between 1979 and 1983 (29,000 or 34%) but it is still a large source of employment and includes a branch with a good export record, high quality knitwear. Employment in the Borders Region is very dependent on the continuing success of the major Scottish firm in knitwear, Dawson International.

Food and drink is another very important sector in Scottish manufacturing. It includes a big export-oriented branch in whisky, but one which has lost market share through weak, traditionalist marketing. Employment in 1983 was around 20,000, more than 5,000 down on 1979. It remains to be seen if performance improves. Whisky has its own high value-added sector in malt whisky, whose growth in output is another encouraging aspect of the Scottish economy. Food processing is the bigger source of jobs in the food and drink industry. Fish products, meat products and bread-baking stand out, but it is a sector of small to medium-sized firms, too small for efficient marketing (sales are mainly in Scotland, or at least the UK). Output recovery has been weak and job losses continue.

2. *Service Industries*: Scotland's service industries increased their employment between 1979 and 1985 by 60,000 jobs. But this was only partial recompense for the loss of jobs in production and construction. It

also represented a halving in the growth of service jobs compared with the preceding 6 years when 118,000 had been added. And the increase could be entirely accounted for by part-time jobs. Part-time female jobs grew by 76,000 between 1979 and 1985. These would not all be in services, but at the time of the 1981 Census of Employment 90% of part-time female jobs were in services.[41] The biggest users of part-time staff in Scotland, according to that Census, are retail distribution 79,000 out of 192,000, hotel and catering 57,250 out of 107,000, health services 55,500 out of 145,300 and education 38,250 out of 135,600. The Community Programme also accounts for some 25,000 of these part-time jobs.

Banking and finance is the service sector which had the biggest percentage rise in employment in Scotland between 1979 and 1985, 17% or an extra 21,000 workers. This sector's share of service employment is lower than in Britain as a whole (11.3% compared with 14.2%), reflecting the predominance of the City of London, but Scotland's employment growth was only marginally lower.

Scotland did relatively better than the rest of Britain between 1979 and 1985 in retail distribution and in public services. In retailing, jobs in Scotland increased by 16,000 (8%), whereas with the GB % increase (2%) it would have been 12,000 less. In education, health and other services jobs in Scotland increased by 29,000 (7%) – a saving of 10,000 jobs compared with the GB %. Even in public administration, where the number of jobs in Scotland fell by 5,000 (3%), this was half the total British rate of decline.

Strategies for Change

Analysis of the problems of both unemployment and employment in Scotland reveals the urgent need for radical measures to tackle the lack of employment opportunity and to combat the hardships and poverty of unemployment. Britain may be 'entering the sixth successive year of sustained economic growth' in the view of the Secretary of State for Employment[42] but the 'recovery' has brought few new jobs to Scotland in comparison with the massive losses. What gains have been made have been largely in part-time or self-employed work in the service sector while manufacturing continues to shed jobs despite the gains in output. The end of 1985 and the first half of 1986 have seen further falls in employment, particularly in the oil-related industries.

Priority must be given to halting and then reversing the deindustrialisation of the Scottish economy. This is not primarily for the sake of the jobs in production industries themselves, but to avoid an economic squeeze forced on the country to correct a payments imbalance with lower oil revenues. Industrial policies are needed which will increase both innovation and investment in high value-added products with export potential. Macroeconomic policies can help through a lower pound and lower interest rates, but the scope for reflation is limited by the great loss of capacity that Scottish industry has suffered.

This first aim has to give priority to economic regeneration. Protection of employment must be primarily seen as a longterm, not shortterm, aim. This means raising output by making it more saleable rather than lowering productivity to achieve job protection. Scotland has some policies for this aim already, notably the Scottish Development Agency. A tribute to the SDA's work is that it is about to be copied in the Northern Region of England, but the evolution of its policies has brought it some criticism in Scotland, particularly for largely discarding direct investment and shareholding in indigenous firms.[43] Much effort has however been devoted to developing a high technology base for Scotland, although this may have been largely achieved by inward investment. It is important to build on that base using and developing Scottish firms, especially by encouraging research and development in non-defence sectors. But the SDA's work is hamstrung by a budget which has not kept up with inflation since 1981, driving the organisation to be increasingly dependent on rental income from its property.[44] 'Commercial' rents on advance factories may easily contradict much of the 'nurturing' policy.

In public expenditure terms much the most important economic policy for Scottish industry is regional policy. Expenditure on regional incentives, however, when measured at constant prices, is running at less than half that recorded in the early 1970s and the size of Development Areas has been cut. The bulk of the incentives are capital subsidies, some automatic, some discretionary. 'Locate-in-Scotland', the one-door agency, has had some success attracting inward investment to Scotland using these regional grants. There seems to have been some waste in the automatic grants in the 1970s, e.g. to the oil and petrochemical industries for developments they would probably have made in the same localities anyway. The changes in regional incentives in 1984 included a highly desirable cost-per-job ceiling on these grants. Their rationale has thus become an employment one, although the subsidy still goes specifically to new investment.

What scope is there for specifically employment policies? Because of the importance of competitiveness and income generation in private industry, the scope is mainly in the public sector and the public supported voluntary sector. We are convinced that in Scotland there is a willingness to pay taxes for more public infrastructure spending and public services (borrowing finance would also be appropriate for infrastructure investment). This willingness to pay comes from the value of better housing, schools, hospitals, roads, and social services – they would not be just employment policies. Estimates of cost per job, when savings in benefits and increases in tax revenue are taken into account, have been as low as £9,300.[45] This sum should be matchable in value of output. Higher sums are estimated for the cost 'per person off the unemployment register', but we argue throughout this chapter that policy should concern itself with the hidden as well as the registered unemployed. A possible target for these public programmes would be to restore employment in construction to its 1973 level. There would be more than enough need for such numbers for tasks like eradicating dampness in houses and making good the repairs backlog in public buildings. For public services targets must take account of training needs, which would mean programmes to expand, for example, nursery education and home help provision would have to be carefully controlled.[46]

It is also necessary to consider the scope for employment creation through self-employment, small businesses, co-operatives and community enterprises. Scotland has the lowest rate of self-employment in Britain so that there would seem to be scope. The growth of co-operatives and community enterprise and small businesses in areas of unemployment has made a small but helpful contribution and financial support, whether from local authorities, the Manpower Services Commission, Scottish Development Agency or voluntary agencies, is to be encouraged. Most self-employment is in the same line of business as people have been employees, especially craftsmen. In consequence, net job creation from these approaches tends to be limited, for new schemes often act as (subsidised) competition for former provision.

The main emphasis for job generation therefore requires broader approaches of industrial policy and revived public programmes. Given the scale and continuing growth of longterm unemployment, however, there will continue to be a need for special employment measures to help groups most disadvantaged in the labour force. There is no justification for maintaining the part-time emphasis and failing to uprate wages regularly. More effort should be directed towards creating opportunities for the growing number out of work two years or more largely neglected by the present scheme and towards providing longer experience for those with special needs such as the disabled.

The most important change however must be to integrate these schemes with the overall strategy for employment creation. More resources and energy should be devoted to enabling people to move from special programmes on to regular employment rather than back into unemployment as seven out of ten currently have to do. The measures may then help to counter the tendency for any growth in jobs to go to those with the least experience of unemployment, leaving the longterm unemployed further disadvantaged.

Whatever the longterm strategy for creating employment, there is an urgent need for reforms to the income maintenance system so that it may help and support the unemployed and those dependent on them by promoting and preserving their economic and social security. The persistent link between unemployment and poverty must be broken both for moral and economic reasons. Proper compensation is due to those who are forced to bear the costs of economic and industrial change; and failure to provide it is likely to increase the demands on the social services in years to come.

The full social and economic costs of recession are borne disproportionately by those unable to find work but they are by no means the only victims. Those in lower paid work have seen their wages fall further behind and poverty in work is increasing.[47] The benefits of sustained high employment to society as a whole have had to be rediscovered as increased unemployment has led to greater inequality and mounting social problems.[48] The case for action is a strong one.

Neil Fraser, Department in Social Policy and Social Work, University of Edinburgh

Adrian Sinfield, Department of Social Policy and Social Work, University of Edinburgh.

References

The authors would like to thank Dan Finn, Stephen Maxwell, David Raffe, David Taylor and Fred Twine for their help and advice.

1. *The Scotsman* 4 December 1985 second editorial. This was picked up and repeated in another editorial, 17 April 1986.

2. *Unemployment Bulletin*, Summer 1986, pp.14-15.

3. Data provided by David Taylor at the Unemployment Unit.

4. Göran Therborn, *Why Some Peoples are More Unemployed than Others,* Verso, London 1986, p.45.

5. Manpower Services Commission (MSC) *Corporate Plan Scotland 1986-1990*, MSC, Sheffield, 1986, p.50.

6. Statistical Office of the European Community, *Yearbook of Regional Statistics 1985*, CECA, Luxembourg, 1985, Tables II.2 - II.4.

7. *op.cit*, note 5, p.10.

8. *Scottish Economic Bulletin*, June 1985, p.9 and p. 41.

9. MSC, *Labour Market Quarterly Report: Scotland*, May 1986, Table 3.

10. City of Edinburgh District Council, *Unemployment in Edinburgh (Ward data January 1986)*, Planning Department, June 1986, p.3.

11. City of Glasgow District Council, *Research Memorandum: Unemployment within Glasgow by Local Area; April 1986*, Planning Department, June 1986.

12. Central Statistical Office, *Social Trends 1985*, Table 4.26.

13. Central Statistical Office, *Regional Trends 1986*, Table 7.24.

14. David Raffe, 'Unemployment among 16 and 17 year-old school-leavers in Scotland', *Employment Gazette*, July 1986, pp.279 and 277. See also on the labour market experiences of Scottish school-leavers, in their own words, chap.7, Lesley Gow and Andrew McPherson (eds) *Tell Them From Me*, Aberdeen University Press, Aberdeen, 1980 and parts I:8 and II, J M Hughes (ed.) *The Best Years*, Aberdeen University Press, Aberdeen, 1984.

15. *op. cit.*, note 5, p.53.

16. *ibid*, p.54.

17. *ibid*, p.55.

18. DHSS, *Low Income Families*, stencil, July 1986.

19. See for example research summarised in Adrian Sinfield, *What Unemployment Means*, Martin Robertson, Oxford, 1981, Chapters 2.4 and 4.2.

20. Vivien Marles, *UB 40*: A study of the public's attitudes and opinions of the world of the long term unemployed, BBC Broadcasting Research, London, April 1986; DHSS, *Unemployment Benefit Statistics*, Newcastle, Feb. 1986, Table 2 – see also *Scottish Abstract of Statistics*, 1977/78, Table 17(b) and 1985, Table 2.3.

21. Richard Berthoud, *Selective Social Security*, p.81, London, 1986; Duncan Forrester, 'The Fowler Reviews – an Initial Response', *The Welfare State and the Fowler Reviews – A Christian Response*, Shaftesbury Project, Nottingham, 1985.

22. Dan Finn, 'Half Measures', *Unemployment Bulletin*, Summer 1986, p.2.

23. Dominic Byrne, 'New Deal or Raw Deal? – The operation of the Community Programme', *Low Pay Review*, 26, Summer 1986.

24. *op.cit*, note 9, para 31.

25. Hansard, Written Answers, 19 April 1986, cols. 527-8 quoted in Robin Smail and Dominic Byrne, 'Job Start or Job Conscription?', *Low Pay Review* 26, Summer 1986; see also Evelyn Smith, 'Restart – A new deal', *Employment Gazette*, August 1986.

26. Bell, David 'Trends in Scottish Industry' in Hood N. and Young S. *Industry, Policy and the Scottish Economy*, Edinburgh University Press, 1984.

27. Scrimgeour P.A.A. 'Employment in industrial research and development in Scotland and the UK', *Scottish Economic Bulletin* No.29, 1984.

28. Leach D and Wagstaff H, *Future Employment and Technological Change*, Kogan Page, London, 1986.

29. Birtwhistle A and Harvey A J, 'Output-based estimates of gross domestic product for Scotland, 1963-84' *Scottish Economic Bulletin*, No.33, 1986. From OECD figures we calculate the corresponding figures for France and Germany to be: France – 1960-73 5.7%p.a., 1973-1984

2.3%p.a. Germany – 1960-73 4.6%p.a., 1973-84 1.7%p.a.

30. *Fraser of Allander Quarterly Economic Commentary*, November 1985.

31. *Fraser of Allander Quarterly Economic Commentary*, May 1986.

32. *Scottish Economic Bulletin*, no.33, June 1986, p.40.

33. *op. cit.*, note 5.

34. Mackay T, 'The Oil and Oil-Related Sector' in Hood N and Young S, *op. cit.* note 26.

35. Industry Department, Scotland, 'Electronics Industry' in *Statistical Bulletin*, January 1986.

36. *op. cit.*, note 34.

37. Taylor A, 'Overseas Ownership in Scottish Manufacturing Industry 1950- 85', *Scottish Economic Bulletin* No.33, 1986.

38. Young S and Reeves A, 'The Engineering and Metals Sector' in Hood N and Young S, *op. cit.*, note 26.

39. *ibid.*

40. Industry Department, Scotland, 'Industrial Output, 1973-83' in *Statistical Bulletin* No. D 2.1, 1985.

41. McNie W M, and Carmichael D S,'Patterns of work in Scotland' *Scottish Economic Bulletin*, No.31, June 1985.

42. Lord Young, Department of Employment press release, 13 June 1986.

43. *Radical Scotland* 20, April 1986.

44. A H Young, 'SDA "success" hides Treasury cash squeeze', *The Scotsman*, 28 March 1986.

45. Neil Fraser and Adrian Sinfield 'The cost of high unemployment' *Social Policy and Administration*, summer 1985.

46. *op. cit.* note 27.

47. Robin Smail, *Breadline Scotland*, Low Pay Unit, pamphlet no.43, London, August 1986.

48. Adrian Sinfield 'The Necessity for Full Employment', Howard Glennerster (ed.) *The Future of the Welfare State*, Heinemann, London, 1983.

VOLUNTARY ACTION ON UNEMPLOYMENT

Chris Clark

Introduction: unemployment and the social services

The recent history of unemployment in Britain is an object lesson in how rapidly and completely conventional expectations, attitudes and policies can be overturned by events. In the mid 1970s, the numbers of the unemployed began to rise somewhat from the minimal level typical of the postwar years. Ten years ago, the official unemployment level of around 4%[1] was still low enough that few people entertained any serious fear that the Beveridge assumption of full employment was becoming untenable; and on this assumption depended the entire postwar economic strategy for ensuring general prosperity and averting individual poverty. Only a handful of social scientists gave much attention to the phenomenon. But in 1986, with an official figure of 14% (or 15.5% on the old count)[1] the prevalence and seriousness of unemployment is already a commonplace. As Showler and Sinfield[2] put it, "Most groups in society now acquiesce in levels of unemployment that were regarded as unthinkable or just part of economic history less than a decade ago".

This article will focus on responses to unemployment from the voluntary sector, beginning by setting the discussion in the context of the social services generally. I shall describe the implementation and results of a postal survey of certain voluntary organisations in Scotland. It will be shown by reference to a discussion of the literature, and from the survey results, that voluntary action in relation to unemployment can broadly be understood as belonging to one of two types, designated the 'welfare' and 'prevention' models respectively. In the first, the aim is primarily to alleviate the consequences of unemployment for the individual affected while in the second, the main concern is to find new ways, at the local level, of preventing the occurrence of unemployment.

Why is unemployment a relevant concern for social welfare organisations? It might be argued that unemployment is an economic problem and that the proper place to look for a remedy is in changed economic policies. It is of course undeniable that changing economic and political doctrines have had a marked effect on the level of unemployment.[3] But it would be altogether too narrow to treat unemployment as exclusively an economic problem. The social consequences of unemployment are increasingly acknowledged, and some of them have implications for social welfare agencies. Hakim[4] has usefully summarised these consequences, which may be paraphrased under five headings: (i) personal financial effects (ii) damage to health and increased mortality (iii) mental health effects (iv) increased crime and delinquency (v) damage to the social fabric as shown by increased rates of family breakup, homelessness, racial tension, and the like. Now the evidence on the exact nature and extent of these consequences is far from complete. For example, the observed higher morbidity amongst the unemployed in itself tells us nothing about its causation. What is beyond doubt however is that unemployment is associated with an increased incidence and severity of many of the problems that social welfare organisations exist to respond to. A short list might comprise poverty; poor health; depression; loss of meaningful role; family strain. All of these are well within the ambit of the statutory social services. Voluntary social action organisations have not only addressed themselves to mitigating the consequences of unemployment, but also considered what steps might be taken to reduce its incidence.

Despite the prevalence of unemployment, and the evidence that a very high proportion of clients come from families affected by unemployment,the statutory social services are only just beginning to address the issue systematically.[5] One of the main reasons for what is perhaps a rather weak response is that social workers and their agencies have not hitherto been expected to deal with employment-related questions at all. Data on employment status are not routinely and reliably collected by social work agencies. The main emphasis on work with the unemployed appears to have been on welfare rights. This is clearly important; but it is no more than partly adequate as a remedial measure, and does nothing towards meeting the unemployed client's main need simply for a job.

The low response from the statutory social services at local level is paralleled by a lack of policy initiatives in the Scottish Office for supporting either statutory or voluntary sector social services for the unemployed. Some existing programmes including the Urban Programme and the Unemployed Voluntary Action Fund are able to support projects concerned with the effects of unemployment; and inevitably, a large proportion of the users of any social service are likely to be unemployed.

However government is clearly reluctant to become involved in initiatives likely to draw political attention to the issue, whereas voluntary action may well wish to generate interest in the political causes of unemployment as well as attend to its untoward effects.

The growth of interest in unemployment in community work, the voluntary sector, and the trade unions

While the response of the mainstream statutory social services to the problem of unemployment has so far been slight, the same cannot be said of the voluntary sector or of community work; here there is a ferment of activity. It will be convenient to review this activity under a number of headings.

Community work

Community workers were perhaps the first in the social welfare sector to take a serious interest in unemployment. The Association of Community Workers' annual conference in 1978 was devoted to the theme, and a collection of conference papers was published[6]. In the following year a volume in the National Institute for Social Work community work series was concerned with the links between community work and employment issues[7].These events do not signal the beginning of community workers' interest in unemployment, however. It may be traced at least as far back as the Community Development Projects. The history of the CDPs has been thoroughly documented and a brief comment will suffice here.[8] The CDPs were originally set up to combat deprivation in local communities by bringing about a more intensive and better coordinated delivery of the standard social services. The projects carried out detailed and wide-ranging studies of the problems of their local areas. The common theme to emerge from these studies was that the poverty and deprivation the projects were set up to alleviate did not originate primarily from within the communities affected. These problems were rather the consequence of much broader economic, political and social processes, and any work carried out at the local level could only have a mildly remedial effect at best. One of the key factors seen as affecting local prosperity was of course the success, or lack of it, of local industry, which in turn had to be seen not in isolation but in context as part of the international capitalist system. This analysis had major implications for the whole running and future of the CDPs because, among other things, it rejected the theory of essentially localised social deprivation upon which they had originally been set up.

In the aftermath of CDP some community workers began to explore the possibility of links between community work and trade unionism. As an occupation, community work represent a number of rather disparate interests but in terms of its major ideologies and practices, its sources of legitimation and its sponsoring bodies, it has been dominated in Britain by the social welfare 'industry' in general and more particularly by social work. With this background, the idea of linking up with trade unions represented something of a new departure for community workers. An attractive argument stimulated this exploration. On the one hand, social welfare and community work had long been concerned with the domestic and community sphere of life; personal, home and family concerns predominated. On the other hand, trade unionism was concerned with the public sphere of production and economic policy and its locus was the workplace and the party meeting. A class analysis however, would require the recognition of an identity of basic interests between those involved in community action and those involved in industrial issues. The point of bringing together action in the two spheres would lie in the belief that action in either one alone was considered unlikely to result in any significant basic improvement in the circumstances and life chances of the working class.

At the local level, problems in communities tend to be concentrated in precisely those areas most seriously affected by industrial decline; the community and the workplace are closely interdependent. According to some versions, community work and trade unionism practised in isolation from each other might actually be counterproductive in that they would merely facilitate the continued operation of the exploitative capitalist system.

Towards the end of the 1970s there were, then, ample grounds for community workers to take a professional interest in employment issues as a result of the recent history of community work[9]. Their interest was further stimulated by the arrival of job creation schemes sponsored by the Manpower Services Commission. In their continual attempts to devise suitable, but not too costly, programmes at very short notice the MSC staff turned both to the statutory social services and to voluntary social welfare agencies to sponsor the projects they did not themselves have the resources to devise, initiate, plan or manage in detail. Community workers were very often involved in originating and managing these schemes. A powerful incentive drove this involvement: at a time when funding in both statutory and voluntary sectors of social welfare was becoming more difficult than at any time since the late sixties if not longer, the MSC disbursed its relatively ample funds at an almost reckless rate. In community work and in the voluntary sector doubts have been raised about the political desirability and practical wisdom of accepting such relatively massive inputs from government[10]; but despite these doubts the usual pattern has been to protest somewhat feebly about undesirable aspects of the schemes, and then take the money.

Intermediary bodies

Intermediary bodies were identified by the Wolfenden Report[11] as performing a number of distinctive functions within the voluntary sector and in the relationship of the voluntary sector to government. They may be local or national, generalist or specialist. Table 1 provides a pocket guide. Their main role is to support, develop and innovate in the voluntary sector, rather than perform direct services. In view of this it might be expected that unemployment would have emerged as a central preoccupation in the last few years. This would be reinforced by the links with community work, as many of those working for the intermediary bodies could fairly be described – and would describe themselves – as community workers. On the other hand, the councils of voluntary service, and especially the smaller ones, have a not unmerited reputation for sticking to 'safe', traditional, welfare or charitable concerns, and a reluctance to become involved in politically controversial issues.

TABLE 1   Typical intermediary bodies concerned with unemployment

	local	national
specialist	resource centre enterprise trust	Community Business Scotland Centre for Employment Intitatives British Unemployment Resource Network

generalist	council for
	    voluntary service
		Scottish Council for Community
		    and Voluntary Organisations
		National Council for Voluntary
		    Organisations
		Scottish Community Education
		    Council

The policies and literature of the national generalist intermediary bodies do indicate a vigorous interest in unemployment in some quarters at least. Both the National Council for Voluntary Organisations and the Scottish Council for Voluntary Organisations have staff specifically concerned with this area, and NCVO in particular has issued a number of documents arguing the role that local councils for voluntary service should take. Another area of activity has been to speak for the voluntary sector on MSC employment creation programmes. In Scotland the Scottish Community Education Council supported a conference in 1983 dealing with responses to unemployment, and its newspaper SCAN regularly carries items describing initiatives. On the other hand there is some reason to think that currently the national bodies are leading where the local bodies are unsure about, or reluctant to, follow. An 'Employment Project Pack' issued by the Councils for Voluntary Service – National Association noted[12] "Despite the fact that voluntary organisations have been involved in employment issues for a long time, some people regard such activity as illegitimate, irrelevant or downright dangerous".

The emergence of specialist intermediary bodies concerned with employment issues is a sure sign of the increasing interest in this area, more particularly since many of them are of very recent foundation. The British Unemployment Resources Network was set up in 1983 and aimed to provide a national forum and information exchange. The Centre for Employment Inititatives, set up in 1981, "offers a range of services designed to help both policy makers and practitioners respond to the challenge of unemployment and its effects upon individuals and communities"[13]. Community Business Scotland, again founded in 1983 out of a predecessor organisation begun in 1978, and its associated bodies provide an information network and consultancy service. The 'new cooperatives'[14] – workers', neighbourhood, and community cooperatives – whose development has been monitored by the Cooperative Development Agency are centrally concerned with alternative employment schemes. A number of the specialist intermediary bodies are closely tied up with the community business movement, which is discussed in the following section.

Community businesses and local enterprise trusts

In general terms, a community business is a production or trading organisation geared to the perceived benefit of the local community rather than to the usual private sector standards of profitability. It resembles an ordinary commercial business in that it has a product or products and, if it is to survive, must compete successfully in what may well be a difficult market. On the other hand it is community oriented in that its product is seen as beneficial to the local community; it aims to generate employment in what will invariably be an economically depressed area; and its surplus, if any, is applied for the good of the community rather than to private profit. Community businesses often adopt values and operating practices more typically encountered outwith the main industrial sectors, such as a cooperative form of management, accountability to the local community rather than to owners of capital, and an over-riding concern with the wider social benefit of the organisation's activities. These objectives may well, of course, be difficult to reconcile with the commercial disciplines necessary for long term survival.

The community business movement, with its ideology of social benefit, has much in common with the statutory and voluntary sectors of social welfare in general, and with community work in particular. Its starting point is the perception of a set of related social problems centred on poverty, deprivation, and the corrosive social and personal consequences of unemployment. In addressing these problems however, the community business movement takes it as axiomatic that creating socially useful and personally meaningful work is the key to a solution, rather than the provision of traditional remedial or welfare programmes to mitigate the undesirable consequences of economic poverty. The significance of the community business movement therefore is that it borrows some of the methods of both industry and community work, but applies them to ends which, from the traditional point of view in either sector, are at least unconventional if not downright deviant.

Local enterprise trusts may broadly speaking be thought of as local intermediary bodies set up to promote enterprises which embody some at least of the ideals of the community business movement. They are normally situated in highly depressed areas. There is considerable diversity which makes further generalisation of limited value[15].

Scotland has been a leading centre of activity in the community business movement. There are several regionally based intermediary bodies and, at the last published count, about 80 community businesses had been established outside the Highlands up to 1986[16]. These facts, together with the novel ideological aspects of community businesses, make this a particularly interesting context for studying responses to unemployment.

The unemployed as volunteers

Offering one's spare time to do voluntary work is of course a well known and long established feature of British society. Although precise distinctions are not always easily made, especially at the margins, the key feature of volunteering is that the volunteer offers his services through the medium of an agency or organisation which may be either in the statutory or the voluntary sector. The possible attractions of involving the unemployed as volunteers are fairly clear. On the one side, the demand for voluntary social services may seem to be almost infinitely elastic, and the unemployed have time in abundance as well as a range of possibly useful skills. The demand for voluntary help might be expected to increase at a time of increasing poverty and deprivation combined with reductions in the level of state welfare services. On the other side, volunteering might seem to offer the unemployed some of the satisfactions, if not the income, of paid work: a sense of purpose and usefulness, an escape from loss of status, isolation and depression, and the opportunity to participate in shared endeavours with others. In addition, a number of government initiatives including the Voluntary Projects Programme of the MSC and the Unemployed Voluntary Action Fund have actively sought to promote participation in volunteering by the unemployed. In spite of all these factors it is clear that voluntary work is no easy answer to the problems of the unemployed, or indeed to the needs of the sponsoring agencies.[17] In a useful, if hurried, piece of research Gay and Hatch[18] indicate that unemployed people are no more likely than the population as a whole to engage in voluntary work; moreover, the unskilled and lower social class groups who in general have a lower propensity to volunteer are also those who are greatly over-represented amongst the unemployed. An indication of more profound difficulties in channelling the unemployed into voluntary work is the probability emerging from Gay and Hatch's research that the consumers of volunteers are not generally adapted to creating opportunities which fit the distinctive interests and needs of the unemployed, or the time and skills they offer. Agencies tend to define their objectives in terms of the needs of the target group – the elderly, handicapped, etc – rather than in terms of the needs of the suppliers of the service; but "most existing agencies do not have helping the unemployed as one of their objectives"[19].

A form of voluntary work which is specifically adapted to the unemployed is the skills exchange, whereby members offer their time and skills to a common pool from which all may draw as needed. In practice such schemes have been very difficult to sustain[20] and it seems unlikely that in themselves they can offer much benefit. However, a few schemes which combine the idea of a skills exchange with some more structured ongoing activities seem to be in a stronger position[21].

Unemployed workers centres

Unemployed workers' centres represent the main tangible response of the trade unions to the consequences of unemployment. The centres are predominantly of very recent creation. The first was established in Newcastle in 1978. In the summer of 1981 there were estimated to be 70 in

Britain[22]; in summer 1982 a figure of 140 was given[23]. Figures of around 190 have been quoted for 1983[24][25]. In Scotland, the first centre was set up at the end of 1982[26]; and in February 1983 Labour Research reported replies to a survey from 11 Scottish centres, in a UK survey which attained an overall response rate of 56%. The Scottish figure for late 1983 is about 23, while by mid 1986 there were reported to be 24 in Strathclyde[27].

Many of the centres have depended on substantial MSC funding to sustain their activities. This has led to a curtailment of possibly 'political' activities. One theme above all emerges from the commentaries on unemployed workers' centres. Do they exist primarily to offer personal support and welfare services, or should they be concerned with the structural causes of unemployment? As Vivian[25] puts it, "Unemployment centres are caught between two ideals – either to make the best of things, or to be a focal point of protest against the system that creates unemployment". There is much to suggest that the trade unions themselves are deeply ambivalent about work with the unemployed. Although the trade unions portray themselves as one of the key institutions of a broad class-based labour movement, and not merely as workers' representatives at the place of work, they have been largely ineffectual in tackling the interests of their ex-members who have become unemployed. When a worker loses his job, he usually also loses the concern of the main organisation which represented his interests. Similarly, the trade union movement has been reluctant to fund unemployed workers' centres in any way commensurate with the resources it can apply to its traditional activities. Trade unions are defined by their relationship to the world of work; they have been slow to assimilate the new realities of non-work.

Although usually sponsored, at least in part, by the trade unions, unemployed workers' centres have not relied upon them exclusively. The relevance of such centres to this review is that they often entail a coalition of trade union and community work interests. We have here another emergence of the link between community work and unemployment which was discussed above. Some unemployed workers' centres may in reality owe as much to professionals in the social welfare field as to activists in the trade unions. The centres have been a focus of concern for intermediary bodies in social welfare. For these reasons it is important to consider the unemployed workers' centres in any estimation of voluntary social action with the unemployed, even though the trade unions do not constitute a part of what is conventionally regarded as the voluntary sector.

A provisional classification of interventions related to unemployment

The literature reviewed above reveals a wide variety of actual, or potential, forms of voluntary action in relation to unemployment. A relatively small number of themes, however, is discernible. There is direct concern for the plight of the unemployed themselves, who face poverty, isolation, loss of skills, loss of status, and mental and physical ill-health. There is frustration with the direct costs of unemployment, reflected in the list just given and in national economic statistics[28]. There is also a concern with the opportunity costs of unemployment: enforced idleness exists in the midst of such obvious social problems as urban dereliction, bad housing, industrial decline, pollution, racial tension, rising drug abuse, unmet dependency amongst the aged and disabled, and so forth. A further theme is the possible irrelevance or obsolescence of certain social institutions and the need to supplement or replace them. This is expressed, for example, in the actions of some of the intermediary bodies and in the field of community businesses, cooperatives, and other novel forms of production organisation. All this takes place against a backdrop of significant government expenditure on MSC programmes to absorb the unemployed, which the voluntary organisations have taken a major role in implementing.

The following typology of responses summarises the themes evident from the literature. The typology is based on distinctions that may be drawn between different analyses of unemployment as a social problem: that is, it reflects different possible understandings of the causes and effects of unemployment. The classification proposed here therefore embodies, at least in embryo, alternative strategies for dealing with unemployment.

The first distinction then is between

(i)   responses aimed at alleviating the harmful consequences of unemployment for individuals; not addressed to reducing unemployment as such

(ii)   responses aimed at reducing the occurrence of unemployment. These two broad strategies will be referred to as the *welfare* and *prevention* models, respectively.

The two broad strategies may in turn be subdivided. The relationship is shown in Figure 1.

(iii)   The *pure welfare* model aims simply to provide direct services to the unemployed, such as welfare rights advice, alternative activities, or counselling.

(iv) The *augmented welfare* model has somewhat similar basic aims to (iii), but in addition to direct service, favours organised political action on issues affecting the unemployed: for example, campaigns on welfare benefits. Its political aims are relatively narrow in scope.

(v) The *traditional employment* model aims to protect and enhance the availability of conventional employment opportunities within the established sectors of the economy. On this view the best approach to unemployment is simply to create more ordinary jobs.

(vi) The *new work* model also seeks to create new jobs, but is not satisfied with traditional definitions of work. Hence there is interest in new organisational structures (especially community businesses) and new philosophies of work – more leisure, job sharing, different patterns of work over the life span, etc[29]. There is some suggestion here of a broad social movement in infancy.

Within these four models, a number of distinctive activities can also be identified from the literature. Fifteen such activities were identified for the purposes of this research, and these are also shown in Figure 1 as a classified list of the variables which were adopted in the design of the postal survey to be discussed below. It should be noted that the allocation of the various *activities* to one or other of the *models* is presented at this point as a hypothetical representation of the field. The extent to which it is supported by the findings will be discussed later on.

Survey of voluntary action on unemployment in Scotland: design

A postal survey was carried out of all known voluntary organisations in Scotland falling within certain categories. The aims were to gauge the prevalence of the activities identified from the literature, and to gain an initial picture of the number, size, composition, age and staffing of the voluntary organisations which pursue these activities. It was also wished to examine the relationship between types of organisation and activities pursued, and enquire in a preliminary way whether the classification of models and activities proposed above was supported empirically.

The survey was planned during the latter part of 1984 and carried out in March-May 1985. Fortuitously, during the planning period three directories[30] and one descriptive study[13] were published which were

FIGURE 1 Hypothetical models of intervention in relation to unemployment

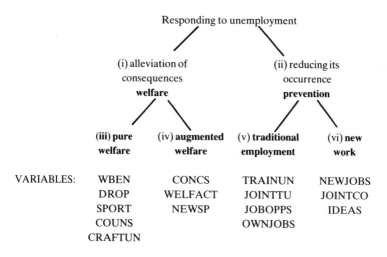

Responding to unemployment

(i) alleviation of consequences
welfare

(ii) reducing its occurrence
prevention

	(iii) pure welfare	**(iv) augmented welfare**	**(v) traditional employment**	**(vi) new work**
VARIABLES:	WBEN	CONCS	TRAINUN	NEWJOBS
	DROP	WELFACT	JOINTTU	JOINTCO
	SPORT	NEWSP	JOBOPPS	IDEAS
	COUNS		OWNJOBS	
	CRAFTUN			

For key to variable names, refer to Table 7

directly relevant to voluntary sector work with the unemployed. This gave rise to the rather unusual opportunity of carrying out a postal survey on the basis of newly compiled directory information in a field which is rapidly changing and difficult to classify. It was therefore possible to aim for a relatively complete 'snapshot' of the situation in Scotland at that time.

The study population

The survey covered four main types of voluntary organisation, plus several minor categories. The types of organisation were selected on the basis that some or all examples of each type were known to have an interest in unemployment, as indicated in the self-descriptions given in the directories mentioned above. The four main groups are: community businesses; unemployed workers' centres; councils for voluntary service; and volunteer bureaux. A total of 200 relevant organisations was identified, and a further 64 were included in the original survey but removed in the light of later information which showed that they did not fall within the designated categories. Table 2 gives a breakdown of the survey population.

Concern about the effects of unemployment is not of course confined to voluntary organisations of the types identified here, and so the decisions

Table 2 Survey population and response of valid members by type of organisation—

	Organisation type:									TOTALS
	CB	UWC	CVS	VB	ARC	Y	O	CO	UNID.	
response N	24	21	32	15	12	8	8	6		126
non response N	28	26	6	4	2	2	1	1	4	74
total N*	52	47	38	19	14	10	9	7	4	200
org. type as % of pop.	26	23	19	9	7	5	4	3	2	(100)—
% response by org. type	46	45	84	79	86	80	89	86		63

* excluding unidentifiable non-respondents
— figures in this row rounded to nearest 1%

Key to organisation type:

CB = community business or local enterprise trust
UWC = unemployed workers' centre
CVS = council for voluntary service
VB = volunteer bureau
ARC = area resource centre
Y = youth unemployment project
O = other
CO = community organisation linked (e.g. tenants' association etc.)
UNID = unidentifiable

about which organisations to exclude are of some significance. Table 3 lists the more important exclusions, with notes on the reason for exclusion. The general principles adopted were to exclude: local authority provision; services which get involved with unemployment *incidentally*, rather than define unemployment as the *central* issue; bodies not directly involved with unemployment.

TABLE 3   Organisations excluded from survey

Organisation type	Reason for exclusion
Grant making charitable trusts	Main role is funding initiatives of other organisations – not involved in direct practice re unemployment
Local authority community education services	(a) Local authorities not in voluntary sector (b) Community and adult education distinguished here from voluntary social action (but there exist affinities with community work)
WEA	See (b) above
Regional or Scottish inter-mediary bodies, specialist and generalist	Survey not designed to explore their role
Educational institutions	Not in voluntary sector
Welfare rights and general advisory services	Not specifically concerned with unemployment
General youth work	Unemployment affects all youth work to some extent; interest reserved for specialist youth unemployment projects
MSC schemes, with some exceptions	Such schemes generally aimed to complement normal activities of organisation. YTS is a training scheme. Projects included where directly addressed to unemployment as in unemployed workers' centres, etc.

Content of questionnaire

The questionnaire was designed to gather information in two main areas: (i) location, structure, funding and staffing of the respondent organisations (ii) activities carried out in relation to the unemployed or unemployment, with some indication of priorities. In order to fulfil the intention of sketching a broad outline of the field, it was desirable to aim for a good response rate and the questionnaire was therefore kept as short and simple as possible. A pilot version was mailed, with a covering letter, to a few organisations of the same type in England. The pilot received a response of 9 out of 13 and indicated that, with one or two minor amendments, the questionnaire would elicit the information required. The main body of the questionnaire asked respondents to say which of the 15 activities identified in Figure 1 their organisation carried out.

Survey results: profile of the organisations

Response

The response achieved is shown in Table 2. The overall net response rate was 63%. It should be noted however that this figure masks an important variation in response rate by type of organisation. Unemployed workers' centres and community businesses achieved 45% and 46% respectively, whereas the response rate for all other types of organisation combined was 83%. In the case of community businesses the low response rate may well be attributable to the fact that about half those included in the survey population were listed as under development rather than actually functioning. The low response rate for unemployed workers' centres is less easy to account for, but it is worth remarking that the total population of 47 is much higher than reported in previous surveys. It is also noteworthy that the unemployed workers' centres and community businesses are very much newer established than the other two main groups, the councils for voluntary service and the volunteer bureaux. It would not be unexpected if the newer organisations were less able to cope with answering even a short questionnaire, partly for reasons of resources and partly perhaps because they were less clear on their position regarding the various matters dealt with in the questionnaire.

Respondents were also asked to include any relevant literature, such as constitution, leaflets, reports etc. This yielded a substantial volume of material, and in some cases there were quite full letters of amplification as well. In general this material served to confirm the picture already built up from the literature. In a number of cases substantial local information was provided.

Age of organisations

The breakdown of age by organisation type is shown in Table 4. The main observations here are that community businesses are young organisations: 71% were less than 3 years old. Much the same is true of unemployed workers' centres, of which again 71% were less than 3 years old. On the other hand the councils for voluntary service were longer established – 74% over 6 years.

Representations from other organisations

Eighteen different kinds of organisation were mentioned by respondents as being represented on their own organisation. However, of these only 7 types were mentioned by more than 10% of respondents. The breakdown by organisation type is shown in Table 5. The most important organisations which supply representatives are clearly the district and regional councils, particularly the latter. In the case of unemployed workers' centres the trades unions provide a major constituency, as would be expected from the fact that the unions have been the main initiators of such centres. The councils for voluntary service draw heavily from local voluntary organisations, as again is to be expected from the nature of their constitutions.

Funding bodies

A somewhat similar pattern emerges with respect to funding bodies as does with regard to organisations supplying representatives. Seventeen different funding sources were mentioned but of these only 6 were named by more than 10% of respondents. The breakdown of funding sources by organisation type is shown in Table 6. In general funding is fairly evenly spread by source and recipient organisations. However, the councils for voluntary service are particularly reliant on SWSG and regional council funding: this is entirely to be expected from the nature of the institutionalised funding arrangements. The MSC is particularly important for unemployed workers' centres, accounting for the fears of curtailment of 'political' activities noted earlier. It is interesting that the main newly established groups, the community businesses and the unemployed workers' centres, are reliant on a diversity of funding sources.

TABLE 4   Organisation type by time established at 1.5.85

Shown thus: N
col %

Organisation type:	CB	UWC	CVS	VB	ARC	Y	O	CO	TOTALS
up to 1 yr	5 20.8	5 23.8	0 0	4 26.7	1 8.3	1 12.5	0 0	1 16.7	17 13.6
2-3 yrs	12 50	10 47.6	5 16.1	4 26.7	4 33.3	5 42.5	4 50	2 33.3	46 36.8
4-6 yrs	5 20.8	6 28.6	3 9.7	4 26.7	6 50	2 52	4 50	3 50	33 26.4
over 6 yrs	2 8.3	0 0	23 74.2	3 20	1 8.3	0 0	0 0	0 0	29 23.2
TOTAL	**24** **19.2**	**21** **16.8**	**31** **24.8**	**15** **12.0**	**12** **9.6**	**8** **6.4**	**8** **6.4**	**6** **4.8**	**125** **100**

For key to organisation type, see Table 2

TABLE 5   Organisation type by bodies supplying representatives

Shown thus: N
      col%

| | Organisation type: | | | | | | | | |
	CB	UWC	CVS	VB	ARC	Y	O	CO	TOTALS
district council	6 25	11 52.4	10 31.3	0 0	5 41.7	1 12.5	0 0	1 16.7	34 27
regional council	10 41.7	11 52.4	18 56.3	6 40	7 58.3	5 62.5	3 37.5	1 16.7	61 48.4
loc. auth. unsp.	3 12.5	3 14.3	6 18.8	2 13.3	0 0	1 12.5	3 37.5	0 0	18 14.3
comm. council	3 12.5	3 14.3	9 28.1	0 0	3 25	1 12.5	1 12.5	0 0	20 15.9
trade unions	1 4.2	15 71.4	8 25	1 6.7	1 8.3	0 0	2 25	0 0	28 22.2
vol. orgs.	3 12.5	2 9.5	31 96.9	6 40	4 33.3	0 0	1 12.5	1 16.7	48 38.1
churches	2 8.3	5 23.8	7 21.9	0 0	0 0	0 0	2 25	1 16.7	17 13.5
local comm. org.	2 8.3	1 4.8	7 21.9	0 0	5 41.7	0 0	0 0	1 16.7	16 12.7

For key to organisation type, see Table 2

TABLE 6 Organisation type by funding sources

Shown thus: N
col%

Organisation type:	CB	UWC	CVS	VB	ARC	Y	O	CO	TOTALS
district council	6 25	8 38.1	10 31.3	2 13.3	3 25	2 25	1 12.5	0 0	32 25.4
regional council	3 12.5	7 33.3	22 68.8	2 13.3	5 41.7	2 25	3 37.5	1 16.7	45 35.7
SWSG	0 0	0 0	24 75	1 6.7	3 25	0 0	1 12.5	0 0	29 23
MSC	3 12.5	9 42.9	1 3.1	8 53.3	6 50	2 25	1 12.5	0 0	30 23.8
urban aid	9 37.5	4 19	1 3.1	0 0	5 41.7	3 37.5	2 25	1 16.7	25 19.8
trusts	2 8.3	0 0	7 21.9	4 26.7	0 0	4 50	4 50	2 33.3	23 18.3

For key to organisation type, see Table 2

Staffing

Respondents were asked to give the number of full time and part time staff working in their organisation. The replies should be treated with some caution since it became clear that the questionnaire did not reliably distinguish between ordinary paid staff and workers on MSC schemes attached to the organisation. Nevertheless the clear picture emerges of predominantly very small paid staffs. Of the respondent organisations 52% had no full time staff, 23% had one and 11% had two. Likewise 85% of respondent organisations had either none or one part time staff. No significant differences between types of organisation emerged.

MSC schemes

Some 32% of respondents were involved in running Community Programme schemes. The vast majority of the schemes were small, employing fewer than five full time and five part time staff. There were no marked variations by organisation type except that the community businesses had a fairly low level of involvement, which is somewhat unexpected.

Very few respondents (about 5%) were involved in YTS schemes, and around 3% ran VPP schemes.

Survey results: activities of the organisations and models of intervention

As previously explained, the body of the questionnaire was designed to gather information about the prevalence and importance of various activites on behalf of the unemployed. Respondents were asked to indicate whether their organisation was involved in the activity on a four point scale, as follows:-

		Coding for analysis purposes
X	= definitely not appropriate to you organisation	1
Blank	= neutral	2
/	= activity your organisation is now involved in	3
//	= vitally important to your organisation's work	4

Scoring was well distributed over the range; in many cases around a quarter of the population fell into each scoring category.

An overall idea of the prevalence of the activities may be gained from

Table 7. Taking the responses coded 3 and 4 (above) together as *positive* responses, it will be seen that in general positive responses in respect of each of the activities were given by between nearly one-third and nearly two-thirds of respondents. There was little difference in the popularity of the eight most popular activities. All activities scored at least 25% positive responses. This confirms that the activities identified from the literature are all widely considered important.

In the analysis of the data, each *model of intervention* was considered to be associated with a number of the activities already discussed, while each *activity* was treated as belonging uniquely to one model. Thus, for example, welfare benefits advice was regarded as indicative of what was identified above as the *pure welfare* model (see Figure 1).

The hypothesis which informs this analysis is as follows. If the various activities are indeed derivations from one or other model of intervention, it would be expected that the various activities linked with each particular model would be highly associated with each other. Thus, in Fig. 1, the five variables WBEN, DROP, SPORT, COUNS, CRAFTUN would *together* tend to score highly in respect of organisations employing a *pure welfare* model.

The relationship of the various activities to each other was explored by means of the gamma statistic. This measures the proportional reduction in error to be gained in the prediction of one variable by reference to another. It is applicable to ordinal-level measurement and takes values between -1 and 1[31]. As the data were well distributed over a four-point ordinal scale it was considered that this would be an appropriate means of measuring any tendency for one activity variable to score high or low along with another activity variable.

If the various activities do tend to be associated with each other, this will be shown up by a crosstabulation of the gamma statistic. This is shown diagramatically in Figure 2.

Table 8 combines the foregoing arguments and applies them to the analysis of the data. It will be recalled that four models were postulated involving respectively 5,3,4 and 3 variables. If the hypothesis of four models entailing these variables is to be supported, Table 8 would show up four corresponding blocks of high gamma scores.

It will be seen from Table 8 that there is no clear evidence for the existence of four distinct models. However, there is good support for a

TABLE 7   **Prevalence of activities**

Activity	Variable name	% respondents ans. positively*	rank order
personal advice and counselling	COUNS	60	1=
helping unemployed people create own job or business	OWNJOBS	60	1=
joint work with local community orgs.	JOINTCO	60	1=
campaigns or projects to create new jobs	NEWJOBS	57	4=
promoting discussions on new ideas about work and employment	IDEAS	57	4=
opportunities for skills and crafts	CRAFTUN	56	6
welfare benefits advice	WBEN	54	7=
training courses	TRAINUN	54	7=
defending job opportunities	JOBOPPS	39	9
drop-in rec. activities	DROP	37	10
organised action on welfare benefits issues	WELFACT	35	11
publish newspaper	NEWSP	33	12
seeking concessions	CONCS	29	13=
joint work with trade uns.	JOINTTU	29	13=
organised sports	SPORT	28	15

* (see page 194) 'Positively' means scores of 3 and 4 combined .

FIGURE 2   Illustration of use of cross-tabulated gamma statistics

Activity variables

	A	B	C	D	E
A					
B					
C		H			
D		H	H		
E		H	H	H	

H = high gamma for cross-tabulated variables
blank = low gamma

In this example, variables B,C,D,E are seen to be highly associated with each other. If listed sequentially on the table they will form a <u>block</u> on the table.

slightly modified hypothesis. If the four models are reduced to two groups – the *welfare* and the *prevention* models – the import of Table 8 is that there is strong support for the existence of a *prevention* model comprising the variables in groups (iii) and (iv) in Figure 1. Similarly, if the variable CRAFTUN (opportunities for practising skills and crafts) is excluded, there is fair support for the existence of a *welfare* model comprising the other variables also listed in Figure 1.

We may now proceed to examine the tendency for *organisations* of a given type to be involved in particular activities or to adopt one or other model of intervention. In Table 9 positive responses (i.e. scores of 3 and 4 combined) are shown for each variable and organisation type, where the variables are grouped into the two models the existence of which is supported from the previous analysis.

Table 10 represents an attempt to indicate how active the various organisation types are within the two models. The following conclusions may be drawn.

TABLE 8 Gamma for two-way crosstabulations

Shown thus: gamma > 0.4 in plain figures; gamma > 0.25 but < 0.4 in brackets; gamma <0.25 blank.

	WBEN	DROP	SPORT	COUNS	CRAFTUN	CONCS	WELFACT	NEWSP	TRAINUN	JOINTTU	JOBOPPS	OWNJOBS	NEWJOBS	JOINTCO	IDEAS
WBEN															
DROP	(.29)														
SPORT	.41	.62													
COUNS	.67	(.25)	(.26)												
CRAFTUN		(.26)													
CONCS	.52	.46	.46	.46											
WELFACT	.63	(.26)	(.35)	.40		.66									
NEWSP	(.28)	(.31)		(.25)		.48	(.39)								
TRAINUN	(.26)			.45	(.27)										
JOINTTU	(.31)			(.27)		(.33)	(.36)		.27						
JOBOPPS				(.27)	.42	.41	.49		(.39)	.49					
OWNJOBS									.50	.54					
NEWJOBS									.53	.42	.64	.53			
JOINTCO	(.32)			.42		.37	.41	(.32)	.52	.71	.59	.41	.51		
IDEAS				(.25)		(.25)	(.26)		.52	(.37)	.63	.61	.61	.64	

For key to variable names, see Table 7.

Hypothetical models (numbered as in Fig. 1):

(iii) **pure welfare** model comprising WBEN, DROP, SPORT, COUNS, CRAFTUN

(iv) **augmented welfare** model comprising CONCS, WELFACT, NEWSP

(v) **traditional employment** model comprising TRAINUN, JOINTTU, JOBOPPS, OWNJOBS

(vi) **new work** model comprising NEWJOBS, JOINTCO, IDEAS

TABLE 9   Organisation type by percent positive scores for activities

Welfare model:	CB	UWC	CVS	VB	ARC	Y	O	CO
WBEN	25	81	44	40	83	62	75	67
DROP	12	76	19	13	42	75	50	67
SPORT	12	67	9	7	42	75	12	33
COUNS	50	90	37	60	58	75	87	67
CONCS	8	67	19	13	25	50	50	33
WELFACT	17	17	44	7	42	25	62	0
NEWSP	25	38	34	13	50	50	37	17

Prevention model:	CB	UWC	CVS	VB	ARC	Y	O	CO
TRAINUN	67	52	37	60	58	50	75	50
JOINTTU	21	67	22	20	33	0	25	33
JOBOPPS	42	57	47	13	42	25	25	17
OWNJOBS	92	62	43	20	58	62	62	100
NEWJOBS	71	52	69	20	67	25	50	83
JOINTCO	75	71	50	33	83	62	50	33
IDEAS	71	52	56	27	58	50	87	67

Notes: For key to organisation type, refer to Table 2.
For key to activity variables, refer to Table 7.

TABLE 10   Organisation type by average percent positive score

Organisation type	Average % positive score:		Rank order:	
	welfare	prevention	welfare	prevention
CB	21	63	8	1
UWC	69	59	1	2
CVS	9	46	6	6
VB	22	28	7	8
ARC	49	57	4	3
Y	59	39	2	7
O	53	53	3	5
CO	41	55	5	4

For key to organisation type, refer to Table 2.
'Average percent positive score' represents average of positive scores, by model, as shown in Table 9.

(i)   Community businesses are strongly involved in the prevention model, as indeed is to be expected. They are markedly unenthusiastic about the welfare model and the contrast is very distinct.

(ii)   Unemployed workers' centres appear to be almost equally involved in the welfare and prevention models. The ambivalence over this has already been commented on elsewhere.

(iii) The councils for voluntary service have by comparison only a rather low level of involvement in work with the unemployed. This is quite significant in view of the emphasis being given to the subject by the national intermediary bodies. As previously suggested, the national bodies have made some attempts to lead where the local bodies are generally still reluctant to follow.

(iv)   The volunteer bureaux also have a relatively low level of involvement with the unemployed. Numbers of respondents commented to this effect in their replies. This finding is of some interest given the high priority attached in some quarters to making voluntary work available to the unemployed, and the unemployed available to potential recipients of their voluntary work.

(v)   The remaining three organisation types each comprised less than 10% of respondents (i.e. less than 12 each) and generalisations on these small groups would be rather risky, especially as there is considerable variety within the three groups. Here it would be advisable to look for further qualitative data.

Conclusions

While interest in the problems of unemployment has a relatively long history in community work circles, it is only very recently that social action on unemployment has begun to emerge as a major theme in the activities of local voluntary organisations in Scotland. The newer bodies specifically concerned about unemployment are more committed to the field than the longer established generalist intermediary bodies or the volunteer bureaux. Nonetheless, in many ways the voluntary sector as a whole is ahead of the statutory services in trying to devise suitable responses to unemployment.

This study has been concerned mainly with community businesses, unemployed workers' centres, councils for voluntary service and volunteer bureaux. The picture which emerges is of a rapid proliferation of small, new and localised bodies pursuing a range of some 15 activities. Two broad orientations can be discerned amongst all this activity. They are the welfare model, where the aim is to mitigate the consequences of unemployment, and the prevention model, where the aim is to reduce its occurrence. Only the community businesses are unambiguously committed to the prevention model; the other groups are divided in their allegiance to one model of the other.

Chris Clark, Department of Social Policy and Social Work, University of Edinburgh

References

1.*Unemployment Unit Briefing* Statistical Supplement, January 1986

2. B. Showler and A. Sinfield, eds, *The workless state*, Oxford, Martin Robertson, 1981, p. 217

3. B. Showler, 'Political economy and unemployment', in B. Showler, and A. Sinfield, *op. cit*

4. C. Hakim, 'The social consequences of high unemployment', *Journal of Social Policy*, 11 (4), 1982

5. For a review of social services responses to unemployment see C. Clark, 'Unemployment, day care and community development' in G. Horobin, ed., *Why day care?*, Aberdeen University Press, 1986

6. Association of Community Workers, *Unemployment: what response from community work*? Papers from the ACW annual conference, 1978, London, ACW

7. G. Craig, M. Mayo and N. Sharman, eds, *Jobs and community action*, London, Routledge and Kegan Paul, 1979

8. See for example, M. Loney, *Community against government*, Heinemann, 1983

9. The adoption by community workers of unemployment as a relevant concern did not however go unchallenged in community work circles; see for example, A. Ohri and L. Roberts, 'Can community workers do anything about unemployment', *Association of Community Workers Talking Point*, 29, London, ACW, 1981; J. Gallacher, A. Ohri and L. Roberts, 'Unemployment and community action', *Community*

Development Journal, 18 (1),1983; G. Hill, 'What community workers can do about employment', *Association of Community Workers Talking Point*, 29, London, ACW, 1981; H. Salmon, *Unemployment: government schemes and alternatives*, London, Association of Community Workers, 1983. However later writings suggest that the controversy is now largely spent; see D.N. Thomas, *The making of community work*, London, Allen and Unwin

10. For a recent critical review of the Community Programme, see D. Finn, 'Half measures', *Unemployment Unit Bulletin*, 19, February 1986

11. J. Wolfenden, chairman, *The future of voluntary organisations*, London, Croom Helm, 1978

12. Councils for Voluntary Service – National Association, *Employment Project Pack*, London, CVS – NA, 1984, p. 5

13. Centre for Employment Initiatives, *Beating unemployment: a practititioners handbook*, London, CEI, 1984, p. 95

14. C. Luyster, *The new cooperatives: a directory and resource guide* (3rd edition), London, Cooperative Development Agency, 1984

15. Community Business Ventures Unit, *Whose business is business?*,London, Calouste Gulbenkian Foundation, 1981

16. Community Business Scotland, *Community businesses in Scotland; 1986 directory*, Glasgow, CBS, 1986

17. See Volunteer Development Scotland, *Volunteering and unemployment*, Edinburgh, VDS, 1986, for a discussion of these issues.

18. P. Gay and S. Hatch, *Volunteering and unemployment*, Sheffield, Manpower Services Commission, 1983

19. *ibid.*, p. 53

20. M. Plouviez, *Skills exchanges: notes on schemes for unemployed people*, Hemel Hempstead, The Volunteer Centre, 1984. Also cf. 'Community swap shop', SCAN, March 1982

21. J. Woulfe, *Working it out: some responses to unemployment in Manchester*, Manchester Council for Voluntary Service, n.d. (1985?)

22. 'Unemployed workers' centres', *Labour Research*, 72 (2), February 1983

23. D. Paul, 'Centres for the unemployed – are they working?', *Voluntary Action*, Summer 1982, pp. 26-27

24. B. Bowden, 'The centres for the unemployed' in S. Etherington, ed., *Unemployment and social work: papers from a BASW study day*, Birmingham, British Association of Social Workers, 1984

25. D. Vivian, 'Unemployed workers' centres' in K. Vincent and T. Davison, eds, *Unemployment strategies: a search for a new way forward*, Edinburgh, Alternative Employment Group in Scotland, 1984

26. Strathclyde Federation of Unemployed Workers' Centres, *Report on Glasgow unemployed workers' centres*, Glagow, 1985

27. M. Allison et.al., Unemployed workers centres in Strathclyde, Paisley, Paisley College of Technology, 1986.

28. N. Fraser and A. Sinfield, 'Can we afford high unemployment', *Unemployment Unit Bulletin* 17, July 1985

29. Cf. C. Handy, *The future of work*, London, Blackwell, 1984

30. British Unemployment Resource Network, *Action with the unemployed: a national directory of centres, groups and projects*, Birmingham, BURN, 1984; Local Enterprise Advisory Project/ Community Business Scotland, *Community businesses in Scotland: 1984 directory*, Glasgow, Strathclyde Community Business Ltd.,1984; Scottish Council of Social Service, *Community development organisations in Scotland: 1984 directory*, Edinburgh, SCSS, 1984

31. For a discussion of the gamma statistic, see e.g. W. Mendenhall, L. Ott, R.F. Larson, *Statistics: a tool for the social sciences*, North Scituate, Massachusetts, Duxbury, 1974

GLASGOW'S NEGLECTED PERIPHERY.

THE EASTERHOUSE AND DRUMCHAPEL INITIATIVES.

Michael Keating & James Mitchell

The Origins of the Peripheral Estates

Glasgow's peripheral estates have achieved fame in Scotland and beyond for their deep-rooted social and economic problems. Yet, unlike many urban crisis points elsewhere in Britain and abroad, they are not a relic of the industrial revolution or the unplanned development of the nineteenth century, but modern housing estates conceived and developed precisely as part of the answer to urban decay and dereliction in central Glasgow. Their origins lie in the housing crisis of post-war Glasgow and the battles fought at that time between the advocates of new towns, dispersal and overspill and those forces within the old Corporation who insisted that Glasgow could solve its housing problems within its own boundaries. The outcome was a compromise. By the early 1950s, the Corporation had conceded the case for overspill and was actively assisting in the decanting of population and industry from the city; but rising pressure for housing and the slow pace of planned overspill kept up the pressure. As a result, large parts of the discredited 1946 Bruce Plan were in fact implemented, with building at the periphery and at ever higher densities to the early 1970s. The periphery, as a result, developed further and faster than had ever been planned, encroaching into the green belt. Easterhouse grew as a single-tenure, one-class estate. Some 95% of the housing was corporation-owned, predominantly in three and four storey tenements and from the start there was a substantial proportion of large families. Such was the urgency to build houses that shopping and community facilities were, in the early years, seriously neglected.

Lack of school building combined with teacher shortages to curtail education provision with children in part-time schooling until the 1970s. In 1963, proposals were first mooted for a Township Centre, combining shopping and social facilities but concern about viability and costs held it up for a decade. By 1966 agreement had been reached with a private developer for a project of 95 shops, 5 supermarkets, a cafeteria, a restaurant, a car showroom, a service station, a post office, library, city factor's office, police station, bowling alley, community hall and dance hall. A year later, the developers cut down the proposals, postponing the ballroom, cinema and restaurant until there was evidence of their commercial viability and halving the number of shops. It was not until 1969 that contracts were placed and in 1972 the first shops in the Township Centre were finally opened. By this time, rising unemployment and continuing low incomes indicated that further development would not be a commercial proposition and the second phase of the centre remains unbuilt. Suggestions that commercial entertainment facilities would have to be subsidised by the council had met a cool response in 1969 when a joint Scottish Office-Corporation report had pinpointed this as a key deficiency of the area. Publicly-owned recreational facilities were developed, with a community centre and a swimming pool in 1971, but these remain limited. It was not until 1983 that a health centre was established and in the same month, the Rogerfield child care clinic was closed. Drumchapel's history was similar. This was envisaged in 1952 as a 'town inside the city', with its own town centre, shops, churches, schools, baths and libraries. It was not until 1968 that the swimming pool was opened, with construction of the shopping centre starting at the same time. Employment opportunities within the areas were also limited. An industrial estate was established at Queenslie but of the 10,000 jobs there less than a third went to Easterhouse residents[1]. Long distances, poor services and high fares on public transport were obstacles to seeking employment further afield in a community in which, by 1981, only some 15% of households were car owners. Drumchapel was better situated in relation to the city centre and the river but the estate itself remained without an economic base, a dormitory area rather than a 'town within the city'.

Almost from their beginnings, Easterhouse and Drumchapel were regarded as 'problem' areas. In the early days, attention was focussed on juvenile delinquency, with gang fights in Easterhouse and vandalism in Drumchapel receiving heavy press coverage. Complaints about the lack of social and shopping facilities were rife and it was widely suggested that the areas had failed to develop any community spirit. The lack of 'community feeling' is an amorphous idea but it was frequently suggested that the social cohesion which had characterised the old inner-city tenement areas had been broken up in the move to the periphery. As the inner-city areas themselves had often been developed extremely rapidly in the nineteenth century, often to accommodate Irish and Highland incomers, it might have seemed reasonable to expect community identification to develop over time and this has been a consistent goal of policy. While there has been some success here, however, the relatively high turnover of houses and the out-migration of the more active and mobile members of the population militated against this from the early days. It has also been increasingly recognised that the tenure pattern in the estates, with nothing but low-cost municipal housing is an obstacle to the development of a balanced community and militates against attempts to attract and maintain even the modestly upwardly mobile.

The impact of the recession in the 1980s has exacerbated the problems of Easterhouse and Drumchapel, as the analysis of the 1981 census for the Easterhouse and Drumchapel APTs shows.[2] In Easterhouse, as befits a postwar development, practically all houses have the basic amenities, but no less than 29.5% are classed as overcrowded, against a Glasgow average of 15.9%. There are 6.4% of households with four or more children against 2.2% for the city as a whole and 15.9% of households contain single-parent families (against 7.0% for the city). Only 1.7% of heads of households are in professional or managerial occupations, compared with 11.0% for Glasgow and 16.2% for the region as a whole; by contrast 39.7% are in low-paid occupations (25.6% for the whole city). Male unemployment is 40.3% overall and 47.8% among the 20-24 age group (19.2% and 24.0% for the whole city). The extent of low incomes can be judged from the fact that some two thirds of households are on housing benefit. 85.1% of households are without a car (70.6% for the city and 54.6% for the region). The population of Easterhouse has been declining along with that of the city. Taking the Greater Easterhouse area as a whole, the population declined from 56,483 in 1971 to 45,708 in 1981[3] but, because of diminishing opportunities elsewhere, this was not as great as had been anticipated in the late 1970s, when it was hoped that population movement could, if not solve the problems of the peripheral estates, at least make them more manageable. The age structure of the population, reflecting that of the scheme, showed an increase in the 17-24 age group and only a small drop in that of 12-16, indicating that the unemployment problem is likely to increase. Overall, Easterhouse retains a younger population than that of the city as a whole and, with low levels of educational achievement, limited prospects of moving into employment outwith the area. Health statistics reinforce the image of deprivation, The perinatal death rate is 23.5% against 18.4% for Glasgow and the infant death rate 22.0%, against 16.3%. Health problems are related to and exacerbated by housing conditions. For Drumchapel, overcrowding stands at 22.9%, with 15.1% of households containing single-parent families. 35.8% of heads of households are in low-paid occupations and 81.5% of households lack a car. The closure of the Goodyear tyre factory in 1979 removed the major industrial employer in the area, further exacerbating Drumchapel's problems.

Overall, then, Easterhouse and Drumchapel exhibit the classic symptoms of multiple deprivation, a finding confirmed by the CES[4] report, which noted that Easterhouse contained 10 of the worst 30 enumeration districts in the city (7 of the others were in the other peripheral estates). Glasgow, in turn, was one of the worst-off cities in Britain in terms of deprivation.

The Impact of Public Policy

By the late 1960s, it was already widely accepted that the policy of building at high density on the periphery had been mistaken, however understandable in the circumstances of the time. The 1971 census showed a slump in the city's population from 1,065,017 to 898,848, less a result of planned overspill than from spontaneous movement, but indicating that an end to the crude housing shortage was in sight. The second review of the Development in 1972 called for an end to overspill and the application of resources to combatting urban decay. This was in tune with the changing national policy agenda, where the 'rediscovery of poverty' had focussed attention on the problems of urban deprivation. National policies in both Scotland and England began to shift from a concern with overspill and physical renewal to an emphasis on the social and economic problems of the inner cities[5]. In England, this was marked by the Inner Area Studies, the 1977 White Paper on the cities and the 1978 Inner Urban Areas Act with its Partnership and Programme schemes. In Glasgow, the shift in emphasis had been heralded with the West Central Scotland Plan of 1974 which had recommended reconsideration of the proposed Stonehouse new town and the establishment of a development agency for the West of Scotland. In 1975 the Scottish Development Agency was set up with both economic and urban renewal responsibilities and, following a further recommendation in the Regional Report of the new Strathclyde Regional Council, Stonehouse was abandoned and its team and resources transferred to the inner-city Glasgow Eastern Area Renewal (GEAR) project. Strathclyde's Structure Plan placed the same emphasis on renewing the older industrial areas and tackling urban deprivation. In the Glasgow conurbation, however, urban decay manifested itself in two types of location. In the older urban and industrial areas, there was the problem of the decline of traditional industries and the flight of the younger and more enterprising sections of the population, often accompanied by poor housing conditions and other symptoms of multiple deprivation. In the peripheral schemes, similar social and environmental problems could be seen but linked here not to the decline of an economic base but to the failure to develop one in the first place.

Attention had been drawn to the plight of the periphery in the second review of the Glasgow Development Plan in 1972. This found, as we have noted, that the crude housing shortage would soon be over but devoted extensive coverage to the extent of multiple deprivation, confirming that this extended well beyond the inner city areas zoned for renewal, to the Corporation's own post-war estates. 34% of all the tenants of Easterhouse had outstanding transfer requests and 58% of these wished to go back to the Gallowgate or surrounding areas in Glasgow's old east end, where social and shopping facilities were available in the ratio of one per 386 persons, against one per 13,850 in Easterhouse.[6] The 1976 Regional Report of Strathclyde Region concurred in giving a high degree of priority to combatting multiple deprivation and Areas for Priority Treatment (APTs) were designated. These were to receive special consideration in the allocation of resources from capital and revenue budgets and to be the location of special multi-agency initiatives to provide a focussed attack on their problems. However, while some of the declining industrial areas were to be designated as Economic Priority Areas with the focus on bringing back industry, the main thrust of the measures for the peripheral estates was in the field of social policy. The development of the Structure Plan shows this up clearly. The first version, in 1979, talked of the need for 'priority for related action in the fields of housing, derelict and degraded land and planning blight both to improve employment opportunities and maintain the progress of renewal' in nineteen areas, including Glasgow's four peripheral estates. The 1981 revision, produced after the Council had developed its economic and social strategies, claimed that ' there is a strong correlation between the Council's APTs, the prospective joint economic initiative areas and the urban renewal priorities identified in the approved Structure Plan'. This coincidence did not, however, apply to the peripheral schemes which, while they were all APTs and 'renewal areas' were not 'early action' renewal areas or joint economic initiative areas. When, for the 1984 revision of the Structure Plan, Glasgow District proposed adding Easterhouse to the list of early action areas, the Region turned down the idea with the delphic comment that in Easterhouse 'the vacant land is concentrated on the periphery, which presents problems associated more with agricultural practice than urban renewal'! At Drumchapel, the potential of the old Goodyear site was blighted by its proximity to the Clydebank Enterprise Zone, showpiece of the Scottish Office's urban economic renewal initiatives. Further evidence of the adverse effect of planning policies came in the early 1980s when proposals for a large retail development on the Goodyear site in Drumchapel and warehousing and retail outlets at Auchinlea Park at Easterhouse were 'called in' by the Regional Council and turned down as contrary to the Structure Plan's emphasis on the city centre and town centres elsewhere in the region – this outweighed their potential for local job creation.

The divergence of the social and economic aspects of urban renewal policy increased after the experience of GEAR. The SDA had been pushed into this rather reluctantly by the Scottish Office (which saw the project as a coordinated attack on all aspects of urban decline), but came increasingly to see the social policy role as a diversion from its main task of economic and industrial renewal. Subsequently, the Agency's area projects focussed more narrowly on the latter, increasingly seeking locations offering the best return on investment rather than those with the most severe social problems (Keating and Boyle, 1986).

We have indicated that, by the mid-1970s, Easterhouse and Drumchapel were recognised as a priority area by local and central government, eligible for additional resources through the Urban Programme and from local authority mainstream capital and revenue budgets. Data on the geographical distribution of expenditure is notoriously difficult to assemble but the District Council has undertaken a series of exercises to assess the impact of capital investment by public and private agencies on the priority areas, GEAR, the Maryhill Corridor and the peripheral estates. The figures for capital spending from 1979-80 to 1983-4 indicate a bias against the estates, with investment per head by all agencies amounting to £586 in Easterhouse and £317 in Drumchapel against £2,415 in GEAR and £1,776 in the Maryhill corridor. For District Council spending alone, the figures are £219 per head in Easterhouse, £271 in Drumchapel, £604 per head in GEAR and £684 in the Maryhill corridor – though these figures exclude the District's non-HRA capital programme which provides grants for private house improvement. Given the lack of private housing in Easterhouse and Drumchapel, inclusion of this would produce a further bias against the schemes. What also emerged was the crucial dependence of the peripheral estates on council spending. While the District Council was responsible for nearly 40% of all investment over the period, in the peripheral estates it is the dominant investor. In Drumchapel, for example, 85% of all investment was undertaken by the District. In Easterhouse, this figure was just 37.5% but this was due to the fortuitous circumstance of the Monkland Motorway passing through the area, increasing sharply the contribution of Strathclyde Region during the road's construction. There is no private investment recorded and only a token amount by the SDA, a finding confirmed by the SDA's own figures, which show Provan and Garscadden as amongst the three parliamentary constituencies with the least amount of SDA current investment as at November 1984.[7] More detailed figures which have been produced by the District Council for selected years up to 1984-5 confirm the picture.

What emerges, then, is that Easterhouse and Drumchapel are critically dependent on public expenditure and, given their preponderance of public sector housing, vulnerable to policies such as prevailed in the early 1980s, when central government sharply diverted housing capital expenditure from the public to the private sector. For the city as a whole, the centrally-permitted expenditure on council house investment (the HRA account) fell from £62.6m in 1979/80 to £51.0m in 1984/5 while that for private sector grants and loans (the non-HRA account) increased from £13.3m to £84.5m. The balance has since been reversed with the heavy cuts in the non-HRA programme, though in real terms council housing investment remains well below the levels of 1979.

Figures on revenue spending are even more elusive. Under Strathclyde Region's anti-deprivation policy launched when the council was set up and refined as the *Social Strategy for the Eighties* the areas are eligible for preferential treatment in the allocation of resources. In education, falling school rolls and the elimination of the teacher shortage has meant that staffing levels could be established on a proper basis and then extra staff under the Scottish Office *Circular 991* scheme allowing 390 additional teachers in Strathclyde's areas of need. In Social Work, too, extra staff have been provided since reorganisation and Welfare Rights workers have been deployed to try and ensure that people get the state benefits to which they are entitled. The fact remains, however, that many revenue services are demand-led so that those areas with more children staying on at school will tend to get more education expenditure and make more demands on the library service.

A major aim of the *Strategy* has been to ensure not simply that resources were available but that the various service delivery agencies cooperated in a joint appreciation of the problems facing them and in coordinated strategies for tackling them. At the same time, the need for community cooperation has been stressed. This stems from a concern that local government professionals tend to see problems in compartmentalised terms and draw a line around their sphere of competence, resisting intrusion by other professionals. The 1972 report by the old Glasgow Corporation had foreseen a problem of coordination when the two-tier local government system came into being, at a time when joint approaches were most needed; but there is also a problem about liaison within authorities, of bringing, for example, teachers, social workers and policemen to share a common appreciation of their problems. Strathclyde's original joint initiatives in seven of the APTs focussed on this problem, with a limited degree of success.

These, then, were the dimensions of the Easterhouse and Drumchapel problem. Over recent years, several initiatives have emerged in the areas of community development, housing, education and social work.[8] The rest of this article is concerned with the latest, the Drumchapel and Greater Easterhouse Initiatives.

The Origins of the Initiative

We have argued that, since the early 1980s, there has been a progressive disaggregation of the physical, social and economic elements of urban policy.[9] At the same time, the main thrust of physical and economic development policy has largely passed the periphery by, leaving estates like Easterhouse and Drumchapel dependent on local social policy initiatives and the limited moneys which can be obtained through urban aid. Concern about them had been building up for some time, however, stimulated by the *Social Strategy for the Eighties*, Glasgow District's area management and decentralisation structures and the work of the Region's Glasgow Divisional Deprivation Group. There was general agreement that 'something should be done' about the peripheral schemes and that an attack should be made simultaneously on the social and economic problems. Just what should be done and how the resources could be found was not so obvious.

In October 1983, proposals were put forward by the Chief Executive's Department of the region identifying the problems, outlining the broad objectives of Joint Economic and Social Initiatives for Easterhouse and Drumchapel and discussing the strategy and programmes. It was stressed that the gestation period for the Initiatives should not be as long as that which preceded GEAR. A steering committee was to be established consisting of elected and senior officers of the two authorities as well as other agencies, the Scottish Development Agency, Greater Glasgow Health Board, and possibly the Scottish Office and Manpower Services Commission. In the event the part played by the central agencies was negligible or, in the case of the Scottish Office, non-existent. Each agency and each department was asked to prepare briefs and various ideas were to be considered in the lead up to the formal establishment of the Initiatives. Community involvement was regarded, at least on paper, as an essential component in the Initiatives not only to lend credibility to the ideas but also to foster community spirit in the areas.

The following year and half or so, to the Summer of 1985, saw very slow progress towards the establishment of the Initiative. Partly because some of the most senior members of both authorities were involved, who were obviously pressed for time, and partly because of the need to seek advice, views and ideas from a range of departments and officials, it took more time in arriving at the point when a formal agreement could be reached. Training seminars were run, consideration of the administrative structure and constitution of the Initiatives and the nature of community involvement were discussed. Until this stage there had been almost no communication with the local communities. However, it is always difficult determining how to *involve* a community and necessarily, in the case of an initiative from a governmental agency, there will be the appearance of presenting a *fait accompli* to the local community. During the Summer of 1985, community conferences were held in each of the areas. In Drumchapel a single conference was held at which six residents were elected to form the Drumchapel Residents' Forum. In Easterhouse, a much larger area, community conferences were held in the constituent neighbourhoods and fifteen residents were elected at these who formed the Easterhouse Residents' Forum. Perhaps inevitably, there were not particularly large turnouts at the community conferences and those who became involved as members of the Residents' Forum were almost all "community activists". This at least ensured that the members of the community who became involved had some experience of committee structures and the workings of the Councils, though obviously the "representativeness" of the individuals might be questioned.

Organisation and Constitution

Interim Planning Groups (IPG) consisting of elected members and officials from the two authorities, other representatives from bodies such as the SDA and GGHB, and some of the members from the Residents' Forum met regularly from Summer 1985, acting as the institutional lead-in to the formal establishment of the Initiatives. The executives of the two Initiatives was further considered and the advertisement for the post of Initiative Director was advertised. This was one of the most contentious matters which developed. The SDA, in one of their very rare examples of involvement in the areas and with the Joint Initiatives particularly, funded a consultant to draw up an advertisement for the post. The result was an advert which was seen by many local people as insulting because of the implication that what Easterhouse and Drumchapel required was a missionary or "superman". The expenditure of the "prime-pumping" budget for the Initiatives was discussed at these meetings.

The formal, legal establishment of the Area Management Groups (AMG) for each of Greater Easterhouse and Drumchapel, replacing the

IPGs, only occurred in April 1986. The AMGs were set up under the provisions of the Local Government (Scotland) Act, 1973 as a Joint Committee of the two authorities. In both cases, equal numbers of Regional Councillors, District Councillors, and Community representatives make up the AMGs. In Drumchapel three members from each of the components make up the AMG of nine members, while in Easterhouse there is a total of fifteen members constituted from five members of each of the components. The chairman and vice-chairman (convener and vice-convener as Drumchapel has chosen to designate these positions) of the AMG cannot come from the same component part of the Group, so for example the convener of Drumchapel AMG is a District Councillor and the Vice-Convener is a resident. Notably, Drumchapel's constitution allows for substitute members to attend meetings of the AMG in the absence of a member with the powers of the absent member, though this is not part of Easterhouse's constitution. In the case of Easterhouse, there would appear to be the need for an amendment given that at the AMG's second meeting, and first to discuss substantive issues, the absence of a number of councillors made the meeting inquorate. The AMGs are to appoint the Initiative Director, a Clerk, a Treasurer and other staff as they may decide, though because the AMGs exist only as Joint Committees of the two authorities and have otherwise no statutorily recognised existence, these officials will officially be employed by the local authorities. Clearly, the relationship between the AMG and its staff will be ambiguous, at least in terms of its legal position though this is unlikely to be of consequence in practice.

The limits within which the AMGs can operate, and indeed exist, as independent entities are obviously prescribed by legislation. The two-tier structure of Scottish local government prevents the devolution of power and responsibilities across authorities to local areas. The perceived need for a body which has Regional and District functions would suggest, at least in areas of concentrated social and economic deprivation, that the two-tier structure in its ideal form may not be applicable. One issue which demands attention and should excite at least academic attention is the role of the local councillor. Each of the local councillors for the areas are members of the AMGs. However the existence of "community representatives" recognises the limited representativeness of the councillors, elected by very small proportions of the electorate. However, the representativeness of the community activists is by no means obvious. Chosen at community conferences which could so easily be manipulated, there are problems of ensuring increased participation across the community as well as ensuring that the community's views are allowed to be expressed by the community.

Aims and Objectives

The aims of the Easterhouse and Drumchapel Initiatives as set out in 1983 when the idea was first being posited were:

1. to generate the facilities and community organisation of the areas, which in the case of Easterhouse especially, was recognised to be comparable to a medium sized town.

2. to meet the aspirations of the population both in the short term and also into the 1990s and beyond.

3. to create jobs and (re)generate the local economy.

4. to involve the local community.

5. to develop the communities of Easterhouse and Drumchapel and their respective individual component communities.

6. to make use of all possible sources of funding, encourage flexibility and innovation.

In effect, the aims come under two broad headings of social and economic development. Under the former, the fostering of a community spirit and participation in their communities is hoped for as well as improved and better coordinated service provision. Under the latter heading of economic regeneration, the most obvious element is the reduction of unemployment.

Each of the areas has particular needs and potentials in respect to these aims. Drumchapel, for example has the best repairs service in the city of Glasgow for its stock of council housing while there would appear to be much more room for improvement on this front in Easterhouse. The Kingsridge/Cleddans scheme in Drumchapel is an example of an innovative approach to housing in one of the most disadvantaged areas where Difficult-To-Let houses were concentrated. There tenant participation has included involvement in a local lettings policy initiative. In Easterhouse, the clearance of the Pendeen Crescent/Sandaig Road area of South Barlanark and the SDA's interest there offers opportunities which the Easterhouse Initiative will no doubt be taking an interest in. The former Goodyear site in Drumchapel has been considered as a potential site for economic development, as has the Queenslie Industrial Estate in Easterhouse.

However, while the Initiative has been described as a Social and Economic Initiative and the local authorities recognise the clear links between the two aspects, the evidence suggests that what is being purposed is, in fact, little more than a social initiative which will also act as a pressure group for greater financial investment in the areas. The employment strategies of the Initiative for each area would appear to envisage the maximum use being made of the various existing funds. The Manpower Service Agency's various "placebo" policies are to be made use of. Training and education are seen as important and this is seen as an area in which the Initiatives could press for support. One important area recognised by the local authorities in which the social and economic aspects of the projects most clearly overlap is that of the encouragement of a local recruitment policy. Not only is there much scope for increasing employment in order to meet the demands caused by the sparcity of services provided, but there would be the encouragement of the employment of those living in the areas by the local authorities. While community businesses can generate employment, the scale of unemployment will require far more ambitious projects and there seems little likelihood that these will come the way of the Easterhouse and Drumchapel Initiatives without the major funding which can probably only be supplied by central government, who have to date shown little interest in, and even less of active part in the establishment of the Initiatives.

Though the SDA has an interest in the South Barlanark development, most likely because it is under pressure from the Treasury and in need of expanding its interests, its interest in Easterhouse and Drumchapel has been negligible. The Glasgow Parliamentary constituencies in which Easterhouse and Drumchapel exist – Provan and Garscadden respectively – are amongst the three constituencies which received the least amount of SDA current investments as at November 1984.[10] Glasgow Central was by far the most fortunate Scottish constituency in terms of investment according to the same answer to the Parliamentary Question. The SDA sponsored *Glasgow Action* is a further example of the preference which that body has for investing in the city centre. The SDA report *The Potential of Glasgow City Centre* may well propose to "put the heart back into Glasgow" but the Agency offers little for the peripheral estates where unemployment is concentrated at its highest levels.

The lack of interest shown by the Scottish Office, especially compared with the activities of the Department of the Environment in many of the inner city developments south of the border, the "placebo" policies of the Manpower Services Commission and the SDA's emphasis on the city centre do not augur well for the prospect of the economic element in the Initiative being successful.

Finances

The finances of the Initiatives will inevitably determine their powers, the extent of their independence and, ultimately, their success. A special pump-priming budget for 1985/86 was established which offered £50,000 to each of the areas. In subsequent years "Area Budgets" jointly funded by the participating authorities will be devolved to the AMGs. Additionally, it is envisaged that greater priority for capital and revenue mainstream resources will feed into the areas as Easterhouse and Drumchapel AMGs articulate their proposals to the local authorities. One of the general principles guiding the local authorities is that there should be no need to declare a large arbitrary sum of money immediately and that the provision of resources should grow in response to the identification of need, specific proposals and activities by and in the community.

A specific block allocation of Urban Aid to Drumchapel and Easterhouse for the financial year 1986/87 was proposed in the report submitted to the Policy and Resources Committees of the Region and District in August 1985. The AMGs would act as the initial approving agency for these sums of over £200,000 for Drumchapel and almost £400,000 for Greater Easterhouse. This effectively means that applications for Urban aid will have a further hurdle to mount though at least there will be a set allocation for the areas. Existing recipients of Urban Aid might well fear this arrangement though this would appear to be the case only if the AMGs, which after all are expected to be closer to the communities than the local authorities, become aware of failings in the existing recipients.

Much talk has been heard of the need for outside financial support. The Greater Glasgow Health Board, the SDA, the MSC, the European Community and the private sector will all, it is hoped, contribute. However, there would appear to be the liklihood of private sector investment only if the private sector see it as in its interests. This may follow from the activities of the public sector funders, notably in providing infrastructure, premises and help with investment finance. It may also, if the Region is serious about bringing in private capital, require some reappraisal of the Structure Plan.

Powers and Responsibilities

Deliberately, the powers and responsibilities of the Initiative are not clearly set out. As a long-term project it is expected that powers and responsibilities will be gained over time. This "rolling devolution" may well involve the need for legislative amendments to Acts of Parliament according to some of those behind the idea. The statutory responsibility of the Region for major areas of education and social work and the District for areas in housing provision mean that these responsibilities will remain under the authority of the local authority. In some respects then, the Initiative will be able to function only at the margins and act more as a pressure group than an administering or governing body. Obviously, the finances available to the Initiative will determine how independent it can be.

The Region and District will have the ultimate power of withdrawing support for the Initiatives and require only to give three months notice in order to do so. Otherwise, the local authorities will maintain a watching brief over the Initiative and there is the intention to devise some method of assessing and monitoring the work of the Initiatives. This could not be by the number of jobs provided or any such criteria which would be affected by variables external to the Initiative's capabilities and measuring such nebulous notions as "community spirit" would, of course cause difficulties. In all likelihood. the Initiative will not be expected to produce any tangible or obvious successes in its first few years of existence. The support in the local communities will act as a measure of success, though not measurable, and also lend credibility and legitimacy to the Initiative's position *vis-a-vis* the local authorities. In that respect, the success of the Initiative may well have a catalytic effect.

One of the most important functions which the Initiatives will be expected to perform will be that of ensuring that their areas are not forgotten. Though the assertion that the Initiatives will be allowed to determine policy has been made, it must be recognised that this will only be permitted within the outlines of the policies of both local authorities. The power of virement within the local service block allocations will be fairly limited because the statutory demands made on the local authorities. This particular power will increase only as the financial resources allocated to the Initiatives over and above the basic levels required to meet statutory requirements increases. It is therefore clear that the Initiatives' role as pressure group on behalf of the communities of Easterhouse and Drumchapel will be crucial.

Conclusion

Much of the rhetoric surrounding the establishment of the Greater Easterhouse and Drumchapel Joint Social and Economic Initiatives suggested that there was going to be a major shift in resources to these peripheral estates ("£ Millions In Action - Boost for city schemes", *Evening Times* headline, 30 August, 1985). In reality, though less of an appealing headline, it would have been correct to state that the Initiative has a long-term potential of gaining increased resources from various agencies but does have the more immediate prospect of improving and coordinating service provision. It has become a cliche that urban economic and social problems are not solved by 'throwing money at them'. If this were all that there is to be said, it would be a comforting thought; but solutions to urban decline do not come free. Large amounts of money need if not to be 'thrown at', then applied to the problem, particularly in areas like Easterhouse and Drumchapel which have been so starved of investment in the past. Providing the resources requires commitment not simply from local government but, critically, from central government which has effectively taken control of local finance. It is worth remembering that both peripheral estates owed their origins to the urban decay and overcrowding of Glasgow city centre which also gave rise to the emergence of the New Towns which were given considerable financial support from the Treasury. Given the lack of support for Easterhouse and Drumchapel over the years since they were conceived, it would seem only just and fair were central government to give their backing to these communities in order that they would be able to develop and prosper to the extent that the city centre is currently receiving the support of central government and the private sector.

Connected with the issue of finance is that of power. The ability of the Initiatives to lever resources out of mainstream budgets will depend on their political 'clout'. Certainly, they have received support from the highest levels in the participating authorities, but the quality of the management structure and the arrangements for local participation will be critical in ensuring that they retain their place in the order of priorities.

Michael Keating, Department of Politics, University of Strathclyde and James Mitchell, Centre for Housing Research, University of Glasgow.

References

1. Centre for Environmental Studies, *Report on Peripheral Estates*, 1985.

2. Strathclyde Regional Council, *Areas for Priority Treatment, Glasgow Division*, Chief Executive's Department, April 1984.

3. Centre for Environmental Studies, *op. cit.*

4. *Ibid.*

5. M Keating and R Boyle, *Remaking Urban Scotland. Strategies for Local Economic Development* (Edinburgh University Press, 1986).

6. Corporation of the City of Glasgow, *Second Review of the Development Plan. Areas of Need in Glasgow* (1972)

7. *Hansard*, 6 December 1984

8. M Keating and J Mitchell, 'Easterhouse – an urban crisis', *Strathclyde Papers in Politics*, University of Strathclyde, 1986.

9. Keating and Boyle, *op. cit.*

10. *Hansard*, 6 December 1984

A SCOTTISH LABOUR MARKET BOARD?[1]

Alice Brown & John Fairley

Introduction

For a government supposedly committed to reducing its role in the running of the economy, the present government has intervened in the labour market to an unprecedented extent. While the underlying objectives of this intervention and the details of the training schemes involved have been open to some debate and criticism, the role of the Manpower Services Commission (MSC) in this strategy has largely gone uncriticised.

Recent developments such as the implementation of a two-year Youth Training Scheme (YTS), the extension of the Community Programme (CP), and the increasing role envisaged for the MSC in education policy require to be analysed and assessed. In addition the commitment of the Labour Party to a Scottish Assembly and the issue of their own policy document on training, highlights the need for urgent debate on a Scottish alternative policy.

This article will, therefore, critically examine MSC practice and suggest an alternative strategy for Scotland based on the democratisation and decentralisation of training policy.

The Growth of MSC

The MSC was set up by the Heath Government's Employment and Training Act of 1973. Its formation, structure and remit were heavily influenced by the TUC. The MSC enjoyed all party support. Since 1973, it has grown from a small coordinating body with about 40 staff to become a major part of the Department of Employment Group with over 20,000 civil service staff and an annual budget of over £2bn[2]. Most of this growth has occurred since 1978 when the Callaghan government began to worry about rising unemployment[3]. Growth has been rapid under the Thatcher Governments, particularly once an initial ideological hostility to the MSC was overshadowed by the pressing need to respond to youth unemployment and inner city riots. However, if Tory attitudes to MSC have changed so too has the Tory approach to economic policy more generally.

Up until 1981/82, the Conservative government's main stated economic objective was the control of inflation. From the 1981/82 period, government statements increasingly referred to the need for strong supply side measures to break up rigidities in the labour market and help make that market function more freely. High real wages and institutional rigidities were held to be responsible for unemployment. In this period, when Norman Tebbit was Employment Secretary, government statements began to endorse either the classical or the new-classical explanations of unemployment[4]. Real wages would have to decline if workers were to "price themselves" back into work. It is within this ideological framework that MSC schemes, which paid subsistence allowances and in some cases undermined collective bargaining, began to acquire a strategic significance.

In 1981, the MSC launched a consultative document on a New Training Initiative (NTI). It is through the NTI that MSC has moved from being a marginal agency providing ad hoc responses to unemployment, to having a central role in the New Right labour market strategy. This new role has helped to bring hundreds of thousands of (primarily) working class people into contact with the MSC, and has shifted the MSC from the margins to the centre of political debate on economic policy[5]. Within months of its launch, the NTI had secured government backing, as Ministers saw in it a vehicle for policies aimed to strengthen the interests of employers in the labour market and reduce wage expectations at least in some sectors of the economy.

The New Training Initiative

The New Training Initiative has been widely discussed and reviewed[6]. Its central objectives are to modernise skill training, to offer some training and work experience to all school leavers not in full time education, and to improve adult training opportunities. Initially these attracted widespread support and very little criticism - although some of the proposals in Norman Tebbit's White Paper[7] which appeared to point to the industrial conscription of young people were vigorously and successfully contested, particularly by the trade union movement[8]. The main programmes of the NTI - the Youth Training Scheme (YTS) the Community Programme (CP) and the Adult Training Strategy (ATS) retain widespread support, but are increasingly criticised as more and more working class people came into contact with them, as employers question the immediate relevance of NTI to their needs, and as sections of the labour movement come to see NTI as a framework for deregulation and privatisation in the labour market and in education.

MSC in Scotland

The closure by government of most of the industrial training boards, the collapse of apprentice training and cuts to further education are tranforming the MSC into the main training agency, even though most of the "training" which it offers is little more than work preparation. In less than 5 years the MSC has acquired a central policy role and completely altered the topography of skill training in Scotland as in the rest of Britain[9].

The MSC is controlled in policy terms from its Sheffield headquarters, and from the Department of Employment. In 1979, in deference to the prevailing national mood, day to day oversight of MSC in Scotland was transferred to the Scottish Office. This does not make MSC policies in Scotland significantly different. It does, however, make Scotland unique in Western Europe in that one Scottish Office Minister is responsible for education, training and industry. The degree of civil service coordination which this should imply may be useful to any attempts to pursue a distinctly Scottish alternative strategy. Only in the overlap between MSC activity and further education is Scotland significantly different from Britain. Here, through the 16+ Action Plan, Scotland is widely praised by government ministers for leading the way in implementing the "new vocationalism"[10] with its clear attacks on comprehensive principles and on general education. The Scottish labour movement generally feels that 16+ arrangements in Scotland have helped keep the MSC at bay to an extent not possible in England and Wales. In England and Wales, where education authorities are felt to be dragging their feet, government gave the MSC direct control over 25% of the budget for Non-Advanced Further Education in 1985 in order to push through the kind of developments already taking place in Scotland.

In Scotland in 1984/85 over 85,000 people entered the main MSC programmes. The increases to the Community Programme which were announced in the Budget speeches of 1985 and 1986, together with the extension of the YTS to a two-year programme from April 1986, will take that figure to well over 100,000 in 1986/87.

Although staffing levels have been squeezed by Rayner-type reviews, the MSC had over 2,300 staff in Scotland in 1984. MSC expenditure in Scotland is substantial, although lack of information on programmes not decentralised to the Scottish Office prevents us from knowing the true total. Identifiable MSC expenditure in Scotland in 1984/85 was £128.9m[11]

The main opposition parties' criticisms of government policy often focus on an alleged under-resourcing of programmes like the YTS. This suggests that non-Conservative governments would set out to plan increases in MSC expenditure. Surprisingly there has been almost no criticism of the philosophy of MSC programmes, and the operation and role of the MSC itself.

What is wrong with MSC?

There is a growing feeling – amongst trade unionists, educationalists and those on MSC schemes – that the current operations of MSC are seriously flawed in a number of respects. Many now feel that MSC itself is so clearly identified with the defects of its own programmes as to make it quite unsuitable as a vehicle for alternative policies likely to win popular support.

MSC schemes are cloaked in rhetoric about "local responsiveness" "local delivery" and the importance of "local labour market needs". Increasingly though MSC is viewed as a highly centralised agency implementing policies determined (often without consultation) at the headquarters in Sheffield or by Department of Employment Ministers. MSC Area Offices are seen simply as conduits for these centrally determined policies. The tripartite advisory Area Manpower Boards are seen as toothless and their appointed members as unrepresentative of community feeling. MSC as a whole is believed to care little about community, local or even regional needs, and in some of its schemes to pose a threat to local democracy. In Scotland, recent opinion polls conducted by the Campaign for a Scottish Assembly have put MSC responsibilities high on the list of matters to be fully devolved to a democratically elected Assembly.[12]

MSC schemes are widely used by private and public employers as a subsidy for temporary labour. The effects of this use are to casualise and destabilise formerly secure areas of work. In some cases MSC "opportunities" actually destroy jobs. The Community Programme in Scotland is 75% based in local authorities with about 25% in the voluntary sector. Within the CP long term unemployed adults are offered a year of low paid, often part-time work experience. The work carried out would in many cases previously have been done by properly employed local authority staff – for example environmental improvement, house insulation, landscape gardening and some personal social services. The Youth Training Scheme is employer-based. In Scotland 75% of places are with employers, and two-thirds are in the private sector. Up to three-quarters of the YTS is "work experience", which is in the work place and is generally unregulated and unmonitored. On the experience of earlier special programmes like the Youth Opportunities Programme, the work experience element in the YTS will lead to employers widely substituting trainees for paid employees. Research commissioned by the Scottish Council Development and Industry on the YTS in Dundee and Renfrew shows that employers may have displaced workers with trainees in over 90% of cases where they considered it a feasible option.[13] MSC's own research shows that as YTS has been introduced for school leavers, the burden of unemployment has been shifted on to older young people.[14] The development of the two year YTS will almost certainly worsen these effects as the "additionality rules" which serve to discourage employers from substituting trainees for workers are to be removed.

In so far as the YTS is a labour subsidy, it is unplanned, possibly irrational, and makes little lasting impression on unemployment. The YTS is not intended to offer vocational skills. Rather it is intended to provide a broad work preparation, as a basis perhaps for subsequent skill acquisition. This makes it difficult to link YTS directly with specific economic sectors. The YTS is organised around "occupational training families" (OTFs) which are groupings of tasks held to have common training requirements. MSC's quarterly analysis for Scotland in December 1984 showed 20% of YTS places in the administrative/clerical OTF, 21% in manufacturing and assembly and 17% in personal service and sales. Given the employer-based nature of the YTS, this pattern seems likely to reflect market demand for low-skilled, low-paid labour, rather than any vision of the economy's changing skill requirements – particularly as MSC has denied aiming at any particular distribution of trainees.[15] In the two-year YTS the proportion of time spent in off-the-job training is about 20%. While this is low, there may be some move towards more vocationally orientated training within this framework.

The MSC's main programmes – the YTS and the CP – offer low level allowances to participants. The allowances have deliberately been allowed to decline in real value since the special programmes began ten years ago. Through these schemes, the MSC may be seen as setting new, low "reference wages" for particular areas of work. The role of the YTS in displacing apprentice training and pay in negotiated national agreements in construction and electrical contracting reinforces this view. This role of the MSC has not been the subject of public or even tripartite discussion. It is not part of a strategy to redistribute income and work more equitably, and in fact bears most heavily on particular groups of the unemployed and the parts of the labour market to which they are closest. Here the MSC seems merely an instrument for government attempts to lower real wages and wage earner expectations, and is consistent with the removal of young workers under 21 years of age from Wages Council Orders under the 1986 Wages Act.

Entry to the largest programme, the YTS, is primarily through recruitment by employers. There is growing evidence that employers' traditional practices and prejudices are being mirrored in the YTS. Given the role of the YTS in preparing young people for and channelling them towards broad areas of work, there are growing fears that the YTS may function as a bridge which consolidates pre-market discrimination in the youth labour market. Evidence of the early experience of young women and young black people supports the view that the YTS tends to institutionalise racism and sexism.[16]

Despite the considerable sacrifices demanded of participants, there is as yet little evidence that they derive lasting benefits. Most CP participants return to the dole after their year on the scheme. The 40-50% proportion of YTS participants who move on to waged work is not markedly different from the proportions who would have been expected to find jobs without the introduction of the YTS. The schemes may though help particular individuals to improve their prospects, and therefore redistribute the opportunities available to the unemployed.

MSC schemes do not offer skill training or the prospect of recognised and valuable qualifications. The CP has no skill training. While it is shortly to be re-vamped and made part of the new Adult Training Strategy (ATS), this will be on the basis of short work preparation courses and remedial education mostly undertaken in the "trainee's" own time. Attempts in Scotland to make SCOTVEC modules widely available to CP participants will ultimately depend upon MSC flexibility in relation to CP rules and resources. As part of the ATS, traditional high-level TOPS courses have been replaced by shorter Job Training courses. The 20 weeks off-the-job education/training to which participants in the two-year YTS are entitled offer little prospect of achieving qualifications which have any currency in the labour market, as MSC's proposed certification will almost certainly take some time to gain employer confidence.

The collapse of skill training – the closure of most ITBs, the rundown of TOPS, the plans to close "uneconomic" skill centres – has occurred alongside the expansion of MSC. MSC schemes do not provide a substitute for proper vocational training facilities lost elsewhere. The NTI shows no evidence whatsoever of any strategic thinking on the economy's future skill requirements. A recent report by the SCDI on the main focus of NTI, the YTS, concludes that "YTS by itself is little use"[17].

The government's view seems simply to be that "the market knows best". NTI received official backing because it was believed to offer employers a framework within which they could take control over the processes of skill formation. The government's view is that employers should be able to identify and pay for all job-related, post-YTS training[18]. There seems little evidence that this is happening. Even in relatively buoyant sectors, eg information technology and electronics, insufficient employer-sponsored training is taking place and skill shortages are emerging[19]

The government's training strategy has produced a very mixed response from employers. Some, notably in construction, have opposed the non-vocational nature of the YTS and advocated publicly funded skill training through the YTS framework. This argument seems to be gaining force now, as the MSC tries to gain employer support for the two year scheme. In other sectors employers have welcomed the YTS, but primarily for its cheap labour provision rather than its training aspirations. In some industries, NTI is supported by employers because of its implications for industrial relations. In engineering both employers associations and unions have a long experience of collective militancy. The Engineering Employers Federation is reported to view the NTI as primarily about industrial relations issues[20]. In industries like construction, road transport, electrical contracting, hotels and catering the YTS has now almost completely extinguished first year apprentice training and its concomitant trade union influence. New national agreements accepted by trade unions recognise YTS as the means of entry to these sectors, removing school leavers from much of the scope of employment legislation and collective bargaining. Indeed whether it was intended or not, the NTI has operated to diminish trade union influence over training and associated labour market policy. Participants on the schemes are unlikely to be directly affected by collective bargaining or to come into contact with traditional trade unionism.[21]

The two-year YTS, which started in April 1986 also brings peculiar difficulties for voluntary organisations and local authorities. The new financial arrangements make it extremely difficult for voluntary organisations to participate in the scheme[22]. The Scottish TUC protested to the Employment Secretary as voluntary sector schemes in West Scotland closed down[23]. At the same time the underfunding of the new scheme by MSC – apparently a deliberate attempt to transfer some of the costs from the Exchequer to employers – created difficulties for financially squeezed local authorities. A survey conducted by the Convention of Scottish Local Authorities on local authority responses to the new scheme showed Annandale and Eskdale planning to withdraw and Dundee, Tweeddale, West Lothian, East Lothian and Dumbarton continuing to participate only if the additional costs were excluded from Rate Support Grant guidelines[24].

Examples from Europe

In formulating an alternative strategy which takes account of the above criticism of MSC, it is important to learn from the experience of other countries. Indeed the present government has used the argument that training is practised more extensively by many of our European competitors as a major selling device for its own scheme:

> "In total just over half of Britain's young people receive any systematic vocational or education training, compared with nine-tenths in Germany and four-fifths in France"[25].

Some would argue that Britain's lack of competitiveness in world markets can be traced back to a lack of a comprehensive training system[26]. But, the government has been most selective in using only certain aspects of other training systems, such as the German system, as a "model" for the YTS.

The "Dual System" of vocational training, which is a combination of practical on-the-job training with an employer and related off-the-job theoretical and general education in a state vocational school, has, it is argued, supplied West Germany's skilled workforce needs with minimal state intervention for many years[27]. The training is provided almost entirely at the employers' expense and they are willing to provide 720,000 training places per year. The length of training varies between occupations, but is normally 3 years and the delivery of training is supervised and controlled locally by Chambers of Industry and Commerce and Trade and Craft Associations, which employers are obliged by law to join and which have tripartite representation of employers, employees and education on occupational training committees. The rights and obligations of employers and trainees are laid down by statute; wages are subject to collective agreement; and the qualification received at the end of the traineeship is nationally recognised[28]. Thus the German system depends on employers accepting a social responsibility for training young people and provides a key role for trade union consultation and participation.

However, the German system was designed and developed in a climate of full employment and a consensual approach to industrial relations, and has had serious difficulties in adapting to the recession and rising unemployment within the new climate of public expenditure cuts[29]. There have been problems in meeting the demand for training places as unemployment has increased; in overcoming the geographical and occupational mismatch between the jobs available and young people's wishes; the system has been slow in responding to changing conditions; and a growing number of trainees have not found jobs at the end of their training[30]. Proposals for changing the funding arrangements from the trade unions and the Social Democratic Party have been strongly resisted by employers and the government. However, the system still has support from those who argue that the level of unemployment would be greater without it.

The German experience illustrates that the problem is not just one of choosing which particular system of training to adopt, but the context within which it is operating. Having a job skill is not a sufficient condition for having a job which, we would argue, requires wider macroeconomic measures and local involvement and initiatives. Webber and Nass argue that the Social-Liberal coalition abandoned its commitment to full employment by the time the coalition collapsed in 1982, and retreated from more active labour market policies not just because of the constraints in formulating and implementing policy, but because of changes in the philosophy of economic crisis management[31].

In comparison, in Sweden, governments have actively pursued full employment and labour market policies, and with unemployment at just over 3%, Sweden has one of the lowest rates of the OECD countries[32].

One reason for the relatively low rate of unemployment in Sweden and other countries put forward by Göran Therborn is:

> "Nothwithstanding other factors, the existence or not of an institutionalised commitment to full employment is the basic explanation for the differential impact of the current crisis"[33].

Therborn argues further that "successful employment countries" have all pursued expansive Keynesian-type policies accompanied by a consistent monetary policy of low interest rates and nationally specific direct interventions in the market economy. In Sweden this intervention has taken the form of active labour market policy measures.

Sweden has a long history of active labour market policy and in providing public funds and introducing measures both to bring jobs to the workers and workers to the jobs. In the 1960s and early '70s there was a strong consensus for the view that, in order to maintain full employment, the government should support the rationalization of private business and the restructuring of industry in a socially acceptable form by providing grants for training and re-training and other measures designed to encourage the mobility of labour between expanding and declining sectors. Thus governments accepted the employment consequences of their "removal policy" by introducing measures to influence both the supply of and demand for labour and 'matching measures' to bring vacancies and job-seekers together. The Social Democratic governments of 1932/76 and 1982 strongly supported an active role in labour market policy and the opposition parties in power from 1976/82 actually increased subsidies to industry as the recession deepened[34].

However, the Swedish model was insufficient to maintain a high rate of employment and in the 1970s there was a change in policy direction towards safeguarding the security and location of existing employment in the local labour market, i.e. a shift from a general policy of providing jobs somewhere in the economy to a selective local policy of protecting existing jobs. Again this shift in policy direction had all party support. Measures were introduced to provide increased job protection and to influence the demand for labour through grants and subsidies and job creation programmes. Therefore, while Swedish governments still recognised the need for industrial re-structuring, flexibility and mobility they also responded to the public demand to provide job protection and security at the local level[35].

Their response to the crisis is in marked contrast to the experience in the UK where the cost of re-structuring, flexibility and mobility is being met by the unemployed. The Conservative government's approach was demonstrated in the Chancellor's 1985 Budget speech which proposed further de-regulation in the labour market (decreased employment protection and reform of Wages Councils);[36] his statements that macroeconomic policy can do nothing for jobs,

"It is a fallacy that changing policy would help employment. A freer and more robust economy is the only sure route to more jobs".[37]

and the 1985 White Paper on Employment which blamed rigidities in the British labour market for the high level of unemployment and which recommended four main ways of improving its operation:- (i) improving the skills of the labour force; (ii) improving costs and incentives; (iii) improving flexibility; and (iv) improving the freedom of employers from regulation.[38]

Sweden's response to the crisis has been to give further security to individuals and restrict the power of employers. In contrast the UK government's proposal is to free employers from regulation and decrease their costs and taxes at the expense of individuals who are paying the cost of the re-structuring process through unemployment.[39]

It is within the above context that the Swedish system of training should be viewed. Labour market training is the joint responsibility of the National Boards of education and of Labour Market Policy and has played an important role within the context of the overall economic strategy (again contrast to the UK where the government is implementing a scheme, without a coherent economic strategy for employment).

The Swedish education and training system is based on the principle of recurrent education which was explicitly established by Parliament in 1975, and provides for a high degree of consumer choice. The adult training programmes aim to provide for recurrent education and training possibilities all through working life. Programmes for the unemployed have been extended to include places for "shortage occupations" and the workers receive bursaries of 80-90% of ordinary income after taxes. Training councils (with representatives from municipal authorities, the labour market administration, employers and trade unions) in the 25 counties annually submit plans for the courses to be arranged in the coming year to the central authorities.[40]

The majority of young people in Sweden (90–95%) enter Upper Secondary Schools after finishing their compulsory schooling at the age of 16. The USS system is organised into "lines", e.g. general, scientific, technical or vocational. Most lines last for two years and others for three or four years. The education system is run with the close involvement of employers and trade unions.[41]

In recognition of discrimination in the labour market attempts have been made at positive discrimination in the compulsory school curriculum since the 1960s, a perceived achievement of this policy being that in 1985 25% of the technology (chemical, mechanical and electro-engineering and building) line students were girls.[42] Further, as a response to concern over the effect of the recession in particular on the employment of young women, the National Board of Education launched a central campaign in January 1982 aimed at making all young persons more aware of the connections between educational choice and employment prospects, building on this campaign in 1983 through advertising, films, TV spots, posters, etc. Their objective was to influence young people and their parents in their choice of subjects and future prospects, and in particular to draw attention to the fact that girls' educational choice may affect their future economic independence:

> "Everybody needs the right to a job and to economic independence and girls must be made aware of the risks they are running through their excessively narrow range of educational and occupational choices".[43]

Specific measures for the disabled, another group often discriminated against in the labour market, have increased in recent years and now account for one-third of total expenditure on active labour market policies.[44]

In 1980 a government commission was appointed to review labour market training. It recommended a stronger decentralisation of decision-making to county boards mainly co-operating with the labour market authorities with lessening of influence by the central school board and stronger attention to the variations in the labour market situation and local needs. Again this is in marked contrast to the situation in the UK, where the trend is towards even further centralisation.

Unfortunately, the alternative policy on offer in Britain from the main opposition and the TUC has largely been confined to criticisms of the details of the present schemes and recommending improvements with no vision of a radical popular alternative.

The Labour Party/TUC Alternative

As discussed above, there existed a remarkable consensus between the political parties and the TUC over training policy. Criticisms from the Labour Party and the TUC were mainly confined to points of detail, e.g. the payment made to the trainees and whether or not their participation in the scheme was to be compulsory. In Scotland the STUC may have distanced itself more from MSC structures, but this of course has little effect on policies which are centrally developed in Whitehall and Sheffield.

"A Plan for Training", published in July 1984 by the TUC-Labour Party Liaison Committee, was submitted to the TUC and Labour Party Conferences in 1984. It criticised the government for "its use of state power to undermine the independence and representative character of the MSC",[45] but overall the document is very pro MSC and the NTI is seen as a bold and progressive step initiated by the MSC and undermined by the government. By implication, everything would be alright with a change of government and if the MSC was left to get on with the job. This view is reflected in some Labour Party publications which argue for improvements to some of the *details* of MSC programmes but assert that:

> "Labour is committed to giving the MSC the resources it needs to get on with the job".[46]

More recently however, Barry Sheerman, Labour's front-bench spokesperson on training policy, has published a pamphlet on the reform of education and training which, to an extent, moves beyond the traditional uncritical loyalty which the TUC and Labour Party have shown to MSC. A number of possible options for a future Labour government are outlined, including the traditional one discussed above. However, the pamphlet as a whole is surprisingly critical of MSC and has central concerns, e.g., equal opportunities and positive action, which are almost completely absent from MSC's agenda. While there is no discussion of the situation in Scotland, one of the options proposes a decentralised system of the type which we favour.[47]

A document produced by the TUC-Labour Party Liaison Committee – "People at Work: Rights and Responsibilities" – for the 1986 Congress and Labour Party Conference, argues for the right of individual workers to establish training committees in their workplaces and the right to paid leave for education and training for the employed and unemployed. In addition the document states that equal opportunities will be a central theme of a new training and retraining strategy with emphasis on positive action to improve employment opportunities for women and black workers.[48] The strategy document adopted by the 1986 STUC contained a section dealing with the labour market and training. It also places considerable emphasis on improving the rights of individual workers, but leaves open the issue of the place of the YTS in future strategy as "still to be clarified·" One of the options canvassed by the document coincides with our view in proposing a more autonomous MSC made directly responsible to a Scottish Assembly.[49]

A Democratic Alternative for Scotland

A Scottish alternative policy needs to recognise Scotland's distinct educational traditions. It also needs, we would argue, to move sharply away from current obsessions with making education more "relevant" to private firms' short-term needs.

Training policy is not merely about educational and labour market objectives. Crucially it is about power in the labour market and in the economy. At present, by building on pre-market discrimination and disadvantage, MSC schemes encourage the reproduction of structural inequalities. These are of course widely and increasingly challenged – by women, by black people and by youth. The left, in its concern to promote a democratic economy needs to recognise that:

> "a training strategy is more than just an economic measure designed to produce the necessary skills in the workforce. It can also be a mechanism for helping to ensure social advance. Both of these aspects are equally important when it is used as one of a number of measures aimed at the development of an equal, full-employment society".[50]

In formulating an alternative policy for Scotland, lessons can be learned from the experience of the GLC. In London between 1981 and its abolition in March 1986, the GLC implemented an alternative job creation and training strategy. The strategy was implemented through two main executive arms[51] – the job-creating Greater London Enterprise Board (GLEB) and the Greater London Training Board (GLTB). The twin objectives promoted by the GLTB were "training for social advance" and "training for skills". The GLTB invested in skill, providing the kinds of high quality training which the MSC was abandoning, and used its initiatives actively to promote the interests of those traditionally denied access to skill training – women, ethnic minorities, and people with disabilities. Although the available resources were limited – £30m and £7m were available annually to the GLEB and GLTB respectively – radical alternatives have been proved both to be possible, and in many cases cheap (for example, in comparison with the cost of unemployment and of some MSC training programmes). The GLTB was a full GLC Committee, yet was also open to broader pressures through co-options from community groups, the regional TUC, the women's movement and the Chamber of Commerce.[52]

We would, therefore, argue, following the GLC, for a strategy which recognises that training must be responsive to the needs of the community, relevant to the needs of the economy, and for training provisions which are closely linked to job creation and investment strategies. The objectives of an interventionist strategy of job creation and investment would be the modernisation and democratisation of the economy. The modernisation we seek is not just concerned with modernising production techniques and improving and up-dating skills to make production more efficient, although this is important. We would wish to go beyond this narrow interpretation and modernise our production to reflect the needs of labour and the whole community. This would be supported by democratising decision making, not only by involving workers within their enterprise, but through the involvement of people as workers and users in the planning of all aspects of the economy, where the provision of goods and services meets their needs and demands and are not delivered in a paternalistic fashion. A broad approach to education and training is an extremely important component of the strategy.

An alternative training programme should also recognise and incorporate the following criteria:

i) The training must be of high quality, of relevance to a modern economy, and be to nationally recognised standards at negotiated rates of pay.

ii) Education and training must be more closely related around consistent and compatible objectives. We must develop a policy for recurrent education for the employed and unemployed with no artificial age or qualification barriers and which offers real choice and flexibility for students.

iii) Vigorous equal opportunity policies are vital, and must include a commitment to positive anti-racist recruitment, flexible hours, part-time courses, and creche facilities. Training methods must recognise and build on trainees' experience, and must be anti-racist and anti-sexist.

iv) All sections of the community, including trainees, should be actively involved in assessing training needs, planning provision and monitoring; and training and educational institutions must be restructured to reflect this new and participative approach.

This will require a fundamental re-think of education and training policy and institutions, the distribution and organisation of work, and the ways in which skill is defined, measured and rewarded. In this respect, the experience of the GLC and other local initiatives is invaluable. They have shown that locally developed and accountable policies can meet skill needs better than employer-led strategies, and help to democratise the economy.

The broad support in Scotland for a Scottish Assembly and the commitment from the Labour Party and the STUC, provides the opportunity to re-think policies in the Scottish context and to move away from the legacy and constraints imposed by the MSC. A Scottish Assembly with strong revenue raising powers and its own Labour Market Agency could develop a new more open labour market policy which is based on the full involvement of workers and users, and which forms the necessary links with its other industrial and employment strategies. Other European countries and the GLTB offer models from which we may draw.

The role of the centre – the Scottish Assembly – is to create a strong framework within which local communities may work towards a genuine democratisation. We see the keys here as the extension of individual legal rights in employment, in education and in training; in the promotion of legislation which encourages (rather than discourages) positive action for women, ethnic minorities and young people; and in the provision of funds. A Scottish Assembly should raise funds specifically for training and job creation. A substantial portion of these funds should be locally available for locally determined projects. However, one obstacle to achieving this decentralisation may turn out to be the traditional centralism of the labour movement itself.

Alice Brown, Department of Politics, University of Edinburgh and John Fairley, Edinburgh District Council.

References

1. The authors would like to thank the workshop participants who discussed an earlier draft of this paper at the 1985 Scottish Socialist Economic Review Conference in Glasgow.

2. See M Anderson and J Fairley, 'The Politics of Industrial Training in the UK.', *Journal of Public Policy*, May 1983, and M Jackson, 'A Seat at the Table?' in C Benn and J Fairley (Eds) *Challenging the MSC*, Pluto Press, London, 1986.

3. Joel Barnet, *Inside the Treasury*, p.141, Andre Deutsch, 1982.

4. For example, Treasury Economic Progress Report No 174. January 1985, See also the White Paper associated with Lord Young, previously

David Young, Chairman of the MSC; Department of Employment, 'Employment, Challenge for the Nation', (Cmnd 9474), HMSO, 1985.

5. Introduction to C Benn and J Fairley, *op.cit.*

6. See P A Dutton, 'The NTI – What are Its Chances?', *Managerial Law*, Vol.23, No 4, 1981, P Ryan, 'The New Training Initiative After Two Years', *Lloyds Bank Review*, April 1984, Greater London Training Board, Review of the NTI 1981-84, GLC 1984.

7. A New Training Initiative, A Programme for Action. (Cmnd 8455), HMSO, 1981.

8. See John Eversley, 'Trade Union Responses to the MSC', in Benn and Fairley, *op.cit.*

9. See J Fairley, 'Industrial Training in Scotland', *Scottish Government Yearbook, 1982.*

10. Phil Cohen, 'Against the New Vocationalism', in I Bake and Others (Eds) *Schooling for the Dole*, Macmillan, 1984.

11. MSC's £2bn budget for Britain would suggest that actual expenditure in Scotland was nearer £200m.

12. *Radical Scotland*, December 1984.

13. Scottish Council Development and Industry, 'Youth Training and Beyond: An Appraisal', Edinburgh, January 1985, p.19.

14. *Times Educational Supplement*, 9 August 1985.

15. P A Dutton, 'YTS – Training for the Future', *Public Administration*, Vol.62, Winter 1984.

16. See A Pollert, 'Ethnic Minorities and the MSC', and S Marsh, 'Women and the MSC', in Benn and Fairley, *op.cit.*

17. SCDI, January 1985.

18. Department of Employment, Training for Jobs, (Cmnd 9135) HMSO, 1984.

19. 'Disappointment over training plea', *Financial Times*, 25 March 1986.

20. H Rainbird and W Grant, 'Employers' Organisations and Training Policy', Institute for Employment Research, Warwick University, 1985.

21. In only a relatively few cases have trade unions been able to negotiate 'top up' to basic allowances for YTS trainees. *Times Educational Supplement*, 21 June 1985.

22. In March 1986, four voluntary organisations, accounting for 37% of Edinburgh's mode B1 places, issued a joint report criticising the new funding arrangements. *Times Educational Supplement*, Scotland, 7 March 1986.

23. *The Scotsman*, 7 March 1986.

24. COSLA Circular, 7 February 1986.

25. *Conservative Party Document 1983*, 'The Youth Training Scheme'.

26. Pat Dutton, *op.cit. Public Administration*.

27. For a critique of the German system see Berndt-George Spies, 'The Dual System', *Transition*, September 1985.

28. J Franklin, 'The Dual System', *Youth Training News*, August 1985.

29. Steve Reardon, 'Supply and Demand Put Pressure on West Germany's Youth Training', *Department of Employment Gazette*, January 1983.

30. Franklin, *op.cit.* and Jean Woodall, 'Youth Training in Europe', *New Society*, 23 February 1984.

31. Douglas Webber and Gabrielle Nass, 'Employment Policy in West Germany', in Jeremy Richardson and Roger Henning (Eds) *Unemployment, Policy Responses of Western Democracies* Sage, London, 1984.

32. Quoted in Goran Therborn, 'West on the Dole', *Marxism Today*, June 1985.

33. Therborn, *op.cit.*

34. The three non-socialist parties (the Moderate Party, the Centre Party and the Liberal Party) were in office from October 1976 to May 1981, except for October 1978 – October 1979, when the Liberal Party formed the government.

35. Roger Henning, 'Industrial Policy or Employment Policy? Sweden's Response to Unemployment', in Richardson and Henning, *op.cit.*

36. The Budget 1985, The Chancellor's Speech in the *Financial Times*, 20 March 1985.

37. Quoted by David Lipsey, *The Sunday Times*, 8 September 1985.

38. White Paper on Employment, 1985, *op.cit.*

39. For a critique of the view that increasing labour market flexibility will automatically reduce unemployment see David Ashton, 'Unemployment and the Flexibility of Labour Market', *Unemployment Unit Briefing*, No.9, June 1985.

40. Gösta Rehn, 'The Role of Training in the Active Labour Market – the Swedish Example'. Paper presented to GLEB Conference in London, 10 May 1984.

41. J Franklin 'Vocational Education and Training in Sweden', *Young Training News*, September 1985.

42. See above.

43. National Swedish Board of Education, Schools and Equal Opportunity, December 1982.

44. Swedish Ministry of Labour, Labour Market Policy Research, *Labour Market Policy Under Reconsideration*, 1984.

45. TUC-Labour Party Liaison Committee, 'A Plan for Training', July 1984, p.2.

46. The Labour Party Scottish Council, Jobs and Industry Campaign – Scotland, p.10.

47. Barry Sheerman, *Education and Training, Options for Labour*, House of Commons 1986, p.31.

48. TUC-Labour Party Liaison Committee, 'People at Work: Rights and Responsibilities', 1986.

49. STUC, 'Scotland at Strategy for the Future', 1986.

50. GLTB, Review of NTI, 1981-84.

51. See the London Industrial Strategy and the London Labour Plan, published by the GLC in 1985 and 1986 respectively. See also *Radical Scotland* January 1985, October 1985 and March 1986.

52. *London Training Legacy*, GLC 1986.

THE PRESS IN SCOTLAND:
ARTICULATING A NATIONAL IDENTITY?

David Hutchison

The media are now firmly at the centre of political debate. This is hardly surprising, for we spend extraordinary amounts of time using them – television viewing and radio listening take up thirty three hours of the average person's week and while it is difficult to get totally accurate figures for time spent reading newspapers and magazines, it seems reasonable to assume that most of us spend about forty hours a week using one or other of the media. This is as much time as many people spend working and would lead any observer to conclude that much of the information we obtain about the world must come via the media. Indeed it is widely believed that the media have considerable impact upon the ways in which we form attitudes and beliefs on a large range of subjects. That is why so many organisations employ public relations consultants, in order to ensure that their 'messages' get across, and why political parties, trade unions and other bodies are continually on the look out for examples of 'bias' and 'misrepresentation'.

It is instructive to look at the way in which the debate on the impact of the media has developed over the last sixty years.[1]

In the twenties and the thirties apparently irrefutable evidence of the ability of advertising, in both the press and the new medium of radio, to persuade consumers to buy particular products led researchers in the USA to postulate causal connections between media depictions of anti-social behaviour and the incidence of such behaviour in reality. Although many researchers would now be reluctant to postulate without qualification such one to one relationships, it is worth noting that the contemporary debate about violence on television is conducted in terms which owe much to the kind of research work done before the war, despite the fact that the results of that work were largely inconclusive.

In more recent times the emphasis on the behavioural effects of the media has given way to an emphasis on the rather more intangible ideological impact. Researchers who have favoured this approach[2], drawing much of their theoretical apparatus from the European Marxist tradition, tend to emphasise the ways in which the media present information within an ideological framework, which is favourable to the status quo – Western capitalist democracy. These critics argue that in such a situation it is extremely difficult for radical views to be heard. What is particularly interesting about this position as it is articulated in the UK is that it encompasses the obvious partisanship of newspapers – which, it is said, all share the same basic ideology within which they are free to champion the political party of their choice – and also the supposed impartiality of the broadcaster, which is seen as a cloak for a continuing process of ideological reinforcement. Indeed the most bitter dispute between academics and media practitioners in recent years has arisen out of the work of a group of researchers based at Glasgow University who have published several analyses which seek to prove this thesis as far as television news output is concerned[3]. Although the debate has been at times unnecessarily vitriolic, it has at least served to focus attention on the meaning of such terms as 'consensus' and 'balance' and to demonstrate the very real difficulties of achieving total 'objectivity' and 'impartiality', no matter how good the intentions.

In the discussion on the Scottish press which follows a number of assumptions will be made. Firstly, and most obviously, that newspapers are products, whose relationship to the world of experience is not simply that of a window through which we gaze on reality. The relationship is more complex: a particular version of reality is being constructed for the reader and the nature of that version will depend on a range of factors, such as the political stance of the paper, the impact of that stance on reporting of events, the nature of the readership as perceived by the paper's staff, and the impact of market forces on the paper. Furthermore, it is assumed that the reader uses his newspaper in various ways. He may be looking for entertainment and diversion as much as information, he may be looking for stock exchange prices or betting tips. If he belongs to one of the more powerful groups in our society, particularly those with a political axe to grind, he is likely to be concerned above all with the way in which that group's interests are represented in the press; if he belongs to a less powerful group, he may be equally concerned to see how the concerns and problems of everyday living, for example, unemployment, damp housing, and crime are being articulated. It is also assumed that readers of newspapers are rather sceptical people. All the surveys tell us that people most certainly do not believe everything they read – indeed a growing proportion are equally distrustful of television news[4]. This distrust is obviously a good thing provided of course that it does not reach epidemic proportions, and gives the lie to the idea that people are simply media fodder willing to swallow any falsehood they are offered, a view all too prevalent in certain quarters. People have a variety of sources of information and can weigh up media information alongside these. Where the media will be at their strongest is where personal experience is at its weakest. Most of us have little direct experience of, for example, serious crime, yet there is a lot of it reported, often in lurid fashion. It is surely not fanciful to suggest that the continual reporting of crime, particularly violent crime, could create a climate more favourable to authoritarian measures than our personal experience would lead us towards. What is true of crime is likely to be true of other aspects of experience. Newspapers may not push us overtly in a particular direction, but by creating a climate of opinion, they may well help to incline us towards that point of the compass. This assumption about the ideological significanct of the press, its ability to influence what is discussed and how it is discussed, is the final crucial one made in the ensuing discussion.

The most immediately striking characteristic of the Scottish newspaper market is that most of the morning and Sunday newspapers read in Scotland are produced here. Because separate Scottish circulation figures for the Fleet Street titles are not produced by independent auditors, totally accurate figures are difficult to come by, but it would appear that during the week the five Scottish produced papers have about two thirds of the market, while the remaining one third is shared by the nine English produced titles, including the Manchester produced *Scottish Daily Express*.

As Table One demonstrates, the market is dominated by the *Daily Record*, which sells one copy for every seven people in the country. By way of comparison it should be noted that the biggest selling UK morning paper, the *Sun*, sells one copy for every thirteen people in England and Wales. The circulation figures achieved by the other four papers, which all hover around the 100,000 mark, compare very favourably with the regional English newspapers, none of which attain the Scottish figures. Of the English produced nationals the *Sun* makes the biggest impact in Scotland selling over 200,000 the *Scottish Daily Express* is not far behind, while the *Daily Star* tails below the 100,000 mark. The combined circulation of the Fleet Street broadsheet dailies at just over 60,000 is less than a third of the combined circulation of the *Glasgow Herald* and the *Scotsman*, the two broadsheet papers which circulate throughout Scotland.

The situation on Sundays is rather similar. Between them the *Sunday Post* and the *Sunday Mail* account for over seventy per cent of sales. The truly astonishing circulation of the *Post* – see Table Two – is inflated by significant sales in the north of England, but it is still remarkable that a newspaper should achieve such a high penetration of its market.

TABLE 1

Circulation of Morning Newspapers in Scotland

Aberdeen Press and Journal	111,512	
Daily Record	758,169	
Dundee Courier	129,522	
Glasgow Herald	118,545	
Scotsman	96,017	
Total Scottish produced	1,213,765	(67%)
Daily Mail	36,267	
Daily Mirror	25,440	
Daily Star	93,934	
Daily Telegraph	24,224	
Financial Times	8,600	
Guardian	13,649	
Scottish Daily Express	178,142	
Sun	210,000	
Times	15,106	
Total English produced	605,362	(33%)

Sources – Audit Bureau of Circulation for Scottish titles and the Express. Other sources for English titles. The figures relate for the most part to the period January to June 1985; *Today* did not appear till 1986.

Although the *Mail's* figures pall beside those of the *Post* they too are strikingly high. Of the English produced papers, the *News of the World* makes most impact in Scotland, while the *Scottish Sunday Express* and the *Sunday People* both clear the 100,000 mark. The combined circulation of the three broadsheet Sundays is just over 180,000, considerably higher than the figure achieved by English broadsheets during the week, though hardly surprising given the absence of any Scottish paper for that segment of the market.

The obvious question which arises is why in a highly centralised country like Britain, which is geographically compact and has a reasonably effective transport system, the Scots insist on buying Scottish produced newspapers.

TABLE 2

Circulation of Sunday Newspapers in Scotland

Sunday Mail	822,394
Sunday Post	1,503,854
Total Scottish produced	2,326,248 (75%)
Mail on Sunday	44,383
News of the World	242,096
Observer	63,000
Scottish Sunday Express	133,438
Sunday Mirror	46,040
Sunday People	140,905
Sunday Telegraph	27,840
Sunday Times	91,364
Total English produced	789,066 (25%)

Source –   As for Table One.

Historically it can be argued that this preference was a Hobson's choice, in that even with printing facilities in Manchester English papers had difficulty in distributing throughout Scotland[5]. The argument runs that if English papers had been able to crack the distribution problem at the beginning of the twentieth century the Scottish press of that time might have had difficulty in surviving. Alternatively it can be argued that once Scottish newspapers began to emphasise their Scottishness in various ways, and to carry much more information about what was happening in Scotland, a process which has accelerated since 1900, then it was unlikely that Fleet Street titles would ever make a large impact on the market. The Scottish newspaper buyer does seem to want his newspapers to talk about Scotland and it is very difficult for English titles to do that in a very satisfactory way. It should be noted however that the development of new technology makes it feasible for small proportions of a newspaper's output to be separately editionised at no great cost.It is therefore possible to envisage a situation where a paper could produce twenty different editions tailored to the needs of different parts of Britain. But although the production cost would be relatively low, the cost of employing the journalists to write the relevant copy would not be, and it is hard to see Fleet Street managements, even after they have made the breakthrough to low cost technology, considering the Scottish market ripe for attack in this fashion, although the English provinces might well be a different matter.

However it should be emphasised that there are very real fears in the Scottish newspaper industry about some current developments. Before the dispute between Rupert Murdoch's News International and the print unions broke out in early 1986, the Scottish newspaper industry was very apprehensive about the printing plant which had been constructed by that company at Kinning Park in Glasgow. It was felt that if the plant were to be used to print a northern edition of the *Sun*, which was the ostensible reason for its construction, then that paper would be in a better position to attack the market leader, the *Daily Record*. This argument does demonstrate a certain lack of confidence in the *Record*. It is hard to see how the *Sun*, even if it produced a Scottish edition, could get over the mismatch between its very obvious political ideology and the very different ideology which prevails in Scotland. Its current circulation in Scotland is impressive – and after the commissioning of the Kinning Park plant much less expensive to distribute for News International which used to air freight copies from London – but it must be close to the maximum possible in the Scottish market. If it were to increase that circulation the cause would lie as much in changes taking place in the make up of the *Daily Record* as in any other factor. But given the extraordinary and unnecessary dispute which blew up at the *Record* and *Mail* headquarters at the beginning of 1986, and the bizarre behaviour of the paper's proprietor, it would not now be surprising if either paper were to embark on an editorial course which damaged its own market position.

If it is the case that the newspapers Scots buy are for the most part Scottish produced it is most definitely not the case that they are Scottish owned. The *Record* and *Mail* are part of Mirror Group Newspapers which Reed International sold to Robert Maxwell's Leichenstein based company in 1984, while the *Glasgow Herald* and *Evening Times* are owned by Lonrho, the international trading company. The Aberdeen and Edinburgh morning and evening papers are owned by the International Thomson Organisation, originally a newspaper based company, but now with interests in a variety of other spheres including travel and North Sea oil, and based in Canada. Only D C Thomson of Dundee, who own the city's morning and evening papers, and the *Sunday Post*, are a Scottish based company, and one which has continued to take most of its income from newspapers and of course from its famous comics and magazines. All of these companies have interests of varying size in commercial broadcasting.

The Scottish pattern is not very different from what is to be found south of the border. Murdoch's News International, which can be regarded as either Australian or American, but certainly not British, owns the

Times, the *Sunday Times*, the *Sun*, and the *News of the World*. The Canadian entrepreneur Conrad Black recently acquired a controlling interest in the *Daily Telegraph* and *Sunday Telegraph*, Lonrho has the *Observer* and acquired a controlling stake in Eddy Shah's *Today* in mid-86, a few months ater the paper's launch, and Maxwell the three Mirror Group titles. The other Fleet Street papers are owned by newspaper companies or conglomerates and in one case, that of the *Guardian*, a trust.

While it is true to say that most newspaper readers could not apparently care less who owns the paper they buy, it has to be insisted that there are important public policy issues involved. It is not a coincidence that under Murdoch the *Times* and *Sunday Times* have become much less willing to challenge the established order of things, nor that under Maxwell the Mirror Group titles have become much more trivial than they once were. These two men are examples of dominant proprietors, who seek to use their papers to thrust their own views and tastes down their readers' throats or to trumpet their own supposedly important initiatives and contributions to the life of the nation. The current editor of the *Times*, a Murdoch appointee, apparently while in his previous post as executive editor, sent the foreign department a memorandum which began 'The foreign pages generally seem to be short of two distinct types of stories .... sex stories and computer stories'.[6] Murdoch is apparently very keen on both. During the miners' strike readers of the *Record* and the *Mirror* were treated to detailed accounts of Maxwell's pompous and hopeless attempt at mediation.

Faced with such obvious abuse of proprietorial power one has to say that the way in which conglomerates like the International Thompson Organisation and Lonrho run their newspapers is preferable by far, although it has to be said that there is evidence of some pressure being brought to bear on the editor of the *Observer* by its parient company over its coverage of events in Africa, a continent where Lonrho has substantial interests. The Thompson Organisation for its part is however credited with a policy of benevolent non interference, provided its newspapers are making money. Indeed that organisation lost a fortune on the *Times* before it sold the paper and its Sunday stablemate to News International. Furthermore, it can be argued that if companies like these two were not prepared to take over ailing newspapers and give them an infusion of capital then they might simply disappear.

It is difficult to dissent from the obvious pragmatism of such an argument, but it is necessary to put another case. Newspapers are fundamental to the operation of democracy. At their best they provide the citizen with a wide range of information about what is going on in his society, and they challenge those who hold power whether in government, industry, the trade unions or elsewhere. Macaulay and others said that the gallery in the House of Commons, to which newspaper reporters finally gained admittance in the latter part of the nineteenth century, had become a 'fourth estate of the realm'. This rather grand notion of the importance of the journalist may seem a little anachronistic in the days of bare breasts and bingo, but it is worth holding on to, for it provides us with a useful basis on which to judge the present pattern of control and ownership.[7] If journalism is to be the fourth estate, then it is vital that those who practice it have a commitment to truth and to scepticism. It is equally vital that the environment in which they work is one which promotes such a commitment. It therefore follows that the patterns of newspaper ownership to be encouraged should be those which lead towards these objectives. Newspaper companies ought to be just that, they ought to be restricted in the number of titles which they own, should be home based, and the market ought to be a competitive one to which access for new titles is not well nigh impossible to all except the wealthy. The kind of situation envisaged here would be one where newspapers would certainly have to survive in the market, and that means attracting both readers and advertising, but would be able to pursue their responsibilities to the public, in relative freedom.

Such a declaration will of course produce world weary sighs from those who would claim that idealism has no place in a discussion of the newspaper industry. Realism dictates a different order of things. To which there is a simple answer. Virtually all of our neighbours in Western Europe have recognised that there are serious problems for democracy if market forces are allowed to hold sway in the press, and have taken various measures to discourage concentration or foreign ownership, and to encourage a diversity of titles. None of these countries has found a magic solution, but they have tried and are continuing to try. In this country the governing party appears totally indifferent to what has been happening lately, while the opposition parties criticise individual developments but have yet to produce coherent proposals which would command wide assent. The hour is getting late.

The point was made in the preceding paragraph that even in a more intelligently organised newspaper market, papers would have to survive by attracting both sales and advertising revenue. It should be added that any perceptive media policy would have to take account of the distortions which the pattern of advertising can produce and to seek ways of remedying that distortion so that papers with a reasonably sized readership but sparse advertising would have some chance of survival. Newspapers have always taken advertising. What is striking about the contemporary situation is the way in which the pattern of advertising has accentuated the polarisation of the market into broadsheet quality on the one hand and popular tabloid on the other. Both are capable of attracting enough advertising to survive, but any paper which sought an intermediate editorial position would face considerable financial difficulties. In the current situation the quality newspaper is able to charge rates proportionately higher than the popular because it is able to offer the advertiser access to a readership which is not only wealthier than the popular one, but a substantial proportion of which is spending money on behalf of its employers in addition to its own personal spending. By way of example, Table Three shows the average net cost of advertising in the nationally circulating Scottish dailies.

TABLE 3

	Single Column Centimetre	Full Page	Circulation
Daily Record	£25.25	£6612	758,169
Glasgow Herald	£13.20	£5750	118,545
Scotsman	£11.00	£4800	96,017

Source: British Rate and Data January '86

One important consequence of this situation is that the broadsheet paper depends for over half of its revenue on advertising, which explains the growth of the special supplement whose editorial material is a thinly disguised public relations exercise in favour of the principal advertiser around whose activities the supplement is organised. The tabloid paper on the other hand depends for over half its revenue on sales, which explains why sales wars between tabloid titles are much more ferocious than those between broadsheet ones.

Overall it is doubtful if there is much scope for substantially expanding the total of Scottish advertising. The ill-starred *Scottish Daily News* came up against this hard fact as did the equally ill-starred *Sunday Standard*. Both newspapers attempted to fill definable readership gaps, and the *Standard* was a newspaper of considerable worth, but there just was not enough advertising around to provide the necessary financial bedrock. When the *Standard* closed in 1983 its circulation was 116,000, more than either the *Herald* or the *Scotsman*, but it did not have the equivalent of the pages of classified property and employment advertising these dailies carry.

The economic limitations imposed by the size of the Scottish market also have their effect on the content of papers. It is often asserted that Scotland is rather a parochial country and that is why foreign news is not given the prominence it is given in a paper like the *Guardian*. The *Scotsman* carries a regular page, the *Herald* a half page. It has to be said that foreign news is not cheap if a paper wishes to use its own correspondents. The *Scotsman* has a European correspondent and a regularly used freelance in America, while the *Herald* has no foreign correspondents, though it uses 'stringers' in various parts of the world. But there is no way in which a Scottish newspaper could easily find the resources to offer a comprehensive foreign coverage. Nor indeed can a Scottish paper employ a large number of specialist writers and commentators. This problem is in part overcome by using outsiders as columnists. Academics, for example, frequently write on matters which a Fleet Street paper would expect members of its staff to cover.

Where of course Scottish newspapers are at their strongest is in their reporting and commenting on the affairs of Scotland. Although the concern in this essay is with the political and economic spheres it should be emphasised that Scottishness is articulated in a number of other areas such as sport, crime and entertainment. These aspects tend to dominate in the tabloids. Indeed when one looks at the kind of package the *Record* offers its readers, it seems to have more in common with an evening's television viewing than the kind of package offered by the *Scotsman* or *Herald*. This is not just because a lot of the material is television related – background stories on the private lives of the stars, prospective developments in soap opera story lines and so on, little of it of specifically Scottish interest – but because so much of what is in the papers is of a light hearted entertaining nature. Hard news is often seriously under represented in the *Record*, a tendency which has been accentuated under Maxwell's ownership. Paradoxically the *Record's* sister paper, the *Sunday Mail*, although having the magazine like nature of all Sunday papers, does still offer a higher proportion of hard news and feature material than the *Record*, though within a very popular framework. When the *Sunday Standard* began publication in 1981 the *Mail* decided that it ought to go a little down market, but since that paper's sad demise it appears to have decided to move slightly up market again in a bid to partially fill what is a major gap in the Scottish scene.

Both the *Glasgow Herald* and the *Scotsman* seek to cover the affairs of Scotland as a whole, although it is possible to detect biases towards the affairs of their cities of origin, but these are not significant enough to detract from the claims which both papers make to being 'national' Scottish newspapers. One would not expect the other two Scottish mornings, the *Dundee Courier* and the *Aberdeen Press and Journal* to make similar claims. The *Courier* still gives over its front page to classified advertising, and while inside there is a mixture, sometimes a conglomeration, of local, Scottish, British and international news, the accent is firmly on what is happening on Tayside. The editorials often range widely, but the news coverage does not. Concessions to the fashions of contemporary journalism are few – the paper now carries a 'Wednesday Girl', sometimes on page three at that, but the photograph is a head and shoulders shot of a fully clothed young woman. The *Press and Journal* is a more modern looking paper and it has a similar mix of contents to the *Courier's*, though with a more systematic coverage of world and national affairs. Its style is livelier than the *Courier's*, but it lacks the sensationalism of the tabloids. Indeed the healthy circulation of both papers suggests that there is a public appetite for news presented in reasonably straightforward fashion about without the hectoring and bawling tones which more and more characterise the tabloid press.

The same point might be made about the evening papers which are produced in Scotland. They are all essentially local papers but they offer some coverage of national and international affairs. The evening paper market has suffered most grievously from the growing dominance of television, but the six evenings produced in Scotland do seem to have achieved a position of relative stability in recent years. Their circulations vary widely, as Table Four demonstrates, and there is naturally a huge gap between the Glasgow *Evening Times* and the Paisley and Greenock papers but the evenings appear to have weathered the competition for advertising revenue which commercial radio represented. Whether they could survive further erosion of that revenue by cable television, is another matter. But then it is far from clear that there is any great public appetite for cable and it could well prove a licence to bury one's money in the streets.

TABLE 4

Circulation of Scottish Evening Newspapers

Aberdeen Evening Express	81,739
Dundee Evening Telegraph	49,052
Edinburgh Evening News	124,624
Glasgow Evening News	181,608
Greenock Telegraph	21,853
Paisley Daily Express	13,220

Source: As for Table One

The ultimate concern of this essay is with political reporting in the Scottish press and in order to examine the coverage of the final stages of the campaign to save the Gartcosh steel plant from closure has been looked at in some detail.The Gartcosh campaign has been chosen because it raised important issues as well as economic and social ones.

The campaign to save Gartcosh reached its conclusion in January 1986. At the beginning of that month a small group of marchers led by shop stewards convenor, Tommy Brennan, set off on the journey to London in order to bring their case to a wider public and to make one last appeal to the Government for a reprieve. They did not succeed, and at the end of January the workers at the plant, confronted with irrefutable evidence that it would soon close, voted to begin negotiating redundancy terms.

The three nationally circulating Scottish dailies gave extensive coverage to the march, although it is clear that at times the turbulence in Mrs Thatcher's cabinet over the Westland affair had the effect of relegating Gartcosh stories to less prominent places than they might otherwise have enjoyed. For example when the workers voted to accept redundancy that occupied the back page of the *Record*, while Leon Brittan's resignation occupied the front page. However, despite the Westland furore, the Scottish papers managed to find space both to report the march and to discuss its ramifications. The *Record* covered the start of the march and gave en route reports. It used a stop at Corby to run a large feature on how that town had tried to cope with the run down of its own steel industry, and it reported on the continuing fears for Ravenscraig which surfaced during the march.

As one would expect, photographs were an integral feature of the *Record's* coverage, as they were of all the papers' approach. Bleak photographs they were, for the marchers were few and the conditions none too pleasant. A photograph on the back page of the *Herald* on the 6th January for example conveyed a particularly embattled and lonely feeling. As part of its coverage the *Herald* gave considerable attention to the tensions within the Conservative Party: one constituency association, South Cunninghame, threatened to disband (although some nifty footwork by the party prevented that actually happening); two back bench MPs refused to support the government. The *Herald* commissioned its own System Three poll on attitudes to the closure among the Scottish electorate and used the results – 80% of those polled wanted the plant kept open and had little faith that Ravenscraig would survive if Gartcosh went – as the basis for an editorial on 17th January which pointed out that 64% of Conservative supporters wanted Gartcosh retained and had thus parted company with their leaders on the issue. The editorial went on to argue that the "prospect of another Conservative government, with an ever diminishing base in Scotland seems highly likely to prompt a renewal of interest in constitutional change". A week earlier on the 11th January the *Herald* had urged Malcolm Rifkind, the new Secretary of State, to study the Scottish select committee's report on Gartcosh with more sympathy than George Younger had shown, but it was soon clear that was not going to happen.

What is interesting about the *Herald's* commissioning and use of the System Three poll is the way in which it focussed on the fortunes of the Conservative Party in Scotland. The *Herald* is no longer a Tory paper – it is not always clear which party it now supports although it leans to the centre – but clearly there is a residual concern with the Tory Party's position, and below the surface one suspects there is a wish that it was still the party of MacMillan and Heath to which support could more easily be offered.

The *Scotsman* also addressed the position of the Tory Party, in an editorial a week after the *Herald's* on that subject appeared. After listing all the issues which have been causing the party trouble in Scotland it focussed on Gartcosh and argued that as far as Ravenscraig is concerned "nobody is deceived by British Steel's assurances, except the Government which is committed to a three year reprieve and nothing more." The editorial went on to argue that support for devolution is greater among Tories than the party likes to admit and that "thoughtful Tories" who do not like the Labour Party now have other alternative parties to defect to, the Alliance, and the SNP. Again, the constitutional issue was raised. The *Scotsman* has of course been committed to devolution for a very long time. A week earlier the *Scotsman* too had suggested that Malcolm Rifkind should look again at the situation or at least come clean on his position.

> "Mr Brennan and his marchers have asked him if he thinks there is a future for steel in Scotland. He should have the courage to reply, either by telling them what kind of future it has or by explaining how he is planning to ensure that the economy can endure a future without it."

When the final moment came – the vote by the workers to accept redundancy – all three papers put the emphasis not on the constitutional implications but on the emotion of the moment and the fears for Ravenscraig. "Gartcosh battle ends with tears" was the *Scotsman's* headline on 25th January over its story on an inside page, inset in which was a head and shoulders photograph of Tommy Brennan in tears. "Steelmen rally forces after Gartcosh defeat" was the headline over the *Herald's* front page report which carried a much larger photograph of Mr Brennan. The fears for Ravenscraig were again highlighted. The *Record's* back page story had the heading "Gartcosh: it's the end – NOW THE BATTLE BEGINS" and it too emphasised the Ravenscraig situation. All three reports quoted Dr Jeremy Bray's fears for the future of the Motherwell plant, while both the *Record* and the *Herald* gave space to the views of Ian Lawson who left the Tory Party over the Gartcosh issue and was now claiming that the Tories would suffer electorally for what had been done.

The *Record* used photographs extensively – a large picture of Tommy Brennan over the quote "We won't give up the fight for Ravenscraig", a picture of a father and son who lost their jobs over the caption "ON THE SCRAPHEAP" and a boxed head and shoulders shot of another worker who is quoted as saying "Any Scots who vote for the Tories now must be off their heads". As one would expect it was the *Record*, which supports the Labour Party, and like all tabloids has long since given up pretending that there should be a distinction between report and comment, which slanted its material in the most anti-government fashion. It also focussed on the human aspect of the closure. Three redundant workers were quoted and pictured in its report and on an inside page over the heading "A Family in tatters" the human aspect was again emphasised as the effects on one family were examined. The *Herald* took a similar approach in an inside page story headed "Bitter-sweet blow ends uncertainty". The piece appeared to argue that the steelmen felt relief that the battle was over and took consolation from the fact that the fight for the steel industry was continuing. It was a strange piece, for alongside the accounts of the effect on three families of the closure, there was the statement "Management and workers, shoulder-to-shoulder, relived the good and the bad times yesterday afternoon at the Gartcosh Works Social Club". There was almost an air of nostalgia pervading the report, contrasting with the bitterness of the *Record's* coverage.

The most interesting coverage of the Gartcosh closure was, perhaps surprisingly, in the *Sunday Post*. In the first place it devoted far more space to the issue than did its rival the *Sunday Mail*. The latter usually mentioned the campaign each week and on 19th January carried an editorial which argued strongly that the fight for Ravenscraig must go on until there was a binding commitment from all political parties that its future is secure. However for most of the time the *Mail* concentrated on other stories, including its own successful campaign to persuade petrol companies to stop charging higher prices in Scotland than they do elsewhere. Of course since the *Record* and *Mail* are sister papers with a shared political stance it would be a reasonable editorial assumption that many of the *Mail's* readers had already heard all that they needed to hear about Gartcosh.

The *Post* managed to work in some reference to Gartcosh in all of its January editions. The coverage culminated in an astonishing front page on the 19th. Headed "THE CASUALTY LIST", it gave the names of the seven hundred workers who had lost their jobs with the closure and explained that such casualty lists had not been published by newspapers since the First World War.

> "It may serve to remind everyone involved that the unemployed are not numbers. Not statistics. Not percentages. Not seasonally adjusted. Not underlying trends. Not the jargon of Whitehall or Westminster. They are people – and here are their names:-"

The *Post's* middle page comment article the same week was also devoted to the Gartcosh issue. It argued that the works had no more right to survive than "a worked out pit or a bankrupt business" but insisted that something must be done about the growing number of unemployed. Of course the government had introduced various measures which the *Post* approved of, of course high unemployment is here to stay "but something must be done quickly to reduce the dole queue if only as an act of faith in the future. Especially for our young people". The editorial asserted that "This is not to argue for either nationalism or the spendthrift excesses of socialism" and credited the government with curing inflation, but nonetheless declared "The cure must be seen to go hand in hand with compassion. The treatment of casualties doesn't stop with the surgery!". The following week the same centre page space was handed over to Councillor Lawrence McGarry, the Chairman of Strathclyde Region's Economic and Industrial Development Committee, who set out the consequences the closure of Ravenscraig would have for the Scottish economy, and argued that the battle to prevent closure must succeed.

The *Post's* coverage illustrates very clearly the ideological tensions which Thatcherism has produced in Scotland. Here is a paper, which is essentially conservative, confronted with a radical Tory government which has waged war on many of the paper's favourite targets, but in the process has turned parts of Scotland into industrial wastelands, as many of the *Post's* own readers would be able to testify. Thatcherism does not seem to be a viable ideology in the Scottish context, for north of the border there are very few of the apparent successes of that approach of the kind which can be pointed to in southern England. When an MP of the St Andrews monetarist school like Michael Forsyth attempted to articulate the case for closure of

Gartcosh, he was well enough reported in Scottish newspapers but in the context of the criticism which had descended on his head. It is not sympathy with Mr Forsyth's ideological fervour that does make one wonder if there are not dangers in the relative unanimity of the Scottish press when confronted with the Gartcosh closure. There is a case to be made that the Scottish steel industry in the long term cannot be sustained without substantial public support and that such support can only be at the expense of other kinds of investment. The problem with Thatcherism is that it has not sought to present the choice in these terms, indeed it is clear that the kind of massive public sector investment in advanced technology, which has characterised other economies, is regarded as ideologically unacceptable by the present government. What this means is that the Scots are forced back on defensive arguments about saving Gartcosh or Ravenscraig or Prestwick or Govan Shipbuilders, and that can have the effect of inhibiting discussion of alternative industrial strategies, which might offer a more secure long term future. In the coverage which has been examined here there is certainly evidence of such thinking but mainly in the form of sub-textual, hints rather than fully articulated proposals. If the choice appears to be between Thatcherism and support for dying industries it is not easy to object to the latter without appearing to endorse the former.

The basic point to be made about the political stance of Scottish newspapers at the present time is that support for Thatcherism is non-existent in the nationally circulating titles. This means that the Scottish picture is very different from the Fleet Street one, for there Mrs Thatcher and right wing views are given substantial coverage and endorsement. This could be regarded as one more illustration of the deep seated differences between Scotland and England. Or it could be regarded as striking evidence of the way in which Mrs Thatcher has split Britain into two, a wealthy south and an impoverished north. Or of the hopelessly unrepresentative nature of the Fleet Street papers. It is certainly the case that in Scotland the distaste for Thatcherism to be found in the press *is* representative, for the opinion polls tell us that the vast majority of Scots would vote for parties other than the Tory Party.

The Scottish broadsheets are however reasonably even handed in their reporting of the affairs of all the political parties operating in Scotland. They may both incline to a centrist position editorially, but that does not mean that the affairs of the non-Alliance parties are unreported. Nuances can be detected in the writing of the various journalists who comment on political affairs – the *Herald's* Political Editor, Geoffrey Parkhouse, for example seems more sympathetic to the Tories than his opposite number at the *Scotsman* – but if the Fleet Street broadsheets all followed the example of their Scottish counterparts the Left might not complain so much about the way in which its affairs are reported.

As far as the tabloids are concerned, the *Post* with its magazine style of content and its relatively limited overt interest in politics, is something of a special case. The *Record* and *Mail*, although they do not engage in gutter journalism fail to be even handed in their political reporting. The fact that the Fleet Street tabloids are tarred with the same brush does not make the offence any less intolerable. It is perfectly possible to produce reasonably fair popular political journalism, though the tabloids behave as if it were not. There is not much complaint about this situation in Scotland, since the *Record* and *Mail* support the Labour Party which remains the largest party north of the border. So left wing politicians reserve their ire for the *Sun*. But this really is hypocrisy. It is in the interests of democracy that all newspapers separate reporting and commenting. Alas it is not going to happen. Unless of course the Press Council suddenly acquires teeth and uses them. Or unless some of our journalists and proprietors decide to become reformed characters.

Scottish newspapers then do report the affairs of their home patch and in times of crisis tend to rally round in defence of what they perceive to be threats to the national well being. In that sense they can be said to be articulating a national identity, and the opinion poll evidence cited earlier certainly suggests that as far as Gartcosh is concerned they were totally in tune with their readers' views. The difficulties of self criticism in the present climate have been alluded to, but it would be a worrying development if the need to defend beleaguered parts of the Scottish economy prevented our papers from exploring more openly than they have felt able to do of late the options which will confront the Scottish economy, with or without Thatcherism, when the oil starts to run out and adjustments have to be made to that reality. Thatcherism has produced a fair degree of unity in our national newspapers, but so far that unity is sustained by distaste for what is happening rather than by an alternative vision of where the country should go. It would be a brave individual who prophesied the result of the next British General Election, but if the Conservatives are returned for a third time with their faces firmly set against devolution and reflation, then our papers are going to have to make some hard choices as to where they stand on the constitutional future of Scotland.

David Hutchison, Senior Lecturer in Communication Studies, Glasgow College of Technology.

References

1. For a thorough discussion see J Curran et al *Mass Communciation and Society*, Arnold, London, 1977.

2. *Op.cit.*

3. Glasgow University Media Group *Bad News* RKP 1976 *More Bad News* RKP 1980 and subsequent publications.

4. See Martin Collins, 'Perceptions of Bias in Television News' in *BBC Broadcasting Research Findings* no.10, BBC Data, London 1985, a study which contrasts attitudes of respondents to television and the press.

5. See Myra Macdonald 'The Press in Scotland' in ed. D Hutchison, *Headlines...the Media in Scotland*, Polygon, Edinburgh, 1978.

6. Martin Huckerby 'Why I could not board the bus to Wapping!' *UK Press Gazette* 3.2.86.

7. For a discussion of the evolution of the concept see George Boyce 'The Fourth Estate: the reappraisal of a Concept' in ed. Boyce et al *Newspaper History: from the Seventeenth Century to the Present Day*, Constable, London, 1978.

TELEVISION IN SCOTLAND: A fair day's programming for a fair day's pay?

Peter Meech

Peacock has pronounced, ministers and Whitehall mandarins are meditating, and in due course the Government will decide which of the committee's recommendations to implement. But whatever course of action it chooses to take, including the improbable option of "business as usual", television in this country is likely to alter radically in the near future as a result of technological change. The new delivery systems, broad-band cable and satellite, though not widely known here yet, are poised to extend their reach. Both present a challenge to one of the basic justifications for state regulation of the airwaves: the limited range of available frequencies. Over the years the options have increased, but at present the majority of us are still restricted to four channels. However, soon anyone with a dish aerial, of modest dimensions and cost, will be capable of receiving unscrambled television signals from whatever source first "uplinked" them to its transponder. At governmental level, the recent EEC Commission draft directive on future European television policy argues strongly in favour of maximum deregulation of transnational services, subject to such minimum controls as the quota on EEC programming. The sky, it seems, positively eggs on the newcomers to European television, the Murdochs, the Maxwells and the Berlusconis, to extend still further their already huge media empires. But these moguls will have to reckon with determined competition from our existing broadcasting institutions, above all the BBC and ITV, which from early 1987 aim to be "up there" too via Superchannel, providing continental Europe with round-the-clock, UK-produced television fare.

In this futuristic context the set of issues that this essay addresses could appear minor. A concern with regional television policy as it relates to Scotland is in danger of seeming somewhat parochial against the global backdrop of battling multimedia conglomerates and state broadcasting services. But getting the relationships right within the domestic system must be seen as an economic and cultural prerequisite for involvement on the international scene.

In a speech before Easter 1986, the late Stuart Young put forward his views on the EEC draft directive on "television without frontiers". With all the authority of Chairman of the BBC Board of Governors he declared that "the way to reinforce the broadcasting culture of a continent is to ensure that there is vigorous, responsible and diverse national broadcasting activity in every country". As an implicit warning of the threat of insipidity, irresponsibility and sameness of programming that could result from the commercial needs of appealing to a pan-European audience, the statement was timely and met with widespread support. Europe will indeed be better served in its broadcasting by a recognition and celebration of the distinctiveness of its several parts, rather than by appealing to a spurious cultural unity via safe, entertainment-led programming.

Stuart Young's ringing words address a broadcasting system that has yet to be, though Sky Channel (Murdoch) and Cable News Network (Turner) are, for example, by now established satellite channels in Europe. By contrast it is now (November 1986) exactly 50 years since the BBC began transmitting a regular high definition television service to the public. This half-century anniversary, together with a number of recent developments, make 1986 an appropriate year in which to consider Young's recipe for a healthy broadcasting culture against the realities of the current situation, in particular as far as Scottish television is concerned. But before stock-taking of this sort, the term itself requires comment.

"Scottish television" presents something of a problem. Is it programming made in Scotland exclusively for Scots, or, a variant of this, television produced here for United Kingdom audiences? Or, again, is it everything that viewers in Scotland can see when they switch their sets on, guided by the Radio Times and TV Times? For the purposes of this article, the first two definitions provide the focus within a framework set by the third.

Having said that, there remains the additional complication that an individual company arrogated the term as its name in 1960 and has significantly returned of late to using it at all times in its full, rather than abbreviated form. Scottish Television plc has been the holder of the ITV franchise for Central Scotland since commercial television came to Scotland. With a potential of over 3.5 million viewers, it has the largest audience of the three Scottish contractors. Grampian Television, based in Aberdeen, broadcasts to viewers in the North and as far south as Perth and Glenrothes, as well as parts of the East Lothian coastline. Of all ITV companies in the UK it serves the largest geographical area. The smallest and most vulnerable of the three franchise holders, Border Television, is distinctive in that it serves not only the Scottish Borders but also parts of Cumbria and Northumberland and the Isle of Man.

The franchises are a statutory entitlement to a local monopoly on commercial broadcasting in a specified area and are allocated and monitored by the Independent Broadcasting Authority (IBA). Every eight years they have to be readvertised and thereafter either renewed with the existing contractors or awarded to new companies. The next round of franchise reallocation is scheduled for 1988, but there are signs that the Home Office, the ministry with the main responsibility for domestic broadcasting services, may decide to extend the current term for at least two further years, safely beyond the next general election.

Together with the three ITV contractors, BBC Scotland makes up the "comfortable duopoly" (Peacock) that dominates television north of the Border. From its headquarters in Glasgow, it runs both television and radio (the latter at regional and local level) with the help of studios in Edinburgh, Dundee, Aberdeen and elsewhere. Formal control of the policy and content of programmes primarily intended for Scotland lies with the Broadcasting Council for Scotland, whose members are appointed by the BBC and whose Chair sits on the Board of Governors. Effective control, however, is exercised by the full-time management in consultation with the Council.

As yet the coming of broad-band cable has proved less successful than its more enthusiastic supporters in the industry and in government would have wished. Aberdeen Cable Services, the pioneer in Scotland, has made slow progress since it began its service in May 1985, exacerbated by the effects of the fall in oil prices on the local economy. Clyde Cablevision, the holders of the North Glasgow franchise, has also experienced an early short-fall in its customer targets, while Edinburgh's Cablevision (Scotland) has had to postpone its launch till late 1987 at the earliest. Overall, then, the recruitment of subscribers to the new cable services has to date been disappointingly modest, with the result that the overwhelming majority of Scottish viewers continue to receive their television directly from the conventional transmitters of the BBC and IBA.

How do we come to be offered what we are? What are the principal aspects of media politics and economics that determine programme making and scheduling?

For all their many differences of funding, structure and ethos, the BBC and ITV have certain things in common. In particular, both are wedded, as a consequence of their commitment to public service broadcasting, to the concept of an essentially uniform, UK-wide television service. This is to oversimplify the situation – it leaves out of account the opportunities for regional programming – but the general point still stands. The BBC and ITV both speak of the "network" with reference to their respective UK-wide service and of regional "opt outs", though the detailed arrangements differ between the two organisations.

In the case of ITV the strategic decisions affecting which peak viewing programes are made, by which company, and when they are to be screened are made by the Network Programme Committee. This body is composed of the chief executives of all the ITV companies, the editor of Independent Television News, senior IBA staff and the directors of programmes of the "Big Five" (Thames, London Weekend Television, Central, Yorkshire and Granada). With the exception of Yorkshire, which was added to this group in 1968, these companies, or, in the case of London and Birmingham, their predecessors have taken responsibility for determining the network schedule since the start of commercial television in the 1950s. Being first in the field and based in major centres of population, they negotiated themselves an arrangement which has guaranteed them regular preferential treatment as regards access for their own products to the nation's screens. In 1984-85, for example, the five "majors" made 46.5% of networked or part-networked programmes and the ten regional companies 8.5%.[1] (The remaining 45% comprises ITN bulletins, British feature films, EEC and overseas quota material etc.) In other words, the majors made nearly 85% of home-produced networked programming, or 5 out of every 6 hours.

In justifying the continuance of this system, apologists point out that the Big Five's substantial investment in staff, studios and equipment requires to be properly used if they are to remain economically viable. Also, large-scale projects entailing massive budgets (such as Granada's "Jewel in the Crown") need advance guarantees of network transmission – and hence intercompany sales – before they can go into production. And finally, publicity and promotional work (for example, the "TV Times" and advertisements in the national press) are facilitated by a more or less standardised provision.

The Broadcasting Acts of 1954 and 1981 specify that a proportion of programmes are produced for local consumption by each of the ITV regional companies. As administered by the IBA, this requirement obliges Scottish Television to screen a minimum of 9 hours, Grampian 5.75 hours and Border 4 hours every week. The IBA's responsibilities extend also to stipulating the inclusion of educational/factual programmes at peak viewing times and imposing a maximum quota on foreign programming. Such regulatory controls – and there are others besides – help to underpin our system of public service broadcasting, thereby guaranteeing that even in commercial television a concern for maximum audience ratings is not the sole determinant of output. Irksome this may be for some ITV schedulers, paternalistic for some libertarians. Yet there is a real risk that the wholesale deregulation and exposure of broadcasting to market forces alone could lead, for example, to increased reliance on cheap, but popular imported continuous serials and action-adventure series, thereby reducing opportunities for programming other than light entertainment and for the expression of dissenting views.

"Opting out" of the network allows regional companies to go their own way, substituting their individual choice of locally produced programmes (and other material) for that selected by the network. The practice has its obvious attractions for the regions, allowing them as it does the freedom to shape their offerings to the perceived needs and interests of the communities they serve. But the current system ensures that this happens less frequently than it otherwise might. Opting out of the network for reasons that are felt to be perfectly legitimate to a regional company but not to the network planners runs the risk of possible discrimination against the offending company's future products. In this way regional companies are constrained in the programming policy by the Big Five.

The structure of ITV, a federation of small to large companies, geographically dispersed and commercially independent, contrasts with the huge, monolithic BBC. Nevertheless, the tension that exists between the needs of the parts and of the whole in the ITV system has similarities with the situation at the BBC.

Since its earliest days the BBC has advanced the claim to being a national institution, centred on London, it is true, but providing a service for the UK as a whole. However, there have long been reservations about the implicit assumption underlying the notion of a national culture. The same is true of a perceived metropolitan bias deriving from largely centralised policy making and programme production. The issue surfaced again of late in connection with the BBC's restructuring of its English regions and, in an impassioned way, at the industry's own Edinburgh International Television Festival in August. But what exactly is the relationship between the Corporation's London-based and regional production and how, specifically, does Scotland fare?

Altogether the BBC produced 11,437 hours of television in 1984-85, not counting feature films, Open University and bought in programmes.[2] 6,008 hours (or 52.5%) were made in London and the remainder by the English regions, by Scotland, Wales and Northern Ireland. In terms of total number of hours of programmes transmitted BBC Scotland is well ahead of most production centres outside London. With 757 hours of output in 1984-85 it was exceeded by only Manchester (867) and Wales (1,066, of which 567 hours were for S4C). The previous year Pebble Mill in Birmingham had beaten Scotland into fourth position in the regional league table. From a Scottish perspective this state of affairs appears on the face of it to be very satisfactory. But is it in reality?

The answer depends on your view of BBC Scotland's role in the UK-wide BBC system. If you think that it should chiefly be producing programmes for consumption north of the Border, then the 544 hours so allocated (out of the annual total of 757) may seem generous when compared with the local output in the South, currently running at about 200 hours per area. If, on the other hand, you take the view that Scotland has at least as much right as Birmingham, for instance, to be making programmes for the network, then these figures tell a sorrier tale. For whereas Manchester produced 668 hours for UK-wide screening in 1984-85, Pebble Mill 541 and Bristol 310, Scotland's contribution amounted to 213 hours. Or, to put it another way, the proportion of networked programmes in relation to total output was 61% for Bristol, 73% for Pebble Mill and 77% for Manchester. By contrast, the figure for BBC Scotland was a mere 28%. (The comparable figures for 1975-76 were: Bristol 53%, Pebble Mill 70%, Manchester 70%, Scotland 26%.)

The explanation for this seeming discrimination is that the five English regions have never been expected to produce very much more than a restricted amount and range of local interest programming, typically a 30 minute news magazine every weekday and little besides. This modest commitment has thus allowed Birmingham, Manchester and Bristol in particular to concentrate on developing specialist areas of programme making for the network. However, BBC Scotland, in common with BBC Wales and BBC Northern Ireland, is recognised as having a special responsibility to reflect the cultural identity of the "national region" to its people. To a greater extent than Wales and Northern Ireland, this involves BBC Scotland in an attempt to do justice to the nation's distinctive institutions (educational, legal, church, sport etc), as well as providing a Gaelic language service, in little over 10 hours per week. This severe pressure on resources militates against production for the network in any way commensurate with Scotland's proportion of UK television licence holders (1 in 12, 1985 figures). However, BBC Scotland's own view is that simply to seek to boost the quantity of network output would be a mistake. Far better to build a reputation by producing high quality programmes and in this way attract extra commissions and resources. For the present it seems as if this cautious strategy has been at least partially vindicated, as will be seen later.

Perhaps the most significant consequence of the Annan Report on the Future of Broadcasting was the addition of a fourth, nationally networked television channel in 1982. Annan had recommended five years previously, among many other things, that there should be greater diversity of content and format on British television and that one likely solution lay in increasing the broadcasting opportunities for UK independent producers outwith the BBC and ITV. That recommendation was implemented from the start and continues, four years later, to determine much of the distinctive character of the channel through the 24% of programming acquired from the independent sector.

An ingenious financial arrangement effectively separates the activities of revenue raising from that of editorial decision-making. Channel 4 and its Welsh counterpart Sianel 4 Cymru (S4C) are largely funded by an IBA administered subsidy levied on the ITV companies, which in return sell the available advertising airtime in their franchise areas, in addition to, and often in special packages with, that on ITV 1. The two Fourth Channel companies are thereby assured an important degree of autonomy to commission and schedule their own programmes, without undue pressure to achieve high audience ratings for particular slots such as affects both ITV 1 and the BBC. Initially, viewing figures for the new channel were low and sales of airtime disappointing. Audience ratings have gone up, but more interestingly there is a growing recognition on the part of certain advertising agencies and their clients that Channel 4 audiences have demographic characteristics of interest to them, insofar as they tend to be young, up-market and discriminating.

The ITV companies still pay hefty subsidies (related to their profits) to Channel 4 and S4C – Scottish Television contributed over £9m to the former and £2m to the latter in 1985, with smaller, but still significant amounts from Grampian and Border. But these and other contractors' involvement with the Fourth Channel is not limited to the sale of advertising time and the subsidy. They are also major suppliers of its programmes. These programme sales naturally generate extra revenue as well as gaining very desirable screentime for less mainstream projects. Also, should any of these programmes prove especially popular, there is the bonus for ITV of having the right to repeat them on the other channel. During the year 1984-85 33.75% of Channel 4 transmisions were of ITV or ITN origin. Not unexpectedly, maybe, a similar though less startling[3] imbalance exists here too between Big Five programming (12.5 hours per week) and that of the ten regional companies (6.25 hours). This provides another cause of resentment for some of the latter, who argue that Channel 4 has become more and more metropolitan in outlook and inequitable in its commissioning of work from the regions. Last year, for instance, Grampian paid £554,000 in subsidy and earned nothing by way of programme sales, and even Scottish Television received only £291,000 in return for its £9.1m subscription. To demand an exact match between subsidy and sales[4] would clearly be unrealistic, especially within the space of a single financial year – Channel 4 needs the guarantee of financial security, yet specific programme ideas may simply not appeal to its commissioning editors. But a substantial and continuing discrepancy between the two is another matter. Allied to this is a sense of grievance concerning the obligatory payment to S4C for its Welsh language programming, which in the case of Scottish Television amounts to over 10 times more than it can find to spend on its own Gaelic programmes.

Discussion of the financing and programme policy of Channel 4 leads naturally to the area of independent production, one of the main justifications for its creation. In 1983-84, the Channel's first full financial year, independent productions accounted for 936 hours and 29.4% of C4's airtime.[5] By 1985-86, during which period the total airtime had grown considerably, the independents' hours (at 974) had increased rather more modestly, to represent a proportion that has declined to 24.9%. Over the same period there was an increase in real, though not proportional terms of ITV/ITN programming, but "acquired material" (feature films and foreign programming) leaped from 33.5% to 45.2%.

Disappointed with the opportunities presented by Channel 4, the independent producers, or "indies" as they are known, have for some time been lobbying for access to the other channels. In this they have had the support of the Peacock Committee, which, aiming among other things at reducing the costs of television (for which it holds the broadcasting unions, principally at ITV, responsible) has been anxious to further their activities. The Committee took the view that the work of independent producers, free of the restrictive practices associated with in-house production, should be increasingly incorporated in the BBC and ITV schedules. This could be expected to lead to a reduction in permanent staff, especially in London, and a consequent curb on the power of the unions, the ACTT in particular. (Such a proposal has obvious attractions for the present Government.)

Thus the Committee recommended that within a decade no less than 40% of BBC and ITV transmissions should come from the independents, although they themselves, through the Independent Programme Producers Association (IPPA) are currently campaigning for the lower, but still substantial figure of 25%. Even this degree of access, however, is regarded by the BBC and ITV as quite unrealistic and, indeed, counterproductive. David Elstein, independent poacher turned Thames Television gamekeeper, takes a position that is shared by other ITV executives:

> "Even the 25% quota for which some of the Independent Programme Producers Association members are currently campaigning means substituting independent production for nearly half of ITV's current in-house effort: a campaign with such an effect will only serve to alienate many of those people who would otherwise be sympathetic to the declared objective of stimulating greater efficiency and creativity in the industry".[6]

Over and above the issue of staff redundancies or increased internal unit costs which would affect both the BBC and ITV companies if such a quota were to be imposed, the latter have another argument: they are already obliged to subsidise Channel 4 (as noted above) to enable it to commission independent productions. Why, they ask, should they have to pay the indies a second time? Be that as it may, the advent of "daytime" broadcasting brings with it the need for additional programming. Clearly this presents the independent sector with an opportunity to demonstrate that it can not only make the kind of programmes that the BBC and ITV are looking for, but can do so at competitive prices.

In addition, the BBC indicated early in 1986 that one of its priorities for the figure will be to nearly double the number of programmes made by, or in collaboration with, UK independents, to a minimum of 150 hours per year by 1988. A budget of modest proportions has been earmarked for this purpose and the development has been cautiously welcomed by the independents as a step in the right direction, especially if editorial control is ceded. A less attractive alternative for them, because of reduced autonomy, is involvement on a freelance basis. (The BBC is currently employing increasing numbers of freelance directors and producers for specific projects.)

So much for the broad outlines of the organisation and financing of television in this country. But does the criticism of it that claims that it works to Scotland's disadvantage amount to any more than a form of nationalist paranoia? How could television in Scotland benefit from changes to the system? And what, if any, are in the offing?

In the first place, greater access to the networks would give Scottish programme-makers the professional satisfaction of a wider domestic audience, a more visible showcase for foreign sales and enhanced career prospects. As it is, one still encounters the claim that a patronising attitude prevails among some network programme controllers and other senior executives towards Scottish output, which accounts for a feeling that it is screened nationally more as a concession than as of right. Despite this, there is evidence of increased self-confidence among Scottish television programme-makers and management, who, resentful of the suggestion of second class status and asserting production values comparable to those obtaining elsewhere, are anticipating a greater UK impact than hitherto.

Enhanced programme sales (ITV) and increases to centrally determined budgets (BBC) would allow production centres in Scotland to grow, thereby providing extra employment and pulling in more of the creative and technical talent that is currently wasted or that has to travel either to the south or abroad to find work. This could either involve additional staffing at existing institutions – not a likely prospect – or it could mean contracting out work to, or more co-productions with, the Scottish independent sector. In either case it would also be of more general benefit to local economies – Grampian Television, for instance, estimates that it currently contributes approximately £8m per annum to the North East.

Over and above the benefits that a "new deal" might have on quantity of output, staff morale, employment prospects and local prosperity, it would create opportunities for a specifically cultural impact both at home and abroad. Structural changes, in other words, could be decisive in helping to promote a more authentic view on television of Scotland and "Scottishness". Back in 1977 Annan had observed that:

> "Something is wrong with the image of Scotland which television projects to the rest of the United Kingdom. The national culture is reflected too much by hackneyed symbols, and too little importance is given to the new opportunities and hopes, the shifts in pattern of industry and occupations, as well as the dour problems and grim realities of life in some parts of Scotland today".[7]

Part of the problem lay in the perceived need to make programmes that would appeal to television controllers based in England and to English audiences. This involved a heavy reliance on material that drew on a restricted set of representations of Scotland. Such "typically Scottish" programmes employed what John Caughie has called "the frozen discourses of Tartanry and Kailyard" to suggest "a petrified culture with a misty, mythic, and above all, static past". Representations of this[8] kind, repeated and recycled ad nauseam on UK television screens, simply reinforced the old cultural stereotypes that pre-dated the coming of the medium. Demands have often been made that this process be reversed, so that the realities of contemporary – and indeed, historical – Scottish life are more accurately reproduced in all its many-sided and contradictory forms. To date this has mainly applied to domestic television. With the advent of pan-European broadcasting there will be new, enlarged and disparate audiences to appeal to. The danger here is that the goal of international audience maximization could entail playing safe and relying on conventional themes and approaches, a return to a set of discourses that must be resisted in the interests on Scotland's television culture and image abroad.

In the meantime, there have been recent developments at both the institutional and programme level which hold out the hope of a more vital Scottish television industry, one that is better attuned to current realities affecting the nation and, at the same time, more adept at staking its legitimate claim to international attention.

Drama is flourishing, though such are the high production costs involved that no broadcasting organisation can any longer afford to make plays for screening in Scotland alone. The recruitment of Bill Bryden to Queen Margaret Drive to head the BBC's Drama department has had a predictable and marked impact. Coming from the National Theatre in London, Bryden is described by a colleague as " 'noisy' and very, very pro-Scottish". These qualities plus a formidable reputation as a man of the theatre have already been largely instrumental in securing for BBC Scotland overall responsibility for the "Play for Today" season. Of the 13 dramas in this revival of the Corporation's commitment to innovative single plays, no fewer than 7 are being made in Scotland. Across at Cowcaddens, Scottish Television has had its own success with single plays for the network, while its mini-series "Taggart" continues to earn not only critical acclaim but also excellent ratings at prime time throughout the UK. A fourth series is, as a result, currently in production.

Gus Macdonald is another Scot to have returned from England in recent months to a key broadcasting post. Of the new Director of Programmes at Scottish Television it has been said that he has a veritable sense of mission to increase the amount, raise the standards and broaden the scope of local interest programming. Certainly, he quickly attracted journalists of repute from outside to sharpen up local news coverage. Current affairs have also received a boost, as have the arts, beginning with a multi-faceted celebration of the 1986 Edinburgh Festival. All of this has been well publicised in the national press, for a high profile strategy is something that Macdonald believes his company should adopt both within Scotland and beyond. He himself has been prominent in campaigning for a fairer deal for regional ITV companies with the network and is confident of making headway in this. Within Scotland the influence of a revitalised Scottish Television now seems set to galvanise the whole industry to produce programmes that harness creative imagination to technical innovation, treat viewers consistently with respect, and give expression to the rich diversity of Scottish contemporary life.

Despite, or perhaps because of, their previous under-representation on Channel 4, Scottish producers have lately been breaking new ground on the channel. Grampian, for instance, in an enterprising co-production with the Norwegian Broadcasting Corporation made a series of 8 one-hour documentaries, entitled "Oil", on the industry world-wide, which was screened in Autumn 1986. And of several projects from the independent sector, "Down the Line" deserves mention on two counts. It is the first regular current affairs programme from a distinctively Scottish perspective and a collaborative venture, involving not only the Skyline and Scotquest production companies, but up to ten other local independents. The studio shoot takes place at Picardy Pictures, Scotland's first hire-only facilities house, open in Edinburgh in early 1986, which also has responsibility for editing and post-production. Including such other companies as In-Video, SSK and Scope, the facilities industry has grown over the past three years to the point where Scotland could be said to be self-sufficient for present needs.

It can be argued that a general resurgence of nationalism and demands for a devolved assembly find their broadcasting inflection in the pressures that are building up for a better deal for Scottish television (in the first two senses discussed above). If so, there is obvious political capital to be gained here for a government which, while rejecting devolution proper, might well favour a less centralised BBC and an ITV system less monopolised by five large companies. It is not necessary here to rehearse the likely motives behind the setting up of the Peacock Committee, the appointment of both the present Chairman of the Board of Governors and of his predecessor and the formation of the Conservative Central Office media monitoring unit, to make the point that the government wishes to bring the Corporation to heel. Some structural changes, it is true, have been introduced in recent months by the BBC. But the initiative involving the new English regions, which, with their modest budgets and no right of opt out, are predicted in the short term to produce only 0.5% of additional network programming, seems more like a sop than a shake-up. Nevertheless, fingers are crossed at BBC Scotland that this move may in the longer term lead to a commitment on the part of the Corporation to increased regional autonomy and opportunities for regional production. In its turn, the IBA has publicly acknowledged the strains in the system it regulates, but has yet to show any apparent willingness to promote effective improvements. Only from Channel 4 is there the hint that Scotland is due for a fairer deal.

Meanwhile, pressure is growing for an overhaul to satisfy the legitimate regional aspirations of today and in the imminent future of transnational broadcasting. If the BBC, the IBA and the ITV companies refuse to participate constructively in this process, they might yet find that change of a far more radical and less welcome variety is pressed on them.

Peter Meech, Department of Film and Media Studies, University of Stirling.

References

1. *Television and Radio 1986*, IBA, London, 1986, p.187.

2. *BBC Annual Report and Handbook*, BBC, London, 1985, p.147.

3. *loc.cit.*

4. S Taylor, *Broadcast*, 15 August 1986, p.5.

5. S Griffin & B Comely, *Broadcast*, 27 June 1986, p.21.

6. D Elstein, *Guardian*, 15 September 1986, p.7.

7. *Report of the Committee on the Future of Broadcasting*, HMSO, London, 1977, p.409.

8. J Caughie, 'Scottish Television: What Would It Look Like?', in C McArthur, *Scotch Reels. Scotland in cinema and Television*, BFI, London, 1982, p.116.

RADIO SCOTLAND: A SHORT SURVEY

Catherine Lockerbie

INTRODUCTION: The Position of Scotland in the Media

It has been said that Scotland was "the last nation in Europe, if not the world, to acquire its own radio service".[1] This immediately begs an important question. Within most broadcasting media infrastructures, Scotland is very far from having the status of a nation. BBC Scotland represents a particular *region* within the BBC; though the actual term used is "national region" which sounds suspiciously like a contradiction in terms. ITV works on a federal system: Scottish Television competes on ostensibly equal terms with Yorkshire, Granada and the rest, an arrangement which Gus MacDonald, Director of Programmes for Scottish Television, feels is fair in essence but possibly disadvantageous to Scotland in pracdtice. The independent radio network is not in the business of broadcasting to nations: their various stations in Scotland, including Radio Clyde, Radio Forth and Radio Tay officially have a forty-mile limit on their transmitters (although Clyde can be and is picked up on the other side of the open space of the Atlantic).

There is only one broadcasting institution which purports to speak to and for the whole country, seven days a week, at least 12 hours a day; and that is Radio Scotland, the self-designated "national network".

BBC and ILR

Radio Scotland then claims to see Scotland as an entity, cultural, geographical and perhaps even political, and sets itself up to provide a broadcasting service for that entity. Given the traditions and practices of the BBC, two problems instantly spring to mind. The first is that here is an institution claiming autonomy in name but which is in reality entirely linked to and subject to BBC Headquarters in London. The second is that the BBC's radio strategy, at least for the past forty or so years, has been that of audience streaming, broadcasting to communities of interest rather than wide geographical communities (local radio, a recent development, targets its catchment areas much more precisely). Radios One, Two, Three and Four know pretty well *who* they are catering for. Who is Radio Scotland to cater for? And is "the Scots" a sufficiently strong answer?

It is in this area that Independent Local Radio (ILR) has a much easier task. This chapter will concentrate on the development of Radio Scotland; but it should be remembered that the biggest radio success story of the past decade has been in the independent sector. Radio Clyde's popularity with public and therefore advertisers has been such that they have been able to finance for themselves the only custom-built radio studios to be constructed in Britain in the last 50 years, at a cost of £2½ million. Clyde will be referred to at various points below: Radio Scotland was started very much in its wake, and it was considered by many that the BBC was trying to "beat the commercial stations at their own game".[2] Radio Clyde, however, benefits from its luxurious, well-equipped studios, while Radio Scotland, particularly in Edinburgh, struggles with cramped conditions and poor equipment. Radio Clyde also has a far more homogeneous catchment area, which it has certainly exploited with aggressively effective imagination. It has the concomitant advantage of small size (total staff of about 70) and flexibility, emphasised in its daily working life. Free from the institutional dead weight of the BBC, it has made its own structures at least apparently more democratic. It pays high wages – on a par with those on offer in television, always a more lucrative field than radio. It has also chosen to dispense with unions – there is little specialisation, producers being their own presenters, their own technicians.

The report of the Peacock Committee and the government's perceived view that advertising might be carried on the BBC (with Radio One and Two, which Peacock suggests selling off, being in the front line for any such development) are however causing some alarm to Independent Local Radio Stations. Despite its success, Radio Clyde, in common with its smaller colleagues, is suffering from a lack of growth in advertising revenue. It does look though in the wake of the Peacock Report and the mixed reception given to it, as if the present status quo will be maintained for quite some time yet.

The Importance of Radio Scotland

Radio Scotland has had both the distinction and the burden of purporting to represent its country. Before its inauguration, in late 1978, hopes inevitably ran high, but were speedily dashed as soon as it became clear just what the new station was going to be like. I intend here to look at some aspects of the evolution of the "national network" of a non- nation: a network whose early debacle coincided with the debacle of the devolution referendum to the point where irate letter-writers to *The Scotsman* were calling it "Teddy Taylor's secret weapon", and where the editor of the Scottish Review was moved to remark: "Wide dissatisfaction with the poor quality of much of its output(...) leaves little doubt that the sudden revelation of how sheerly awful Scottish mindlessness could be was another weapon on behalf of the "No" side."[3]

SOME BACKGROUND: The Situation Before 1978

The centralisation of programmes, especially serious programmes and news, in London – which can be dated from 1939 with the creation of the Third Programme[4] – had obviously long been a matter of some grievance in Scotland. A Saltire Society report of 1946 bemoaned the general lack of and poor quality of Scottish features – and added, in a fit of the self-doubting paranoia which may have returned to haunt the early listeners to Radio Scotland: "There is a question whether there is not perhaps missing from the typical Scottish make-up the adaptability and easy manner before a microphone which seems to come naturally to English people."[5]

Over ten years later, similar complaints were being made in the Saltire Review: complaints about the trivialisation of Scottish material, about the assumption that serious discussion or news coverage is somehow not Scottish, about the "horrifying familiarity of almost every programme."[6] An SNP report of the same year highlighted the same issues, but considered it part of a plot to maintain the Tory and Labour parties in power. And of course, all of this was happening at a time when radio was still by far the most widely available broadcast medium.

Alternatives did emerge to the BBC monopoly, but they were precarious or illegal. Radio Free Scotland impressed listeners and journalists by its audacity in transmitting nationalist material through the early sixties; while the first Radio Scotland, in the mid-sixties, was a pirate station, a boat anchored offshore, lively but short-lived.

During the 1970s, there was a crescendo of calls for local radio franchises which the government was offering. At one stage *The Scotsman* reported that there could be "200 applicants for local franchises in Scotland".[7] In the event there was only one – Edinburgh – and it failed due to lack of support.

Scotland was left with a radio service emanating from London, with certain Scottish appendages – notably, education, religion and drama. It was far from ideal. As Stewart Conn, now Senior Producer of drama for Radio Scotland has explained[8], under the opt-out system he and his colleagues *either* had to produce for the whole of Britain and therefore with

English sensibilities in mind (no difficult dialects, for example); *or* produce plays they felt specifically suited to Scotland and block out the Radio 4 coverage while broadcasting them (there being only one wavelength available.)

It was against this background of dissatisfaction, the feeling of being stuck in a rut of second-best, and against the prevailing mood of pre-devolution optimism and national aspiration, that the new Radio Scotland was conceived.

THE BIRTH OF RADIO SCOTLAND

Instantly, there were those who felt that this particular conception should never have been allowed to come to term. There had been much debate about what form the new Radio Scotland would take. Would it be like Radio 2? like Radio 4? a "mother ship" for local stations, as one member of the broadcasting council suggested? The form it did take was something of a Frankenstein's monster: hulking, ham-fisted, well-meaning in intent but, in the view of many, teetering between destructive and laughable in practice.

The man appointed as Head was John Pickles, who had been working as station manager at BBC Oxford. He quickly made clear what he envisaged. In a preview entitled "Hail Ceilidhdonia", he was reported as declaring: "We have got to come down from our pedestal".[9] He announced schedules including radio bingo, one-arm bandit quizzes and The Tartan Terror Show (a frighteningly awful concoction, still going strong). The formats for the main daily programmes were as follows: music and consumer questions; music and entertainment; music and chat; music and current affairs(!); and music and chat again.

It was clearly a desperate attempt to court popularity, a desperate attempt to be the proverbial and impossible all things to all men. Within a few days, even hours, it was the listeners who were desperate. Below is presented a small array of some of the comments greeting the new programmes and policies. It should be stressed that there has been no selective editing here, no painstaking search for the negative: complaints, sometimes of astonishing virulence, flooded in. The Scottish press had never before acted as such a forum for views on radio; and it was bitterly disappointing that the awakened interest should be so wholly damning. Defenders of Radio Scotland, most notably of course John Pickles, responsible for setting the tone as well as the content of the proceedings, were eager to point out the over-hastiness of the reaction (some of the criticisms which follow were issued *before* the station came on air). Undoubtedly, there was an element of "how-can-the-BBC-descend-to-this" snobbishness in some of the criticism; there was also a real sense of anger at a squandered opportunity. The foundations of the criticism rested on the perceived vulgarity and triviality of the programmes, and particularly on the confused and parochial news presentation – this "new-look" format had already been given a trial run before the station proper started up in the last week of November 1978.

A Few Comments

– "If the BBC Scottish Symphony Orchestra were even making a token appearance in Radio Scotland's opening concert, I would be more confident that it was the dawn and not the twilight of responsible radio in Scotland."[10]

– "Some august member of the BBC hierarchy should tell Mr Pickles that the corporation is not in business to play bingo. In fact, this tawdry innovation merely illustrates the disgusting way in which the BBC is whoring around like an aging prostitute trying to seduce clients from the commercial broadcasters by offering them even more vulgar delights."[11]

– "As well as being too inward-looking, Radio Scotland is much too anodyne... The central question of whether it will become a national service – embracing the world – or a local anaesthetic – soothing its listeners – remains to be answered."[12]

– "This Radio Kailyard or Back Green Calling is what Hugh MacDiarmid at his deadliest called "an ugly bird without wings", a speckled hen whose horizon goes no further than the end of the little minister's glebe(...). There is an ugly German word, "Verduemming". It means: the making stupid of someone. Is the new sound of Queen Margaret Drive the noise of a Verduemmingsmachine in first gear?"[13]

– "...our hamming, shamming Radio Scotland.(...)
Don't let his learning put you off,
He's just oor ain wee tartan Prof."
(Proposed jingle for Radio Scotland.)[14]

Maurice Lindsay's comment about the "sudden revelation of how sheerly awful Scottish mindlessness could be", quoted in the Introduction will also be recalled, as will the notion that the abysmal failure of the new schedules to live up to even the most modest expectations sapped Scottish confidence in Scottish ability and seriousness at a time – that of the devolution referendum – when that confidence might have been most needed.

The list of criticisms could extend and extend. Let the above-quoted suffice to give an idea of the feelings aroused. (One line of defence was to protest that it was only professional critics and intellectuals who felt this way – the "ordinary" or "average" listener like the new programmes perfectly well. It seems at best a poor and at worst a grossly patronising line of argument). The prevailing sentiment was then that of an opportunity woefully missed; and to add to the woe, the wavelength changes introduced to bring Radio Scotland onto medium wave, thereby banishing Radio 4 to long wave, met with wide dissatisfaction too. A cartoon in *The Scotsman* depicts a distraught wifie, a tear on her cheek, in front of the wireless, lamenting: "I've twiddled and twiddled, but it's nae use – I still get Radio Scotland".[15]

In fact, the difficulties over poor reception of Radio 4 on Light Wave forced some early changes which were generally welcomed. *World at One*, which for a time had been blocked out by a farming programme (good idea but very bad time) was restored to medium wave, and plays and concerts were scheduled for Monday and Thursday evenings. Any added cultural weight, Mr Pickles made clear, was not as a response to any criticism of programming policy, but an expedient measure to rectify an over-optimistic assessment of long wave reception throughout Scotland.

Despite these minor improvements, the critics continued to keep up the pressure. It was still felt that the mix of programming – admittedly, as stated above, a complex task given the size and diversity of the geographical community – had not yet even begun to get the balance right: not so much all things to all men, as "a crash course in audience alienation."[16]

In the midst of all this, an event occurred which, in retrospect, seems in keeping with the character of those times. The duty announcer in Glasgow, Robert Sproul-Cran, received an internal call saying that the Queen was dead. Deciding to check, he did not broadcast the message. John Pickles and his assistant Les Robinson, the perpetrators of the "joke", were relieved of their duties. It was less than a year since the birth of Radio Scotland.

A FRESH START

Clearly, a change of gear and mood was needed. (It is tempting to speculate what would have happened if the "Queen is dead" message *had* been broadcast by a less thorough or experienced announcer: might it have brought the London axe which was certainly poised over Radio Scotland at that time crashing down?) A new Head of Radio Scotland, Chris Irwin, was named in April 1980. In the early months of that year, Pat Ramsay, the controller of BBC Scotland, and Pat Walker, his assistant (as well as Chris Irwin, already in line for his new appointment) would have had at their disposal at least three pieces of documentary proof of the problems they faced. The first was an internal report, supposedly secret but widely leaked. The second was a survey done by a BBC audience research team from London. The third was the latest set of audience statistics.

a) The Internal Report

News of a highly critical report compiled by Bob Atkins, a senior producer with the World Service, appeared in September 1979. A notice appeared on Radio Scotland notice-boards stating that "there will be more talk and less blether and there will be a move away from wallpaper music." Pat Ramsay announced further changes, recognising that Radio Scotland had failed to attract large audiences or to generate "that enthusiasm which legitimises small audiences."[17]

b) The Survey

The results of this survey were summarised in The Scotsman in December 1979. While some caution might be thought necessary before attaching too much importance to the conclusions of a visiting team from London, unfamiliar with the daily context of Scottish listening – they did, for example get certain names and titles wrong – the survey nonetheless had some interesting points to make not only about specific programmes but also about wider questions of perception of national identity. The researchers stated, for instance that "an impression could be gained that these respondents showed an acute self-consciousness about their provincialism and it was as if Radio Scotland sometimes exposed that in a distressing way." Moreover – and particularly worrying for the aspirations of Radio Scotland: "While Scots clearly have a sense of national identity they do not – at least so far – seem to wish to identify this in terms of a radio station."[18] This, if at all true, was surely the attitude which the post-Pickles regime had to alter.

c) The Audience Figures

By late 1979 the BBC was spending over £2 million a year on Radio

Scotland (its starting budget had been £750,000). Yet, at the end of its first year, the station still had fewer listeners in Scotland than Radio 4, and less than when Scottish programmes were an adjunct of Radio4. Audience research figures presented by Pat Walker, Assistant Controller of BBC Scotland in December 1979 showed the average daily patronage, expressed as a percentage of the population, as follows:

Radio Scotland	4.6%
Radio 4	5.7%
Radio 1	18.8%
Radio 2	9.6%
Radio 3	Less than 1%
Radio Forth and Clyde	9.7%[19]

That last figure for the independent stations might be put into clearer perspective if it is remembered that the Forth and Clyde transmitters officially have a radius of only 40 miles. A quick cross-reference to Clyde's own figures for earlier that year, for the West of Scotland, show their assessment for their listening area as follows:

Radio Clyde	46.89%
Radio 4	5.38%
Radio Scotland	5.88%

It should be said that these figures are uncontested, as the BBC did not supply their own for that period; but the general pattern in Strathclyde has been consistently and overwhelmingly in Clyde's favour – up to nine times greater than Radio Scotland's audience.

d) The Response

The new bosses of Radio Scotland, once accused of being a "look-alike" Clyde but patently without the success, decided in response to these poor figures and the comments contained in the internal report and the audience survey, to adopt a policy which still holds good in 1986: to place far greater emphasis on news and current affairs. This was one of the areas which had attracted the greatest criticism when the station had started: the news presentation, with its one presenter, its dilution by music in "Rhythym 'n' News" were widely seen as one of the grossest failures of vision and responsibility of Radio Scotland, providing, in the words of Neal Ascherson, only "a frosted window on the world".[20]

In the re-vamped, tightened schedules now proposed for 1980, news and current affairs would form the backbone of programming, being broadcast for anything up to 6 hours a day at a time when the total output was being reduced to about 70 hours a week. (It started with 90, and Pickles had hoped to push it up to 120 as soon as possible).

The Radio 4 element was increased; radio bingo was dropped; and by the second anniversary of Radio Scotland in 1980, things were, at last, beginning to look up. In response to one of Bob Atkins' criticisms Good Morning Scotland, the main early day news programme now had two presenters instead of one, and was reaching 125,000 listeners at any one time (a respectable amount in radio terms). A good mixed range of features was being presented; "minority" programmes were being developed, notably those catering for specific musical tastes, such as "Take the Jazz Train" and "Travelling Folk".

As against this, the "Tartan Terror Show" was still alarmingly present; and the programme which drew perhaps the greatest acclaim for Radio Scotland, indeed upon which a large part of its new worthy reputation was based, had next to nothing to do with Radio Scotland and was even rejected by them. "Odyssey" was a quite excellent series of oral history, conceived and produced by the writer and broadcaster Billy Kay – a freelance, who sold to the station the idea for which they received such praise. When, however, a second series was proposed, no-one it seemed had the energy or initiative (or, they claimed, the money) to take up the offer. It was only through the intervention of Stewart Conn, senior producer of drama, that Billy Kay was attached incongruously to the drama department, there to produce his entirely documentary series. Thanks to Conn's vision and action, and Kay's tenacity, the project survived; the second series was broadcast to further acclaim; it was commissioned for television and turned into a popular book; and Radio Scotland reaped the critical reward of that for which they had been unwilling to make space.

THE PRESENT

"The Tartan Terror Show" with its frenetic garbling of pseudo-Scottish chat ("waggle yer wellies, Granny, och aye" etc.etc.) is still firmly in place in the Radio Scotland schedules, dismaying many who inadvertently switch it on and presumably pleasing many others. Billy Kay is still firmly in place as one of Radio Scotland's most respected external contributors: his personal but thorough assessment of "The Scots Tongue", over 6 weeks, was one of the documentary highlights of 1986.

The anomalous mix subsists; but there is no doubt that Radio Scotland has, in eight years, learned how to build on some of the talents available to it. In February 1983, Stan Taylor was appointed successor to Chris Irwin as Head of Radio Scotland. As a previous Head of news, Taylor has maintained and increased the importance of proper news reporting and analysis as the essential backbone of the station. "Focus", a current affairs investigative half-hour, has been reinstated Newsweek is an hour-long news review early on Saturday mornings. The depressing swathe of light music and chat in the afternoons has been broken up by – in this writer's opinion – the best discussion show on the wavelength, "Taking Issue With Colin Bell" the eponymous Bell, a political pundit, broadcaster and writer of considerable verve, has transformed the hour between two and three into an energetic and witty forum for matters of topical importance.

In other areas too, Radio Scotland has been edging forward out of the unhappy debacle of its birth. The BBC Scottish Symphony Orchestra, threatened with extinction, has not only been saved – it, or at least, three of its members, was the moving force behind Classical Aid, one of the many fund-raising efforts inspired by Bob Geldof's Band Aid. This ambitious event, staged at the Scottish Exhibition Centre in Glasgow, carried off two major prizes at the New York International Radio Festival.

Another recipient of awards has been the drama department. This small creative nucleus existed well before Radio Scotland; but with the increased posibilities now available to it in terms of programming (although not in terms of studio space or equipment), it has produced consistently thoughtful and occasionally excellent work. It is here perhaps that the advantages of the small scale of Radio Scotland operations can be seen to their best advantage. Radio 4, which broadcasts at least one play a day, receives its material through the medium of a script unit, whose purpose is solely to read and to pass scripts on to directors or to discard them. Radio Scotland can avoid this distancing, conveyor-belt approach. The staff of three or four read scripts personally, discuss them in detail with the writer, are in a position to offer commissions, and produce nothing to which they are not fully committed. For the writer, this collaborative process is highly helpful. Stewart Conn believes that the remit of his department is not only to produce good material for broadcast, but to support the infrastructure of Scottish creative life by their presence; and without exaggerating the *scale* of what they are able to do, he is justified in this belief.

There are other elements contributing to the station's gradual success. The education department which also, like drama, existed before Radio Scotland, and which also, like the BBC SSO, was threatened with the axe, continues to produce high quality material for Scottish schoolchildren (giving additional employment to many Scottish-based writers and actors in the process). Documentary series have also been produced within that department and broadcast on "adult" Radio Scotland. The Talks and Features Department is also coming into its own. Programmes on the veterans of the Spanish Civil War, the hunger marchers of the 30s, the above-mentioned "Scots Tongue" and other such projects supplement the weekly cultural review "Prospect" and the programmes made for network (i.e. Radios 3 and 4). A Radio 3 "Scottish Season" in November 1984 was a showcase for Scottish production of music, drama, poetry, music, and talks. The critical reaction to this in England[21] was, it must be said, cautious, but critics in Scotland, less taken up with issues of accent etc. considered the season to be made up of demanding and worthwhile work. The inevitable question, however, arose: why a season on Radio 3? Why can such productions not be scheduled in the normal weekly course of things on Radio Scotland?

The answer to that resides in the complexities of Radio Scotland's conception, and the fact that here, uniquely within the BBC, is a station serving a country which has to combine the various divided functions of Radios 1,2,3,4 and independent radio. It will be recalled that one of the earliest criticisms of Radio Scotland was of its lack of identity, its confusion of styles. In 1986 one of the ways in which a strong attempt has been made to create a cohesive corporate identity is to insist on its being called "the national network". (This is to some extent wishful thinking. As mentioned in the Introduction, the BBC designates Scotland as a "national region"). Along with this goes a new theme tune "Alba", a piece using symphony orchestra and bagpipes, composed by George MacIlwham and first heard in "Classical Aid".

In tandem with this increased emphasis on "national" identity, which it is hoped may surpass and gather together the various programming styles (somewhat wishful thinking also…), attempts are being made to develop the international perspective from that ostensibly strong Scottish base. "Triple Alliance" is a non-metropolitan discussion programe, seeking to explore issues in common to Scotland, Wales and Northern Ireland, outside the usual BBC embrace of London. The executive producer responsible for that, Michael H Shaw, also plans to begin a world series – exchanging programmes directly with other countries.

THE FUTURE

The range and quality of the provision of programmes have greatly improved since 1978; it might sourly be said that they could hardly have got worse. However, Radio Scotland has new obstacles to overcome, not entirely, this time, of its own making.

With Radio Clyde basking in its custom built studios in Clydebank, Radio Scotland is still muddling through with cramped space and often inadequate equipment, especially at the Queen Street premises in Edinburgh. The solution to this was going to be the big new BBC building in Edinburgh: a project already anticipated in 1978 when John Pickles was setting out his plans for the station. In 1986, with the licence fee being set at £58 instead of the requested £63, the BBC decided, to the horror of both its patient staff and the Edinburgh authorities, to cancel this long and eagerly-awaited development.

As part of the same cutbacks, Radio Scotland has been asked to "save" £500,000 a year, and also self-operated contribution studios which were going to be set up throughout Scotland to increase the democratic and geographically diverse input to programmes, have had to be curtailed.

Again, within the same cutbacks, staffing is being "rationalised" by uprooting the Edinburgh news and current affairs staff and sending them to the increasingly powerful and centralised Queen Margaret Drive in Glasgow.

With no new and vitally needed facilities; with a half million pound slash through the budget; and with gross under-representation in Scotland's capital, it's hard to envisage how Radio Scotland can establish itself as a respected force in the future.

Catherine Lockerbie, *The Scotsman*.

References

1. *The Scotsman*, November 18th 1978, Allen Wright.

2. *ibid*.

3. Maurice Lindsay, *The Scottish Review*, No.14, May 1979.

4. George Bruce, *Ethics of Broadcasting in Scotland*, 1977.

5. *Saltire Society Report on Broadcating*, 1946.

6. David MacEwen, *Saltire Review*, Summer 1957.

7. *The Scotsman*, November 20th, 1970.

8. C. Lockerbie, *Cencrastus*, Spring, 1985.

9. *The Scotsman*, November 1978.

10. *The Scotsman*, November 18th, 1978, Allen Wright.

11. *The Scotsman*, November1 15th, 1978, Ian Nowatt.

12. *The Scotsman*, November 25th 1978, Allen Wright.

13. *The Scotsman*, November 22nd 1978, Neal Ascherson.

14. Robert Garioch, Letter Page, *The Scotsman*, December 19th, 1979.

15. *The Scotsman*, November 28th, 1978.

16. *The Scotsman*, November 24th, 1978.

17. *Glasgow Herald*, September 13th, 1979.

18. *The Scotsman*, December 12th, 1979.

19. *The Scotsman*, December 19th, 1979.

20. *The Scotsman*, November 22nd, 1978.

21. Which the present writer believes was as motivated by prejudice as anything else. See, *Cencrastus*, Spring, 1985.

THE 'LEADERSHIP CLASS' DISMISSED:
HUMES' CRITIQUE OF SCOTTISH EDUCATION

Charles D Raab

Broad-ranging interpretations of Scottish policy systems are not so common as to pass unremarked across the field of vision of those who are concerned to understand how Scotland is governed. At a time of great turbulence in Scottish education, a study of the workings of the educational system is bound to gain further prominence from the heightened political interest in the subject of its analysis. When that analysis is as provocative as that offered by Walter Humes in his book, *The Leadership Class in Scottish Education* (Edinburgh: John Donald, 1986), its publication becomes something of an event within the system itself, and its reception by those who figure in the analysis provides further data to test the thesis.

Humes' full frontal assault upon those whom he believes run Scottish education has, not surprisingly, brought down upon his head their counter-attack: not so much a closing of ranks by the 'leadership class', as an aggregation of protest from the bruised. In consequence, a book which held the promise of opening up the question of how Scottish education is run risks the dismissal of that question as a subject of research along with the rejection of its specific findings. The bath-water won't wash; out goes the baby as well. We would then be left the poorer in two senses: first, that complacency would too easily be restored; and second, that the effort spent by academics on the study of power would be construed as a time-wasting diversion from 'real' education policy research, or, worse, as an opportunity for mischief, when what is needed is for academics to rally round the flag. Our impoverishment would be regrettable because, as Humes knows, the critical scrutiny of the actions, inactions, and relationships of the leading figures and the main institutions is sadly underdeveloped in Scotland. We don't know ourselves sufficiently to change ourselves. We need more studies of the sociology and culture of government in education and in other fields; more, but far better than this one.

The principal argument of Humes' book is that Scottish education is run by a coterie of persons who hold top positions in the bureaucracies of central and local government, in appointed educational bodies ('quangos'), and as education college Principals. This 'leadership class' is neither monolithic nor omnipotent, but it controls the educational policy agenda and powerfully influences the making and execution of policies. Patronage gives some hand-picked ordinary teachers access to the decision-making processes controlled by the leaders. But they play very subordinate parts in the machinery through which the top professionals and bureaucrats pursue their own organisational or personal interests. The leadership class, moreover, uses masks and perpetuates myths and ideologies to conceal, disguise, or facilitate the realisation of its purposes.

Thus its members invoke the Scottish educational 'tradition' of democracy and equality, and they cling to the assumption that education in Scotland reflects the supposed autonomy and distinctiveness of Scottish society, culture and politics. They proffer a description of power relations in educational governance in terms of a pluralistic distribution of authority amongst a consensual 'partnership' of the Scottish Education Department (SED), the education authorities and the teachers. And, for a variety of unworthy ends, they exploit a shabby rhetoric of 'professionalism' that plays upon the susceptibilities of teachers. The result of this "bureaucratic expansionism, professional protectionism and ideological deception" is that "much of Scottish education is now run, not for the benefit of pupils, their parents and the community at large, but to serve the interests of those who occupy senior positions in the hierarchy" (p.201). Only by exposing these causes and effects, and by dislodging this class, can we begin to rescue Scottish education from its malaise. Only by reconstructing Scottish politics and culture can the job be completed; but the prospects for that are gloomy.

Humes is informative and insightful about a wide range of institutions and relationships, for one of his purposes is to replace the obsolete textbooks of the 1960s and 1970s on the Scottish educational system. He does not achieve this in any comprehensive way, but the refreshing iconclasm of his selective descriptions suits his main purpose, the illustrative demonstration of his thesis. This makes a good, cathartic read. No doubt, it was a good, cathartic write as well, calculated to attract attention. One can't escape notice if one runs amok with a long knife. But this is where this book is badly flawed. Humes pursues vendettas across ten chapters, building up his case against the 'leadership class' from an assortment of examples, suppositions, close-ups, and accusations which sometimes border on the slanderous. Little use it is, on one of the last pages of the book, for him to beg indulgence on the grounds that he was employing "deflating irony" at many points ('if we shadows have offended...'). For the gratuitous insults and innuendoes, the sour carping, the intemperateness and the gossip have, by then, done their work and, alas, their damage. Not, I fear, to the objects of the attack: if they are, by hypothesis, the impregnable panjandrums of state and professional power, one will neither wound nor change them. The damage is done to the kamikaze pilot himself and, perhaps worse, to the aircraft he flies, the enterprise of the sociopolitical analysis of power.

How has that analysis been done? This is the crux of the matter. Humes addresses the question of method in Chapter 1. There he mentions three methods of investigation. The first involves Acts, facts, and the study of policy-making processes. The second is sociocultural, and has to do with the "complex fabric of norms, values, beliefs and traditions which combine to produce particular responses to specific educational issues" (p.2). The third is phenomenological: by going inside the system to elicit "the subjective experiences of men and women closely involved in its day-to-day workings", the researcher could "construct a picture of channels of communication, networks of influence, and the machinery of decision-making" (p.2). But it is puzzling that Humes sees these as alternatives, for it is clear that only the third is a method whilst the other two are subjects to which that, and other methods, could be applied. Moreover, the "picture" to be constructed phenomenologically seems to be synonymous with "policy-making processes". Yet Humes points out the pitfalls of phenomenology. One is journalistic reportage, but Humes has certainly not scrupled here. Another is the non-representativeness of informants, but Humes does not say how one would know when they *were* representative. So the proposal of an eclectic approach to the subject compounds the confusion.

Humes identifies what is needed in order to fathom the actions of a 'leadership class', or indeed of any power group that is institutionally defined: "Some of the most interesting aspects of bureaucratic organisations can...only be understood if attention is focused on the *interaction* between administrative and personal aspirations" (p.17; emphasis in original). Related to this is another essential duality, that between conceptions of leaders as conscious conspirators or as hapless, falsely-conscious victims of their socialisation into the ways of bureaucracy. One fruitful avenue of analysis could be to explore these and other sets of alternative explanations by intepreting events in terms of them. Indeed, much of what Humes presents as a descriptive account of the system, and as case-studies of its working, bears the imprint of such an attempt. However, these presentations too often betray the wide gulf that separates author from subject; not the sort of distance that helps to preserve detachment and objectivity, but one that betokens an estrangement that undermines the argument. The giveaway is Humes' retreat into armchair speculation about motives, the result of which seems to be an attribution of psychopathology and a stereotyping of what 'bureaucrats' or 'professionals' do under the spell of a restless, ideologically-driven search for yet more power. And all this on the basis of their public pronouncements, of written sources, and of circumstantial evidence.

Humes claims to have talked to many people who work in the system, but has found direct access to what goes on in central and local government difficult. And indeed it is. But before the book was published, Humes admitted, in an academic seminar, that he didn't *seek* to interview members of the 'leadership class' themselves, for three reasons. First, because he had little confidence that they would give him straight answers; second, because he didn't want to be contaminated by the chummy atmosphere of self-congratulation; and third, because it would be adequate to use their utterances in the public print. What this means, of course, is that no purchase can be gained on leaders' "lived experiences" (p.2), nor on their beliefs or values, nor on their perception of the interation between situational, personal and organisational factors that produces actions on specific policies. We have to make do, instead, with deductions from highly generalised theories. Or with jejune reconciliations: thus the answer to the question whether conspiracy theory or false-consciousness best explains the behaviour of officials is that "[t]he truth, in the majority of cases, probably lies somewhere between the two"(p.19). This tells us precisely nothing at all. It is the result of the 'if I were a horse' school of social science, and it is impoverished. We also have to make do with personal insults and lampoons, although Humes says he wants to avoid *ad hominem* argument (p.20). This is the 'yah, boo' school of social science, and it is unworthy of the author and of his subject.

Apart from their apparent subscription to the Scottish educational 'myth', we learn little about the leaders' educational thinking concerning particular policies or patterns of provision. Their 'ideology' is about power and status, not about the substance of education. Thus the relationship between authority and educational policy is left obscure just where a trenchant critique of Scottish education needs to illuminate. One way in which more could have been brought to light is if Humes had abandoned his misplaced fastidiousness and had talked in depth to his 'leaders'. This is not a trouble-free methodological solution. It is labourious and epistemologically problematical. But especially where the analysis of policy-making and power is said to depend crucially upon an understanding of motives, confidence in the conclusions drawn from the analysis is seriously weakened by its absence.

It is true that the political temperature of education has been high in recent years partly because decision-making, policy development and implementation have been inept. But what of the policies themselves, and the events, the demographic and economic changes, and the coming-home-to-roost of yesterday's policies, that have shaped the agenda of the present day? To what extent can these all equally be laid at the doorstep of SED officials, local authority directorates, Principals, quangocrats, and teachers' spokesmen, whether taken singly or in some combination which Humes fails to delineate? Is it control, or lack of control, that more accurately expresses the educational policy predicament?

In a sense, there is too much going on, and 'leaders' struggle, with inadequate resources of power and knowledge, to ride a tiger whose joints are disarticulated enough to upset predictions of its motion. The principal riders Humes shows are central government officials. He is perceptive in highlighting some of the strategies they use to stay on top: the suborning of the research process (ch.8); the 'rationalisation' of the examination system, tertiary education, and other parts (ch.9), and the use of patronage in the appointments system (*passim*). What is evident, however, is that success in these ventures is limited and comes at a high price of effort and odium. Central officials may work towards the incorporation and harnessing of other power centres, and, to the extent that they succeed, may gain the potential for policy control. But their rationality, their rationalisation, and their corporatist endeavours are all bounded.

In part, they are bounded by the wider, and often more influential, circles of British social, economic and educational policy. These work through the likes of the Department of Education and Science, the Manpower Services Commission, the Cabinet and the Treasury. These are insufficiently recognised, or even omitted, from Humes' account, but they need fuller understanding as the framework within which Scottish leadership acts. In part, action is also bounded by the decisions of parents, classroom teachers, and pupils whose influence may be strengthened by, respectively, enfranchising politicians, recalcitrant trade unions, and the soles of the feet. The 'leadership class' needs to govern by some consensus, by some consent of the governed. Perhaps the leaders bear a heavy responsibility for having eroded these, and the proof of this erosion is the current whirlwind, which lends strength to Humes' argument. In a Postscript to the book, Humes notes of the continuing teachers' dispute over salaries and conditions of service: "When a settlement is finally reached, there will be a need to reassess the relations between teachers, parents, local councillors, members of the directorate, civil servants and Scottish Office ministers" (p.212).

That reassessment will go on, if it does, in the world of politics and administration. An *academic* reassessement will need to be served by first-hand accounts of actions and perceptions. It will need to be contrasted with what went before, so that we can see the trajectory of those relations across issues and structures that have an increasingly better-known past. Do bureaucrats and professionals act differently today and tomorrow from the way they did yesterday? If so, what becomes of 'bureaucracy' or 'professionalism' as analytic categories? Are the prospects for rationalisation and for corporatism greater as we approach the 'nineties than they were when we emerged from the 'fifties?

Whatever the answer, what does it suggest about Scottish culture, politics, society and education? Humes has made an important contribution by implicitly positing these as four sides of a geometric figure whose precise angles and lengths remain to be discovered through research. The figure moves through time, but its rate of change may be uneven and the sides may sometimes part company with each other. How are we to learn about this, about Scotland and about ourselves? Humes has framed the government and politics of education as a focus of research that is as worthy of investigation in Scotland as it has for many years been in England and elsewhere. Its neglect, perhaps through the Scottish self-satisfaction that Humes decries, may be part of our current predicament. For all its inadequacies, there is a sufficient ring of truth in this book for it not to be ignored. Humes has showed us the keyhole; it is for others to find the key; and there are plenty of people around who might know where it is, if only they were asked.

Charles D. Raab, Department of Politics, University of Edinburgh.

THE ORIGINS AND IMPACT OF THE PARENTS CHARTER*

Michael Adler, Alison Petch and Jack Tweedie

This paper is in two parts. In the first part, we attempt to put the parental choice provisions in the 1981 Act into a historical context by considering the development of public education in Scotland since 1945; we examine the enactment of these provisions in the Scottish legislation and compare them with analagous provisions in the English legislation; and we assess the extent to which the Scottish legislation has altered the balance between individual parents and education authorities. In the second part, we describe the early implementation of the legislation by education authorities; we examine the take-up of placing requests and their impact on parents and the admission of pupils to schools; and look at the effects of decisions of appeal committees and sheriffs on regional policy and practice in an attempt to assess whether the legislation has found the right balance between the interests of individual parents and the policy concerns of education authorities.

PART 1

THE 1946 ACT

The Education (Scotland) Act 1946 established a framework for the development of public education in the post-war period. It was a consolidating act and incorporated the reforms contained in the Education (Scotland) Act 1945. Among the most important of these were:

1. education was made compulsory from 5 to 15

2. education was to be organised as primary, secondary and tertiary education, all pupils were to proceed from primary to secondary and (unless exempted) from secondary to (part-time) tertiary education until the age of 19

3. education was to be free with the proviso that education authorities could charge fees in some or all classes in a limited number of schools

provided that this did not prejudice the provision of free education in other schools.

Considering its importance, the 1946 Act was not a particularly substantial document[1]. This is because, like most other educational legislation in the UK, the Act was, in large measure, an enabling Act. As such, it created a statutory framework and conferred broad powers on education authorities which were responsible for the provision of education. Thus, a statutory duty was imposed on authorities

> to ensure that adequate and efficient provision is made throughout their area of all forms of primary, secondary and further education[2].

The 1946 Act imposed a further duty on authorities 'to prepare and submit for the approval of the Secretary of State a scheme or schemes for the exercise of their powers and duties'[3], and the Secretary of State could either approve or ask the authority to revise or modify its scheme[4]. The Secretary of State was also given powers to declare an education authority in default of its duties and order the authority to discharge the duty[5].

Parents were given a duty under the 1946 Act to provide education for their children, either by sending them to school regularly or, otherwise, by providing efficient education suitable to the 'age, ability and aptitude' of the child[6]. Moreover, if they failed to discharge this duty, they could find themselves liable to a criminal prosecution[7]. It is, of course, true that, under s28, the Secretary of State and education authorities were 'to have regard to the general principle that, so far as is compatible with the provision of suitable instruction and training and the avoidance of unreasonable public expenditure, pupils are to be educated in accordance with the wishes of their parents'. However, this did not mean, nor was it intended to mean, that pupils were necessarily and in all cases to be educated in accordance with the wishes of their parents. As Lord Denning said of the analogous provisions in Section 76 of the Education Act, 1944 in one of the leading English cases:

> (the Act) only lays down a general principle to which the (authority) must have regard. This leaves it open to the (authority) to have regard to other things as well and also to make exceptions to the general principal if it thinks fit to do so. It cannot be said that an (authority) is at fault simply because it does not see fit to comply with the parents' wishes[8].

Lord Denning's opinion is generally accepted as the correct

interpretation of Section 76 of the English Act. A number of Scottish decisions likewise made it clear that Section 29 of the Scottish Act placed Scottish education authorities under a duty to take parents' wishes into account but did not require authorities to give effect to them[9].

The idea that parents (to say nothing of children) might have been given rights as well as duties in respect of education was quite foreign to the spirit of the legislation and to the spirit of the times. A legal right is a legally enforceable claim which is made against some person or persons who seek to deny its enactment. In the case of education, a parental right would, in practice, have been enforced against an education authority or, possibly, against the Secretary of State. However, the legislation entrusted education authorities to promote the educational well-being of all pupils and, in the event of an authority failing to do so, gave the Secretary of State powers to declare an authority in default of its duties and require it to discharge them. It made little sense to give parents rights to use against education authorities when their interests in their children's were, in effect, being enhanced by the progressive expansion of educational opportunities.

As we have seen, education authorities were required to prepare and submit for approval to the Secretary of State a general scheme of educational provision. In addition, they were required to prepare and submit for approval a 'promotion scheme' (subsequently known as a 'transfer scheme') describing how pupils were to be promoted from primary to secondary schools and the basis on which children were to be allocated to different schools[10]. The Act contained no indication of the kinds of schools which authorities might develop at each stage of education, or the criteria for allocation which authorities might develop and apply.

DEVELOPMENTS IN THE LIGHT OF THE 1946 ACT

There is always and inevitably pressure to fill a vacuum and this was indeed the case with the 1946 Act. In 1947, the Advisory Council on Education published its blueprint for the reconstruction of secondary education in the post-war world[11]. The Council recommended the omnibus school, providing for all pupils from a fixed area throughout their compulsory secondary education, seeing this as 'the natural way for a democracy to order the post-primary schooling of a given area'. Although the Council believed that, by the age of twelve pupils differed so much in academic potential that they should be streamed for all academic subjects, its view did not prevail. This was in part because of the SED's belief that only a minority of children were academic and its long-standing commitment to the principles of separate educational provision for academic and non-academic children known as 'bi-partism', which was thought to provide a socially efficient model of schooling and to be the legitimate descendent of the Scottish democratic tradition. But it was also in part because of strong attachments by education authorities to their local academies and to the meritocratic system of schooling of which they were a part. Thus, the 1946 Act did not lead to the introduction of omnibus schools in urban areas but resulted instead in a new form of bi-partism in which 'junior secondary schools' were developed alongside the well-established 'senior secondaries' and in which 'promotion' arrangements were increasingly based on intelligence testing. The Advisory Council's report notwithstanding, this continued commitment to bi-partism reflected a consensus of opinion between the major institutional actors; between Labour and Conservative parties, between ministers (of either party) and the SED, between the SED and the education authorities, and between local councillors and Directors of Education.

The post-war period has been one of fairly sustained expansion in education. Taking the UK as a whole, public expenditure on education as a proportion of GDP doubled (from 2.8% to 5.6%) between 1948 and 1967, reached a peak of 7.0% in 1975 but has been falling back since then[12]. At secondary level, there was a steady expansion in the proportion of pupils admitted to selective schools. This was, in part, a response to rising aspirations and an increasing local demand for selective schooling. However, as McPherson and Raab point out[13], this expansion unwittingly contributed to the undermining of confidence in the bipartite system:

> As higher proportions of successive age groups were selected for senior secondary courses, so the number of dissatisfied 'borderline' cases was statistically bound to increase. Moreover, an expanding senior secondary sector continued to drain junior secondary schools of resources, teachers and esteem.

Education authorities responded in a variety of ways. Some Labour controlled local authorities started to establish comprehensives. However, this was on a piecemeal, one-off basis; such schools co-existed with senior secondaries which still creamed off their intakes and, as far as we know, no authority attempted to introduce comprehensive schooling 'across the board'. Elsewhere, authorities 'upgraded' junior secondaries, again on a one-off basis, by adding senior secondary classes and thereby creating an 'omnibus' school. The SED also responded in a number of ways. Through the Advisory Council, education authorities were asked to reduce the proportion of pupils embarking on senior secondary courses. At the same time, in an attempt to stem the wastage from senior secondary courses (which increased as more and more pupils embarked upon such courses), the 'O' grade was introduced. Paradoxically, by designing 'O' grades on the assumption that one-third of the age group would succeed, the SED unwittingly put additional pressure on the system, since it followed that as many as half the age group would need to embark on the course.

SECONDARY SCHOOL REORGANISATION

By the early 1960s, it was clear that the consensus was beginning to break down; the return of a Labour government committed to the abolition of selection and the reorganisation of secondary education along comprehensive lines brought the matter to a head. Pressures for such a change, which had been party policy for some time, came largely from south of the border and there was relatively little indigenous pressure for change (even from staunchly Labour education authorities) from within Scotland itself[14]. Nevertheless, it was soon clear that the government wanted this policy to be applied in Scotland as well as in England. It was equally clear, given the lack of impetus for change at local level and the continuing support for selective schools in many areas (which included traditional working class communities like Fife and Lanarkshire, as well as the big cities) that some form of central direction would be necessary.

In Circular 600/1965[15], the Labour government presented the case for reorganisation as a natural development in an evolving Scottish tradition of common education and of common opportunities to acquire certification. All that was absolutely required of local authorities without exception was that they should 'no longer ... allocate pupils to 'certificate' and 'non-certificate' courses when they start the secondary stage'. Logically this seemed not so much to require abolition of selection as postponement from 12 to 14 and a number of authorities submitted proposals for secondary school reorganisation along these lines. However, in contrast to the DES which stated a preference for the all-through 11-18 comprehensive school but also endorsed five other ways in which comprehensive schooling could be organised on a non-selective basis, the SED advocated a single final form of organisation, the six year all-through comprehensive for 12-18 year olds, although it did concede that some variant on the two-tier system might be an unavoidable interim solution especially in scattered, rural areas. The match between the political complexion of central government and the majority of local authorities helped the SED to get its way. On occasion, local councillors over-ruled the Director of Education; on other occasions, the SED used its powers to amend the local authority's proposals: in the end, after extensive negotiations with 35 local authorities, the large majority opted for all-through 12-18 comprehensives.

Secondary school reorganisation in Scotland is best understood as a political rather than an educational initiative, as a British policy developed and applied to Scotland rather than a Scottish policy. Paradoxically, it was implemented more uniformly and more comprehensively than the parallel policy in England and Wales – mainly because the majority of local authorities were Labour controlled and the minority who weren't did not hold out. In many cases the Directors went along with the changes, although in few cases did they actively take the lead. The means chosen by Ministers (north and south of the border) was that of 'government by circular' – education authorities were told how they were expected to exercise their statutory duties under the Act and, as a last resort, the government could withhold its approval or use its default powers to achieve its ends. Section 29 of the 1946 Act (which had now become section 29 of a new consolidating act,the 1962 Act) was not deemed to be relevant to these changes – parents could not insist on the retention of selective schools because they wished to send their children there. At the same time, no one suggested that parents should be given a right to a non-selective secondary education for their children (Such a notion is, in any case, intrinsically problematic, not least because rights are individual claims while the organisation of schooling is a collective policy).

REORGANISATION OF LOCAL GOVERNMENT

Leaving aside the raising of the school leaving age, the next major policy change to affect the organisation of schooling was not the result of an educational initiative at all. The reform of local government in 1975 was intended to improve regional planning, enhance the quality of the professional input at the local level (not least through its commitment to corporate management) and improve the calibre of local councillors. With education allocated to regional (and islands) authorities, the number of education authorities was reduced from 35 to 12. Many authorities were immediately faced with the problem of harmonising the disparate administrative arrangements and transfer schemes of the various antecedent authorities. The immediate effect was to disturb a rather settled pattern of relationships, e.g. with the SED, but its long-term effect was to alter the balance of power between central and local government inasmuch as the largest of the new authorities must now constitute a powerful countervailing force to the centralising tendencies of the SED. Or, so it seemed until recently.

THE BACKGROUND TO THE 1981 ACT

We now turn to our main concern, which is with the Education (Scotland) Act 1981 and in particular with the provisions of Section 1 (inserted into the 1980 Act as Section 28A) which strengthen the rights of parents to select schools for their children and curtail the discretion of the local authority with regard to school allocation. In presenting an account of this measure, it is instructive to make some comparisons with the secondary school reorganisation 15 years previously. Among the differences is the fact that the 1981 Act was brought in by a Conservative government which, unlike the Labour government in 1966, could not exploit 'same party' control over the large majority of education authorities. The financial and demographic contexts were very different too. In 1966, school rolls were increasing and educational expenditure was expanding; by 1981, both these trends had gone into reverse – falling school rolls had been affecting primary schools for some years and were about to have an impact on secondary schools while public expenditure on education had passed its peak and was declining in real if not in absolute terms. This latter development, which reflected the government's ideological hostility to public expenditure in general and to the 'welfare state' in particular, had already begun to sour the relationship between central and local government. Foremost among the similarities was the fact that there was virtually no impetus for change at the local level in Scotland and the pressure for reform came, once again, from south of the border. All education authorities in Scotland allocated children to schools on a catchment area basis or, in the case of secondary schools, in terms of their 'feeder primaries', and gave parents who were unhappy with the allocated school an opportunity to request an alternative. Most authorities, including the Conservative controlled authorities, were reasonably flexible although one or two authorities adopted rather strict 'neighbourhood school' policies and only allowed pupils to attend schools other than the ones to which they were allocated in special circumstances, e.g. if they had a sibling at the school or for medical reasons. There certainly was political pressure on Scottish Ministers to confront the more restrictive authorities but the pressure was local rather than national. This pressure was undoubtedly strongest in Edinburgh and in 1980 prompted the Secretary of State to use his powers under the existing legislation to call in and amend Lothian's transfer scheme[16].

By contrast, the situation in England and Wales was very different[17]. There, the issue of parental choice had been on the political agenda for some years. In 1969, the Labour government had raised the possibility of establishing an independent appeals system for parents as part of a new Education Bill. Somewhat surprisingly, the proposal received only moderate support, even from parents groups. Preparations for consultation were set in hand but these were cut short by the election called in 1970. The issue did not surface again during the lifetime of the Conservative government from 1970-1974 (while Margaret Thatcher was Secretary of State for Education). However, after the defeat, of the government in February 1974, pressure grew among Conservatives for a re-evaluation of their education policies. Norman St John Stevas was appointed Education Spokesman and was charged with developing new policy initiatives that would lead to a new and distinctive Conservative education policy. He and his colleagues quickly realised the potential appeal of parental choice, which had the added advantage of being consistent with the values

Conservatives traditionally placed on freedom from state control and on parents' responsibilities for their children. St John Stevas announced the Parents Charter in August 1974 and a Charter of Parents Rights was included in the Conservative Manifesto for the October 1974 election[18]. Subsequently they twice put forward legislation based on the Parents Charter while in opposition: a Conservative backbencher put forward a Private Member's Bill in 1974[19] and in 1976, the Conservatives introduced a set of new clauses relating to parental choice as amendments to Labour's Education Bill in an attempt to publicise their concern with parental choice and to stall the Bill. Whereas the rationale for parental choice had initially emphasised freedom from state control and the assumption of parental responsibilities for their children, it was now presented as a means of improving educational standards – the introduction of market forces would force unpopular (poor) schools to close and enable popular (good) schools to expand. It was also seen to appeal to those parents whose children would previously have gone to grammar schools and who were disenchanted with comprehensive schooling, and to those who were alarmed at the growth of radical educational ideas and would welcome an attempt to cut the teaching profession down to size.

Although none of these parliamentary initiatives met with any success, they did help to put pressure on the Labour government to propose some form of parental choice legislation of its own. Eventually, after issuing a consultation paper[20], the Labour government included a number of parental choice provisions in its 1978 Education Bill. Although the primary effect of these provisions was to give LEAs statutory powers to control school numbers, the Labour government certainly claimed that it was establishing and enhancing parental choice. Be that as it may, the Bill died in Committee when the election was called.

While the Conservative opposition and the Labour government both attempted to legislate for parental choice in England and Wales, there were no comparable attempts at legislation for Scotland. The dearth of politicians with strong interests in education among the depleted ranks of Scottish Conservative MPs after the party's defeat in the 1974 election, meant that Scottish interests were not represented among those Conservatives who set out to create a new and distinctive approach to education. Although the 1974 Parents Charter quickly became official Conservative Party policy, it was really an English policy which did not easily take root in Scotland. Several Scottish Regions had experienced disputes with parents who objected to the Regions' refusals to admit their child to the school they preferred, but these disputes were seen as regional matters, not matters which called for a statutory resolution. Largely for this reason, the Labour Party in Scotland did not find it necessary to propose its own form of parental choice legislation and the Scottish Office took the view that provisions analagous to those in the 1978 Education Bill were not needed for Scotland[20a]. In any case, there was less public concern in Scotland with educational standards or with the introduction of comprehensive schooling, and less support for an attack on collectivism in practice or the espousal of an individualistic ethic. However, when the Conservatives were returned in 1979 on a Manifesto which included a clear commitment to legislate for parental choice[21], it was clear that the situation had changed. As with the proposals on secondary school reorganisation 15 years previously, the government wanted legislation on parental choice to apply to Scotland as well as to England.

THE MAKING OF THE 1981 ACT

In 1979, the new Conservative government immediately set about revising the statutory rights of parents and the duties of education authorities with respect to parental choice in England and Wales. By this time, however, the new Secretary of State for Education and Science, Mark Carlisle, considered that strengthening the rights of parentys to choose schools should be qualified by concerns for reducing authorities' expenditure on education. Thus, although the Education Act 1980 gave English and Welsh parents a right to choose schools, education authorities could refuse a parent's choics of school if complying with that choice would "prejudice the provision of efficient education or the efficient use of resources." Parents could appeal against an authority's decision to a local appeal committee, but the appeal committees would be appointed by the eduation authorities and could contain a majority of education authority members.

The SED moved quickly to follow the English legislation. Alex Fletcher had been appointed Under-Secretary of State for Education and Industry in May 1979 and the onus fell on him to implement his party's Manifesto pledges. The first indication of his intentions came when he met members of the COSLA Education Committee on 17 August 1979[22]. One of the principal items on the agenda was the government's proposal for a Parents Charter[23]. The discussion was only of a preliminary nature. The Minister said that falling school rolls presented an opportunity for relaxing school catchment areas and widening parental choice of school and expressed the view that an extension of the rights and responsibilities of parents would be good for overall educational standards. He stressed the need for more information, including details of examination results, to enable parents to make informed choices and invited comments on a two-tier appeal system under which parental applications would be considered first by school councils and subsequently by an appeals committee with an independent element, which would be administered locally by the education authority. COSLA's response was unenthusiastic. Dr Malcolm Green (Chairman of the Education Committee) pointed out that authorities were already required to 'have regard to' parental wishes and argued against the imposition of a uniform system. He could see no problem about making more information available but pointed to some of the difficulties which increased parental choice might create for authorities, emphasising that limits would have to be placed on the number of places available at each school.

At the end of the meeting the Minister suggested that further discussions should take place at official level between the SED and COSLA in order to clarify the issues involved, investigate likely difficulties and possible means of resolving them, and set out (possibly in the form of a draft circular) the steps that might be taken by authorities to implement the proposals he had in mind. Thus, at this stage, it would appear that the Minister was not yet thinking in terms of legislation. Dr Green accepted the invitation, on the understanding that the COSLA officials would merely feed in their expertise without committing themselves or COSLA in advance to whatever proposals the government came up with, and nominated six Directors to participate in the discussions as representatives of COSLA. When the group met on 2 October 1979, it was made clear that the SED's aim was now to produce a Consultative Paper on which COSLA and other interested parties would be asked to comment in due course. Whether or not this would be followed by legislation would depend on the outcome of the consultations and the willingness of authorities to enter into voluntary arrangements. Discussion focussed on the scope for authorities to relax their existing policies on admissions and catchment areas so as to enhance parental choice of school, the possibility of a two-tier system of appeals, the feasibility of pilot schemes in which parents would be asked to choose one of a number of schools within an enlarged catchment area, and the information parents would require in order to exercise choice. SED officials acknowledged that problems would arise but reiterated the Minister's hope that authorities would no longer refuse parents if space was available at the school of their choice. They also accepted that any new arrangements should still preserve the general principle that priority should be given to parents who wished their children to be educated at the local school and take into account the desirability of ending the use of annexes and temporary accommodation and the need to determine the optimum annual intake, with some capacity retained for incomers to the area. COSLA's nominees participated in the discussions as individuals rather than as representatives and no attempt was made to reach a consensus. However, it is significant that, at this and a subsequent meeting on 19 October 1979 when a number of background papers, including papers on admissions and transfers in Manchester and the ILEA were considered, there was very little enthusiasm for the idea of 'free choice' even on a pilot basis.

Prior to the publication of the Consultative Paper, the Minister had outlined his ideas to COSLA and the SPTC and a series of discussions had taken place between SED officials and COSLA representatives. The Minister had some contact with the Conservative Group on Lothian Regional Council but there appears to have been very little contact between the SED and the DES. Policy was developed independently by a small group of officials within the SED who met regularly with the Minister. Alex Fletcher was almost certainly more 'bullish' than his officials and had to compromise on a number of issues. However, his officials experienced little difficulty in supporting the principle of parental choice or in translating this into a workable policy.

The Consultative Paper which was issued in March 1980 was the fourth in a series of papers issued by the Minister[24]. At a press conference to launch the paper, Alex Fletcher questioned whether low rates of exceptional admissions and transfers in Scotland reflected widespread satisfaction with the existing arrangements (as the education authorities, in particular, insisted) and claimed that it indicated a high level of apathy, which was engendered by existing practices. He also invoked the beneficial consequences of market forces, asserting that 'a touch of consumerism is no bad thing for a nationalised industry'[25]. The introduction to the paper made it clear that account had been taken of the need to reduce existing levels of educational expenditure, and claimed that the proposals would enable disadvantaged children to escape from the deprived areas in which they were currently trapped. The paper itself did not propose the abolition of zoning schemes or catchment areas but argued that, pending legislation to this effect, 'all authorities should accept an obligation to meet parents' wishes if this can be done within the existing accommodation and staffing resources of the school in question'[26]. It accepted COSLA's argument that authorities needed to determine planned capacity and annual intake limits for each school, agreed that the former could be less than the school's physical capacity where an authority wished to end the use of annexes, temporary buildings or other unsatisfactory accommodation and sought views on whether or not places should be reserved for incomers to the catchment area. In order to deal with oversubscribed schools, authorities would be required to devise guidelines for determining which cases should be given priority. Priority would still be given to children from the catchment area but where some children from outside the catchment area were refused admission, authorities were to set up appeal procedures involving, in the first instance, school councils and subsequently committees of the authority with the same constitution and powers as those proposed in the (English) Education (No 2) Bill which was then before Parliament. The Consultative Paper also listed the information (including examination results) which authorities would have to provide for parents and concluded by giving local authorities, teachers associations and bodies representing parents twelve weeks in which to submit their comments.

The content of the Consultative Paper reflected a number of developments in the government's position. First, legislation was promised, if not immediately then at least at some time in the future. This reflected the Minister's wish to enable parents to exercise choice at all stages of education; his conclusion that education authorities would not all agree to this voluntarily; and the fact that his powers were limited under the existing legislation to amending an authority's policy on transfer to secondary school. In addition to these general considerations, it was no doubt also influenced by the concurrent dispute between the Secretary of State and Lothian Region over Lothian's transfer scheme. Second, although the Consultative Paper encouraged authorities to consider adopting wider catchment zones, it no longer contained any specific references to the piloting of 'free choice' schemes. Likewise, although it encouraged schools to develop their own ethos, it was noticeably cautious about curricular diversity. These two changes can be taken to reflect the influence of the SED. Third, in borrowing only one provision (on the constitution and powers of appeal committees) from the English legislation, strong evidence is provided for the independent elaboration of policy on this issue for Scotland.

The Consultative Paper was given a fairly cool reception. Altogether, some 15 organisations responded, of whom four were teachers' unions and three were headteachers' associations[27]. There was general support for the retention of catchment areas (and again little enthusiasm for the adoption of wider catchment zones); for giving authorities the power to set admission limits; for reserving places for incomers to the catchment; and for the provision of information. On the other hand, there was widespread criticism of the government's approach on the grounds that it would raise expectations which would not be satisfied; a general concern about its effects on the reputations of individual schools, especially in deprived areas, and on staff morale, and a widely-expressed concern that among secondary schools it would result in the return of a 'two-tier' system. Many reservations were also expressed about the publication of examination results. COSLA took the view that the existing legislation satisfied the 'broad interests' of parents and pupils. It opposed the imposition by statute of standard practices and procedures, e.g. in relation to appeal procedures, on local authorities and criticised the Consultative Paper for tipping the balance too far in favour of individual parents[28]. On the other hand, the SCC argued that in some respects the Consultative Paper did not go far enough. Thus, it criticised the govenment for ignoring the issue of under-age admissions to primary schools and argued that parents should be given a statutory right of appeal to the sheriff which would eliminate the undesirable practice of keeping children out of school in order to invoke the attendance order procedure[29].

On 29 July 1980, in a written parliamentary answer, Alex Fletcher announced that he proposed to introduce legislation much along the lines of his Consultative Paper, the only major change being that provisions of an appeal to the sheriff by a parent who was aggrieved by a decision of an appeal committee. COSLA was provided with a confidential paper outlining the government's proposals for legislation, which was discussed at a further meeting between Alex Fletcher and the Convention's Education Committee on 22 August 1980. A number of questions were raised, in particular about the additional expenditure which might be incurred by education authorities and about the appeals procedures, which the Minister promised to look into, but because Dr Green was concerned that the legislation would not sufficiently take into account COSLA's representations, a Working Group of three Directors[30] was asked urgently to produce a paper setting out in precise terms the amendments the Convention would wish to propose[30].

The Education (Scotland) (No 2) Bill, which was laid before Parliament on 20 December 1980, contained few surprises[31]. Education authorities would still be able to allocate children to schools, but parents would be given a right to make a placing request for another school and the authority would be required to grant such requests unless one of seven grounds for refusal applied. The most important of these exceptions to the authorities' duty to comply with placing requests applied to circumstances where this would 'exceed the planned admission limit for that school or that stage of education'[32], 'require engaging an extra teacher in the school or give rise to significant expenditure on extending or otherwise altering the accommodation at or facilities provided in connection with the school, ... or be likely to be seriously detrimental to order and discipline in the school or the educational well-being of the pupils there'[33] or 'if the education normally provided is not suited to the age, ability or aptitude of the child'[34]. However, the authority could still grant a placing request even if one of the grounds for refusal existed. Education authorities would be required to publish their admission arrangements and the order of priorities which would apply if a school is oversubscribed. Where a placing request is refused, parents would be able to refer the case to an appeal committee[35] and subsequently to the sheriff. The powers of the appeal committee and the sheriff were to be identical with those of the authority and, where an appeal is upheld, the decision would be binding on the authority. The only provision in the Bill which was not foreshadowed in Alex Fletcher's parliamentary answer in the draft of the legislative proposals was a novel requirment that where an appeal was upheld and analagous placing requests have been refused, the authority must review their decisions in such cases and, where they do not reverse their decision, the parents would be given a further right of appeal.

Of the 15 organisations which responded to the Consultative Paper, only a handful made detailed criticisms of the Bill and prepared detailed amendments[36]. The Bill was given its second reading on 12 February 1981 and, during March, it was considered by the First Scottish Standing Committee. The government successfully moved one amendment, to the effect that authorities could only refuse a placing request if they had to take an additional teacher into employment; by contrast the opposition moved a large number of amendments but none of them was successful. The whole impact of the Bill, and the balance it sought to strike between the rights of individual parents and the collective responsibilities of education authorities, was fundamentally altered by the government's late deletion of the clause that would have allowed authorities to fix admission limits for their schools and use those admission limits to justify refusing parents' requests[37]. The admission limits had been included in the Bill at the request of education authorities who were concerned that they should be able to refuse parents' choices in order to take unsuitable annexes and temporary accommodation out of use, and in order to avoid operating under-enrolled schools which would require higher expenditures and offer lower quality education to children in disadvantaged areas. The clause was removed during the Bill's Third Reading on 18 June 1981, too late for the authorities to protest effectively. Alex Fletcher removed the clause when he realized that authorities could use it to restrict parents' ability to choose popular schools and force them to send their children to unpopular schools, artificually keeping such schools open instead of closing them. He belatedly came to the conclusion that authorities could not be trusted to use the admission limits for legitimate purposes without restricting parental choice. He also realised that the statute would provide no effective way for parents to challenge any artificially low admission limits that the authorities might adopt. The clause in the Bill would have allowed authorities to justify a refusal simply by asserting that it would breach a schools' admission limit. Parents could not have challenged that limit at an appeal committee or in an appeal to the sheriff. An amendment along these lines had been proposed by the SCC and the SPTC, who pointed out that authorities could have used the provision to reinforce rigid catchment area policies and to deny or seriously restrict choice, and the government may well have been influenced by this. COSLA was incensed, not only by the amendment but also by the stage at which it was introduced. Their co-operation with the government had throughout been on the understanding that any legislation would contain such a provision. However, despite intensive lobbying, it was clear that the government would not back down on this issue. The Bill went to the Lords on 25 June 1981. A number of further amendments were moved but only one was successful. This had the effect of debarring members of the education committee from serving as chairman of an appeal committee. This amendment was accepted by the government and the Bill received its Royal Assent on 30 October 1981, some 14 months after the statutory enactment of parental choice in England.

COMPARISONS WITH THE ENGLISH LEGISLATION

The general structure of the parental choice provisions of the Education (Scotland) Act 1981 is in many ways similar to that of the Education Act 1980. In Scotland, as in England, parents were given the right to request that their children are admitted to a particular school or schools; education authorities are required to comply with parental requests unless a statutory exception to this general duty applies; dissatisfied parents have the right to appeal to a statutory appeal committee and, if the latter finds in favour of the parent, its decision is binding on the authority; and education authorities are required to provide parents with information about the school to which their child has been allocated and about any other school if the parents ask for it. However, there are also some important differences between the two pieces of legislation. First, the statutory exceptions to the authorities duty to comply with parents' requests are broad and general in England but much more specific in Scotland[38]. In England, the primary exception, which applies when compliance with the parents' request would 'prejudice the provision of efficient education or the efficient use of resources', enables the authority to justify a refusal by referring to conditions at schools other than the one requested by the parents or to conditions in their schools generally. By contrast, in Scotland, where the primary exceptions apply when compliance would entail the employment of an additional teacher or significant extensions or alterations to the school or 'be likely to be seriously detrimental to order and discipline at the school or the educational well-being of the pupils there', the authority can only refer to conditions at the school requested by the parents. Second, parents in Scotland can appeal an adverse decision of an appeal committee to the sheriff[39] while parents in England have no further right of appeal. Thirdly, where an appeal committee or a sheriff upholds an appeal in Scotland, the authority must review the cases of all parents in similar circumstances who did not appeal and, if its decisions are unchanged, it must grant the parents a further right of appeal[40]. There is no comparable provision in the English legislation.

It is somewhat ironic that, although the primary impetus for parental choice legislation came from England, the Scottish legislation appears to establish stronger rights for parents. The explanation for this irony lies partly in the different perspectives of the Ministers responsible for the legislation, partly in the relative influence of English and Scottish local authorities and partly in the different historical antecedents. The English Secretary of State, Mark Carlisle, was rather lukewarm in his support for parental choice. Although he recognised the government's Manifesto commitment and was committed to the principle of parental choice, he was concerned that it should not give rise to additional spending or result in the inefficient use of resources. Moreover, at the end of the day, he was prepared to trust the English LEAs to implement the legislation in good faith. On the other hand, the Scottish Education Minister, Alex Fletcher, was very strongly committed to parental choice[41]. Having been closely involved in the disputes over parental choice in Edinburgh, it is clear that he did not trust the education authorities and was thus anxious to specify precisely in the legislation all the exceptions to the authority's general duty to comply with parental requests. He was able to do so, in part because COSLA (which was Labour controlled) had less influence over the Scottish Office than the English local authority associations, in particular the Association of County Councils (ACC) which was Conservative controlled, had over the DES. Thus COSLA was unable to prevent the government from removing at a very late stage in the parliamentary process, a key provision in the Bill which would have allowed education authorities to fix the maximum number of pupils to be educated at a school or at a stage of education in a school and to refuse a placing request where the maximum number has already been reached. COSLA's lack of influence with the government, and the government's own populist tendencies, allowed organisations representing parents (SPTC) and consumers (SCC) to exercise considerable influence over the government and it is significant that these two organisations lobbied for all three amendments which were accepted by the government[42]. Those who had come to regard themselves as 'insiders' in the policy process strongly resented the influence of these two 'outside' organisations[43]. The inclusion of a further right of appeal from appeal committees to the courts in Scotland (but not in England) can, in part, be explained in this way but is also due to the fact that the sheriff already played a role in the Scottish (but not the English) attendance order procedures[44].

COMPARISIONS WITH PREVIOUS SCOTTISH LEGISLATION

Like secondary school reorganisation in Scotland, the introduction of parental choice in Scotland can also best be understood as a political rather than an educational initiative, and as a British policy developed and applied to Scotland rather than a Scottish policy. However, it differed from it in two important respects. Although consensus for the legislation was initially lacking in both instances, in the case of secondary school reorganisation, the government worked hard to obtain and finally achieved an impressive consensus on the issue; in the case of parental choice, the attempt to achieve a consensus was not only somewhat half-hearted but was abandoned at the last moment, the result of which was that a solution was imposed by statute. Objections can be raised to the comparison on the grounds that the two issues are not really comparable, and that one of them (secondary school reorganisation) is arguably much more important than the other. It is also true that it is very much harder for a Conservative than for a Labour administration in Scotland to achieve a consensus with local authorities. Nevertheless, the contrast is still very striking. The second respect in which the parental choice legislation differed from secondary school reorganisation was in the implied relationship between the individual and the education authority. From 1945 onwards, it has been assumed that the interests of the individual coincided with those of the authority, thus the best way of promoting an individual's rights was to improve the provision of education. Now, for the first time, the interests of the individual and the concerns of the authority were seen, atleast in some respects, to conflict and the individual was seen to be in need of protection from the authority. We can sum up these changes as follows:

TABLE

date	policy focus	relations between SED and education authorities	relations between interests of parents and those of education authorities
1945	development of secondary schooling	initial consensus between SED and local authorities – consensus subsequently broke down	
1965	secondary school reorganisation	initial consensus between SED and local authorities lacking – consensus finally achieved through negotiation	interests of individual thought to coincide with those of the authority
1981	parental choice of school	initial consensus between SED and local authorities lacking – solution imposed by legislation	intersts of individual thought of conflict with those of the authority

It is not part of our argument to suggest that, because the 1981 Act is best understood as a piece of political legislation, or because its origins are to be found south of the border, it is, for either of these reasons deficient. However, the belated deletion of the provision which would have enabled authorities to fix admission limits and refuse to admit pupils in excess of these limits not only magnified their initial antipathy to the legislation but also seriously restricted their capacity to discharge their statutory duty to promote 'adequate and efficient education' for all children[45]. It is important to try to find a balance between the interests of individual parents and the collective concerns of statutory authorities. In exercising choice, a parent has only to think about his/her child. An education authority, on the other hand, is less interested in which school a particular child attends and more concerned with the distribution of all children among its schools. Thus, the interests of individual parents and the concerns of an authority with collective responsibilities may well not coincide. The problem is to find the right balance and a question which must now be asked is whether the 1981 Act has succeeded in doing so.

PART 2

EARLY IMPLEMENTATION

The parental choice provisions of the 1981 Act came into effect on 15 February 1982. Considering the nature of the legislation and the manner in which it was enacted, it is not surprising that few authorities greeted it with enthusiasm. Nonetheless, the appropriate statutory requirements were fulfilled and each region formulated policies and adapted its procedures to allow for the exercise of choice. New administrative procedures were devised, guidelines (or, at least, a set of criteria) for determining priorities when there were more applications than places at a school were formulated, appeal committees were set up, and information booklets were designed and distributed. Although these activities must have generated substantial demands in terms of manpower and resources, our impression is that the initial implementation of the legislation proceeded without major problems. It should, however, be noted that because admission to primary school in Scotland is based on a system of catchment areas, and because allocation to secondary school is either based on a similar system or on attendance at a 'feeder primary' school, the system of allocation which exists in Scotland is much simpler than some of the 'free choice' systems which operate south of the border[46].

TAKE-UP

Over the four years since the placing request provisions of the 1981 Act came into effect, the number of placing requests doubled from 10,456 in 1981-82 to 20,795 in 1984-85[47]. 96% of the requests have been for children of school-age and 4% for under-age children, but the number of requests for under-age children has increased quite markedly from 261 (1.5% of the total) in 1982-83 to 1,844 (8.8% of the total) in 1984-85. Among children of school age, more than half the requests (56%) have been for primary school and less than half (44%) have been for secondary school. After increasing steadily from 1981-82 to 1983-84, the number of placing requests for primary schools levelled off in 1984-85 while the number for secondary schools actually declined somewhat. Thus it could well be that a plateau has now been reached.

Over the four years 1982-1985, 97.4% of requests for primary school and 93.8% of requests for secondary school were granted, either at the initial stage or at appeal committee or on appeal to the sheriff. However, there was a downward trend between 1982-83 (when 98.5% of primary requests and 97.3% of secondary requests were granted) and 1984-85 (when the corresponding figures were 95.7% and 90.3%), reflecting the growing practice of a number of authorities to restrict admissions to schools which would otherwise be oversubscribed. By comparison the success rate for under-age placing requests was much lower – 1,001 out of the 2,618 requests submitted over the period 1983-1985 (38.2%) were refused.

At both primary and secondary levels, the majority of requests are for children entering the first year of school. Thus, in 1984-85, 55.2% of primary requests (6,390 out of 11,561) were for P1 while 68.7% of secondary requests (5,767 out of 8,390) were for S1. The 1984-85 figures are not yet available but in 1983-84, 8.9% of P1 pupils and 8.1% of S1 pupils had made placing requests.

National figures, such as those mentioned above, mask considerable regional and local variations. At primary level, the regions with the highest placing request rates are Tayside (15.4% of P1 pupils in 1983-84), Lothian (11.0%) and Grampian (10.0%). For Strathclyde Region, the overall rate was 9.1%, but the rate for Glasgow Division (12.7%) was substantially higher. The Highlands and Islands have the lowest placing request rates: Highland (1.6% of P1 pupils in 1983-84), Western Isles (1.3%), Orkney (0.8%) and Shetlands (0%). At secondary level, the pattern is very similar. Tayside (13.3% of S1 pupils in 1984), Lothian (11.8%) and Grampian (11.0%) again had the highest rates; Strathclyde (7.8%) was somewhat lower but the rate for Glasgow Division (10.3%) was again higher. The regions with the lowest rates were Highland (1.9%), Shetland (1.3%), Orkney (0.7%) and Borders (0.7%).

It is clear that the more urbanised regions, where schools have relatively small catchment areas and children can easily get to several schools, have higher placing request rates than rural regions where this is usually not the case. Within regions, the same relationships are to be found and placing request rates are highest in the cities and lowest in rural areas. Thus, for example, in 1983-84, 21.1% of the P1 entry and 19.8% of the S1 entry in Dundee had made placing requests[48] compared with rates of 15.4% and 13.3% in Tayside. Because, in many parts of Scotland, Catholic schools have larger catchment areas than non-denominational schools, we would expect the percentage of placing requests for Catholic schools to be lower and this is, in fact, the case. In 1984, the P1 placing request rate for Catholic schools in Dundee (5.4%) was only 38.0% of the rate for non-denominational schools (14.2%); likewise the S1 placing request rate (12.3%) was only 56.4% of the non-denominational rate (21.8%).

The pattern of under-age requests is completely different. In 1984-85, Strathclyde accounted for 1,476 out of 1,844, i.e. 80.0% of such requests. In the previous year (1983-84), when the number of under-age placing requests was much less, the authority with the highest rate (3.4% of the P1 entry) was Highland Region.

IMPACT ON PARENTS

What kinds of parents have made placing requests for their children and what were their reasons for doing so? The University of Glasgow Parental Choice Project found[49] that placing requests have been made by parents across the entire social class spectrum and not predominantly by a middle class minority. This finding is confirmed by our own survey research[50]. However, although we were unable to identify any factors which differentiated between parents who had made a placing request (requesters) and those who had not (non-requesters) when we analysed the entire sample of 1,000 respondents, relationships did emerge when the sample was broken down by geographical location and by school catchment area. Thus, the fact that no overall pattern has emerged does not imply that no identifiable patterns exist at a local level.

A very large majority of all parents seem to have been aware of their rights to request a school different from the one allocated to their child by the education authority. Although there were variations between geographical areas, and between the parents of children who were about to enter primary or secondary school, large majorities of non-requesters were aware of their right to select another school. For all parents, the most common source of their knowledge was an official communication from the education department or the school. A large majority of requesting and non-requesting parents were aware that placing requests could be refused. The most common reason was believed to be overcrowding or lack of accommodation at the school and parents overwhelmingly agreed that requests should be turned down in these circumstances. Nearly all the requesters and a large majority of non-requesters were aware of their right to appeal. Overall, parents seemed very well informed about their rights under the 1981 Act.

In presenting a brief account of the ways in which parents used their rights and selected schools for their children, we present our conclusions separately for entry to primary[51] and admission to secondary[52]. At P1 entry, about 60% of parents who made a placing request were concerned to avoid sending their child to the catchment area school. However, whether or not this was a consideration, the concerns of parents tended to be pragmatic and pastoral in nature. Proximity and safety (on the one hand) and a concern with the 'happiness' of their child were the dominant concerns. Although the latter may conceal as much (if not more) than it reveals, there was little evidence that parents were influenced by what the child was likely to learn or by the style and quality of teaching at the school. Parents were less concerned with the specifics of educational provision and more concerned with the external attributes of the school, e.g. with 'rough and rowdy' children whose contact they wished to avoid or with overcrowding and accommodation which they regard as inappropriate for their children.

Many of our findings at secondary level replicate those for admission to primary school. At S1 entry, almost 70% of requesting parents were concerned to avoid the district school. Although there were again variations between different areas, there was a similar emphasis upon factors which related to practical and pragmatic considerations rather than to an assessment of educational provisions. Among reasons for rejecting a school, for example, inconvenient location again featured prominently together with the suggestion that the child him/herself did not wish to go to the district school. Thus the question of the child's happiness again appeared to be a dominant factor. Poor discipline was another consideration which was cited frequently – in all geographical locations it was among the top three reasons. In giving their reasons for choosing a school, parents in all areas most frequently said they were choosing a particular school because they thought that their child would be happier there. Siblings who were already at the school, friends who were going there and proximity were all mentioned frequently. On the other hand, there was only occasional reference to the subjects on offer at the chosen school or to the school's educational record in terms of its published examination results. Our general conclusion was that the majority of parents have in mind a broad general agenda in selecting a secondary school for their child and are as much if not more concerned with social considerations than with educational ones.

At both primary and secondary levels, about two thirds of all the parents who made placing requests only considered one school other than the district (catchment area) school. Since about the same proportion of requesting parents were motivated by a concern to avoid their district school, it is clear that, for most requesters, choice involves a process of 'satisficing', in which rejection of an unsatisfactory district school is followed by selection of a satisfactory alternative[53]. There were very few examples of parents trying to pick the best available school – even at the secondary level, only 10% of requesting parents considered three or more schools (including private schools).

Overall, our evidence suggests that parents are rather well-informed about their rights; that, although this may not be the case at a local level, those who have exercised their right to make a placing request are a reasonably representative cross-section of parents in terms of social class, income, education, housing, political affiliation etc., but in making a placing request, parents are influenced more by psychological and social considerations over which the school may have little control than by a concern with the education on offer at the school.

IMPACT ON SCHOOLS

As we would expect, placing requests have had a very differential effect on local authority schools. Some schools have experienced substantial net gains while others have incurred substantial net losses; many have been affected hardly at all and, in a smaller number of cases, gains have been matched by losses. Our research on the effects of parental choice on admissions to schools in Dundee[54] and Edinburgh[55] suggests that, at the primary level, most of the movement between schools involved a move to an adjacent school (this was the case for 83% of all requests in Edinburgh and 85% in Dundee). Although there are extreme differences in the social composition of school catchment areas in both cities, similar schools tend to be grouped together in certain areas of the city. Because of the local nature of the majority of P1 requests, movement is predominently within these areas, which are homogeneous with respect to social composition and housing tenure. In both cities there is evidence of a set of sub-systems of movement, usually within these areas.

The main factors which influenced movement between primary schools were similar in the two cities. Movement tended to be towards larger schools (although this could have been because they had gained pupils in the past) and away from schools which are located in areas of social and economic deprivation. In Dundee, there was no evidence of movement away from schools on housing schemes, but there was some slight evidence of this in Edinburgh. In Dundee and Edinburgh, the much smaller number of moves to non-adjacent schools were clearly very different. They tended to be away from local authority housing schemes and towards schools in middle class areas. In both cities, the impact of placing requests on primary school intakes has resulted in sharp gains and losses for a number of primary schools. Some schools are in danger of becoming overcrowded, and as a result, Lothian and Tayside Regions have had to restrict entry to a few schools. At the same time, other schools are seriously undersubscribed.

However, because of the local nature of movement between schools and the social geography of the two cities, placing requests have probably not had a very marked impact on the social composition of school intakes.

Geographical factors were also important at secondary level. In Dundee and in Edinburgh, the greatest amount of movement was between schools which are a fairly short distance apart. After allowing for distance, school attainment measures were the strongest predictors of movement followed by census variables. Thus, movement tended to be towards schools with better SCE results and higher staying-on rates, and towards schools in more middle class areas. In Edinburgh the three schools which gained large numbers of pupils were all located in middle class areas (and were all previously selective schools), while the three schools which lost most pupils were all on local authority housing schemes in areas characterised by a high incidence of social and economic deprivation. In Dundee, the three gaining schools were all previously selective schools, two of which were located in old, inner- city areas, but the two losing schools were both on local authority housing schemes. In one or two cases, particularly in Edinburgh, placing requests have had an effect on the social composition of the intake to the gaining school. In both cities, some of the losing schools now have S1 intakes of less than 100 and their viability must therefore be called into question. Entry to the three gaining schools in Edinburgh has now been restricted (in order that they can abandon annexes and replace temporary accommodation) but access is still unrestricted in Dundee. Overall, the advantages for some children of attending larger secondary schools with more balanced intakes and higher staying-on rates appear to have imposed substantial costs on other children whose curricular choices and wider educational opportunities have been further restricted.

IMPACT ON AUTHORITIES

We can only really comment on three authorities (Lothian, Fife and Tayside) where we have carried out research and studied the impact of the legislation in some detail. In Lothian, the legislation resulted in a radical transformation of the region's policy on school admissions. Prior to the 1981 Act, Lothian's policy on school admissions was one of the most restrictive in Scotland. Under a Labour administration, the region adopted a strong commitment to neighbourhood schools and sought to strengthen the ties between secondary schools and the primary schools within their catchment area. Children were allocated to their local (catchment area) school and, although parents could request an alternative school, such requests were usually refused unless the child involved already had a sibling at the chosen school or there were documented medical reasons which made it appropriate for the child to be offered a place. The number of transfer requests was fairly small (391 in 1981) but about one-third of them (126 or 32.2%) were refused, although there was frequently room at the school. It was this restrictive policy which led to the confrontation with the Secretary of State soon after the return of the Conservative government, which ended in 1981 when the Secretary of State amended Lothian's transfer scheme and ordered the region to grant parental requests at transfer to secondary school if there was room at the chosen school. This allocation policy inevitably meant that the region would be strongly opposed to the government's legislative proposals. The Labour controlled region accepted the Secretary of State's amendments to its transfer scheme but the 1981 Act completely transformed the existing allocation policy. In the first three years after the Act came into effect, Lothian (which had a minority Conservative administration from May 1982 to May 1986) took the view that the 1981 Act prevented it from refusing any parental requests unless it was clear that the admission of another child would cause 'serious detriment' to the school and the well-being of its pupils. Thus, it accepted virtually all parental requests for non-district schools. As we have already seen, some primary and secondary schools in Edinburgh gained substantial numbers of pupils and became overcrowded, while others lost large numbers of pupils and became seriously undersubscribed. As a result, the intake to some secondary schools has dropped to a point where it has become difficult for them to maintain a wide range of curricular choice.

Lothian undertook a re-evaluation of its policy for secondary schools in 1984. It concluded that it could impose intake limits on overcrowded schools, in particular where it wished to phase out annexes or replace temporary accommodation, but that no direct action could be taken to protect undersubscribed schools. Admission limits were imposed on the three schools which had received most placing requests in 1984-85 and in this year Lothian refused almost 100 requests for the schools in question. 12 parents appealed and three appeals were upheld on the grounds that the region had not properly applied its own criteria for determining priorities. However, there was no challenge to the region's imposition of intake limits. This was also the case in 1985-86 – 94 placing requests were refused for the three intake limited secondary schools, 11 parents appealed but this time none were successful. Lothian also refused a number of placing requests for primary schools, including requests from latecomers to the catchment area. Placing requests have been refused where the admission of another child would breach a contractual agreement on maximum class sizes[56] and require the appointment of an additional teacher once staffing allocations have been made, or where accommodation restrictions call for a limit on class size lower than the normal maximum. In nearly every case where the parent has appealed, the appeal committee has upheld the region[57]. There has only been one appeal to the sheriff; this concerned admission to a purpose-built primary school where the design of the building required class sizes to be lower than the normal maximum[58]. In this case too, the sheriff upheld the region.

Not surprisingly, in the light of this experience, Lothian has concluded that it can protect schools from overcrowding. However, since there has only been one appeal to the sheriff, and the circumstances of that case were somewhat atypical, the region cannot be sure that its general policy of imposing intake limits on oversubscribed schools would be upheld by the courts. Although the new Labour administration is committed to developing links between secondary schools and the primary schools within their catchment areas, and to grouping secondary schools together in consortia[59]it remains to be seen how successfully these policies will protect the curricular choices and wider educational opportunities of pupils at secondary schools which have lost a large proportion of their intake. If they fail, the fears of the critics that the 1981 Act would lead to the reintroduction (by the back door) of a two-tier system of secondary education will have been borne out.

The picture in Fife differs from that in Lothian in a number of respects. In the years immediately following reorganisation, the policy in operation at primary and secondary levels was one of rigid zoning by catchment areas. This policy was fairly strictly applied although some exceptions were made. School rolls were on the whole near to capacity and there was a desire to minimise movement across catchment area boundaries. However, at the beginning of 1978, the attitude of the authority towards parental choice began to shift. Falling rolls in primary schools created greater scope for flexibility and, anticipating that legislation was very likely, the region decided to proceed with the implementation of a scheme for parental choice in primary schools from August 1980. Perhaps because of this initiative at primary level, Fife (which had a Labour administration) was distinctly more favourable than some other regions in its response through COSLA to the government's legislative proposals. At secondary level the authority was somewhat more cautious, concerned at the damage that parental choice could inflict on a balanced comprehensive system. However, with the passing of the legislation Fife proceeded to implement the requirements in a fairly routine manner. The region is committed to accommodate all district pupils within the district school and only in one primary school has it been found necessary to refuse placing requests because of lack of space. This is also the only school where any appeals have been pursued, and no parent has made a further appeal to the sheriff. The nature of the movement resulting from placing requests has been less dramatic than in some other regions, e.g. Lothian and Tayside, and there have been no problems of overcrowding which have necessitated action of the type experienced in Lothian. There is, however, some increasing concern emerging at the effects that are becoming evident at the least popular secondary schools. Two schools in particular are losing a substantial proportion of pupils. Moreover, pupils are not only opting out on entry to secondary but are applying to attend a primary school within the catchment area of the desired secondary school at an earlier stage, in the belief that this will secure them admission to the secondary school later on. The legislation has accentuated an already vulnerable position in that both of these schools had initial weaknesses but the authority has yet to determine whether, and if so, how it intends to deal with the problem.

The picture in Tayside is different again. After reorganisation, the region adopted a catchment area system and children were allocated to the primary or secondary school which served the catchment area in which they lived. However this policy was operated flexibly and the relatively small numbers of requests for admission to schools other than the catchment area school were granted where space was available. There appears to have been general satisfaction with these procedures and, for this reason, Conservative controlled Tayside was unenthusiastic about the need for legislation.

The main effect of the legislation has been to increase substantially the number of requests for admission to schools other than the catchment area school. As we have seen, this has been particularly marked in Dundee. Nevertheless, in spite of the consequences (the growth of composite classes in primary schools and substantial imbalances in secondary level intakes) Tayside has, until recently, continued to operate a policy of laissez-faire. However, this policy was brought to an end when it got in the way of other (more important) policy concerns. Thus, in selecting primary schools for closure the region did not appear to give much weight to parental choice[60]; once the schools had been closed, it then imposed a limit on admissions to adjacent schools; and, in deciding on the future capacity of a secondary school which was to be substantially rebuilt, a limit below its current intake was fixed in order to protect a neighbouring school.

The three regions provide a number of interesting contrasts. They differed, for example, in political control (Fife has always been Labour; Lothian switched from Labour to Conservative in 1982 and from Conservative to Labour in 1986; while Tayside has, until the 1986 regional elections, always been Conservative) and in their attitudes to parental choice (under Labour, Lothian took a hardline approach; likewise Fife, although it had adopted a more flexible policy for primary school admissions prior to the 1981 Act; while Tayside under the Conservatives was always very flexible). However, the Act itself has had a similar impact on all three authorities. Particularly in the cities, it has produced substantial imbalances in school intakes which have serious staffing and curricular implications. Surprisingly Conservative controlled Lothian Region probably went furthest in the direction of imposing limits on parental choice, although the legality of its attempts to protect schools from overcrowding still remains to be tested in the courts.

THE IMPACT OF APPEALS

The 1981 Act severely curtails the discretion of education authorities to formulate their own allocation policies by granting parents the right to request a school of their choice and placing a duty on authorities to grant any placing request unless one of a small number of grounds for refusal applies. However, it does not remove the authorities' discretion altogether, since they are still free to formulate their own policies within the constraints imposed by the legislation. Under the Act, parents are given a right of appeal against refusal first to an appeal committee and then to the sheriff. Although an authority might be prepared to live with an occasional reversal by an appeal committee, especially if it were on grounds of 'appropriateness' and did not threaten its general policies, it would have to take very seriously any adverse decision by a sheriff. Most authorities have taken a broad view of sheriffs' judgments and have sought to bring their general policies into line with them; those that have taken a narrower view, and have not amended their general policies in the light of sheriffs' decisions in individual cases, have nevertheless had to make exceptions to their general policy whenever a parent has appealed to the sheriff. Thus, the extent to which adverse decisions are appealed and the outcome of these appeals is central to an understanding of the impact of the legislation on policy and practice.

The number of cases taken to an appeal committee has increased from 85 in 1982-83 to 321 in 1984-85[61]. Of the 321 appeals in 1984-85, 182 referred to requests for secondary schools, 90 to requests for primary schools for school age children, 47 to requests for early admission from under-age children and 2 to requests for special schools. Overall the total represented 27.6% of parents whose placing requests were refused by the authority, although this proportion was considerably higher for P1 refusals (77 out of 155 or 49.6%) and S1 refusals (157 out of 500 or 31.4%) than for under-age cases (47 out of 376 or 12.5% refusals). The proportion of appeals upheld was about one quarter for each type of appeal (12 out of 47 for under-age cases, 19 out of 77 for P1 and 2 out of 13 for P2-P7, 39 out of 157 for S1 and 17 out of 25, i.e. rather more, for S2-S6). Appeals to the sheriff have been far fewer in number. Between 1981-82 and 1985-86, less than 50 cases have been heard, and most of these have been decided in favour of the parents. Thus, the number of appeals to the sheriff has been small but not insignificant.

During the course of our research we were able to observe appeal committees in operation in one authority and to compare them with accounts of their operation in another authority[62]. Focussing here on appeals for oversubscribed schools, neither of the two sets of appeal committees appeared to consider the question of whether the authorities' admission limits are justified in terms of the 1981 Act. In fact, they appeared to consider questions about admission limits as irrelevant to their concerns – in one authority they assumed that admission limits were near-absolute barriers to upholding appeals, whereas, in the other, they considered exceptions without regard to the admission limit, although they did appear to think that too many exceptions would be wrong. Thus, in the first authority, appeal committees saw their role as supportive of the authority. The main emphasis was on explaining to parents why they could not have a place at the school. Appeal committees were also, on occasion, concerned to ensure that the authority had properly applied its own policy and the only appeals which have been upheld in this authority have related to circumstances in which they were of the opinion that the authority had not applied its own policy fairly. In the second authority, appeal committees have seen their task as one of evaluating the circumstances of parents and upholding appeals where the parents put a particularly strong case. Thus, they have been more prepared to make exceptions to the authority's policy. Interestingly, the approaches of the two appeal committees have matched those adopted by the authority. In the first authority, parents are not interviewed and the Placing Request Sub-Committee[63] makes a fairly cursory look for special circumstances, its main concern being to apply the Council's guidelines in such a way as to offer places within the school's admission limit. In the second authority, where a school is over-subscribed, all parents are interviewed by the School Council, which makes a real effort to identify special circumstances, and exceptions are made to those admission limit in many cases. Thus, in both cases, appeal committees function as an extension to the procedures and in neither case do they really function as an effective check on the authority.

Our examination of sheriffs' judgments[64] suggests that they have adopted two different approaches to adjudication. In the 'single child' line of decisions, sheriffs have interpreted the statutory grounds of refusal restrictively, holding that parents' appeals must be upheld unless the authority can show that a ground of refusal exists in the case of the single child involved in the appeal. Thus, they have refused to allow the harmful effects of overcrowding at the school to justify refusal[65]. In the 'school-level' line of decisions, sheriffs have been prepared to look at the conditions in the school and have taken into account the fact that other parents may have requested the same school and been turned down. These sheriffs have rejected the single child approach, arguing that it makes it virtually impossible to refuse any requests, and have instead examined the authority's justification for limiting admissions, which has usually referred to overcrowding and its detrimental effects on education at the school[66].

Which of the two approaches sheriffs adopt is obviously of considerable importance to an authority. Where a sheriff adopts the first approach, an authority can be reasonably confident that if it can justify the imposition of admission limits, it will be able to enforce them. Where a sheriff adopts the second approach, the authority can have no such confidence and, although it may still wish to impose admission limits in appropriate cases, it cannot expect to be able to enforce them. In Lothian, there has only been one appeal to the sheriff so far and in this case the sheriff adopted a 'school-level' approach to adjudication and, in doing so, found in favour of the authority. On this basis, and because the appeal committees have been prepared to go along with it, the region feels confident about the legality of its policy of determining and enforcing admission limits on schools it regards as oversubscribed. There have been no appeals to the sheriff in Fife or Tayside, although there may well be appeals to the sheriff in Tayside now that the region has imposed admission limits on some of its schools. The main contrast with Lothian is Strathclyde, where there has been a string of appeals to the sheriff and where all the sheriffs have adopted the 'single child' approach to adjudication. In doing so, they have consistently found in favour of the parents. The main consequence of this is that, although the region continues to set admission limits for its schools, it can no longer enforce them if and when parents appeal to the sheriff. As a result, Strathclyde Region now concedes most appeals as soon as they are lodged with the sheriff[67]. The 1981 Act prevents all authorities from taking any direct steps to protect their undersubscribed schools; in Strathclyde one consequence of the string of shrieval judgments is that the authority can, in effect, no longer protect its oversubscribed schools either.

EARLY AGE ADMISSIONS

The increasing focus on the admission of under-age children to primary education is a development which was not foreseen by those who initiated the 1981 legislation. Few areas adjusted their policy towards early age admission in the light of the Act, and, in all but one of the education authorities, applications were treated separately from placing requests. The major effect of this being to deny any access to the appeal procedures. However, this practice was called into question in an opinion by the Sheriff Principal in Aberdeen in a test case (the Boyne case)[68], in which it was ruled that education authorities were under a duty to treat requests for under-age children as placing requests in terms of the Act.

This interpretation had initially been resisted by most authorities and on the initiative of Lothian Region steps were taken to make representation through COSLA to the Secretary of State that the legislation should be modified specifically to exclude requests for under-age children. However, the SED had, by this time, already responded to the Sheriff Principal's decision in the Boyne case by issuing Circular 1108/1984[69]. This made it clear that applications for early admission were to be treated as placing requests and threatened action under section 70 of the 1980 Act if education authorities did not comply[70]. In doing so, the Secretary of State intimated that the judgment in the Boyne case accurately reflected the legislative intention of the government that parents of under-age children should have the right to make a placing request and access to the statutory appeal procedures if that request is refused. Not only is this a very questionable interpretation of the legislation, it is also a rather unusual way for the government to make policy. Nevertheless, the majority of authorities reluctantly capitulated to the demands of this Circular, although at least one continues to be less than explicit over the right of appeal in its explanatory leaflet.

We have already referred to the increasing number of requests for early admission and the increasing number of under-age appeals. The placing request rate varies considerably between authorities. We have already seen that the largest number (1,476 out of 1,844 or 80% of the total in 1984-85) came from Strathclyde. However, as a proportion of the P1 population Highland (97 cases, 3.4% of P1 intake in 1983-84) and Borders (25 cases, 2.1% of P1 intake in 1983-84) are also higher than most other regions. The policies of the authorities also differed a great deal: whereas Strathclyde granted 63.4% of under-age placing requests in 1985, Tayside granted 24.3% (6 out of 25) while Lothian only granted 8.1% (3 out of 37).

These differences, which are again replicated in the approach to under- age cases taken by appeal committees, also reflect differences in their interpretation of the statutory grounds for refusing such requests. Children who are under the statutory age of entry may be refused admission if 'the education normally provided at the school is not suited to the age, ability or aptitude of the child'[71]. While most authorities (including Strathclyde) consider the terms 'age', 'ability' and 'aptitude' in the phrase 'age, ability or aptitude' conjunctively, arguing that age on its own is not a ground for refusal and must be considered along with ability and aptitude; some (including Lothian) interpret the phrase disjunctively and regard age as a sufficient ground for refusal. The second interpretation does not put an end to the matter since the Act gives authorities (and likewise appeal committees and sheriffs) the power to grant a placing request even where the ground for refusal applies if they consider it appropriate to do so[72]. Although the first approach was adopted by the sheriff in a recent appeal in Highland Region[73], in another recent appeal (this time in Lothian Region)[74] the sheriff accepted the view of both parties that the word 'or' implied that the terms could be used disjunctively with the result that the appeal was refused on the grounds of the child's age alone. Thus, the issue remains unresolved and different authorities persist with their different interpretations.

This being so, Lothian and Strathclyde adopt approaches to under-age admissions which parallel their approaches to requests for oversubscribed schools. Lothian has a policy of refusing applications from under-age children and is very reluctant to make exceptions to it. Strathclyde on the other hand (and Tayside to a lesser extent) is much more prepared to assess the ability of the child to benefit from a school education and has seen fit to admit a substantial number of under-age children. In each case, the region's policy is replicated by its appeal committees. These differences in policy in part reflect differences in interpretation of the relevant statute. However, they also reflect a different stance towards the legislation largely imposed upon the authorities by different kinds of shrieval judgments, as well as more mundane considerations such as the extent of nursery school provision in the respective regions. This notwithstanding, the cost to Strathclyde of admitting large numbers of under-age children is quite substantial – figures have been published to the effect that the region has had to employ 44 extra teachers at a cost of £200,000[75] – and the authority is concerned about the administrative and financial implications. Others have expressed concern at the long-term educational implications of this development[76].

CONCLUSION

Having considered the impact of the parental choice provisions in the 1981 Act on parents, schools and education authorities, we are now in a position to assess whether the legislation has achieved a satisfactory balance between the rights of individual parents and the duties of education authorities with collective responsibilities for all children. The rights granted to parents under the act appear to be widely understood; parents who have made placing requests do not seem to have experienced any difficulties in doing so; the extent of take-up, particularly in urban areas, has been quite substantial; and placing requests have been made by parents across the entire social class spectrum. In choosing schools, most parents have emphasised psychological and social concerns rather than educational ones. They have, in many cases, been concerned to avoid their district school and have opted for a more satisfactory alternative. In doing so, they have been influenced more by the general reputation of the schools than by any careful assessment of the education they provide. Thus, there is a good deal of evidence for 'incremental problem solving' but considerably less for 'rational choice'[77].

In many areas, the exercise of choice has imposed few, if any, costs but, in other areas, the costs have been quite considerable. In a few cases, the exercise of choice by some parents has deprived others of the opportunity to send their child to their local (catchment area) school. Elsewhere, it has caused overcrowding which, in spite of the provisions in the act which were intended to prevent it, has undoubtedly caused 'serious detriment' to other children. It has, likewise, resulted in some very under-subscribed schools. This is of particular concern at secondary level where curricular choices and educational opportunities for pupils at such schools may be seriously affected. In the case of under-age children, the exercise of choice by some parents may not be in the long-term interests of their own children and may, in addition, impose costs on the other (school- age) children in the class. Although parents' rights may not be seen to be in need of much protection, there is little evidence that appeal committees provide such protection when it is needed or that they function as an effective check on the powers of education authorities.

While the parental choice provisions of the 1981 Act have substantially enhanced the rights of parents, they have, at the same time, seriously curtailed the powers of education authorities. Thus, Scottish education authorities (unlike their English counterparts) have no powers to protect under-subscribed schools. Although the act did give them powers to protect over-subscribed schools, where one of the statutory exceptions to the general duty to comply with placing requests applies, their ability to do so is largely dependent on the approach to statutory interpretation adopted by sheriffs in the small number of appeal cases that have been taken that far. The same applies to the authorities' ability to say 'no' to the admission of under-age children. There are no sanctions for authorities which choose to adopt a laissez-faire approach to school admissions, but those which do not may find their decisions struck down by the courts. Appeals to the sheriff have not removed inconsistencies in statutory interpretation, nor are they likely to do so since sheriffs have disagreed on all the key issues they have had to consider, and this, as much as differences in the policies of the authorities, results in substantial diversity of practice. In urban areas, the act has caused serious imbalances in school intakes and, particularly at secondary level, there is evidence that it has not only increased educational inequality but that it is also leading to the reintroduction (in another form) of the old (and discredited) two-tier system of schooling. Thus, although placing requests have been unproblematic in many areas, our overall conclusion is that the 1981 Act has not achieved the right balance between the rights of individual parents and the collective duties of education authorities. Moreover, we do not think the right balance will be achieved unless and until education authorities are given more powers to control admissions to school, subject to effective safeguards which would ensure that these powers are used responsibly to prevent parental choice from prejudicing equality of educational opportunity or the duty placed on education authorities to promote 'adequate and efficient education' for all.

*This paper is based on a programme of research on parental choice in education, funded initially by the ESRC and latterly by the SED, and we would like to thank both these organisations for their financial support. We would also like to thank our secretary, Valerie Chuter, for her forbearance and for her practical help in a variety of ways. In addition, we would like to acknowledge the considerable assistance we have received from many individuals who helped us by giving us their time, answering our questions, providing us with data or with access to their files. Without their assistance our research could not have been undertaken. A shorter version of this paper was presented at the annual conference of the Scottish Educational Research Association, held at the University of St Andrews, 25-27 September 1986.

Michael Adler, Department of Social Policy and Social Work, University of Edinburgh.

Alison Petch, Social Work Research Centre, University of Stirling.

Jack Tweedie, Department of Political Science, State University of New York at Binghamton.

References

1. The 1946 Act runs to 109 pages and contains 144 sections and 6 schedules. It is about the same length as the (English) Education Act 1944, which runs to 109 pages and contains 122 sections and 9 schedules.

2. Education (Scotland) Act 1946, s 1(1).

3. *ibid*, s 7(2).

4. *ibid*, s 65.

5. *ibid*, s 66.

6. *ibid*, s 31.

7. *ibid*, s 35.

8. Watt v Kesteven County Council (1955) 1 QB 408. See also, Paul Meredith (1981), 'Executive Discretion and Choice of Secondary School', *Public Law*, pp 52-82.

9. C M G Himsworth (1980), 'School Attendance Orders and the Sheriff', *Journal of the Law Society of Scotland*, pp 450-455.

10. Education (Scotland) Act 1946, s 30.

11. Scottish Education Department (1947), Secondary Education : a Report of the Advisory Council on Education in Scotland, Cmnd. 7005, Edinburgh: HMSO.

12. In the financial year 1983-84, public expenditure on education came to 5.2% GDP.13. Andrew McPherson and Charles Raab (1987), *The Making of Scottish Educational Policy*, Edinburgh: Edinburgh University Press (forthcoming). Our account of early post-war developments is based on theirs.

14. Our account of secondary school reorganisation also draws very heavily on McPherson and Raab, *op cit*.

15. Scottish Education Department (1965), 'Reorganisation of Secondary Education on Comprehensive Lines' (Circular 600).

16. This was the only one on which the Secretary of State used his powers to amend an authority's transfer scheme.

17. The following account is based on research carried out by our colleague Jack Tweedie. See Jack Tweedie (1986), 'Parental Choice of School: Legislating the Balance' in Andy Stillman (ed) (1986), *The Balancing Act of 1980: Parents, Politics and Education, Slough: National Foundation for Educational Research*, pp 3-11.

18. The Conservative's Election Manifesto for October 1974 included the following: A CHARTER OF PARENTS' RIGHTS: An important part of the distinct Conservative policy on Education is to recognise parental rights. A say in how their children are to be brought up is an essential ingredient in the parental role. We will therefore introduce additional rights for parents. First, by amending the 1944 Education Act, we will impose clear obligations on the State and local authorities to take account of the wishes of parents. Second, we will consider establishing a local appeal system for parents dissatisfied with the allotment of schools. (The Charter goes on to promise parental representation on boards of governors, an obligation to form parent-teachers associations, and a requirement that schools publish prospectuses.)

19. Education (Parents' Charter) Bill, 1974.

20. Department of Education and Science (1977), 'Consultation Paper – Admission of Children to the School of their Choice'.

20a. According to a Scottish Office *Press Notice*, issued on 24 November 1978 "In England and Wales, the law on school admissions is confusing and to some extend contradictory, and the extent to which parents can express a preference varies widely from area to area. No similar need for legislation exists in Scotland."

21. The 1979 Conservative Manifesto stated: Extending parents' rights and responsibilities, including their right of choice, will also help raise standards by giving them greater influence over education. Our parents' charter will place a clear duty on government and local authorities to take account of parents' wishes when allocating children to schools, with a local appeals system for those dissatisfied. Schools will be required to publish prospectuses giving details of their examination and other results.

22. This was the first of several meetings between Alex Fletcher, SED officials, elected members of the COSLA Education Committee and Directors of Education (in their role as advisors to the Committee) at which the Minister outlined the government's thinking in general terms and

sought a response from the Convention.

23. Other items on the agenda were the need to monitor educational standards and the assisted places scheme.

24. Scottish Education Department (1980), 'Consultative Paper: Admission to Schools – A Charter for Parents'. The other Consultative Papers dealt with curriculum development, education for the 16-18s, and the assisted places scheme.

25. *Times Educational Supplement (Scotland)* (1980), 'Fletcher Unveils "The New Spirit"', 7 March, p 1.

26. Scottish Education Department (1980), *op cit*, para 6.

27. Alastair Macbeth, David Strachan and Caithlin Macaulay (1986), *Parental Choice of School in Scotland*, Department of Education, University of Glasgow, chapter 3.

28. Confederation of Scottish Local Authorities (1980), 'Observations on the Consultative Paper "Admission to School – a Charter for Parents"'.

29. Scottish Consumer Council (1980), 'A Charter for Parents – the SCC's Reply to the Government's Proposals'.

30. The particular concerns of the Working Group, comprising I G Halliday (Depute Director of Education, Strathclyde), D G Robertson (Director of Education, Tayside) and W D C Semple (Director of Education, Lothian), related to the appeal arrangements information for parants and the proposal to use regulation rather than advisory circulars.

31. Other important provisions contained within the bill dealt with special educational needs, the assisted places scheme, changes in the powers of the Secretary of State and the duties of education authorities, and a number of miscellaneous matters.

32. Education (Scotland) (No 2) Bill, clause 28A(3)(a)(i).

33. ibid, clauses 28A(3)(a)(ii) to (v).

34. ibid, clause 28A(3)(b).

35. Comprising 3, 5 or 7 members. Members of the authority or its

education committee could not outnumber those who were not by more than one. Although the appeal committees were to be set up by the authorities, they were nevertheless placed under the general supervision of the Scottish Committee of the Council of Tribunals.

36. COSLA, the EIS, the SCC and the SPTC all prepared detailed amendments to the Bill.

37. Education (Scotland) (No 2) Bill, clause 28A(3)(a)(i).

38. Compare section 6(3) of the Education Act 1980 with section 28A(3) of the Education (Scotland) Act 1981.

39. Education (Scotland) Act 1981, s 30.

40. ibid, ss 28E(5) and 28F(6).

41. In September 1978, together with John MacKay, MP, Alex Fletcher published a Conservative Party paper entitled 'Scottish Education – Regaining a Lost Reputation' in which he stated his strong support for greater freedom of choice of school.

42. The introduction of a right of appeal to the sheriff, the removal of the provision enabling authorities to set admission limits and refuse plaing requests when these are reached, and the requirement that appeal committees should be chaired by one of the independent members.

43. John Pollock, General Secretary of the EIS, was quoted as saying: 'The government is using outside organisations in order to slip through vital amendments which would fundamentally affect Scottish education in years to come, without consultation and with the minimum of fuss'. It is clear that he was complaining that 'inside' organisations had not been consulted.

44. Education (Scotland) Act 1980, s 1(1).

45. For an analysis of the role of the sheriff in Scotland, see C M G Himsworth (1980), op.cit. In England, the Secretary of State was empowered to alter the terms of an attendance order under section 37(3) of the Education Act 1944. For an account of the English provisions, see Paul Meredith (1981), op cit.

46. On the much greater variety of allocation procedures in England, see Andy Stillman and Karen Meychell (1986), *Choosing Schools: Parents,*

LEAs and the 1980 Education Act, Windsor: NFER-Nelson, chapter 3.

47. Most of the data in this section are taken from Scottish Education Department (1986), 'Placing Requests in Education Authority Schools', *Statistical Bulletin*, No 5/B6.

48. Data for Dundee Division were provided by Tayside Region Education Department.

49. Alastair Macbeth, David Strachan and Caithlin Macaulay (1986), *op cit*.

50. Alison Petch (1986a), 'Parental Choice at Entry to Primary School', *Research Papers in Education*, 1(1), pp 26-47; and Alison Petch (1986b), 'Parents' Reasons for Choosing Schools' in Andy Stillman (ed) (1986), *The Balancing Act of 1980: Parents, Politics and Education*, Slough: National Foundation for Educational Research, pp 28-35.

51. Alison Petch (1986a), *op cit*.

52. Alison Petch (1986b), *op cit*.

53. H A Simon (1965), *Administrative Behaviour*, New York: The Free Press.

54. Michael Adler and Gillian Raab (1986), 'Survival of the Fittest? the Impact of Parental Choice on Admission to Primary and Secondary Schools in Dundee', Department of Social Policy and Social Work, University of Edinburgh (unpublished paper).

55. Gillian Raab and Michael Adler (1986) 'Exploding Some Myths about the Uniqueness of Edinburgh: the Impact of Parental Choice on Admission to Primary and Secondary Schools in Edinburgh', Department of Social Policy and Social Work, University of Edinburgh (unpublished paper).

56. The 'normal maximum class size' is set at 33 in the conditions of service for teachers. Although the size of the class may exceed the 'normal maximum', where this is held to be 'reasonable', Lothian region does not consider increases resulting from placing requests to be reasonable. The absolute limit on class numbers is 39.

57. Five appeals for one 'open plan' primary school, where the authority wished to reduce the size of P1 classes from 33 to 30 to avoid overcrowding,

although the 'normal maximum' had applied in previous years, were upheld in 1983. Over the five year period 1982-1986, 32 other appeals (from school age children) for admission to primary school were all refused. These data were supplied by Lothian Region Education Department.

58. Forbes v Lothian Regional Council (1982), (Edinburgh Sheriff Court, 29 October), unreported.

59. *Times Educational Supplement (Scotland)* (1986), 'Lothian to Step Up Consortia' 16 May, p 1. Strathcyde Region has operated consortia arrangements for some time.

60. Michael Adler (1985), 'Falling Rolls and Risig Conflict', Department of Solcial Policy and Social Work, University of Edinburgh (unpublished paper).

61. See Scottish Education Department (1983) 'Placing Requests in Education Authority Primary and Secondary Schools', *Statistical Bulletin*, No 9/B6; and Scottish Education Department (1986), *op cit*.

62. Jack Tweedie, Michael Adler and Alison Petch (1986), 'The Rights and Wrongs of Education Appeal Committees', Department of Social Policy and Social Work, University of Edinburgh (unpublished paper).

63. Where there is space in the school, places are allocated by the Education Department. However, where the number of applications is greater than the number of available places, decisions are taken by a sub-committee of the Education Committee.

64. Jack Tweedie and Michael Adler (1986), 'Parental Choice: Liberty or License', *Journal of the Law Society of Scotland,* pp 305-310.

65. The majority of sheriffs have adopted the 'single child' approach in their decisions. Among the early cases, see the following: Mrs M Y v Strathclyde Regional Council (1982), (Glasgow Sheriff Court, 16 August); Mrs A B or K v Strathclyde Regional Council (1982), (Glasgow Sheriff Court, 16 August); Mrs A K v Strathclyde Regional Council (1982), (Sheriff Principal, Glasgow Sheriff Court, 9 September); Duggan, Murray and Paul v Strathclyde Regional Council (1983), (Glasgow Sheriff Court, 17 August), and Easton v Strathclyde Regional Council (1984), (Ayr Sheriff Court, 27 August); all unreported. The decision by the Sheriff Principal in Mrs A K v Strathclyde Region was particularly influential.

66. Three sheriff's decisions have followed the 'school level' line of reasoning: Forbes v Lothian Regional Council (1982), op.cit; X v Shetland Islands Council (1983), (Lerwick Sheriff Court, 19 October), and D v Grampion Regional Council (1984), Aberdeen Sheriff Court, 29 August); all unreported.

67. During the school year 1984-1985, Strathclyde Region conceded more than 40 appeals in this way. In the period August-December 1985, there were six further appeals to the sheriff in Strathclyde Region. In the first two cases (involving the same school), the Region concluded that it would be unable to establish its case and did not contest the actions. The Region decided to treat the third appeal as a test case but, when the sheriff upheld the appeal, the Region did not contest the two other appeals for this school. In the sixth appeal (for another school), the Region again concluded that it would be unable to establish its case and did not contest the action.

68. Boyne and Boyne v Grampian Regional Council (1983), (Sheriff Principal, Aberdeen Sheriff Court, 29 October), unreported.

69. Scottish Education Department (1984), 'Placing Requests: Under-Age Children', (Circular 1108).

70. Under s 70, "If the Secretary of State is satisfied...that an education authority...have failed to discharge any statutory duty imposed on them by the 1980 Act, he may make an order declaring them to be in default in respect of their duty and requiring them before a date specified in the order to discharge that duty".

71. Education (Scotland) Act 1981, s 28A(3)(b).

72. *ibid*, s 28A(3).

73. Mackay v Higland Regional Council (1985), (Inverness Sheriff Court, 11 September), unreported.

74. Coates and Coates v Lothian Regional Council (1986), (Linlithgow Sheriff Court, 3 January), unreported.

75. *Times Educational Supplement (Scotland)* (1985), 'Strathclyde Stretched by Early Placings', 8 November, p 3.

76. The Association of Directors of Education in Scotland (ADES) and COSLA have both made rep-resentations to the SED. In addition, it was

one of the main issues raised at the 1986 Annual Conference of the Association of Headteachers (Scotland). Under-age admissions are equally a problem south of the border and it is significant that the DES has recently sponsored a review of existing under-fives research (from Professor Margaret Clarke of Birmingham University), and the NFER is currently carrying out a survey of (English) education authorities' policies towards children starting school at four years of age.

77. David Braybrooke and Charles E Lindblom (1963), *A Strategy of Decision*, New York: The Free Press.

POLITICAL EDUCATION IN SCOTTISH SCHOOLS

Gordon Lawrie

At each General Election called by a full-term government, some two-and-a-half to three million new voters become eligible to vote. Since May 1969, when the voting age was reduced to eighteen, this has meant that that number of eighteen to twenty-three year olds have been asked to participate in deciding the United Kingdom's political course for the immediate future. Considering how influential such a number of voters can be in determining the results of elections, it is remarkable how little attention has been given as to what factors determine the voting patterns of this "new elector" group. Moreover, experience of previous generations has suggested that voter preferences, once established in favour of any given party, are hard to alter, so that these first-time voters may be establishing a trend for their particular generation which may continue throughout its lifetime.

If we accept the assumption that voters tend to vary their votes at least partly according to the performance, and events during the lifetime, of the outgoing government (an extension of the old "oppositions don't win elections, governments lose them" adage), then we can see that the years leading up to the election – anything up to five, in some situations possibly even more – are vital in shaping the views of this new electorate. In turn, what this means is that some new voters are being asked to judge the record of an outgoing government which took ofice when they, the voters, were as young as thirteen – in other words, in their early years at a Scottish secondary school.

Britain has an education system which ensures captive pupils and students between the ages of five and sixteen, and provides for a further variety of educational experiences in schools and colleges up to and beyond the age of eighteen, yet it is the case that, particularly in Scotland, very little is known about the ways in which young voters receive the rudiments of a political education in these environments, or even about the level of commitment that the state gives to developing political literacy in schools.

This article will attempt to begin to fill some of these gaps. It will try to examine and assess the contribution of the Scottish education system towards creating a politically educated electorate – the historical development of political education in Scottish schools, the nature and provision of this political education, and, finally, some of the political and financial influences in Scottish schools. Throughout this article, we will assume, rightly or wrongly, that it is desirable that the electorate should be politically literate so that it can play a full part in a democratic system of government. Schools have a unique – and almost certainly the best – opportunity to ensure this aim is achieved. Yet as we shall see, the development, provision, and nature of political education in the school curriculum apears to depend less on the educational justification of preparing pupils for playing a full role in adult society than it does on expediency, economic viability, and, in some cases, actual political pressures. In short, this article will examine the politics of political education in Scotland.

The Historical Development of Scottish Political Education

Historically, there is little tradition in Scotland of schools making a conscious attempt to include any form of political education at any level of compulsory schooling before the 1950's and 1960's. Parents and teachers alike tended to assume that, like one or two other important things in life, children would eventually "pick up" the important bits of information if they needed to. Some teachers did feel that their pupils should know about their contemporary environment, though, so that, for example, some primary classes made regular studies of the news – cutting out newspaper articles and putting them on a wall and so on. In secondary schools, such little political education as there was could appear virtually anywhere, usually reflecting individual subject teacher's interests at the same time, but most often occurring in english, history, geography, or religious education lessons. Almost without exception, secondary school political education dwelt on current affairs and had almost one aim only – to show that what happened in the news, however boring it might seem to the adolescent child, was in fact rather "important" and could even be quite interesting from time to time. Except in perhaps a few cases, no attempt was made to study political processes, either of the United Kingdom or of foreign governments. Such matters were treated as almost trivial because they were so "modern". These were the days, after all, when history courses in Scottish schools stopped at 1914.

It would be nice to think that the changes in thinking which took place in the 1960's and early 1970's were purely the result of an educational renaissance which thrust political education more into the limelight.

However, it is probably truer that some more basic factors were of greater significance, though it would be wrong to write off totally the work done by educationalists in the field. Three important factors combined around this time to make circumstances ripe for a re-appraisal of the need for some kind of direct "preparation for society". Firstly, in the 1960's, the Scottish system of secondary education was reorganised to usher in a truer comprehensive education. What this in effect meant was that most of the old junior secondary schools closed, and merged with the senior secondary schools into large "high schools". Secondly, population trends in general – and the post-war baby boom in particular – bulged its way through secondary schools at this time, so that school rolls swelled still further. Finally, in the early 1970's, the school leaving age was raised to sixteen, by and large compelling all children to stay at school until the end of their fourth year at secondary school.

These changes did three things. The raising of the school leaving age increased the number of reluctant school attenders dramatically, and it was clear that such pupils, who were only in school because they had to be, simply would not tolerate yet another year of education unless it was at least of clear relevance in preparation for outside life – the old traditional curriculum simply would not do. Early in the 1960's, recognition had already been made of the need to provide certification for more school leavers with the discontinuation of "Lower" Grade examinations, sat in the fifth year[1] of secondary school, and its replacement by "Ordinary Grade", sat a year earlier. This created an examination framework in which new ideas could be developed. Secondly, the emergence of schools with bigger rolls created an environment in which a greater variety of courses became viable, and so, of course, new courses could also be considered for inclusion in the curriculum for the first time. Finally, although the secondary schools grew in size, there were fewer of them, and this created a shortage of promoted posts in schools, including at departmental head level. In the field of social studies there was, in some parts of Scotland at any rate, an immediate need to find jobs for many teachers of history and geography which acknowledged their experience in the junior secondary schools. The answer to all these problems was the development of a new subject in the Scottish curriculum – Modern Studies. The choice of the name itself was significant. It was neutral, could mean virtually all things to all people, and – most of all – the word "modern" suggested relevance and usefulness. Thus because early heads of Modern Studies departments were converted history and geography teachers, the subject itself was at the outset simply a mixture of both; it was very much associated with the less able end of the pupil spectrum; and it was confined to pupils in their last years of schooling.

However, the early efforts of many of these new Modern Studies teachers brought a great deal of praise, especially in that it forced curriculum thinkers to rethink the purpose of social studies provision in schools. Modern Studies rapidly ceased to be merely a history/geography hybrid, since the concentration on contemporary history and social geography clearly led teachers and examiners of the subject[2] towards the areas of politics, sociology, and political economics. Teachers emerged new out of teacher training college with degrees and backgrounds in sociology and, especially, political science, and by the late 1970's Modern Studies had clearly identified itself as the subject of "politics and a bit more". Its protagonists, keen to advance the cause of their subject, began to articulate the value of educating pupils to understand political institutions, political processes, and the important contemporary issues. The status – and profile – of political education rose enormously in these years; and in 1977, the Munn Report declared that

> "It is of the utmost importance that pupils, as members of a society, should be made fully aware of the forces which shape it, and that they should come to understand the operation of our own social and economic institutions, and the pattern of life in other human communities as well. A democratic society needs citizens who have been properly educated in these matters."[3]

Other endorsments of political education came from businessmen, trade unionists, and government ministers, and served to emphasise the fact that, officially at least, political education was both educationally valuable and academically respectable. The Pandora's Box of political education had been opened.

The Nature and Provision of Political Education in Scottish Schools

When analysing any programme of political education, however formal or informal it may be, it is always worth bearing in mind that what is understood by "political education" can be subdivided into different types. There are various ways of doing this, but since this article is not the place for debates on educational theories, we can restrict our categories of political education to two crude types.[4] Firstly, the student, however young or old, can be informed of, or given an understanding of, the political processes of governmental systems. This area is often known as "civics", and would normally include such elements of the United Kingdom system as voting procedures, powers of the Prime Minister and Cabinet, role of the Member of Parliament, functions of local government, House of Lords; and it might also include a study of other systems of interest – the EEC, United Nations, the USA, the Soviet Union, or China, to give but a few examples. The second type of education can be described as "current affairs" and would cover contermporary issues, which students discuss and about which they may or may not be invited to reach conclusions – this can be absolutely anything from political policies or the role of women in society, to nuclear disarmament or the roles of the superpowers in the third world. These two elements make up the body of knowledge on which political education draws, but in the course of their study, students should also be attempting to develop certain political skills to a greater or lesser degree – skills such as "critical analysis", "reporting", "decision-making", and "problem-solving".

The opportunity to begin political education, whatever type it is, begins, of course, in primary schools. Exactly what happens here is very hard to determine, and certainly varies not only from region to region but also from school to school. It would appear that any political education which takes place does so because of the personal interest of a local headteacher, or even of a class teacher. Most commonly, current affairs are discussed in a "what's in the news?" lesson, a lesson about newspapers or television, or in a classroom debate. This type of education hardly ever seems to have system or structure, and the express aim of "developing political literacy" certainly does not exist. Even the most enlightened teachers seem to justify such political education as they do in the classroom as an attempt to "to put classwork into perspective" or "keeping the children informed of the world about them". One might even say that this kind of activity is best described as a subsection of an environmental studies programme which might also include science, geography and history. No Scottish authority claims to have any specific policy pertaining to political education in primary schools. This is surprising – and possibly even a little irresponsible – given that most educationalists agree that the primary school provides essential frameworks and foundations for all future learning experiences. The danger of failing to offer guidance in political education at least to classroom teachers is that it opens the door wider still to uncontrolled political indoctrination; yet education authorities seem to take the view that this will not happen in primary schools, perhaps on the questionable grounds that children of that age are somehow not fertile for political moulding.

But in the secondary sector, the situation is very different. Here we have the formal, as well as the informal, aspects of political education to consider, because one of the most important features of the development of Modern Studies as a school subject has been that it offers the outsider a method of measuring fairly precisely any given school's commitment to formal political education – the element wholly absent at primary level – and also to examine the nature and structure of such courses.

The provision of Modern Studies in secondary schools seems to vary greatly from school to school and from region to region, but, broadly, one typical pattern can be identified. In the first two years of secondary education some schools include Modern Studies as part of the curriculum for all pupils; while at third, fourth, fifth and sixth year levels Modern Studies is offered as an optional choice (in most schools as an alternative to history or geography). What this means is that, from third year (roughly aged fourteen) onwards, formal political education is only given to those who already show an interest – in other words, those arguably most in need of "political educating" are allowed to opt out of it. In first and second years, while this is not the case, Modern Studies is available only at the whim of each individual school. Generally, though, some regions clearly offer much better provisions than others; it appears best in Grampian, Strathclyde, Central and Fife, and patchiest in some of the smaller, and island, authorities. Even size, though, is no guide; Lothian, which one would expect to have a provision similar to that of Grampian or Strathclyde, was reported as having 20% of its secondary schools with no Modern Studies teaching whatever.(see table)

THE PROVISION OF MODERN STUDIES IN SECONDARY SCHOOLS
(Selected Scottish Regions)

Region	No of Secondary schools	% schools offering Mod. Studies	% schools offering S1/2 Mod. Studies	% schools with full status Mod Studies departments
Borders	9	100	56	22
Central	19	89	63	53
Fife	20	90	90	85
Grampian	39	97	90	85
Lothian	51	78	65	35
Strathclyde	189	88	55	46
Tayside	32	88	44	41

(Information as supplied by regions listed.)

Part of the problem for Modern Studies is that formal political education in Scotland suffers from something of an identity crisis. In allowing itself to be identified as "a social science" it tends to fall into competition in schools with history and geography (and occasionally economics) as an academic discipline, yet because the subject is called

Modern Studies – a name which fails to appear in the tertiary education sector, or anywhere in England for that matter – it lacks an air of total academic acceptance at times. Indeed the subject has experienced difficulties with universities, even north of the border, which have been reluctant to grant Scottish Examination Board examination passes the same status as their equivalents in history and geography. Partly in an attempt to gain greater credibility, the SEB revised the Higher Grade Modern Studies syllabus for the 1981 examination, but in so doing, created a test which has proved monstrously difficult for school-age candidates. Yet despite successive years of poor results, it still seems impossible to provide an examination which both satisfied the expectations of employers and universities, and also offers students a fair chance of passing. What this suggests is that the educational establishment is unable to accept that the levels of political literacy which teachers currently help their pupils to achieve are actually worthy of proper recognition. Presumably this also casts a shadow of doubt over their ability to accept political education in general.

It is also worth noting what kind of political literacy is encouraged by the examination system. Since teachers tend, rightly or wrongly, towards achieving success in an examination rather than to a specific syllabus, the formal examinations in Modern Studies tend to dictate the style of political education which takes place. By and large, the examination system encourages a passive observation of the institutions and issues deemed relevant in the modern world, rather than an active participation in them. Pupils, for the most part, analyse, criticise and discuss, and without doubt these are important; generally, though, they develop few of the skills necessary to play a directly productive role in a democracy. There are a few exceptions.

The Ordinary Grade examination includes a project in which direct research (including such items as survey and interviewing techniques, and letter writing) is assessed, as are features such as originality and presentation; the Sixth Year Studies Examination includes a decision-making exercise; and it is possible that, if suitable resources are made available, some of the new Standard Grade courses in Modern Studies will move a little more in this direction. But it is clear that pupils taking Modern Studies examinations are expected to demonstrate that they know why their world is the way it is rather more than they know how to change it. As a result, attempts to develop the skills of political participation – debating, decision-making, visual and oral presentation of cases, and even voting – are largely only seen in areas of the curriculum where outside examinations are not dominant. This usually limits such experiments to the first and second years.

Pupils are also informally politically educated, of course, in the secondary sector throughout the school day and in all types of subjects. Many teachers feel free to express their own political views in classrooms, and those that do not almost certainly do so despite themselves. Certain issues seem particularly popular subjects for classroom discussion, in particular nuclear defence and unemployment, for the obvious reasons that these seem most relevant to adolescent school students. Teachers are naturally concerned to emphasise the relevance of school work in general, and their subject in particular, in order to maintain class morale, and this trend becomes even more marked as pupils progress up the school. It is safe to assume, then, that even in schools where Modern Studies is not part of the curriculum, the political awareness of the pupils is, after a fashion at least, being developed.

The problem with relying on such informal education, however, is that it is hard to be sure exactly what political education is being taught. A structured course of any sort has recognisable aims and objectives, and attempts can be made to measure the extent to which these have been attained; moreover, the type of political education taught in this way can be altered and controlled in a visible way. Unstructured, informal education processes, on the other hand, are as uncontrollable as they are indefinable. Another factor is that Modern Studies in Scotland is taught by specialist registered teachers, who have had some degree of specialised training in political education and are aware of some of its pitfalls. Teachers of other subjects, lacking this background, are less aware of the dividing line between political education and political indoctrination, and may drift across it quite easily. The irony is that many individuals in influential positions in education suspect that formal political education and political indoctrination are one and the same thing; yet by excluding Modern Studies from the curriculum they may in fact be creating the very seed-bed for political education which they seek to avoid.

Political and Financial Constraints on Formal Political Education

When examining the politics of political education, it is hard to escape the influences of finance on the curriculum. We have already seen that formal political education developed rapidly only when schools found themselves in a position of expansion in general; as school rolls fall, and pressure is made on schools to trim staffing levels to match, so subjects find themselves competing with each other to maintain the viability of their courses and departments. Modern Studies, History and Geography departments regularly find themselves struggling to share a shrinking market of third and fourth year pupils, and since Modern Studies is frequently taught less than the other social subjects in first and second years (or not at all), pupils often perceive Modern Studies as a "less important" subject as well. Surveys by the Modern Studies Association in Strathclyde and Lothian have shown a direct link between a school's level of commitment to formal political education in the first two years, and the numbers of pupils opting to continue study in later years. Naturally, all teachers wish to protect their own jobs, so that, by and large, the further expansion of Modern Studies in first and second years – at the expense of other subject teaching time – is quietly resisted. This especially applies to history and geography teachers, who feel, perhaps rightly, that they have most to lose.

Another problem caused by the lack of finance is the lack of money available to create separate Modern Studies departments, with fully paid promoted staff responsible, in all schools. As with the provision of Modern Studies in general, the region-by-region position is very variable. Comparing two fairly similar-sized regions, for example, reveals that Lothian has only 18 separate departments of Modern Studies with fully-paid heads out of 51 secondary schools (as opposed to 49 history and 50 geography), while Grampian claims such departments in 38 out of its 39 schools. In many schools, formal political education is the responsibility of either the history or geography department – for whom, as we have already noted, flourishing Modern Studies courses are a decidedly mixed blessing.

Although commitment to Modern Studies programmes varies from authority to authority, it is less easy to establish a definite statement that political education is actually a "party political" issue at local level. The Labour Party in Scotland appears to have shown more interest in developing political literacy than the other parties, but individual politicians of all parties, when asked, say that they believe that political education, usually Modern Studies, should be in the school curriculum. However, the process of transferring this informal support into a written commitment has proved more difficult. It seems that in only one instance has such a statement been made – albeit an important one; Strathclyde Labour Party included a strong commitment to Modern Studies in their most recent regional election manifestos. Yet even such a commitment still has, at time of writing, to be fulfilled by the Labour Strathclyde Regional Council.

It is probably true to say that Modern Studies is more likely to prosper in a high-spending education authority than in a low-spending one, and that of course Labour councils tend to be associated with high spending more than other parties. Parties' enthusiasm or otherwise for Modern Studies seems less important than their willingness or capacity to spend money to create the conditions in which it can flourish. Contrary to what one might expect. political education courses can be quite expensive to run, because of the ephemeral nature of their content; in concrete terms, Modern Studies books get thrown out because they go out of date, not because they wear out. In particular, it is hard for schools to build up satisfactory reference libraries, so that they depend on the proximity, convenience, and co-operation of good public libraries. Specialist "Modern Studies" books as such are in any case rather thin on the ground because there is no direct equivalent in England, and the schools market in Scotland alone is too small for publishers to be able to make a reasonable profit margin.

The fact that, in England, there is less tradition of teaching political education in general, and no direct equivalent of Modern Studies in particular, no doubt partly explains why political education is so little taught in the independent secondary sector, since many independent Scottish schools still prefer to offer GCE 'A' Levels and 'O' Levels than SEB examinations. Modern Studies is taught in some schools, but rarely throughout all six years, and more usually the subject is offered as an alternative "interest" option for senior pupils. Perhaps, of course, the lack of enthusiasm in the independent sector also reflects a parental suspicion of a subject which many still feel is either frivolous or even in some ways subversive. Yet it has to be said that parents in general tend only to ask questions about political bias in teaching, or else they ask for reassurance that qualifications will count for entry to careers; thus it often seems that headteachers worry more about what parents think of political education than they really need to.

We have seen, then, that parental pressure and party political attitudes have so far been less important influences on the development, degree, and style of political education in Scottish schools than are the financial constraints and education structure. But it would be a mistake to see formal political education in Scotland as being totally free from political direction. If there is one common aim that almost everyone involved in the education of individual children can unite upon, it is success in examinations. These examinations, along with the skills and knowledge that they test, are in Scotland devised by what may well be the most powerful policy-making organ of educational policy – namely, the Scottish Examination Board. If the Scottish Education Department wants to change the emphasis or styles of teaching, then its most effective method is to encourage the examination board to alter the examinations so that those candidates being taught the approved topics in the approved manner will score the highest marks.

In the first instance the Scottish Education Department sees the function of education, and in particular of political education, as being to prepare pupils to "take their place in society" and "play a full part in the British democratic system". Yet as Colin Wringe has pointed out[5], this is in itself a very political objective, since this aims to produce future citizens who will have perceptions of democracy and of society which broadly match those of existing society. It is, in short, a very conservative objective, and one which implies that many educationalists, especially in government circles, feel that a pupil population which is being politically educated in this way is likely to add stability to our current social structure. Yet it is at least arguable that pupils should be educated for change in society as much as for its conservation.

This conservatism pervades all political education, particularly the formal type. Teachers are well aware that the public sometimes suspects that political education in schools is really political indoctrination, and tend to "play safe" by stressing relatively "moderate", centrist, or conservative views. Moreover, many teachers also believe that it is harder in practice to gain high marks in SEB examinations by answering questions from an extreme viewpoint that from a centrist one. Certainly, such an approach can be successful, but in general one suspects that only the best candidates have the skills necessary to convince markers that they really understand what they are writing about, whereas more conventional approaches tend to be accepted more readily. Pupils are extremely vulnerable at this stage of their school careers; paramount, of course, is the need to achieve good grades to maximise job and further education prospects, and few candidates are prepared to risk failure for the sake of upholding principles, however strongly felt.

Many assumptions in fact underpin the philosophies of political education as recommended for schools by the Scottish Education Department. Some of these can be seen from the aims and structures of courses in general, while others have to be gleaned from trends in the examinations themselves. SEB syllabuses are highly compartmentalised in their approach to the study of British society – it is clear that "women", "unemployed", "ethnic minorities" and "the elderly" are perceived as four separate topics, for example – and this in turn emphasises the pluralist features of United Kingdom society and, by implication, the suitability of a pluralist democratic system.

The SEB and SED are also quite open in declaring that one aim of

Modern Studies is to create a more racially tolerant society, and while almost everyone accepts that this is a worthy aim, it remains a political objective for all that.

But one of the interesting features of Modern Studies examinations is the way in which certain topics and controversial issues appear. The SEB has obviously always felt that study of the EEC is important, and has rewarded those who do so by including a question on the Common Market in every Ordinary and Higher Grade examination set since the two syllabuses were revised in 1976 and 1981 respectively. By contrast, the examinations show little interest in the problems of the third world, and in general the subject is examined in the context of support from and involvement of the United Nations Special Agencies or the superpowers.

Exactly where the educational establishment (i.e. SED, SEB and the Consultative Committee on the Curriculum) stands on the political spectrum is hard to establish exactly, except that, as one might expect, it apears to have centrist tendencies. Examinations at Higher level, especially, though, have shown a particular interest in the rise of the SDP and the possible unfairness of the electoral system, implying a significance possibly out of proportion to the performance of the SDP at the 1983 General Election. By contrast, the SNP barely rates a mention in the main part of the Higher paper, although there is an optional area of study (not often taken up by teachers) in Scottish politics. Taken along with the previously mentioned compartmentalisation of the syllabus, it seems reasonable to deduce that the SEB's view (at least as represented by the examination panel) is that a pluralist democracy and consensus politics are the most suited to United Kingdom society. The two main parties are clearly seen as fragmented – questions on divisions within the Labour or Conservative parties are far more common than on problems within the Alliance or the SNP – and they are also seen as being increasingly polarised. This is clearly intended as part of the answer to a question such as "Account for the rise of the SDP........", for instance.[6] In general, a thorough study of the examinations of the 1980's would suggest that the SEB – and therefore presumably the SED, since it is in a position to inspect and influence the SEB – believes that the rise of such new centre parties is more significant for students of politics than are the issues and frustrations which led to the Conservative and Labour Parties diverging from the centre in the first place. It is, however, probable that this does not happen consciously; the examining panel does contain teachers, including the principal examiner himself or herself, and a more powerful influence is likely to be the pressure from teachers to make the examination more predictable, and therefore easier to teach towards. This in turn means the examinations tend to keep to "safe" topics (such as the EEC or the electoral system) which they can be sure all teachers will include somewhere in their courses; and of course, their repeated inclusion tends to encourage even more teachers to teach these topics in later years. But to a certain extent, the reasons for the nature of the examinations are less important than the effects of them on political education in Scottish schools, no matter what the cause.

If one suspects that, consciously or subconsciously, the Examination Board promotes the view that a harmonious, consensus-based society is both natural and appropriate to the United Kingdom, then for final evidence one need only look at the SEB's approach to Northern Ireland. Although observers abroad would probably regard this as the United Kingdom's most serious, intractable, and pressing problem, it hardly ever appears in the examination at all – never in the Ordinary grade, only once in each of Higher Grade and Sixth Year Studies papers in recent years. No official statement has ever been made on the subject but many teachers believe that the subject is too sensitive for younger children, especially, to handle. Certainly, omitting questions from the examination ensures that, at least at certificate level, teachers are unlikely to spend valuable class time discussing certain issues. The exclusion of Northern Ireland as a topic – and therefore from the de facto syllabus – also strengthens the image of the United Kingdom as a society in which consensus politics prevails, in stark contrast to the visions of conflict and polarisation elsewhere in the world – the arms race, Middle-East, Central America, South Africa, communist/ capitalist conflicts and so on.

Many Modern Studies teachers believe that the Examination Board itself is suspicious of the academic value of political education. The SEB has its own index of the comparative difficulty of subject examinations, called the Kelly Index, which in recent years at least has shown Examinations in Modern Studies to be of well above average difficulty, particularly in relation to other social subjects.

Despite its own evidence, the SEB has for the most part insisted that the reasons for the low pass rates in Modern Studies are connected with teacher mismanagement of the syllabus and other errors in preparation of candidates rather than any over-difficult examinations or severe marking. The real reasons for this low pass rate may be extremely complex, and may have something to do with the large percentage of mature students who sit the examination and who therefore artificially raise the quality of the "average" paper. But the educational establishment's lack of open attention to the problem still leaves the impression, rightly or wrongly, that it is felt that political education examinations need to be of slightly greater degree of difficulty than for other subjects in order to validate good passes to higher education establishments or employers.

This impression is enhanced by study of the Scottish Education Department's plans for curriculum development at Standard Grade and 16 level. The Munn Report on "The Curriculum in the Third and Fourth Years of Secondary Schools" argued that all pupils should be educated to understand the political, economic, and social influences of our society; but it did not recommend Modern Studies as such for all. A new subject created partly to meet this need, "Contemporary Social Studies", contains no more political education than history or geography, and, more tellingly, is only deemed suitable for the less able. Indeed, the Conservatives' drive towards a technologically-orientated society may have offered one of the few instances of direct party political influence on the development of political education. While the Munn Report, published during the Labour Government's term of office, laid stress on developing political education for all, the suggestion was quietly dropped in the Conservative's plan for implementation in 1982, re-interpreting the Munn Report's statement (see above) as ".....a strong case for courses..........which would broadly be orientated to the study of contemporary society and to preparation for adult life and work".[7] The SED's plans for education after sixteen likewise show political education is held in low esteem – relatively few modular courses are currently prepared for the field of political education, or even public administration.

A final – and perhaps the most significant in the last analysis – influence that the examinations exert over political education is in its general style – namely, it is what was earlier described as a "passive" form. Political education of this nature encourages students to observe trends, implications, and causes, but not, as a rule, to develop the skills of active participation in politics or in becoming an active part of the political system – pressure group skills, canvassing, and so on. Indeed, a preamble to the Certificate of Sixth Year Studies syllabus suggests that students should develop "a healthy scepticism" towards politics. Thanks to the examination system pupils and students spend far more time critically analysing politics at school than they do in offering alternative strategies. It may well be that the current style of political education creates a contempt for politics which discourages some students from taking a more active role in politics in later life; but of course such a suggestion can at present only be mere speculation. Given that most Scots who have formally studied political education already presumably did so because they were already interested enough to choose the subject, it is interesting at least that no obvious link has stood out between those active in one form or another of politics, and those who received a formal political education. This has been studied very little, however, and it surely merits a careful survey in the future.

So what picture of Scottish political education in Scottish schools are we left with? Firstly, we can see that, for all the lip-service and testimony paid to the value of a politically literate society, formal political education remains a low priority and has developed in Scotland only where financial constraints and structure of Scottish secondary schools has suited. Consequently, provision varies from the carefully-considered to cavalier. Secondly, we can see that the Scottish Education Department, deliberately or otherwise, heavily influences the style and content of formal political education in schools, partly through influence on course syllabuses, but more particularly through examinations in Modern Studies. By remote control, it directs a curriculum which is passive in style, concentrates heavily on "civics" and the mechanics of formal government, appears to avoid certain controversial topics, and above all presents a centrist view of a pluralist consensus society with a democracy to match. Moreover, the SED currently appears less concerned with the development of social sciences in general, and political education in particular, than some outsiders have suggested it ought to be.

Finally, we can see that, although the Labour Party seems perhaps marginally more interested and concerned with creating a politically literate electorate, no party has actually done very much, and in fact party politics is a relatively minor influence on political education.

Perhaps this is not so surprising; it is probably true that party machines are less interested in dealing with a politically literate electorate (who might talk back) than a politically *receptive* electorate. Political parties presumably would prefer the electorate to know why things have to be the way they are rather than how to change them. If ever the United Kingdom electorate were to become truly politically educated – in all aspects of politics, in the sense that it could act independently as well as listen – then the party system as we know it might well be in real danger. In the meantime, it may well be that professional politicians would prefer that political education widens from its present extent, but retains its present form.

Gordon Lawrie, Department of Modern Studies, Portobello High School.

References

1. Some readers may not be familiar with the standard Scottish school structure, in which pupils normally attend primary school for seven years (usually termed P1, P2 and so on), then go on to anything up to six years of secondary education (S1-6). Thus pupils normally sit Ordinary Grade examinations in "fourth year", Higher Grade in "fifth year", while in "sixth year" they may take further "Highers", or the Certificate of Sixth Year Studies.

2. The first Ordinary Grade examaination was offered in 1962, the first Higher in 1968.

3. Scottish Education Department Consultative Committee on the Curriculum (Chairman, J Munn), *The Structure of the Curriculum in the Third and Fourth Years of the Scottish Secondary School*, HMSO, 1977, p.25.

4. Although it is not within the scope of this article to discuss political education methodology extensively, readers who wish further reading on this subject are referred to the extensive bibliography in Colin Wringe *Democracy, Schooling and Political Education*, Allen & Unwin, London, 1984.

5. *ibid*.

6. From the Scottish Examination Board Higher paper in 1983.

7. Scottish Education Department *The Munn and Dunning Reports: Framework for Decision*, (consultative paper circulated to schools and other relevant bodies), 1982, p.11.

SCOTTISH LEGISLATION 1985

Hamish McN. Henderson

The Acts of Parliament passed in 1985 were both numerous and voluminous. Of the 76 passed, five were *Scotland only* Acts, about several of the others are not without interest to the student of the government of Scotland.

Contrary to the usual practice, England and Wales had the "bumper supplement", in the long awaited *Insolvency Act*; Part I prescribes the qualifications for the profession of insolvency practitioner, and Part II deals with what is called "Company Insolvency, etc". These provisions apply, for the most part, north and south of the Border. But Part III, dealing with individual insolvency, and many of the miscellaneous provisions of Part IV – together more than half the Act – apply to England and Wales only. It is of course arguable that it is Parts I and II which comprise the "bumper supplement", by extending to Scotland what is essentially an England and Wales Act. Whichever way it is, the Scottish practitioner is going to have to buy a lot of unnecessary paper.

This is of course not the fault of the draughtsmen, but of the rules of parliamentary procedure and the associated pressures of the parliamentary timetable. Now that the prices of Acts of Parliament and all other Stationery Office publications are so high, it would be reasonable for Parliament to adopt a modified version of the procedure followed for consolidation Bills, so that Acts could be passed and printed in a form convenient to the public to which they are addressed, even if Bills from which they derived were arranged in the traditional manner for the convenience of debate.

The same criticism may be applied to the *Law Reform (Miscellaneous Provisions)(Scotland) Act 1985*, which could well have been split up into about 25 short Acts, to suit the diverse interests, and the convenience, of various users. These would have been no briefer than many of the other Acts which found their way on to the statute book in 1985.

There were nine consolidation Acts in 1985; three deal with various aspects of company law and three with housing law, the leading ones in each of these groups running to nearly 750 sections and 25 Schedules and to 625 sections and 24 Schedules respectively. The *Housing Associations Act* is an interesting risotto of Great Britain, England and Wales, and *Scotland only* provisions. These two groups are each accompanied by separate *Consequential Provisions Acts*. This is a useful innovation, because relatively peripheral or transitional matters are not included in the substantive legislation.

An important feature of the *Consequential Provisions Acts* is the fact that, each in its own way, they unambiguously state that the re-enactment of provisions in the consolidation Acts, and the repeal of the old legislation, do not affect the continuity of the law. So, contrary to the view expressed by some authorities, these consolidation Acts clearly do not represent a fresh start. These authorities have deplored the practice of counsel of indulging in legal archaeology when dealing with problems involving the interpretation of consolidation Acts; accordingly, decisions under Acts now repealed by the consolidation process are still relevant and must not be ignored. Legal archaeology will therefore continue to flourish, aided by invaluable tables of derivations and destinations.

The programme of privatisation is helped on its way with the controversial *Trustee Savings Bank* and *Transport Acts*.

The decision in the costly fluoridation case, in which a judge of the Court of Session held, at the instance of an edentulous lady from Glasgow, that it was unlawful to add fluoride to water supplies, was overturned by the *Water (Fluoridation) Act*, for the benefit of the inhabitants of the whole of Great Britain.

Whether the battle to promote a return to Victorian standards will be assisted by the less publicised, and presumably less controversial, three-clause *Betting, Gaming and Lotteries (Amendment) Act*, or the almost as brief *Gaming (Bingo) Act*, is open to question. The former permits us to go to the dogs, or follow the horses, every day except Sundays, Good Friday or Christmas Day, an increase of just under 140% at any one site. The latter gives us the opportunity to reap the benefits of modern technology and so to indulge in multiple bingo and thus to win even bigger prizes.

Chapter Number
16. *National Heritage (Scotland) Act* This Act provides for the establishment of two new boards and amends the law in relation to two others.

The Royal Scottish Museum has, since 1901, been part of the Scottish Education Department, and the National Museum of Antiquities of Scotland has, since 1954, had its own board of trustees.

Under the new Act, we now have the Board of Trustees of the National Museums of Scotland. This takes over the Royal Scottish Museum and the National Museum of Antiquities of Scotland, together with what are usually known as the Royal Scottish Museum's outstations, such as the Museum of Flight at East Fortune in East Lothian, and the Museum of Costume in Shambellie House, near Dumfries.

The Board will have from nine to fifteen members, appointed by the Secretary of State, and will be financed by a grant-in-aid from the Scottish Education Department. Members will have to be suitably qualified, as laid down in the Act, and at least one will be a Fellow of the Society of Antiquaries of Scotland. In turn, the Board will appoint a Director of the National Museums of Scotland, with the approval of the Secretary of State, and other staff.

The Board may work with other, non-national, museums, and bodies such as the National Trust for Scotland, but the precise nature of collaboration is left to the Board itself to decide.

The administration of the Royal Botanic Garden, but not the ownership of the land and buildings occupied by it, is transferred from the Department of Agriculture and Fisheries of Scotland to the Board of Trustees of the Royal Botanic Garden, Edinburgh. This Board will have from five to nine members, appointed by the Secretary of State from persons qualified as laid down in the Act. The Regius Keeper of the Royal Botanic Garden will be appointed by the Queen, and the rest of the staff by the Board.

Despite its name, the Board's activities need not be confined to Edinburgh. Its responsibilities will cover the outstations at the Younger garden at Benmore, the Logan garden near Stranraer and the Dawyck garden near Stobo.

One of the oddities of the Act is the provision that prevents the Board from altering the hours when the Garden is open to the public without the consent of the Secretary of State. But as his consent is also required for the fixing or alteration of any fees charged to members of the public for entry, this is probably meant to protect the public from any action by the Board to try to meet cuts that might be imposed by the government by reducing facilities.

The Board of Trustees of the National Galleries of Scotland is increased, so as to consist of from seven to twelve members, appointed by the Secretary of State, again from persons with suitable qualifications as listed. The Board will appoint a Director of the National Galleries of Scotland, with the approval of the Secretary of State, and other staff.

The constitution of the Board of Trustees of the National Library of Scotland is updated. It will consist of thirty-two members, of whom eleven will be ex officio, such as the Secretary of State, the Queen's and Lord Treasurer's Remembrancer, the lord provosts of the four cities, and others to represent the law and the church. Five will be appointed by the Queen on the recommendation of the Secretary of State; these must include at least one representative of organised labour. As the Library started life as the Advocate's Library, and still serves this purpose, the Faculty appoints five members, while the Scottish universities appoint four, and CoSLA two. The appointment of the Librarian is subject to the approval of the Secretary of State.

Instead of the Keeper of the Records of Scotland being ex officio chairman of the Scottish Records Advisory Council, an outside chairman may now be appointed. The Keeper is given express power to accept responsibility for the safe keeping of records other than public ones, to acquire records and accept gifts and loans of records.

33. *Rating (Revaluation Rebates)(Scotland) Act* Following the revaluation of properties in Scotland in 1985, it became apparent that there had been a substantial shift of rateable value from manufacturing industry towards domestic property. Unless there were an adjustment in the imposition of rates, this shift of rateable value would have caused a corresponding shift of the rates burden.

The Secretary of State sought two remedies. He made an order reducing the level of industrial derating from 50% to 40%, and announced an intention to increase the domestic rate relief first to five pence, and subsequently to eight pence, in the pound. In the commercial sector the overall effect was considered to be neutral, but there were wide variations in individual cases in this sector, some increases being regarded as crippling, or even fatal.

Because these steps did not provide an adequate remedy to the hardship caused by revaluation, the government introduced a Bill to require the making of rebates in certain circumstances.

The Act enables the Secretary of State to make an order obliging rating authorities to grant rebates according to a formula contained in the order. To qualify for rebate, the new rateable value has to be more than three times the old. The Secretary of State indicated that the rebate would be subject to a maximum of £10,000 on any one property.

The rebate scheme does not apply to lands and heritages occupied by local authorities, joint committees and joint boards, for the purpose of their functions. Nor does it apply to those buildings which enjoy partial derating because they are used for livestock production, nor to industrial and freight transport lands and heritages, since they already enjoy industrial derating.

Rebates should be awarded automatically, without the need for the individual ratepayer to lodge a claim, but a claim procedure was envisaged for the benefit of anyone who might fail to receive a rebate through inadvertence.

37. *Family Law (Scotland) Act* This Act is based on two reports on Family Law by the Scottish Law Commission – the Report on Aliment and Financial Provision (November 1981, Scot.Law.Com.No.67) and the Report on Matrimonial Property (June 1984, Scot.Law.Com.No.86). The Act brings the law into line with modern social practices and attempts to deal with the often intractable financial problems arising on divorce.

At common law, the obligation to aliment each other had always existed mutually between ancestors and descendants. In modern times, however, the burden of maintaining elderly parents and grandparents has fallen increasingly on the state. The obligation is now, by this Act, limited to that of parents to aliment their children, and of individuals to aliment children accepted as children of the family, including, for example, step-children. The word "individuals" is used, in order to ensure that the provisions will apply to single-parent families. Children are defined as persons under the age of 18, or, if they are undergoing educational or vocational training, under the age of 25.

Husbands and wives now have a mutual obligation to aliment each other. Formerly, it was doubtful whether a wife had any duty to aliment her husband, if he could maintain himself at subsistence level. The duty applies to the spouses of valid polygamous marriages. It ceases on death or divorce.

Nevertheless, the common law rule, which entitles anyone who is left without support on the death of a relative, who was liable to aliment him or her, to claim aliment out of the estate of the deceased, or against anyone who has benefited from the succession, is preserved. Claims have been rare, presumably because the law of intestate succession and the rules concerning legal rights of surviving spouses and children have effectively covered most situations; families may have made arrangements amicably, or individuals may have relied on state benefits. The common law rule will in future be applicable to the more restricted list of persons to whom the obligation of aliment is now owed.

These rights to claim aliment may be enforced in the Court of Session or in local sheriff courts. Payments of aliment must be made periodically, and not in one lump sum; but extraordinary single payments may be ordered to meet special needs, including child-bearing, funeral and educational expenses. The amount of any award may be fixed by the court, having regard to all the circumstances of the case, including the needs and resources of the persons concerned, and their earning capacities. If the defender already maintains a person voluntarily, such as an aged friend or relative, that fact will be relevant in quantifying liability.

Future liability may be excluded by agreement, but the agreement may be set aside by the court, if it was not fair and reasonable at the time when it was entered into.

In an action for divorce, either party may apply to the court for an "order for financial provision". Readers not familiar with Scottish legal terminology should note that the term "aliment" is used only during the subsistence of a marriage. On divorce, the anglo-american word "alimony" is not used. For the purposes of this Act, actions for declarator of nullity of marriage are treated in all respects as if they were actions for divorce, even for the benefit of the part denying the existence of the marriage.

An order for financial provision may provide for the payment of a capital sum, the transfer of property, such as houses and motor cars, and the making of periodical financial allowances. The power to transfer the ownership of the matrimonial home may reduce the hardship suffered by many women in the past, when the house has been sold "over the head" of the ex-wife. The principles by which the court is to be guided, in order to establish fair treatment of both parties, are set out in great detail.

Only in exceptional circumstances will an order awarding periodical allowances be made to endure for more than three years. This is considered to be long enough to permit the spouse making the application to adjust to the changed circumstances. The order ceases to have effect on the remarriage of the party to whom payments are being made; if the other party dies, the order may continue to operate as a claim against his estate.

The Act is aimed at securing a clean financial break on divorce, and at bringing to an end the concept of periodical payments as a "meal-ticket for life".

During and after a marriage, there is a rebuttable presumption that household goods that are kept for the joint domestic purposes of the spouses – but not money, investments, motor vehicles and domestic animals – are owned by spouses equally. Similarly, any money saved, or property bought with such money, by either spouse out of a housekeeping allowance provided by either of them, is presumed to belong to each in equal shares.

66. *Bankruptcy (Scotland) Act* This Act provides Scotland with a modern code of law on bankruptcy, concerning debtors other than limited companies. So it applies to individuals, living and dead, partnerships, trusts, clubs and the like.

The technical term used throughout the Act to describe "bankruptcy" is "sequestration". "Bankruptcy" appears only in the short title, and in the expression "Accountant in Bankruptcy".

There is plenty of background material for anyone wishing to study the context of this Act. The principal source is the Scottish Law Commission's Report on Bankruptcy and Related Aspects of Insolvency and Liquidation (February 1982, Scot.Law Com. No.68). But the newfangled insolvency practitioners created by the *Insolvency*

Act 1985 (c.65), which deals with company insolvency for the whole of Great Britain, and individual insolvency for England and Wales, appear in the Scottish Act. So it is also useful to have regard to the two reports of the Review Committee on Insolvency Law and Practice – the Cork Committee – (July 1980, Cmnd 7968 and June 1982, Cmnd 8558) and to Bankruptcy: A Consultative Document (July 1980, Cmnd 7967).

The old Scots *Bankruptcy Acts, 1621 c.18 and 1696 c.5* disappear, as does the *Bankruptcy (Scotland) Act 1913 (c.20)*. So "conjunct and confident persons" become "associates", "fraudulent preferences" become merely "unfair preferences" and "notour bankruptcy" becomes "apparent insolvency". Trust deeds for behoof of creditors survive (except that they are now said to be "for the benefit of creditors generally"), as a useful and economical device for gathering in the assets of a debtor. Indeed, they are encouraged, by the introduction of rules whereby they become "protected trust deeds", which will no longer be liable to be superseded by sequestration at the instance of a non-acceding creditor, nor liable to be treated as unfair or fraudulent preferences, as they were under the 1696 Act.

Both the Court of Session and the sheriff courts will have jurisdiction in bankruptcy, but, if proceedings begin in the Court of Session, most of the subsequent procedure will normaly be remitted to the appropriate sheriff.

The newly created Accountant in Bankruptcy, who is responsible for the general supervision of the administration of sequestration and personal insolvency, is in fact the Accountant of Court (i.e. of the Court of Session), who already had certain responsibilities in this connection. He is now required to maintain a register of insolvencies, with details of estates sequestrated and of trust deeds for the benefit of creditors generally which become protected trust deeds.

Insolvency practitioners are defined in the *Insolvency Act*. They are such members of professional organisations recognised by the Secretary of State as are permitted by these organisations to act as insolvency practitioners. Effectively, this means solicitors and accountants.

At the beginning of the sequestration it is the court which appoints a qualified insolvency practitioner, whose name appears on the list of interim trustees maintained by the Accountant in Bankruptcy, as interim trustee, to safeguard the estate of the debtor until a permanent trustee is appointed. Individuals on the list of interim trustees may not refuse office.

Within 28 days, unless the sheriff allows more time, at a statutory meeting of creditors, the creditors elect a qualified insolvency practitioner as the permanent trustee, unless the assets are such as to make the payment of a dividend unlikely. In this case, the court appoints the interim trustee as permanent trustee, and the expenses of sequestration, including his fees, will be met out of public funds. One may expect that even in cases where there is an election the interim trustee will be elected as permanent trustee.

All the property of the debtor rests in the permanent trustee, so that he can deal with it as if he were a beneficial owner. There are, however, restrictions on disposing of the debtor's family home; the authority of the court may have to be obtained to do this. The court will take into account the needs and financial resources of the debtor's spouse, or of a former spouse, of any child of the family, and the interests of the creditors. The interests of the so-called non-entitled spouse under the *Matrimonial Homes (Family Protection)(Scotland) Act 1981 (c.59)* are also protected.

Perhaps the most important step forward taken by this Act is the reduction of the entitlement of the Crown to priority for unpaid taxes, and of local authorities for unpaid rates. Especially in a small community, the bankruptcy of one tradesman could have a domino effect, and pull down other tradesmen with it. The Crown and local authorities have broader backs.

The Scottish Law Commission adopted a root and branch approach, and proposed the abolition of all these antiquated priorities. The Cork Committee found that the ancient prerogative of the Crown was supportable neither by principle nor by expediency, but tolerated it where the debtor has acted as a tax collector and not as a tax payer. The Treasury's attitude was that it was an involuntary creditor – but are not most of us, in the ultimate analysis?

The Bill, as introduced into Parliament, followed the Treasury line, but common sense prevailed. Preferential ranking of Crown debts is limited mainly to deductions of PAYE from the salaries of employees, to social security contributions, and to car tax, referable to the twelve months before sequestration, and to VAT for the six months before this date. Employees have priority in relation to contributions to occupational pension schemes and arrears of pay up to a limit to be fixed in regulations. Rates are no longer granted priority.

In most cases, the debtor will be automatically discharged three years after sequestration. He may obtain a certificate to that effect from the Accountant in Bankruptcy. However, the permanent trustee, or any creditor, may apply to the sheriff at least three months before the end of the three years for deferment of discharge. Deferment may be granted for up to two years, and is renewable. But the debtor whose discharge has been deferred may, at any time, petition the sheriff for discharge.

Sometimes sequestrations go off the rails. Formerly it was necessary to apply to the Court of Session to exercise its equitable jurisdiction, the *nobile officium*, to put things right. Now the sheriff is empowered to cure defects in procedure where any requirements of the Act or relevant regulations have not been complied with, to put it back on the rails again.

73 *Law Reform (Miscellaneous Provisions)(Scotland) Act* This Act concerns many aspects of the law as its name implies, and it is one of the most wide-ranging of the Law Reform Acts passed in recent years. Only a relatively brief, and somewhat selective, outline of its details can be given here.

The Act restricts the power of a landlord of commercial or industrial premises to rely on provisions in a lease which terminate it automatically, or permit him to terminate it, for simple non-payment of rent, without giving the tenant a notice requiring him to pay within a stated time limit. This time limit in most cases will be not less than 14 days. Where the breach of the lease is non-monetary, such as failure in an obligation to carry out repairs, the test will be what a fair and reasonable landlord would do in the circumstances.

Where it is considered that a document, other than a testamentary document (an expression which is wider in meaning than a will), has failed to express accurately the common intention of the parties to an agreement, or the intention of the grantor of a document relating to unilateral juristic acts, such as covenants and other promises, at the date when it was executed, the Court of Session or the local sheriff court may make an order to rectify the document, with retrospective effect.

The court must have regard to all relevant evidence, written or oral. The interests of third parties are protected. Thus, the retrospective effect of a rectifying order may be modified. In appropriate circumstances, the rectifying order may itself be rescinded, or an innocent third party compensated by the person who applied for the order. But an application to the court for rescission or compensation must in all cases be made not later than five years after the making of the rectifying order.

Recent conflicting decisions of the courts have demonstrated the state of confusion of the law of Scotland in relation to negligent misrepresentation. The Act of 1985 attempts to remedy this, and to clarify the law. Formerly, if a person had been induced to enter into a contract by negligent misrepresentation made by, or on behalf of, another party to the contract, he was nevertheless considered by traditional jurists to be prevented from recovering damages from that other party for any loss or damage suffered, if the misrepresentation was merely negligent.

On this view, he had to be satisfied with rescission of the contract, and restitution of property, alone, unless he could prove fraud. It will now be sufficient to prove a duty of care, and the fact that the misrepresentation was negligent. This brings these special cases of negligent misrepresentation into line with the general principle which is the basis of delictual liability, namely, fault, or *culpa*. This brings Scots law roughly into line with that of England, and perhaps also with the developed law of the later Roman Empire.

Under the Act of 1985, all actions based on verbal injury, including the most common form, namely, actions of defamation, must now be brought within three years of the date when publication of the defamatory material first comes to the notice of the pursuer. Formerly the period of time was five years. The new rule brings the time limit into line with that for claims based on personal injury.

The *Matrimonial Homes (Family Protection)(Scotland) Act 1981 (c.59)* has now been heavily amended, to strengthen the right of occupation of the so-called non-entitled spouse (that is, the spouse who does not have a legal title to the home, as owner or tenant). The Act of 1985 removes some technical difficulties that have developed in the conveyancing of houses as a result of the Act of 1981.

Another provision brings Scots law into line with English law, by removing the privilege against self-incrimination in civil proceedings relating to the protection of intellectual property, and to the prevention of "passing-off". This will help the owners of copyright in actions relating to pirating of video-tapes.

In Scotland, consumers have had problems in pursuing their claims in the courts, because of the expense involved and the difficulty which ordinary citizens have found in understanding the existing procedure for summary causes, which was introduced in 1976 under the *Sheriff Courts (Scotland) Act 1971 (c.58)*.

So we now have a new "small claims procedure". The precise descriptions of cases which will fall within the new procedure, including the maximum value of any claim, will be laid down in an order made by the Lord Advocate. The draft order will have to be approved by both houses of Parliament, so that it will not be possible to slip it through without discussion and publicity. This should guarantee that discussions will take place with interested pressure groups before the draft is laid before parliament. The normal rules of evidence will not apply to this procedure. In very small claims (as prescribed by the Lord Advocate), no expenses will be awarded; in others, they will be limited.

The children's hearings, conducted by children's panels, which were established by the *Social Work (Scotland) Act 1968 (c.49)* to replace traditional juvenile courts, have stimulated interest among lawyers, sociologists, criminologists and others in many countries. Several improvements are made to the system, *inter alia*, to facilitate the adoption of children who are subject to supervision under the Act of 1968.

Further provisions deal with the detention of young offenders over 16 but under 18 years of age. It also deals with the functions of the Parole Board in relation to the small number of children under 16 who are detained after a jury has found them guilty of an offence, and the supervision of these children when they are released after the expiry of their detention.

Several new sections are inserted in the *Criminal Procedure (Scotland) Act 1975 (c.21)*. The rules of evidence in trials relating to rape and other sexual offences have, for the most part, been established at common law. These rules have not always been observed in recent cases. The Scottish Law Commission advised that the rules should be reformed. The new sections effectively lay down a code of rules for eliciting evidence in these trials.

Scotland has many serious problems arising from the abuse of drugs. Further new sections are inserted in the *Criminal Procedure (Scotland) Act 1975*. Where a person has been found guilty by a jury of offences concerning the production, supply, possession, importation or exportation of certain drugs, the court is required, in addition to imposing a prison sentence, to impose a fine effectively to confiscate any profits likely to have been made by the offender from the crime for which he has been convicted. If the fine is not paid, the term of imprisonment will be increased by up to two years. It is to be noted that it is only the profits obtained by the individual offender from the particular crime before the court that will be confiscated. Profits obtained by a co-accused, or arising from a previous course of drug trafficking, are immune.

Scottish solicitors (who have traditionally worked together in partnerships) now, for the first time ever, will be permitted to carry on their practices as bodies corporate, called "incorporated practices". Detailed rules as to the management and control of incorporated practices will be made by the Council of the Law Society of Scotland. The shareholders and directors of incorporated practices will themselves normally be practising solicitors, and subject to the usual disciplines of the profession.

Hamish McN. Henderson, Department of Scots Law, University of Edinburgh.

SUMMARY OF OPINION POLLS 1985/86

Allan Macartney

The Opinion Polls appendix follows the by now standard format. Table 1 (System Three [Scotland], published in the *Glasgow Herald*) illustrates the movements of public opinion over the period mid-1985 to mid-1986, with the General Election result two years before that as a yardstick. Table 2 gives, by comparison, the MORI figures of voting intention published in *The Scotsman*. As before, the Conservative and Alliance result in June 1983 still appears as a peak to which they have not returned whereas for the SNP (marginally) and for Labour (more dramatically), their standing has been better in the opinion polls than in the preceding General Election.

Table 3 gives the views of the public on Scotland's constitutional future. For ease of comparison we have followed as far as possible the same method of presentation of the options, although minor variations in wording have occurred over the years.

One of the more intriguing issues for debate during the past year has been the apparent paradox of rising support for Independence coupled with a failure to translate that sentiment into an intention to vote for the only party which promises that outcome. Moreover, the result of the Regional Council elections did not exactly contribute to a solution of the problem: the Scottish National Party came second in terms of the popular vote but well behind Labour, whose showing was closer to its opinion poll rating. Political scientists can of course rationalise such discrepancies by referring to saliency and differential abstention but it does leave some interesting question marks over the development of Scottish politics in the near future, and these seem unlikely to be settled before the next General Election.

Acknowledgements

The Yearbook is again indebted to System Three (Scotland), MORI, the *Glasgow Herald* and *The Scotsman* for permission to publish the data in this section. We are grateful to Edinburgh University Audio-Visual Services for graphical presentation.

Technical Notes

As always, percentages have been rounded, while "don't knows", refusals and "won't votes" have been omitted. The dates given are those of completion of the fieldwork, rather than dates of eventual publication.

Allan Macartney is Staff Tutor in Politics, the Open University in Scotland, and Hon.Fellow in Politics, University of Edinburgh.

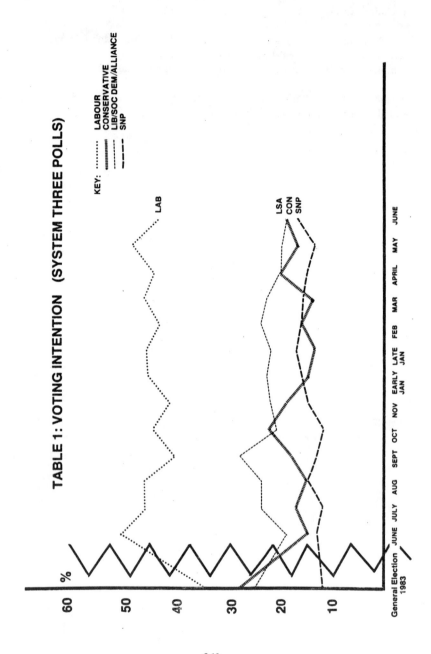

TABLE 1: VOTING INTENTION (SYSTEM THREE POLLS)

KEY:
LABOUR
CONSERVATIVE
LIB/SOC DEM/ALLIANCE
SNP

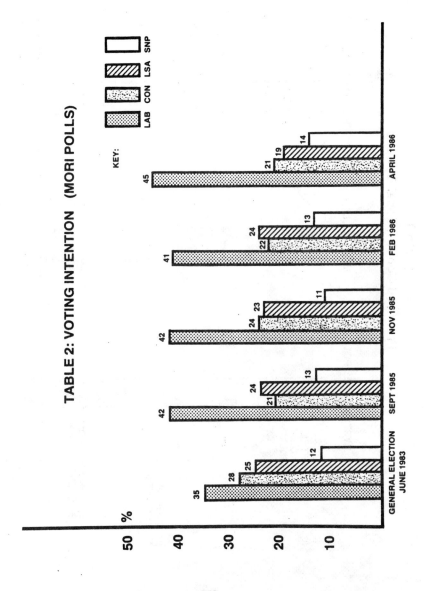

TABLE 2: VOTING INTENTION (MORI POLLS)

Table 3
Preferred Constitutional Options

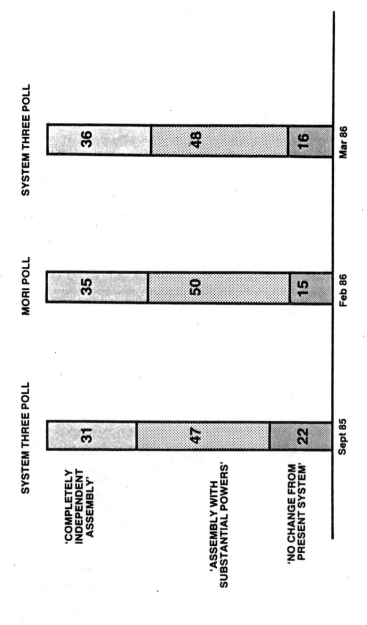

SECTION 1

SCOTTISH OFFICE MINISTERS

Private Secretary*

Secretary of State Rt Hon Malcolm Rifkind MP R S B Gordon Ext
Assistants:
A Rinning DH 8372‡
C Weatherston Ext 4021

Minister of State Lord Glenarthur I S McWilliam
(Health & Social Work, Ext 4023
Highlands & Islands affairs)

Parliamentary Michael Ancram MP I J C Howie Ext 4012
Under-Secretaries (Minister of Local Govern-
of State ment and the Environment)

John MacKay MP D A Stewart Ext 4107
(Minister for Education,
Agriculture & Fisheries)

Ian Lang MP P A D Ritchie Ext 4015
(Minister for Industry
and Home Affairs)

* at New St Andrew's House, Edinburgh EH1 3SX
(031-556 8400) except
** at St Andrew's House, Edinburgh EH1 3DE
‡ Dover House, London (01-233 300)

SECTION 2

REGIONAL COUNCILS

Names and Addresses of Convenors and Chief Officers

	Convener/ Population	Chief Executive	Director of Administration	Director of Finance	Director of Education	Director of Social Work	Director of Planning	Director of Roads
BORDERS Newton St Boswells TD6 0SA 0835 23301	Tom Hunter (Ind) 101,000	K J Clark	R A Macaskill	P Jeary	J McLean	D A Macdonald	D P Douglas	R I Hill
CENTRAL Viewforth Stirling 0786 3111	Charles Sneddon (Lab) 273,000	E Geddes	P W Buchanan	J Broadfoot	I Collie	J A Ross	F Bracewell	G I McCrindle
DUMFRIES & GALLOWAY Council Offices Dumfries 0387 53141	John Jameson (Ind) 144,000	M W D McIntosh	G M Sinclair	J C Stewart 0387 62323	J K Purves 30 Edinburgh Rd Dumfries 0387 63822	8 Gordon St Dumfries 0387 63022	A H Dobbie	H D B Murray
FIFE Fife House North Street Glenrothes 0592 754411	Robert Gough (Lab) 344,000	J M Dunlop	W Breslin	D T Mitchell	M More	M A Gillespie Queensway Glenrothes 0592 756701	W Taylor	J T Rowson (Engineering) Rothesay House North Street Glenrothes 0592 754411

	Convener/ Population	Chief Executive	Director of Administration	Director of Finance	Director of Education	Director of Social Work	Director of Planning	Director of Roads
GRAMPIAN Woodhill House Ashgrove Rd West Aberdeen AB9 2LU 0224 682222	Geoffrey Hadley (Ind) 497,000	J D Macnaughton		T E Carter	J A D Michie	Miss M Hartnoll	T F Sprott	G Kirkbride
HIGHLAND Regional Buildings Glenurquhart Road Inverness 0463 234121	Alexander Russell (Ind) 197,000	R H Stevenson	H Farquhar	J W Bremner	C E Stewart	J G Bailey	R Cameron	G K M Macfarlane
LOTHIAN George IV Bridge Edinburgh EH1 1UQ 031-229 9292	James Cook (Lab) 745,000	G Bowie		D B Chynoweth	W D C Semple 40 Torphichen St Edinburgh EH3 8JJ	R W Kent Shrubhill House Edinburgh EH7 4DP 031-554 4301	1 Parliament Sq Edinburgh EH1 1TU	P J Mason 19 Market St Edinburgh EH1 1BL
STRATHCLYDE Strathclyde House 20 India Street Glasgow G2 4PF 041-204 2900	James Jennings (Lab) 2,373,000	R Calderwood		K R V Paterson	E Miller	F E Edwards	R G Mound	W S McAlonan
TAYSIDE Tayside House 26-28 Crichton St Dundee 0382 23281	John McAllion (Lab) 394,000	J A Wallace		I B McIver	D G Robertson	S J Moxley	H Ramsay	A R Mollison

ISLANDS COUNCILS

	Convener/ Population	Chief Executive	Director of Administration	Director of Finance	Director of Education	Director of Social Work	Director of Planning	Director of Roads
ORKNEY County Offices Kirkwall 0856 3535	Edwin Eunson (Ind) 19,000	R H Gilbert	R McCallum	R H Gilbert	A Bain	H MacGillivray	M Sargent	
SHETLAND Town Hall Lerwick 0595 3535	Alexander Tulloch (Ind) 23,000	M Gerrard	P B Regan 31 Commercial St Lerwick	M Green 4 Market St Lerwick	R A B Barnes Brentham Ho Harbour St Lerwick	P Malcolmson 64 St Olaf St Lerwick	G L Mann Victoria Bldgs Esplanade Lerwick	
WESTERN ISLES Council Office South Beach Stornoway 0851 3773	Sandy Matheson (Ind) 31,000	R MacIver	D Sinclair	D G Macleod	N R Galbraith 0851 3992	Mrs N E Macleod 0851 3664	J R Haworth	

SECTION 3

DISTRICT COUNCILS

Names and Addresses of Conveners and Chief Executives

	Convener/Provost	Chief Executive
BORDERS		
Berwickshire	J Evans	R Christie District Offices, Duns TD11 3DU (03618 2600)
Ettrick & Lauderdale	A L Tulley	C Anderson, PO Box 4 Council Chambers, Paton St., Galashiels TD1 3AS (0896 4751)
Roxburgh	J R Irvine	K W Cramond District Office, High St. Hawick TD9 9EF (04507 5991)
Tweeddale	J Campbell	G H T Garvie District Offices, Peebles EH45 8GH (0721 20153)
CENTRAL		
Clackmannan	J Millar	I F Smith The Whins, Alloa FK10 3SA (0259 722160)
Falkirk	J Docherty	J P H Paton Municipal Buildings, Falkirk FK1 5RS (0324 24911)
Stirling	J Wyles	R Black Municipal Buildings, Corn Exchange Road, Stirling FK8 2HU (0786 79000)
DUMFRIES & GALLOWAY		
Annandale & Eskdale	R G Greenhow	J A Whitecross High Street, Annan DG12 6AQ (04612 3311)

Nithdale   K Cameron   W W Japp
                                    Municipal Chambers,
                                    Dumfries DG1 2AD
                                    (0387 3166)

Stewartry   J Nelson   W L Dick-Smith
                                    Council Offices,
                                    Kircudbright DG6 4PJ
                                    (0557 30291)

Wigtown   D R Robinson   A Geddes
                                    Sun Street, Stranraer
                                    DG9 3JJ (0776 2151)

FIFE
Dunfermline   R Mill   G Brown
                                    City Chambers, Dunfermline
                                    KY12 7ND (03837 22711)

Kirkcaldy   R King   J M Smith
                                    (Director of Administration)
                                    Town House, Kirkcaldy
                                    KY1 1XW (05922 61144)

North-East Fife D Barrie   R Brotherton
                                    County Buildings, Cupar
                                    KY15 4TA (03345 3722)

GRAMPIAN
City of Aberdeen H E Rae   J M Wilson
                                    Town House, Aberdeen
                                    AB9 1AQ (0224 642121)

Banff & Buchan N Cowie   R W Jackson
                                    (Director of Administration
                                    and Legal Services)
                                    St Leonards, Sandyhill Rd.,
                                    Banff AB4 1BH (026 12 2521)

Gordon   J B Presley   A C Kennedy
                                    Gordon House
                                    Blackhall Rd., Inverurie
                                    AB5 9WA (0467 20981)

Kincardine &   D J MacKenzie   T Hyder
   Deeside   Arduthie Rd, Stonehaven
                                    AB3 2DQ (056 92 62001)

Moray	E Aldridge	J P C Bell High Street, Elgin IV30 1BX (0343 3451)

HIGHLAND

Badenoch & Strathspey	J A McCook	H G McCulloch 36 High Street, Kingussie PH21 1JA (054 02 555)
Caithness	J M Young	A Beattie Council Offices, Wick KW1 4AW (0955 3761)
Inverness	A G Sellar	B Wilson Town House, Inverness IV1 1JJ (0463 239111)
Lochaber	C Neilson	D A B Blair Lochaber House, Fort William PH33 6EL (0397 3881)
Nairn	H McLean	A M Kerr (Director of Law and Administration) The Courthouse, High Street, Nairn IV12 4AU (0667 52056)
Ross & Cromarty	G D Finlayson	A Cuthbertson County Buildings, Dingwall IV15 9QN (0349 63381)
Skye & Lochalsh	J F Munro	D H Noble Park Road, Portree IV51 9EP (0478 2341)
Sutherland	Mrs L Mackenzie	D W Martin District Office, Golspie KW10 6RB (040 833192)

LOTHIAN

City of Edinburgh	J H Mackay	M M Duncan City Chambers, High St., Edinburgh EH1 1YJ (031 225 2424)

East Lothian   T Wilson

D B Miller
Council Buildings,
Haddington EH41 3HA
(062 082 4161)

Midlothian   S Campbell

D W Duguid
1 Eskdaill Court, Dalkeith
EH22 1DJ (031 663 2881)

West Lothian   D McCauley

D Morrison
South Bridge St., Bathgate
EH48 1TS (Bathgate 53631)

STRATHCLYDE

Argyll & Bute   D C Currie

M A J Gossip
Kilmory, Lochgilphead
PA31 8RT (0546 2127)

Bearsden &
Milngavie   R W Robinson

A U Laurie
Boclair, Bearsden G61 2TQ
(041 942 2262)

Clydebank   D S Grainger

J T McNally
District Council Offices
Clydebank G81 1TG
(041 941 1331)

Clydesdale   Miss M T Hodgson

P W Daniels
District Offices, Lanark
ML11 7JT (0555 61511)

Cumbernauld &
Kilsyth   J Pollock

J Hutton
Bron Way, Cumbernauld
G67 1DZ (02367 22131)

Cumnock &
Doon Valley   D Shankland

D T Hemmings
Lugar, Cumnock KA18 3JQ
(0290 22111)

Cunninghame   Mrs T Beattie

B Devine
Cunninghame House, Irvine
KA12 8EE (0294 74166)

Dumbarton   R McNamara

L Mackinnon
Crosslet House, Dumbarton
G82 3NS (0389 65100)

East Kilbride	G McKillop	W G McNay Civic Centre, East Kilbride G74 1AB (035 52 28777)
Eastwood	Mrs J M Edmondson	M D Henry Eastwood Park, Rouken Glen Road, Glasgow G46 6UG (041 638 6511)
City of Glasgow	R. Gray	S Hamilton City Chambers, Glasgow G2 1DU (041 221 9600)
Hamilton	S. Casserly	F T Malcolm 102 Cadzow Street, Hamilton ML3 6HH (0698 282323)
Inverclyde	Sir Simpson Stevenson	I C Wilson Municipal Buidings, Greenock PA15 1LY (0475 24400)
Kilmarnock & Loudon	T Ferguson	R W Jenner Civic Centre, Kilmarnock KA1 1BY (0563 21140)
Kyle & Carrick	G MacDonald	I R D Smillie Burns House, Ayr KA7 1UT (0292 81511)
Monklands	E Cairns	J S Ness Dunbeth Road, Coatbridge ML5 3LF (0263 24941)
Motherwell	J McGhee	J Bonomy P.O. Box 14, Motherwell ML1 1TW (0698 66166)
Renfrew	W McCready	W McIntosh Cotton Street, Paisley PA1 1BU (041 889 5400)
Strathkelvin	R M Coyle	C Mallon P.O. Box 4, Kirkintilloch G66 1PW (041 776 7171)

TAYSIDE

Angus	A D Welsh	W S McCulloch County Buildings, Forfar DD8 3LG (0307 65101)
City of Dundee	T Mitchell	J F Hoey City Chambers Dundee DD1 3BY (0382 23141)
Perth & Kinross	J M Mathieson	J E D Cormie 1-3 High Street, Perth PH1 5JU (0738 21161)

SECTION 4

MAJOR POLITICAL AND SOCIAL ORGANISATIONS IN SCOTLAND

1. **Political Parties**
   Communist Party, 44 Carlton Place, Glasgow G5 (041-429 2558)

   Scottish Conservative Party, 3 Chester Street, Edinburgh EH3 7RN
   (031-226 4426)

   The Labour Party (Scottish Council), Keir Hardie House,
   1 Lynedoch Place, Glasgow G3 6AB (041-332 8946)

   Scottish Liberal Party, 4 Clifton Terrace, Edinburgh EH12 5DR
   (031-337 2314)

   Scottish National Party, 6 North Charlotte Street,
   Edinburgh EH2 4JH (031-226 3661)

   Social Democratic Party, 5 Royal Exchange Square, Glagow G1
   (041-221 8871)

2. **Government Agencies**
   Crofters Commission, 4-6 Castle Wynd, Inverness IV2 3EQ
   (0463 23731)

   Glasgow Eastern Area Renewal Project (GEAR), Gear Centre,
   596 London Road, Glasgow G40 (041-551 0011)

   Highlands and Islands Development Board, 27 Bank Street,
   Inverness IV1 1QR (0463 234171)

   The Housing Corporation, Scottish Head Office, Rosebery House,
   9 Haymarket Terrace, Edinburgh EH3 7AF (031-226 3153)

   Manpower Services Commission for Scotland, 4 Jeffrey Street,
   Edinburgh EH1 1UU (031-556 0233)

   Scottish Development Agency, 120 Bothwell Street, Glasgow G2 JP
   (041-248 2700)

   Scottish Special Housing Association, 37-41 Manor Place,
   Edinburgh EH3 7EE (031-226 4401)

3. **Industrial and Social Organisations**
   Church of Scotland, 121 George Street, Edinburgh EH2
   (031-225 5722)

   Confederation of British Industry (Scottish Office), 5 Claremont
   Terrace, Glasgow G3 (041-332 8661)

Scottish Consumer Council, 314 St Vincent Street, Glasgow G3 8XW
(041-226 5261)

Scottish Council (Development and Industry), 1 Castle Street,
Edinburgh EH2 3AJ (031-225 7911)

Scottish Council for Community and Voluntary Organisations,
18/19 Claremont Crescent, Edinburgh EH7 4QD (031-556 3882)

Scottish Trades Union Congress, 16 Woodlands Terrace,
Glasgow G3 6DF (041-332 4946)

SECTION 5

REGIONAL ELECTIONS
MAY 1986

	Seats Contested	Members Elected	% Votes	% vote in Contested Seats
Labour	317	233	43.9	48.3
Conservative	259	65	16.9	22.5
Liberal/SDP	245	40	15.1	20.0
SNP	330	36	18.2	19.8
Independent	110	79	4.8	52.7
Green	69	0	0.5	2.3
Others	25	2	0.6	7.0
Total		445		

Source: Election Studies, University of Dundee

RECENT PUBLICATIONS IN SCOTTISH GOVERNMENT AND POLITICS

C H Allen

The list below covers material omitted from previous listings, and material published since the last list in the period 1.6.85 to 31.5.86. Where a publisher is not specified, the publisher and author are the same. I would be grateful to be told of any errors or omissions.

To make it easier to obtain theses on inter-library loan, I have included where possible the British Library (Lending Division) or University Microfilm numbers; these should be quoted when applying for a loan copy.

As there now exists a current index to the *Scotsman* (contact John Bennett, Scotsman Index Project, 21 Buccleuch Place, Edinburgh), I no longer cite newspaper feature articles in the index. I also do not list reports of investigations by the local Government Ombudsman.

1. ABERDEEN DISTRICT COUNCIL, *Financial statement and abstract of accounts for the year ended 31.3.1985*. Aberdeen, 1985, 36pp.
2. ABERDEEN, J, "Cooperation: the way forward", *New Shetlander* 155 (1986) 8-9.
3. AGNEW, J, "Models of spatial variation in political expression: the case of the SNP", *International Political Science Review*, 6,2 (1985) 171-96.
4. AITKEN, P (ed), *EEC policies for rural areas*. Glasgow: Planning Exchange, 1985, 84pp.
5. ALEXANDER, K, "Appreciation of Jimmy Milne on his retirement", *Scottish Trade Union Review* 30 (1986) 4-5.
6. "The HIDB", *The economic development of modern Scotland*, ed J Saville, 214-32.
7. ALLEN, B, "New towns for oil city?", *Town & Country Planning*, 55,4 (1986) 115-116.
8. ALLEN, C H, "Recent publications in Scottish goverement and politics", *Scotish Government Yearbook* 1986, 299-325.
9. ANGUS, I, *Outside the law? Non-statutory local planning in Scotland*. Glasgow: University of Strathclyde, Dept. of Urban and

Regional Planning (Papers in Planning 5), 1985.

10. ANON, "Giving tenants an equal right to buy", *Scottish Federation News*, Jan. 1986, 8-9.

11. ANON, "Glasgow's revival: a Scots lesson for Liverpool", *Economist*, 7.12.85, 33-34.

12. ANON, "Housing (Scotland) Bill", *Scottish Federation News*, Feb.1986, 3-6, 13.

13. ANON, "Scotland: a special report", *Times*, 27.11.85, 17-20.

14. ANON, "Scotland's rates for 1986-87", *Local Government Chronicle*, 21.3.86, 312-31.

15. ANON, "Scotland's top 100 companies", *Scottish Business Insider*, 3,1 (1986) 2-32.

16. ANON, "The vital support industries" (Microelectronics), *Scottish Economic Development Review* 4, (1985) 11-17.

17. ARKELTON TRUST/ERNEST COOK TRUST, *Future issues in rural development*. Langholm: Arkleton Trust, 1985.

18. ARMSTRONG, A, "Another brick in the wall: the politics of Scottish education", *Radical Scotland* 16 (1985) 13-15.

19. ASCHERSON, N, "Devolution diary", *Cencrastus* 22 (1986) 3-14, 49-54.

20. ASHRIF, S, "What Scotland can learn from 'riots' in England", *The Thatcher revolution* (Modern Studies Association, 1986), 61-64.

21. ATHUGALAGE, T S K, *The Tayside economy: an input-output approach to analysis and planning*. Ph.D. thesis, CNAA, 1983.

22. BAILEY, S, "Rates reform: lessons from the Scottish experience", *Local Goverenment Studies*, 12,3 (1986), 21-36.

23. BALFOUR, A, "Mathewson", *Scottish Business Insider*, 2,11 (1985) 4-7.

24. BALFOUR, A, "Sunrise in the North", *The Director*, 37 (1983) 30-33.

25. BALFOUR, A & BROWN, R, "Tayside: a £100m renaissance starts to make an impact", *Scottish Business Insider*, 3,4 (1986) 32-39.

26. BEARSDEN & MILNGAVIE DISTRICT COUNCIL, *Fifth housing plan November 1985*. Milngavie, 1985, 46pp.

27. BEGG, H & MCDOWELL, D "Regional industrial policy", *Scottish Government Yearbook* 1986, 211-24.

28. BERSS, M, "Silicon Glen", *Forbes Magazine*, 24.10.1983, 167-79.

29. BOCHEL, H M, *The values, attitudes and partisanship of Scottish parliamentary candidates at the 1979 General Election*. M.Sc. dissertation, Strathclyde, 1983.

30. BORDERS REGIONAL COUNCIL, *Annual report on economic development in the Borders region 1985*. Newtown St Boswells,

1986.

31. .... *Financial report and accounts 1984-5.* Newtown St Boswells, 1986.

32. BOYD, G, *Multifunctional community cooperatives in the Western Isles: an oblique view.* M.Sc. dissertation, Aberdeen, 1979.

33. BRAILEY, M, *Women's access to council housing.* Glasgow: Planning Exchange (Occasional paper 25), 1986, 120pp.

34. BREATHNACH, P, *Aspects of rural development in the Scottish Highlands and Islands.* Maynooth; St Patricks College, Dept. of Geography (Occasional paper 4), 1984, 39pp.

35. BREITENBACH, E, "Can Scotland provide independence for women?", *Radical Scotland* 17 (1985) 10-11.

36. .... "Scottish feminism in print", *Cencdastus* 21 (1985) 45-47.

37. BRUCE, S, "Ideology and isolation: a failed Scots protestant movement", *Archives des sciences sociales des religions,* 28, 56/1 (1983) 147-59.

38. BRYDEN, G, "Scottish agriculture", *The economic development of modern Scotland,* ed J Saville, 141-62.

39. BURNS, M, "The ownership of the Scottish press", *Scottish Trade Union Review* 30 (1986) 32-35.

40. BUTT, J, "The quality of life" *Quality of life and human welfare,* ed Pacione & Gordon, 124-33.

41. BUTT, J & GORDON, G, *Strathclyde: changing horizons.* Edinburgh: Scottish Academic Press, 1985, 294pp.

42. BUXTON, N, "The Scottish economy 1945-79; performance, structure and problems", *The economic development of modern Scotland,* ed J Saville, 47-78.

43. BYRON, R, "Buying a share: state institutions and local communities on the periphery – a case from Shetland", *'Nation' and 'state' in Europe,* ed R D Grillo (London: Academic Press, 1980), 137-49.

44. CAMPAIGN FOR A SCOTTISH ASSEMBLY, *Agreeing a Scottish Assembly,* Glasgow, 1986.

45. CAMPBELL, A, "Employment profiles of new manufacturing establishments in Scotland and the HIDB area", *Scottish Economic Bulletin* 32 (1985) 12-15.

46. CAMPBELL, C, "Cooperation at work in Scotland", *Scottish Economic Development Review* 4 (1985) 8-9.

47. CARNIE, J, "Parliament and Scottish moral legislation in the 1970s", *Scottish Government Yearbook* 1986, 46-69.

48. CARTER, H, "Edinburgh: capital and regional city", *Regional cities in the UK 1890-1980,* ed. G Gordon (London: Harper & Row, 1986).

49. CARTER, I R, "Regional policy in New Zealand and Scotland: tentative comparisons", *Australian and New Zealand Journal of Sociology*, 20, 3 (1984) 393-404.

50. CARTY, T, "The HIDB: a vehicle for land reform in Scotland?", *Land for the people*, ed. Evans, I & Hendry, J, 34-40.

51. CAWDERY, J & TAYLOR, A C S, "Branch plant performance in Scotland", *Scottish Economic Bulletin* 32 (1985) 16-21.

52. CENTRE FOR HOUSING RESEARCH, *Low cost home ownership in Glasgow 1977-83*. Glasgow: Glasgow University Centre for Housing Research (Discussion paper 7), 1985, 54pp.

54. C.E.S. LTD., *Outer estates in Britain: Easterhouse case study*. London (CES Paper 24), 1985.

55. CHARTERED ASSOCIATION OF CERTIFIED ACCOUNTANTS, *Assessing local expenditure needs: problems of theory and measurement in the Scottish client group approach*. Dartford: Certified Accountant Publications, 1985, 116pp.

56. CHRISTIE, C, "The way ahead for the Scottish economy", *Scottish Trade Union Review* 30 (1986) 9-10, 27.

57. CLAPHAM, D & KINTREA, K, "Rationing, choice and constraint: the allocation of public housing in Glasgow", *Journal of Social Policy*, 15,1 (1986) 51-67.

58. .... "The social consequences of the allocation process: evidence from Glasgow", *Housing Review*, May-June 1986, 83-84.

59. CLYDEBANK DISTRICT COUNCIL, *Housing plan 7 1986-91*. Clydebank, 1985.

60. CLYDESDALE DISTRICT COUNCIL, *Housing plan 1985-90*. Lanark, 1985, 118pp.

61. COCKHEAD, P, *Strategic planning in Grampian*. Glasgow: Planning Exchange, 1986, 16pp.

62. COCKSHUT, P, *Scotland, Ireland: socialism, nationalism*. Edinburgh: MCM, 1984, 27pp.

63. COLWELL, R, "Scotland sees spark of new lease of life", *Town & Country Planning*, 55, 4 (1986) 109-110.

64. COMMISSIONER FOR LOCAL ADMINISTRATION IN SCOTLAND, *Report...for the year ended 31.3.85*. Edinburgh, 1985, 23pp.

65. .... *Report...for the year ended 31.3.86*. Edinburgh, 1986, 24pp.

66. COMMISSIONER FOR LOCAL AUTHORITY ACCOUNTS IN SCOTLAND, *Tenth report, 1985*. Edinburgh, 1985, 48pp.

67. COMMITTEE OF PUBLIC ACCOUNTS, *Investment activities of the SDA, WDA and HIDB: report*. London: House of Commons paper 600, 1985, 26pp.

68. COMMITTEE ON RESOURCES FOR THE SCOTTISH

TENANTS MOVEMENT, *What price tenants' groups?* Glasgow: TPAS, 1985.

69. COMMITTEE ON SCOTTISH AFFAIRS, *HIDB, The Government's reply to the Committee's second report of session 1984-85.* London: House of Commons paper HC 428, 1985, 9pp.

70. *HIDB. The Government's further reply to the Committee's second report of session 1984-85.* London: House of Commons paper HC 352, 1986, 9pp.

71. *Public expenditure to 1988-89: a commentary on the Scotland programme. Minutes of evidence: Scottish Office.* London: House of Commons paper 290, 1986, 25pp.

72. *The impact of airport privatisation on Scottish Lowlands airport policy: the Government's reply to the Committee's first report of session 1984-85.* London: House of Commons paper 220, 1986, 2pp.

73. *The proposed closure of BSC Gartcosh. Report and minutes of evidence.* London: House of Commons paper 164, 1986, 2 vols (19pp, 174pp).

74. CONFEDERATION OF BRITISH INDUSTRY, "Scotland: special report", *CBI News*, 25.10.85, supplement.

75. COOPER, D, *The road to Mingulay: a view of the Western Isles.* London: Routledge, Kegan Paul, 1985, 226pp.

76. CORRIGAN, S, CUNNINGHAM, C & THORBURN, M, "Fife women stand firm", *The cutting edge: women and the pit strike*, ed. V Seddon (London: Lawrence and Wishart, 1986), 30-49.

77. COSLA, *Scotland's housing crisis.* Edinburgh, 1986, 12 leaves.

78. .... *The case for a Scottish house condition survey.* Edinburgh, 1986.

79. CROFTERS COMMISSION, *Annual report 1984.* Edinburgh: HMSO, 1985, 35pp.

80. CROSS, M, *New manufacturing firm formation and regional development: the case of Scotland.* Ph.D. thesis, Edinburgh, 1983 (BLLDNo.; D48896/84).

81. CUNNINGHAM, C "Warm welcome, sharp realities: relations with the NUM. Fife", *The cutting edge: women and the pit strike*, ed. V Seddon (London: Lawrence and Wishart, 1986), 222-26.

82. DANSON, M, "Poverty and deprivation in the West of Scotland", *Quality of life and human welfare*, ed Pacione & Gordon, 23-34.

83. DEPARTMENT OF URBAN AND REGIONAL PLANNING, UNIVERSITY OF STRATHCLYDE, *Factors affecting the performance of planning authorities in submitting observations on planning appeals.* Edinburgh: Scottish Office, 1986, 133pp.

84. DEVEREUX, R J, *Employment changes in Scottish manufacturing industry (1954-74).* Edinburgh: SEPD (ESU Discussion paper 12), 1980, 31pp.

85. DOLAN, N, "What's wrong with Scottish housing?", *The Thatcher revolution* (Modern Studies Association, 1986), 57-64.

86. DONALDSON, G, *Scottish church history*. Edinburgh: Scottish Academic Press, 1985, 256pp.

87. DONNELLY, C, *Diagnosis: healthy or ailing? The state of private health in Scotland*.

88. "Private health care in Scotland", *Scottish Government Yearbook* 1986, 172-86.

89. DOUGLAS, A, "An introduction to local government finance in Scotland", *Scottish Bankers Magazine*, May 1985, 5-7.

90. DOWLE, M, "The year at Westminster", *Scottish Government Yearbook* 1986, 5-19.

91. DRAKE, B, "Managing as best they can", *Local Government News*, Sept. 1985, 28-29, 32.

92. DRAPER, P, SMITH, I & STEWART, B, "Scottish financial institutions", *Quarterly Economic Commentary*, 11, 2 (1985) 77-81.

93. DRUCKER, N, "Lost in the haar: a critique of Mental health in focus", *Scottish Government Yearbook* 1986, 70-92.

94. DUGUID, J, *Sociological aspects of mass tourism: the case of the Scottish Highlands*. Ph.D. thesis, Aberdeen, 1981 (BLLD No.: D 49074/84).

95. DUMFRIES & GALLOWAY REGIONAL COUNCIL, *Abstract of accounts for the year ended 31 March 1985*. Dumfries, 1985.

96. .... *Annual report 1984/5*. Dumfries, 1985.

97. .... *Transport policies and programme 1985-90*. Dumfries, 1985, 126pp.

98. DUNDEE DISTRICT COUNCIL, *Housing plan 1986-91*. Dundee, 1986.

99. EAGLES, M, "The neglected regional dimension in Scottish ethnic nationalism", *Canadian Review of Studies in Nationalism*. 12, 1 (1985) 81-98.

100. EAST KILBRIDE DISTRICT COUNCIL, *Housing plan 1982-87 (revised edition)*. East Kilbridge, n.d., 93pp.

101. .... *Housing plan. 1984 update*. East Kilbride, n.d., 53pp.

102. ECONOMIC DEVELOPMENT BRIEFING, *Japanese direct investment in the UK 1986-7*. London, 1986, 19pp.

103. EDINBURGH DISTRICT COUNCIL, *Financial report and abstract of accounts 1984-85*. Edinburgh, 1985.

104. .... *Housing in Edinburgh: the public investigation 20-23.5.85*. Edinburgh, 1985.

105. .... *Housing plan 1985-90*. Edinburgh, 1985.

106. .... *Housing plan 4, 1986-91*. Edinburgh, 1985.

107. EDWARDS, R, "Splitting on the sidelines", *New Statesman*,

4.10.85, 15-16.

108. EQUAL OPPORTUNITIES COMMISSION, *Women and men in Scotland: a statistical profile*. Glasgow, 1985.

109. EVANS, I & HENDRY, J (eds), *The land for the people*. Edinburgh: Scottish Socialist Society, 1985, 71pp.

110. .... "The land policies of political parties in Scotland: a commentary", *Land for the people*, ed. Evans, I & Hendry, J, 64-70.

111. EWING, W, "Oblivion or resources: Scotland's choice", *Town & Country Planning*, 55, 4 (1986) 11-113.

112. FALKIRK DISTRICT COUNCIL, *Annual report and financial statement 1984-5*. Falkirk 1985.

113. .... *Housing plan 1986-1991*. Falkirk 1985.

114. FIFE REGIONAL COUNCIL, *Annual report and financial statement 1984/5*. Glenrothes, 1985.

115. .... *Revenue budget 1986/7*. Glenrothes, 1986.

116. FITZPATRICK, T A, *Catholic secondary education in South West Scotland before 1972: its contribution to the change in the status of the Catholic community*. Aberdeen: Aberdeen University Press, 1986, 220pp.

117. FOULIS, M B, *Council house sales in Scotland: April 1979 to December 1983*. Edinburgh: Scottish Office Central Research Unit, 1985, 92pp.

118. FORSYTHE, D, "Urban incomers and rural change: the impact of migrants from the city on life in an Orkney community", *Sociologica Ruralis*, 20,4 (1980) 287-307.

119. FRASER OF ALLANDER INSTITUTE, *The Shetland industrial survey 1982/3*. Glasgow, 1985, 8 volumes.

120. GASKIN, M, "The Scottish financial sector 1950-80", *The economic development of modern Scotland*, ed J Saville, 114-40.

121. GEDDES, E, "Scottish revaluation: a worthwhile exercise", *Municipal Journal*, 15.11.85, 1856-60.

122. GEDDES, M N, *The political economy of regional development: the Scottish HIDB*. Ph.D. thesis, Sussex, 1984, 370pp (BLLD No.: D 57785/85).

123. GB PETROLEUM CONSULTANTS, *The impact of offshore oil and gas related activity on the economic development of the Shetland Islands*. Lerwick: Shetland Islands Council, 1986.

124. GIARCHI, G G, *Between McAlpine and Polaris: a social inscape study*. Ph.D. thesis, Glasgow, 1981.

125. GIBB, A & MACLENNAN, D, "Policy and process in Scottish housing 1950-80", *The economic development of modern Scotland*, ed J Saville, 270-91.

126. GIBSON, J S, *The thistle and the crown*. Edinburgh: HMSO, 1985,

198pp.

126a. GIBSON, R, "Buried nationalism or re-emergent state?", *Nationalist Left Review* 2 (1985) 7-8.

127. GILCHRIST, J A, *The Motherwell Project: a study of agency intervention in urban renewal*. Glasgow: University of Strathclyde Dept. of Urban and Regional Planning (Papers on Planning 6), 1985.

128. GLASGOW DISTRICT COUNCIL, *Annual housing review 1984*. Glasgow, 1985, 374pp.

129. .... *City profile*. Glasgow, 1985, 151pp.

130. .... *Community ownership in Glasgow*. Glasgsow: GDC Housing Dept. (Briefing paper), 1985, 43pp.

131. .... *Economic development plan (monitoring statement Oct-Dec 1985)*. Glasgow, 1986, 8pp.

132. .... *Housing plan 8*. Glasgow, 1985, 2 vols.

133. .... *Mortgage default in Glasgow*. Glasgow: GDC Housing Dept. Policy Research Group (Research memorandum 5). 1985, 20pp.

134. .... *Peoples and households in Glasgow: current estimates and expected changes 1984-91*. Glasgow, 1985, 17pp.

135. .... *The impact on the local community of the contraction of British Rail Engineering Ltd., Springburn*. Glasgow, 1985, 41pp.

136. GODMAN, N A, *Historical and contemporary issues in the catching sector of the British fishing industry*. Ph.D. thesis, Heriot-Watt, 1982.

137. GOODLAD, J, "The Shetland fishing industry", *New Shetlander* 156 (1986) 7-9.

138. GORDON, G, "The city of Glasgow", *Strathclyde: changing horizons*, ed J Butt & G Gordon, 53-78.

139. GORDON, I, "The cyclical interaction between regional migration, employment and unemployment: a time series analysis for Scotland", *Scottish Journal of Political Economy*, 32, 2 (1985) 135-58.

140. GORDON, J C, *The temperance movement and the Labour Party in Glasgow 1920-76*. M.A. dissertation, Newcastle, 1983.

141. GRAMPIAN REGIONAL COUNCIL, *Annual report and accounts 1984/5*. Aberdeen, 1985, 37pp.

142. .... *Development programme for upland agriculture: the case of Grampian*. Aberdeen: GRC Agriculture Committee, 1985.

143. GRIMES, A, "The welfare state, privatisation and the voluntary sector", *Scottish Government Yearbook* 1986, 157-71.

144. GRANT, R & CURRIE, H, *The use and impact of housing improvement and repair grants in Scotland*. Edinburgh: Scottish Office Central Research Unit, 1985, 65pp.

145. GRAY, C, "Effect of central government policies in Strathclyde

Regional Council", *The Thatcher revolution* (Modern Studies Association, 1986), 67-69.

146. GREENHALGH, G (ed), *Rural economic development: policies and initiatives*. Glasgow: Planning Exchange (Occasional paper 20), 1985, 67pp.

147. GRIEG, N J, *A planning critique of local government reorganisation*. M.Sc. Dissertation, Strathclyde, 1983.

148. HAGUE, C, "Housing privatisation in practice", *Housing and Planning Review*, 40,3 (1985) 16-18.

149. HALLWOOD, P, *The offshore oil supply industry in Aberdeen: the affiliates, their characteristics and importance*. Aberdeen: Aberdeen University Dept. of Political Economy (North Sea Study Occasional paper 23), 1986.

150. HAMILTON, C M, *An examination of the efficiency of the Housing Management Department of the Glasgow District Council*. M.Sc. dissertation, Strathclyde, 1983.

151. HAMILTON, J, "Give us a future, give us our jobs!", *The cutting edge*, ed. V Seddon (London: Lawrence & Wishart, 1986), 211-21 (Monktonhall Colliery).

152. HAMILTON, R T, "Closure rates in Scottish manufacturing industries", *Scottish Journal of Political Economy*, 32,3 (1985) 333-42.

153. .... "Entry and exit of businesses in Scotland", *Success and failure in small businesses*, ed. L Lewis et al (Aldershot: Gower, 1984), 57-69.

154. .... *Measures and determinants of entry and exit rates of businesses in Scotland*. Ph.D. thesis, London, 1982.

155. HAMPSON, S F, *Recent trends in the Scottish energy market*. Edinburgh: SEPD (ESU Discussion paper 1), 1977, 54pp.

156. HARE, P, "Land ownership in Scotland and Eastern Europe: a comparison", *Land for the people*, ed. Evans, I & Hendry, J, 56-60.

157. HARRIS, A H et al, *Dependence, displacement and deterrence: the employment implications of oil in Aberdeen*. Aberdeen: Aberdeen University Dept. of Political Economy (Discussion paper 85-04), 1985, 42pp.

158. .... *The distributional impact of incoming industry: Aberdeen*. Aberdeen: Aberdeen University Dept. of Political Economy (Discussion paper 85-06), 1985, 31pp.

159. HARRISON, D, "The case for Gartcosh and Ravenscraig", *Scottish Trade Union Review* 28 (1986) 7-9.

160. HART, D M, *A review of community councils in Scotland 1983-84*. Edinburgh: Scottish Office Central Research Unit, 1986, 75pp.

161. HARTLEY, J, *Transport and accessibility in a small area of Grampian Region*. M.Sc. dissertation, Aberdeen, 1983.

162. HARVIE, C, "The Appleby Version", *Scottish Government Yearbook* 1986, 20-22 (review).

163. HAUG, P, "US high technology multinationals and Silicon Glen", *Regional Studies*, 20,2 (1986) 103-116.

164. HAYTON, R, "Supporting community business", *Local Government Policy Making*, 12.2 (1985) 15-20.

165. HENDERSON, D S, *Consumers expenditure in Scotland 1962-77*. Edinburgh: SEPD (ESU Discussion paper 9), 1980, 46pp.

166. HIGHLANDS AND ISLANDS DEVELOPMENT BOARD, *Accounts 1984-85*. London: House of Commons paper.

167. .... *Annual report 20*. Inverness, 1986.

168. .... *Community councils in the HIDB area*. Inverness, 1980, 26pp.

169. HIGHLAND REGIONAL COUNCIL, *Economic review 4*. Inverness, 1985, 15pp.

170. .... *Structure plan review issues paper*. Inverness, 1985, 52pp.

171. HOLLAND, G, "A note on high technology manufacturing industries in Scotland", *Scottish Economic Bulletin* 32 (1985) 10-15.

172. HOPE, K, *As others see us: schooling and social mobility in Scotland and the US*. Cambridge: Cambridge University Press, 1984, 306pp.

173. HOWE, M, "Aspects of social malaise in Scotland", *Quality of life and human welfare*, ed Pacione & Gordon, 91-102.

174. HUGHES, J, "Policies and practice: the Scottish experience", *Planning and development in rural areas*. ed P M Jess et al (Belfast: Queen's University Institute of Irish Studies, 1984), 179-95.

175. HUMES, W, *The leadership class in Scottish education*. Edinburgh: John Donald, 1986, 238pp.

176. HUNTER, D J, *Managing the NHS in Scotland: review and assessment of research needs*. Edinburgh: SHHD, 1986.

177. HUNTER, J, "Urban renewal in Glasgow: a comprehensive strategy", *Housing Review*, 34,4 (1985) 125-29.

178. HUNTER, L, "The Scottish labour market", *The economic development of modern Scotland*, J Saville, 163-82.

179. HURWITZ NADEL, J, "Stigma and separation: pariah status and community persistence in a Scottish fishing village", *Ethnology*, 23,2 (1984) 101-115.

180. INDUSTRY DEPARTMENT FOR SCOTLAND, *Index of industrial production and construction for Scotland: detailed industry series 1973-83*. Edinburgh: IDS (Statistical Bulletin D2.1), 1985, 7pp.

181. *The electronics industry in Scotland*. Edinburgh: IDS (Statistical Bulletin C1.1), 1986, 9pp.

182. INNES, J, "The powers that be", *Land for the people*, ed. Evans, I & Hendry, J, 49-55.

183. INSTITUTE OF HOUSING (SCOTTISH TRAINING UNIT), *House sales: the management implications*. Edinburgh, 1986.

184. JENKINS, B & MINNERUP, G, *Citizens and comrades: socialism in a world of nation states*. London: Pluto, 1984.

185. JOHNS, P M & LEAT, P M K, *An approach to regional economic modelling: the case of Grampian*. Aberdeen: North of Scotland College of Agriculture, 1986, 77pp.

186. JONES, C & MACLENNAN, D, *North Sea oil and the Aberdeen housing market*. Glasgow: North Sea Oil Panel, 1983.

187. JONES, H, "Peripheral counter-urbanization...in Northern Scotland", *Regional Studies*, 20, 1 (1986) 15-26.

188. JONES, J B & KEATING, M, "Labour's territorial strategy", in their *Labour and the British state* (Oxford: Clarendon, 1985), 105-39.

189. KEATING, M, "Community-owned housing in Glasgow facing 'suffocation'", *Municipal Journal*, 20.12.85, 2058-59.

190. .... "Islands councils: authorities with unique responsibilities", *Municipal Journal*, 30.8.85, 1432-33.

191. .... "Public sector housing: the Scottish experience", *Municipal Journal*, 2.8.85, 1289-90.

192. .... "Will a 'poll tax' prove a pole-axe for the Conservatives North of the border?", *Municipal Journal*, 28.2.86. 309-309.

193. KEATING, M & WATERS, N, "Scotland in the European Community", *Regions in the European Community*, ed. M Keating & B Jones (Oxford: Clarendon, 1985), 60-88 (corrected entry).

194. KENDRICK, S, "Occupational change in modern Scotland", *Scottish Government Yearbook* 1986, 240-72.

195. KEREVAN, G, "Sao Paulo by the Forth", *Radical Scotland* 17 (1985) 15-16.

196. LAUGHLIN, S & MCKINNON, D, "Scotland's health service of the future", *Radical Scotland* 16 (1985) 10-11.

197. LEVER, W & MOORE, C, *The city in transition: policies and agencies for the economic regeneration of Clydeside*. Oxford: Oxford University Press, 1986, 173pp.

198. LEVY, C (Comp.), *A very hard year: the 1984/5 miners strike in Mauchline*. Glasgow: Workers Educational Association, 1985, 34pp.

199. LEVY, R, "The search for a rational strategy: the SNP and devolution 1974-79", *Political Studies*, 34,2 (1986) 236-48.

200. LIVINGSTONE, L H, *Vacant land in Glasgow's East End: history, recent policies and potential uses*. M.Phil dissertation, Edinburgh, 1983.

201. LOTHIAN REGIONAL COUNCIL, *Annual report and accounts 1984-85*. Edinburgh, 1985, 55pp.

202. .... *Census 1981: analysis of multiple deprivation in Lothian Region*. Edinburgh, 1984, 52pp.

203. .... *Structure plan 1985 (written statement)*. Edinburgh, 1985, 69pp.

204. .... *Transport policies and programme 8: 1985-90*. Edinburgh, 1985, 57pp.

205. LOVE, J & STEVENS, J, "The SDA since 1979", *The Thatcher revolution* (Modern Studies Association, 1986), 23-26.

206. .... "The Scottish steel industry", *The Thatcher revolution* (Modern Studies Association, 1986), 30-35.

207. .... "Scottish steel at the crossroads", *Quarterly Economic Commentary*, 11, 3 (1986) 61-65.

208. LYDDON, D, "Hope for Scotland after the oil", *Town & Country Planning*, 55, 4 (1986) 107.

209. LYTHE, C, "Government and economy in modern Scotland" (review article), *Scottish Economic and Social History* 6 (1986) 69-73.

210. .... "The rise of the Strathclyde Region", *Strathclyde: changing horizons*, ed J Butt & G Gordon, 23-42.

211. MACARTHUR, A, *The community business movement in Scotland: contributions, public sector responses and possibilities*. Glasgow: Glasgow University Centre for Urban and Regional Research (Discussion paper 17), 1984.

212. MACARTNEY, W J A, "Summary of opinion polls 1984/5", *Scottish Government Yearbook* 1986, 283-86.

213. "The Scottish islands debate", *Islands of Europe*, ed. W J A Macartney (Edinburgh: Unit for the Study of Government in Scotland, 1984), 7-24.

214. MACASKILL, K, "Tasks of the national left", *Nationalist Left Review* 3 (1986) 5-6.

215. MACASKILL, K, HALIDAY, R & REID, C, *A new image for a new age*. 1985.

216. MCCONNELL, J, "Governing with the people", *Radical Scotland* 19 (1986) 22-23 (Stirling District Council Labour Group).

217. MCCREADIE, J, *Enterprise agencies and local economic development*. Glasgow: Planning Exchange (Occasional paper 17), 1985, 52pp.

218. MCCRONE, G, "The role of government", *The economic development of modern Scotland*, ed J Saville, 195-213.

219. MCCRONE, G & RANDALL, J N, "The SDA", *The economic development of modern Scotland*, ed J Saville, 233-44.

220. MCDOWALL, S, "Coal, gas and oil: the changing energy scene in Scotland 1950-80", *The economic development of modern Scotland*, ed J Saville, 292-311.

221. MCGARRY, M, *Housing facts and figures*. Edinburgh: Age Concern, 1985, 32pp.

222. MACGREGOR, B, "Rural land development and land policy: some problems and opportunities", *Land for the people*, ed. Evans, I & Hendry, J, 25-33.

223. MACGREGOR, B D, "Crofting demography and land use: case study of N W Sutherland", *Scottish Geographical Magazine*, 102, 1 (1986) 46- 56.

224. .... *The Highland problem: the difficulties and development in a remote rural area*. M.Sc. dissertation, Heriot-Watt, 1978.

225. .... *The role of land in the economic development of the Scottish Highlands*. Ph.D. thesis, Cambridge, 1984.

226. MACGREGOR, K, "Waiting for the winds of change", *Radical Scotland* 18 (1986) 8-11.

227. MCINTOSH, S, "New Towns' success record provides a hard act to follow", *Scottish Business Insider*, 3, 2 (1986), 22-26.

228. MACKAY, T, "The deregulation of local bus services in Scotland", *Scottish Government Yearbook* 1986, 187-210.

229. MCKENZIE, J, "Trade unionism and Shetland", *New Shetlander* 155 (1986) 22-24.

230. MACLENNAN, D, "Urban housing rehabilitation: an encouraging British example", *Policy & Politics*, 13,4 (1985) 413-29.

231. MACLENNAN, F, LAMONT, D & MUNRO, M, *New private housing in the GEAR area*. Edinburgh: SDA, 1982.

232. MACLENNAN, D & O'SULLIVAN, T, "Scottish housing policy and spending since 1979", *The Thatcher revolution* (Modern Studies Association, 1986), 45-54.

233. MCNICOLL, I, "Input-output planning in Shetland", *The Planner*, June 1986, 39-42.

234. .... *Shetland: economy and industry 1982/3*. Lerwick: Shetland Islands Council, 1985, 34pp.

235. MACPHERSON, T, "The greening of Scotland", *Scottish Economic Development Review* 6, (1986) 8-9.

236. MALANCZUK, P, *Region und unitarische Struktur in Grossbritanien*. Berlin: Springer, 1984, 296pp.

237. MALCOLM, J F (ed), *Local authority rates: new research*. Glasgow: Glasgow Univrsity Centre for Urban and Regional Research (Discussion paper 19), 1985, 59pp.

238. MANPOWER SERVICES COMMISSION, *Corporate plan for Scotland 1985-89*. Edinburgh, 1985, 50pp.

239. MARSHALL, L, "A canteen worker on strike", *The cutting edge*, ed. V Seddon (London: Lawrence & Wishart, 1986), 97-108 (Killoch Colliery).

240. MARTLEW, C, "Consulting nondomestic ratepayers in Scotland: the first year", *Local Government Studies*, 12, 1 (1986) 57-66.

241. MARTLEW, C & KEMPE, S, *The councillor's working environment in Scotland and West Germany*. Glasgow: Planning Exchange, 1986, 118pp.

242. MARTLEW, D & NASSMACHER, H, *Training and development for councillors in Scotland and West Germany*. Glasgow: Planing Exchange (Occasional paper 18), 1985, 50pp.

243. MATTHEWS, C P, *Integrated development as a concept in the Western Isles*. M.Sc. dissertation, Aberdeen, 1983.

244. MAXWELL, S, *Facing the facts*. Edinburgh: SCCVO (Briefing paper 1), 1985.

245. .... "The 79 Group: a critical retrospect", *Cencrastus* 21 (1985) 11-16.

246. .... "The fall and fall of Toryism in Scotland", *Radical Scotland* 15 (1985) 7-9.

247. MEWETT, P G, "Economic brokerage and peripheral underdevelopment in the Isle of Lewis", *Sociological Review*, 31, 3 (1983) 327-52.

248. MIDDLETON, A & MCELDOWNEY, J T, *Small scale economic activity and regional decline in Northern Ireland and Strathclyde*. Edinburgh: Edinburgh University Dept. of Urban Design and Regional Planning (Occasional paper), 1986.

249. MIDWINTER, A, "Local government in Strathclyde", *Strathclyde: changing horizons*, ed J Butt & G Gordon, 43-52.

250. MIDWINTER, A MAIR, C & FORD, C, "The politics of rate support grant distribution", *Scottish Government Yearbook* 1986, 23-35.

251. MILES, R & MUIRHEAD, L, "Racism in Scotland", *Scottish Government Yearbook* 1986, 108-36.

252. .... *Racism in Scotland: a comparative approach*. Coventry Polytechnic, Institute of British Geographers Study Group Conference, 1986.

253. MILLAN, B, "Scotland, the S.O. and the UK economy", *A maverick institution*, ed. C Blake & C Lythe (Dundee: Dundee University Dept. of Economics, 1981).

254. MILLAR, A, *Strathclyde (British PTE's, 1)*. Shepperton: Ian Allen, 1985, 128pp.

255. MITCHISON, R, "The hidden labour force: women in the Scottish economy since 1945", *The economic development of modern Scotland*, ed J Saville, 183-94.

256. MONIES, G, *Local government in Scotland*. Edinburgh: W Green, 1985, 88pp.

257. MOORE, B, et al., *The effects of goverement regional economic*

policy. London: HMSO, 1986, 82pp.

258. MOORE, C & SKINNER, V, "Community business: a new synthesis", *Public Administration Bulletin* 46 (1984) 54-70.

259. MORTON, J, "Cooperative refurb - Glasgow style", *Local Government News*, July 1985, 38-39.

260. MOTHERWELL DISTRICT COUNCIL, *Annual economic review 1985*. Motherwell, 1985, 58pp.

261. .... "The threat to Ravenscraig", *Motherwell District Economic Review* 6 (1985) 8pp.

262. MULHOLLAND, L, "Membership of the EEC means sellout of nationalism and socialism", *Nationalist Left Review* 3 (1986) 3-4.

263. MULHOLLAND, M, "The sense of nationality in Scotland", *Nationalist Left Review* 2 (1985) 4-6.

264. MUNRO, M, *The use of discretionary grants by owner-occupiers in Glasgow*. Glasgow: Glasgow University Centre for Housing Research Discussion paper 5, 1985, 23pp.

265. .... "Who uses improvement and repair grants?", *Housing Review*, 34,6 (1985) 191-94.

266. MUNRO, M & LAMONT, D, "Neighbourhood perception, preference and household mobility in the Glasgow private housing markets", *Environment & Planning* A, 17, 10 (1985) 1331-50.

267. NABARRO, R et al, *Local enterprise and unemployment*. London: Gulbenkian Foundation, 1986.

268. NAIRN, A G & KIRWAN, F X, "The economy of Strathclyde Region", *Strathclyde: changing horizons*, ed J Butt & G Gordon, 134-51.

269. NATIONAL UNION OF MINEWORKERS; DYSART STRIKE CENTRE: *Coal in Fife: the facts and the fight for the future*. Bathgate: West Lothian Labour Party Publications, n.d., 28pp.

270. NITHSDALE DISTRICT COUNCIL, *Annual report and financial statement*. Dumfries, 1985.

271. NORTH EAST FIFE DISTRICT COUNCIL, *Council house sales in NE Fife*. Cupar, 1985, 17pp.

272. .... *Housing plan 1986-91*. Cupar, 1985.

273. NURMINEN, E & ROBINSON, G M, *Demographic changes and planning initiatives in Scotland's Northern and Western isles*. Edinburgh: Edinburgh University Dept. of Geography Research Discussion paper 20, 1985, 86pp.

274. NORRIE, C B, *Aspects of regionalism and nationalism: recent Scottish experience*. M.Sc. dissertation, Manchester, 1977.

275. OGUNFIDODO, O A, *Statutory local plans and development control; a case study of the Bishopbriggs local plan*. M.Sc. dissertation, Strathclyde, 1983.

276. OLIVER, N, "An examination of the organisational commitment in six workers' cooperatives in Scotland", *Human Relations*, 37, 1 (1984) 29-46.

277. PACIONE, M, "Inner city regeneration: perspectives on the GEAR Project", *Planning Outlook*, 28, 2 (1985) 65-69.

278. PACIONE, M & Gordon, G (eds), *Quality of life and human welfare*. Norwich: Geo Books for Royal Scottish Geographical Society, 1984, 120pp.

279. PAGE, E, "Local government in Scotland", *Local democracies*, ed. M Bowman & W Hampton (Melbourne: Longman Cheshire, 1983), 41-60.

280. PARRY, R, "Privatisation and the tarnishing of the Scottish public sector", *Scottish Government Yearbook* 1986, 137-56.

281. PARSONS, D W, *The political economy of British regional policy*. London: Croom Helm, 1986, 294pp.

282. PATTERSON, K, "Scottish RSG settlement", *Public Finance and Accountancy*, 24.1.86, 7-9.

283. PAYNE, P L, "The decline of the Scottish heavy industries 1945-83", *The economic development of modern Scotland*, ed J Saville, 79-113.

284. PLANT, S D, "A subculture of parasuicide", *Human Relations*, 38, 4 (1985) 257-97.

285. .... *Cultural aspects of parasuicide: an empirical investigation*. Ph.D. thesis, Edinburgh, 1984.

286. RADICAL SCOTLAND, "Cold climate settles over Scotland's Tories", *Radical Scotland*, 18 (1986) 6-7.

287. .... "Kinnock's 'new realism': what's left for Labour in Scotland?", *Radical Scotland* 16 (1985) 7-9.

288. .... "SNP: on the march again?", *Radical Scotland* 20 (1986) 6- 8.

289. .... "The SDA: Living under an illusion", *Radical Scotland* 20 (1986) 12-15.

290. RANDALL, J N, "New Towns and new industries", *The economic development of modern Scotland*, ed J Saville, 245-69.

291. RENFREW DISTRICT COUNCIL, *Annual report and financial statement 1984/5*. Paisley, 1986.

292. ROBERTSON, A, "Devising a local strategy for a deprived housing area: Ferguslie Park", *Quality of life and human welfare*, ed Pacione & Gordon, 65-74.

293. ROBERTSON, D S, *Revitalising Glasgow: Glasgow's improvement programme 1964-84*. Glasgow: Glasgow University Centre for Housing Research (Discussion paper 3), 1985, 40pp.

294. ROBERTSON, D S & CUNNINGHAM, C, "Selling out the Housing Associations", *Radical Scotland* 16 (1985) 22-23.

295. .... "Sold down the river", *Housing*, Sept. 1985, 10-11.

296. RODGER, J S, *A critical sociology of the local public enquiry system: a study of the formulation and presentation of opposition to North Sea oil and gas onshore development.* Ph.D. thesis, Edinburgh, 1983.

297. ROGER TYM & PARTNERS, *Integrated development operation for Strathclyde: preparatory study. Final report.* Glasgow, 1985.

298. RURAL FORUM, *Annual report 1985.* Perth, 1985, 14pp.

299. .... *Scotland's rural housing.* Perth, 1985, 10pp.

300. SALMOND, A, "Disinvestment and industrial change", *Scottish Government Yearbook 1986,* 225-39.

301. SAVILLE, R (Ed), *The economic development of modern Scotland.* Edinburgh: John Donald, 1985, 316pp.

302. SCOTSMAN, "The Scottish Office 1885-1985", *Scotsman,* 3.7.85 (supplement, 10pp).

303. SCOTT, M & CUTHBERT, M, *Reviewing industrial aid programmes: (1) the Invergordon smelter case.* Glencorse: David Hume Institute (Hume paper 2), 1985, 31pp.

304. SCOTT, D, "Local v central government: the spending conflict", *Scottish Government Yearbook 1986,* 36-48.

305. SCOTTISH COUNCIL (DEVELOPMENT & INDUSTRY), *Annual report 1984-5.* Edinburgh, 1985, 44pp.

306. .... *Export survey report 1984.* Edinburgh, 1986.

307. .... *Marketing of financial services: consultative paper.* Edinburgh, 1985, 22pp.

308. *Rates: a consultative paper on the Scottish Council's response to the government's Green Paper.* Edinburgh. 1986, 14pp.

309. SCOTTISH COMMISSION FOR RACIAL EQUALITY, *Annual report 1984/5.* Glasgow, 1985.

310. SCOTTISH DEVELOPMENT AGENCY, *Annual report 1985. Agency of change.* Glasgow, 1985, 83pp.

311. SCOTTISH DEVELOPMENT DEPARTMENT, *Homelessness in Scotland 1979-84..* Edinburgh: SDD (Statistical Bulletin HSIU 17), 1985, 15pp.

312. .... *Housing condition survey of private sector interwar stock in the four Scottish cities 1983.* Edinburgh, 1985, 408pp.

313. .... *Home improvement in Scotland: a new approach.* London: HMSO (Command 9677), 1985, 27pp.

314. .... *Lothian Region structure plan: Secretary of State's proposed modification.* Edinburgh, 1985, 6pp.

315. .... *Public sector rents 1984-85.* Edinburgh: SDD (Statistical Bulletin HSIU 14), 1985, 7pp.

316. .... *Public sector rents 1985-86.* Edinburgh: SDD (Statistical Bulletin

HSIU 21), 1986, 7pp.

317.   .... *Radioactive waste management policy in the UK (with special reference to Scotland)*. Edinburgh, 1985, 28pp.

318.   .... *Sales of public sector houses 1984*. Edinburgh: SDD (Statistical Bulletin HSIU 15), 1985, 10pp.

319.   .... *Strathclyde structure plan: second review and alteration. Secretary of State's approval with modification*. Edinburgh, 1985, 20pp.

320.   SCOTTISH EDUCATION DEPARTMENT, *Future strategy for higher education in Scotland*. Edinburgh: HMSO (Command 9676), 1985.

321.   SCOTTISH HEALTH SERVICE PLANNING COUNCIL, *Report for 1984*. Edinburgh: HMSO, 1985.

322.   SCOTTISH HOME AND HEALTH DEPARTMENT, *Health in Scotland 1984*. Edinburgh: HMSO, 1985, 88pp.

323.   SCOTTISH INFORMATION OFFICE, *Local government in Scotland*. Edinburgh: SIO (Factsheet 28), 1985, 39pp.

324.   SCOTTISH OFFICE, *Paying for local government: the community charge. Operational issues*. Edinburgh, 1986, 13pp.

325.   .... *Paying for local government: the Scottish approach*. Edinburgh, 1986, var.pag.

326.   .... *Public expenditure to 1988/9: a commentary on the Scotland programme*. Edinburgh, 1986.

327.   .... *Register of research*. Edinburgh, 1985, 31pp.

328.   .... *Rate support grant (Scotland) (no.4) order 1985*. London: HMSO, 1986, 10pp.

329.   SCOTTISH SOCIETY OF DIRECTORS OF PLANNING, *Annual general meeting and conference 1985*. Glasgow: Strathclyde regional Council Dept. of Physical Planning, 1985.

330.   SCOTTISH SPECIAL HOUSING ASSOCIATION, *Annual report for the year ended 31.3.85*. Edinburgh, 1985.

331.   SCOTTISH TRADES UNION CONGRESS, *88th annual report*. Glasgow, 1986, 377pp.

332.   SCOTTISH TRANSPORT STUDIES GROUP, *Annual report 1985*. Glasgow: Glasgow University Centre for Urban and Regional Research, 1985, 28pp.

333.   SECRETARY OF STATE FOR SCOTLAND, *Housing support grant (Scotland) order 1986: report*. London: House of Commons paper 137, 1986, 10pp.

334.   .... *Housing support grant (Scotland) order 1986: report*. London: House of Commons paper 136, 1986, 11pp.

335.   .... *Rate reduction (City of Edinburgh District Council) 1985-86. Report*. Edinburgh: HMSO, 1985, 144pp.

336. .... *Rate support grant (Scotland) (No.4) order 1985: report.* London: House of Commons paper 139, 1986, 37pp.

337. SHARPE, L J, "Devolution and Celtic nationalism in the UK", *West European Politics*, 8,3 (1985) 82-100.

338. SHELTER, *Who needs empty houses?* Edinburgh, 1985, 59pp.

339. SHETLAND ISLANDS COUNCIL, *Housing plan 1984-89* Lerwick, 1983, 40+28pp.

340. (SHORT, A), "Community councils speak out", *Community Councils Communique* 15 (1985) 8-13.

341. SHUCKSMITH, D M, "Community councils as a medium for public participation", *Journal of Rural Studies*, 1, 4(1985) 307-319.

342. SHUCKSMITH, D M et al, *Preparing for the plan: preparing community groups for the Grampian Regional Council rural area structure plan.* Perth: Scottish Council of Social Service, 1983, 13pp (corrected entry).

343. SILLARS, J, *Scotland: the case for optimism.* Edinburgh: Polygon, 1986, 191pp.

344. SIM, D "Local authority influence on the private home building industry", *Housing Review*, 34, 5 (1985) 166-69.

345. S.L.A.N.T. *Housing needs within Scottish New Towns.* Bathgate: Scottish Local Authorities within New Towns, 1986.

346. SPENCE, G J, *The oil money: survey of Shetland's oil revenues.* Lerwick: Shetland Council of Social Service, 1985, 72pp.

347. STANFORTH, J, MALCOLM, J & MACLENNAN, D, *The delivery of repair services in public sector housing in Scotland.* Edinburgh: Scottish Office Central Research Unit, 1986, 96pp.

348. STEWART, G, "Health in Glasgow: the influence of behaviour and environment", *Quality of life and human welfare*, ed Pacione & Gordon, 103-110.

349. STEWART, J C, *Why devolution?* Cupar: Rowan, 1984(?), 46pp.

350. STIRLING DISTRICT COUNCIL, *Housing plan 1985/90: working group report.* Stirling, 1984, 51pp.

351. STRATHCLYDE COMMUNITY BUSINESS, *The last LEAP year. Final report of the Local Enterprise Advisory Project.* Glasgow, 1986, 125pp.

352. STRATHCLYDE HOUSING LIAISON GROUP, *Provision of capital allocations and revenue support to council housing in Strathclyde (1986/87). Report 5.* Glasgow: Council Housing: the Need for Investment, 1986.

353. .... *The need for increased investment in council housing in Strathclyde (Oct. 1985 edition).* Glasgow: Council Housing: the Need for Investment, 1986, 18pp.

354. STRATHCLYDE REGIONAL COUNCIL, *Annual report and*

financial statement 1984/5. Glasgow, 1985.

355. .... *'Paying for local government': interim report on the implications for Strathclyde.* Glasgow, 1986, 8pp.

356. .... *Population, household and housing projection 1984 base: main report and technical notes.* Glasgow, 1985.

357. .... *Strathclyde structure plan: monitoring report 1985.* Glasgow, 1986, 116pp.

358. .... *Transport policies and programme 6b: 1985-90.* Glasgow 1984, 171pp.

359. .... *Transport policies and programme 6c: 1986-91.* Glasgow 1985, 193pp.

360. .... *Unemployment: implications for regional services.* Glasgow, 1985, 82pp.

361 .... *Unemployment in Strathclyde: June 1985.* Glasgow, 1985, 6+11pp.

362. STRATHKELVIN DISTRICT COUNCIL, *Sixth housing plan 1986-91.* Kirkintilloch, 1985.

363. STRAWHORN, J, *The history of Irvine: Royal Burgh and New Town.* Edinburgh: John Donald, 1985, 263pp.

364. SUTHERLAND, I, "The sacked miners of Scotland", *New Society*, 5.7.85, 7-9.

365. .... "Ulster comes to town", *New Society*, 6.12.85, 405-406.

366. TAYSIDE REGIONAL COUNCIL, *Annual report and accounts for the year ended 31.3.85.* Dundee, 1985, 19pp.

367. .... *Transport policies and programme 1984-89: first supplement.* Dundee, 1985, 51pp.

368. THOMPSON, F, *Crofting years.* Barr: Luarth, 1984, 141pp.

369. TINGLE, R, *Housing and mobility in Scotland.* London: Aims of Industry, 1986, 15pp.

370. TODD, G, *Investing in Scotland: public policy and private enterprise.* London: Economic Intelligence Unit (Special report 218), 1985, 108pp.

371. TODD, G & BAGGOTT, M, "The development dilemma", *Scottish Economic Development Review* 6 (1986) 14-17.

372. TOLSON, A & MCKIE, D, "Cashing in the current account? Current affairs at the BBC", *Cencrastus* 21 (1985) 43-44.

373. TUCKETT, A, *The STUC: the first 80 years 1897-1977.* Edinburgh: Mainstream, 1986, 444pp.

374. TURNER, A B S, "State, civil society and national development: the Scottish problem" *Australian and New Zealand Journal of Sociology*, 20, 2 (1984) 161-82.

375. VARIOUS AUTHORS, "Migrazione", *Affarri Sociali Internazionali*, 11, 4 (1983) 55-167 (includes piece on Italian migrants

in Scotland).

376. WALLACE, J, "The SIC and local development", *New Shetlander* 156 (1986) 27-29.

377. WANNOP, U, "Glasgow/Clydeside: a century of metropolitan evolution", *Regional cities in the UK 1890-1980*, ed. G Gordon (London: Harper & Row, 1986).

378. .... "The New Towns of Strathclyde", *Strathclyde: changing horizons*, ed J Butt & G Gordon, 79-101.

379. WESTERN ISLES ISLANDS COUNCIL, *Housing plan 1984-89*. Stornoway, 1985, 136.

380. WILKS, S R M, *Government and the motor industry, with particular reference to Chrysler (UK) Ltd*. Ph.D. thesis, Manchester, 1980.

381. WILLIAMS, N J, "Crime patterns in Aberdeen", *Scottish Geographical Magazine*, 101, 1 (1985) 49-59.

382. WILSON, G, "The impact of North Sea oil on the British economy since 1979 and its effect on Scotland", *The Thatcher revolution* (Modern Studies Association, 1986), 35-38.

383. .... "The Scottish contradiction: a nation in limbo", *Contemporary Review*, 247 (Aug. 1985), 57-61.

384. WILSON, J L, "The two-tier mistake", *Scots Magazine*, Dec.1985, 269-71.

385. WILSON, J N, *Pragmatic and romantic incomers: a study of power and influence on Orkney*. Ph.D. thesis, Edinburgh, 1983 (BLLD No.: D48943/84).

386. YATES, C AB, *A sociological and demographic analysis of patterns of church membership in the Church of Scotland in the urban city*. Ph.D. thesis, St Andrews, 1985, 495pp. (BLLD No.: D66027/86).

387. YATES, K, "Strathclyde's strategy to combat deprivation", *Quality of life and human welfare*, ed Pacione & Gordon, 35-49.

388. YOUNG, J D, "Nationalism, marxism and Scottish history", *Journal of Contemporary History*, 20,2 (1985).

389. YOUNG, R, "Decentralisation in Strathclyde", *Local Government Policy Making*, 11, 1 (1984) 25-29.

C H Allen, Department of Politics, University of Edinburgh

INDEX TO BIBLIOGRAPHY

Women: 33, 35,36,76,81,108,151,239,255.

THE SCOTTISH GOVERNMENT YEARBOOK 1976-7
Ed. by M.G. Clarke and H.M. Drucker
CONTENTS

THE SCOTTISH GOVERNMENT YEARBOOK 1978
Ed. by H.M. Drucker and M.G. Clarke
CONTENTS

THE SCOTTISH GOVERNMENT YEARBOOK 1979
Ed. by N. Drucker and H.M. Drucker
CONTENTS

THE SCOTTISH GOVERNMENT YEARBOOK 1980
Ed. by H.M. Drucker and N. Drucker
CONTENTS

Colin Wiseman
10. More and Less Coercive Ways of Settling Debts – Mike Adler and Edward Wozniak
11. The Scottish Fishing Industry: Technical Opportunities and Political Constraints – John Godfrey and Norman Godman
12. Energy Demand and Energy Policy in Scotland – G.A. Mackay

THE SCOTTISH GOVERNMENT YEARBOOK 1981
Ed. by H.M. Drucker and N. Drucker
CONTENTS

1. The Political Physiognomy of Jekyll and Hyde – The Editors
2. The Select Committee on Scottish Affairs – Donald Dewar
3. The Year at Westminster – James Naughtie
4. The Social Structure of Modern Scotland – David McCrone
5. Scotland's Public Expenditure 'Needs' – David Heald
6. The Rise and Fall of Civil Service Dispersion to Scotland – Richard Parry
7. COSLA: A Silent Voice for Local Government? – Carol Craig
8. Subverting Housing Plans: Some Institutional Realities – Paul Crompton
9. Policy-making in Area Health Boards: The Role of the Board Member – David Hunter
10. Children's Panels: A Strathclyde Member's View – Alf Young
11. The Birth and Development of the Shetland Movement 197780 – Martin Dowle
12. Scotland in Europe – Ian Dalziel
13. Parties' Progress: The District Council Elections of May 1980 – John Bochel and David Denver
14. Scottish Legislation in the Seventies – H. McN. Henderson

THE SCOTTISH GOVERNMENT YEARBOOK 1982
Ed. by H.M. Drucker and N. Drucker
CONTENTS

1. Valedictory – The Editors
2. The Year at Westminster – James Naughtie
3. Braking Mr Younger's Runaway Train: The Conflict Between the Scottish Office and Local Authorities over Local Government Expenditure – D.A. Heald, C.A. Jones and D.W. Lamont
4. Reflections of a Scottish Office Minister – Malcolm Rifkind

SCOTTISH GOVERNMENT YEARBOOK 1983
Ed. David McCrone
CONTENTS

SCOTTISH GOVERNMENT YEARBOOK 1984
Ed. David McCrone
CONTENTS

SCOTTISH GOVERNMENT YEARBOOK 1985
Ed. David McCrone
CONTENTS

SCOTTISH GOVERNMENT YEARBOOK 1986
Ed. by David McCrone
CONTENTS

SCOTTISH VOCATIONAL EDUCATION COUNCIL

The Scottish Vocational Education Council (SCOTVEC) was established by the Secretary of State for Scotland on 29 March 1985.

SCOTVEC is responsible for developing, administering and assessing the new NATIONAL CERTIFICATE, introduced in August 1984 and for continuing and refining the system of advanced courses at HNC and HND level, affered by its predecessors SCOTBEC and SCOTEC.

Membership of the Council reflects the many interests – professional, educational, technician, industrial and commerical – which are served by its activities.